P9-AFI-424

There Are Two Errors in the the Title of This Book

There Are Two Errors in the

There are two errors in the the title of this book : a sourcebook of philosophical puzzles, problems, and paradoxes
33305233979776
6an   05/16/16

the Title of This Book

a sourcebook of philosophical puzzles, problems, and paradoxes

REVISED AND EXPANDED (AGAIN)

Robert M. Martin

broadview press

© 2012 Robert M. Martin

All rights reserved. The use of any part of this publication reproduced, transmitted in any form or by any means, electronic, mechanical, photocopying, recording, or otherwise, or stored in a retrieval system, without prior written consent of the publisher—or in the case of photocopying, a licence from Access Copyright (Canadian Copyright Licensing Agency), One Yonge Street, Suite 1900, Toronto, Ontario M5E 1E5—is an infringement of the copyright law.

Library and Archives Canada Cataloguing in Publication

Martin, Robert M.
    There are two errors in the the title of this book : a sourcebook of philosophical puzzles, problems, and paradoxes / Robert M. Martin. — Rev. and expanded (again)

Includes bibliographical references.
ISBN 978-1-55481-053-6

    1. Paradoxes.   2. Semantics (Philosophy).   3. Reasoning.   I. Title.

BC199.P2M37 2011   165   C2011-904836-1

Broadview Press is an independent, international publishing house, incorporated in 1985.

We welcome comments and suggestions regarding any aspect of our publications—please feel free to contact us at the addresses below or at broadview@broadviewpress.com.

North America
PO Box 1243, Peterborough, Ontario, Canada K9J 7H5
2215 Kenmore Ave., Buffalo, New York, USA 14207
Tel: (705) 743-8990; Fax: (705) 743-8353
email: customerservice@broadviewpress.com

UK, Europe, Central Asia, Middle East, Africa, India, and Southeast Asia
Eurospan Group, 3 Henrietta St., London WC2E 8LU, United Kingdom
Tel: 44 (0) 1767 604972; Fax: 44 (0) 1767 601640
email: eurospan@turpin-distribution.com

Australia and New Zealand
NewSouth Books
c/o TL Distribution, 15-23 Helles Ave., Moorebank, NSW, Australia 2170
Tel: (02) 8778 9999; Fax: (02) 8778 9944
email: orders@tldistribution.com.au

www.broadviewpress.com

Broadview Press acknowledges the financial support of the Government of Canada through the Canada Book Fund for our publishing activities.

Copy-edited by Martin Boyne

This book is printed on paper containing 100% post-consumer fibre.

Design and composition by George Kirkpatrick

PRINTED IN CANADA

Contents

ACKNOWLEDGEMENTS • 19

ABOUT THIS BOOK • 21

CHAPTER I: DIFFERENCES THAT MAKE NO DIFFERENCE • 25

1. THE UNANSWERABLE • 25
   William James and the Squirrel • 25
   Empty Questions • 27
   More Empties • 28
   Something or Nothing? • 29
2. YOU CAN NEVER TELL • 30
   Double or Nothing? • 30
   The Right-Handed Universe • 31
   Fake Antiques • 31
3. SENSATIONAL PROBLEMS • 33
   Mildred's Peculiar Sensations • 33
   Another Inversion in Mildred • 34
   The Cheezy Puzzle • 35
   Taste-Tests • 35
4. THE TRUE AND THE USEFUL • 36
   It's Practically True • 36
   What's So Good about True Beliefs Anyway? • 37
   INTO THE MAINSTREAM OF PHILOSOPHY • 38

CHAPTER II: GOD • 41

1. RELIGIOUS BELIEF • 41
   The Invisible Gardener • 41
   Industrial Prayer • 42
   The Anti-Flu Flight • 43
   I Believe in One Outpouring of Existence Itself • 44

Religious Truths • 45
   (1) Divine Geology • 45
   (2) One Hell of a Rainstorm • 45
Faith • 46
Brainless Spirituality • 47
The Philosophy Poll • 47

2. GOD'S DIFFICULTIES • 48
Gods Made Me Do It • 48
God Knows! • 48
God the Counterfeiter • 49
A Proof That Everything Is Hunky-Dory • 52
God When He Was a Baby • 52
The Fawn in the Fire • 53

3. ODDBALL THEORIES OF RELIGION • 55
How There Got to Be Only One God • 55
God Is Love? • 56
Where Heaven Came From • 57

4. PROVING THE EXISTENCE OF GOD • 57
God as the Tortoise on the Bottom • 57
The Miracle on the Expressway • 58
Unusual Arguments for God's Existence • 58
Miraculous Evidence • 59
I Believe in Love • 61
God and the Printing-Factory Explosion • 61

5. BETTING ON GOD • 62
Why Believing in God Is a Good Bet • 62
Why Believing in God Is Not a Good Bet • 63

6. WHAT IF THERE ISN'T ANY GOD? • 64
INTO THE MAINSTREAM OF PHILOSOPHY • 64

CHAPTER III: TAKING CHANCES • 67

1. SOME PROBABLE FACTS • 67
Rosencrantz Flips a Coin • 67
to be or not to xq • 68
Another Surprising Sequence • 69
You're On a Roll! • 69
Why We're All Nasty • 70
Psychic Powers in Your Classroom • 71
Your Extraordinary Ancestors • 72

How Many Ancestors Do You Have? • 72
The Miracle of You • 73

2. SOME PROBABILITY SURPRISES • 73
One-Third of Two • 73
How to Play Russian Roulette • 74
Happy Birthday Dear You-Two • 74

3. UNHEALTHY MISTAKES • 75
Canada's Colonic Sweetheart • 75
Hazards to Your Mental Health • 77
Guess the Percentages • 77
Sweinfeld: The Epidemic about Nothing • 78

4. YOU'RE WRONG • 79
The Trouble with Taxis • 79
The Basketball Blunder • 80
Better Pay or Worse? • 81
Why It's Not Certain That You'll Be in a Plane Crash • 82
Predicting Priscilla • 83
INTO THE MAINSTREAM OF PHILOSOPHY • 84

CHAPTER IV: MAKING CHOICES: Decision Theory • 85

1. LOTTERIES AND OTHER GAMBLES • 85
The Proof That Lots of People Are Crazy or Stupid • 85
A Good Lottery Strategy • 87
How to Go Home a Winner • 88

2. GETTING MONTY'S GOAT • 90
The Monty Hall Paradox • 90
In Which I Try to Convince You That I'm Right • 91
Pigeon Reasoning • 92

3. MORE PROBABILITY PUZZLES • 93
The Paradox of the Three Prisoners • 93
The Other Envelope Is Always Better • 93
The Sleeping Beauty Conundrum • 94
Paradoxical Babies • 95

4. PREFERENCES AND VOTING • 96
Why You Shouldn't Vote • 96
Fred's Confusing Preferences • 96
How Not to Choose a Movie • 97
How to Win at Dice • 99
Rock, Scissors, Paper • 101

5. SLIPPING DOWN THE SLOPE • 102
      The Elusive Wine-Bottle • 102
      Why You Should Always Have Another Glass of Beer • 102
      Why Everyone Is Poor • 103
   INTO THE MAINSTREAM OF PHILOSOPHY • 104

CHAPTER V: LOGIC AND PARADOX • 107

1. THE ILLOGIC OF ENGLISH • 108
      "Or" Confusions • 108
      Nothing If Not Complicated • 108
      "The" Confusions • 109
      Much Ado about Nothing • 110
      The Messy Counterfactual • 112
2. THINKING IN CIRCLES • 113
      The Divine Circle • 113
      There's Always a Catch • 114
      The Münchhausen Trilemma • 114
3. THE UNSPOKEN IMPLICATION • 115
      It Never Turns Blue Either • 115
      Has the Present King of France Stopped Robbing
         Banks? • 116
4. IMPOSSIBLE SURPRISES • 117
      The Surprise Quiz That Never Happens • 117
      Why You *Can't* Pick Any Number • 118
      The Surprising Meatloaf • 118
      Why All Numbers Are Interesting • 119
5. PARADOXES OF SELF-REFERENCE • 119
      The Non-Existent Barber • 119
      The Trouble with Adjectives • 120
      The Troublesome Statement in the Box • 121
      A Silly Proof of God's Existence • 121
      Self-Referential Jokes • 122
      On Being a Member of Yourself • 122
      This Is Not the Title of This Item • 124
      There Are Two Errors • 125
6. OH NO! *MORE* SILLY PROOFS OF GOD'S EXISTENCE! • 126
      The Universal Prover • 126
      God Knows That He Exists • 128

7.   ZENO'S PARADOXES • 129
         The Speedy Tortoise • 129
         The Runner Who Never Gets to the Finish • 129
         Supertask: Able to Leap Short Time-Intervals • 130
         How to Finish an Autobiography • 131
         Thinking about Changing? There's a Lot to Do. • 131
     INTO THE MAINSTREAM OF PHILOSOPHY • 132

CHAPTER VI: BELIEF, LOGIC, AND INTENTIONS • 135

1.   BELIEVE IT OR NOT • 135
         Why You Should Never Change Your Mind • 135
         The Zen of Chicken-Sexing • 135
         Be Careful What You Believe • 136
         Knowing Nothing about Birds • 138
         The Hobgoblin of Little Minds • 139
         You'll Believe Just Anything • 141
         Impossible Beliefs • 142
2.   IT HAS TO BE TRUE • 144
         Descartes's Thought • 144
         The Unexamined Life • 145
         A Guaranteed True Belief • 146
3.   SELF-FULFILLING / SELF-DEFEATING • 146
         The Power of Positive Thinking • 146
         How to Fail at Baseball • 147
         The Pursuit of Happiness • 148
         Fooling Yourself • 148
         Sorry, I'm Not Free Right Now • 149
4.   MENTAL IMPOTENCE • 150
         Believe or I'll Shoot! • 150
         How to Intend to Kick Your Cat • 150
     INTO THE MAINSTREAM OF PHILOSOPHY • 151

CHAPTER VII: GOOD AND BAD REASONING • 153

1.   THOUGHT-TRAPS FOR THE UNWARY • 153
         The Price of a Ball • 153
         Splitting Up the Diamonds • 154
         The Disappearing Dollar • 155

Free Beer • 155

Nobody Works at All • 156

The Disappearing Day • 157

Who's Looking? • 158

The Jelly-Bean Peculiarity • 159

The General Makes Some Bad Choices • 159

More Math Troubles • 160

His Father's Son • 161

The Card Mistake • 161

Roses and Mice • 163

2.   THE REASONING OF OTHER CULTURES AND PAST CULTURES • 164

Azande Witches • 164

Camels in Germany • 165

If We Had Three Nostrils, Would There Be Eight
Planets? • 166

Nobody Could Be *That* Wrong • 168

Charity for All? • 169

Warning for Tourists: Watch Out for Extreme
Politeness • 171

3.   THINKING IN GROOVES • 174

Ungroovy Thinking • 174

(1) The Boy with Two Fathers • 174

(2) How to Win a Camel Anti-Race • 174

(3) Thinking Straight about Roman Numerals • 175

(4) Reducing Speeding Violations • 175

(5) Smashing a Fly • 175

(6) The Enormous Tiddly-Wink Tournament • 176

(7) Notes from the Underground • 177

Thinking Outside the Box • 177

Getting Out of the Box • 178

The the Title of This Book • 179

The Mushroom Hunt • 180

INTO THE MAINSTREAM OF PHILOSOPHY • 181

CHAPTER VIII: LEARNING FROM EXPERIENCE • 183

1.   WHAT'S KNOWLEDGE? • 183

Justification • 183

Lucy the Baseball Oracle • 184

Galileo as Scientist • 184
Kekulé's Dream • 185

2. SCEPTICAL DOUBTS AND PUZZLES • 185
Life Is But a Dream • 185
The Stuff That Dreams Are Made On • 186
The Brain in a Vat • 188
What Pink Socks Tell You about Ravens • 189
Something Even Worse about Pink Socks • 190
Ravens in Rutland • 191
Chicken Induction • 192
How Long Will This Keep Going On? • 192
The Inevitability of Scientific Error: Another Circle • 193
Dunno • 195
No Future to Know • 195

3. SCIENTIFIC SURPRISES • 196
The Depressing Sample • 196
Your Popular Friends • 197

4. SCIENTIFIC MISTAKES • 197
Bad Predictions • 197
The Board of Miseducation • 198
True Scotsmen • 199

5. CAUSE AND EFFECT • 200
Cause and Correlation • 200
The Tickle Defence • 201

6. SCIENCE AND NON- • 204
Too Good to Be True • 204
I Dreamed That Would Happen! • 204
Is It a Boy or a Girl? • 206
The Wisdom of the Noble Savage • 207
The Wisdom of the Dumbest Yokel • 208
INTO THE MAINSTREAM OF PHILOSOPHY • 209

CHAPTER IX: KNOWING WITHOUT EXPERIENCE • 211

1. THE A PRIORI AND DEFINITIONS • 211
Why Your Sisters Are Female • 211
Truth "By Definition" • 213
The Dictionary with Very Few Definitions • 213
Sisters without Language • 215

Honest Abe and the Sheep • 216
The Disappearing Planet • 216
2. CONCEPTUAL TRUTHS • 218
I Forget What I Saw Before I Was Born • 219
More on Conceptual Existence • 220
3. THE SYNTHETIC A PRIORI • 221
The Incompetent Repairman • 221
Kant on the Synthetic A Priori • 222
Nothing Made That Happen • 222
The Butterfly That Destroyed Oakland • 223
The Tribe without Arithmetic • 226
$7 + 5 \neq 12$ • 227
The Numbers Made Me Believe That • 229
Bizarre Triangles Discovered in Space • 230
4. A PRIORI SCIENCE • 231
Bad Physics • 231
The Infinity of Space • 232
Why It's Dark at Night • 232
Thinking about Falling • 233
The Shadow Knows • 234
The Mirror Problem • 236
More Thoughts about Falling • 237
INTO THE MAINSTREAM OF PHILOSOPHY • 237

CHAPTER X: THINKING, SAYING, AND MEANING: The Philosophy of Mind and
of Language • 239

1. THINKING MACHINES • 239
Could a Machine Think? • 239
Artificial Insanity • 240
The Turing Test • 241
How to Think Like a Computer • 243
Don't Try This Recipe at Home, Kids! • 243
A Robot Has Feelings, Too • 244
The Mystery of Meat. • 245
Let's Not Get Physical • 247
What Zombies Tell Us • 248
Mildred Again • 249
The Material Girl (and Boy) • 250
The Astonishing Hypothesis • 251

Angels and Superman • 251
Believing in Angels • 252
Why Picnics Don't Obey the Laws of Physics • 253
2. THE THOUGHTS OF ANIMALS • 254
Dog-Zombies • 254
Fido's Logic • 255
Fido's Mendacity • 256
Language Requirements? • 258
3. MEANING • 259
What Could They Have Meant? • 259
Saying What You Don't Mean • 261
Thinking about Vienna • 262
The Incredible Swampman • 263
Thinking about Santa Claus • 264
INTO THE MAINSTREAM OF PHILOSOPHY • 265

CHAPTER XI: HERE AND NOW; YOU AND I • 267

1. TIME TRAVEL • 267
Not Killing Grandpa • 267
Meeting Yourself • 268
UFOs Contain Visitors from Planet Earth • 269
Time Travel and the End of Humanity • 269
2. WHEN, WHERE, AND WHO • 270
Telling Space Aliens What Day It Is • 270
I'm Here Now • 271
Fred Finds Himself in the Library • 272
What Two Gods Don't Know • 274
3. THE IDENTITY OF THINGS • 275
Two Ways to Be the Same • 275
The Same Lump • 278
The Identity of My University • 279
The Disappearing Boat • 280
Three Odd Buildings • 281
(1) The Gold Pavilion Temple • 281
(2) The Hôtel de Glace • 282
(3) The Ugly Apartment House • 282
Puzzling Rivers in Klopstokia • 283
4. THE IDENTITY OF ANIMALS AND PEOPLE • 284
My Organism Is Bigger than Yours • 284

Rover and Clover • 285
The Adventures of Amoeba-Man • 287
Getting Someone Else's Body • 288
Keeping Your Own Body • 289
Two Places Are Better than One • 290
What It Takes to Be in Heaven • 291
5.   IDENTITY AND ESSENCE • 293
What Makes You You • 293
What Makes Us Us • 294
INTO THE MAINSTREAM OF PHILOSOPHY • 295

CHAPTER XII: WHY SHOULD I BE MORAL? • 297

1.   WHAT'S IN IT FOR ME? • 297
Change for a Dollar • 297
The Ring of Gyges • 298
Rationality • 298
2.   RELATIVISM AND REALISM • 299
Finger-Lickin' Good and Evil • 299
It's All Relative • 300
Can Ethics Be Taught? • 301
The Gurgling Wave • 301
When God Tells You to Do Evil • 302
Biblical Guides to Conduct • 303
3.   THE PRISONER'S DILEMMA • 306
A Deal for the Prisoners • 306
The Tragedy of the Commons • 308
Coca-Cola Morality • 309
Why We Should Hire a Dictator • 309
Why People in Small Towns are Nicer • 311
Toucha Smasha • 311
4.   THE PARADOX OF DETERRENCE • 312
Bombing the Russians • 312
When It's Sane to Be Crazy • 314
The Swerving Chicken • 315
INTO THE MAINSTREAM OF PHILOSOPHY • 316

CHAPTER XIII: HOW TO THINK MORALLY • 319

1. JUSTICE AND DISTRIBUTION • 319
    Why You Should Give Away Your Shoes • 319
    Sell Whatsoever Thou Hast, and Give to the Rich • 321
    Why You Don't Have to Give Away Your Shoes • 321
    Your Shoes and Your "Families" • 322
    Supererogatory Acts • 323
    Schadenfreude • 324
2. PUNISHMENT • 324
    Getting Back at Eichmann • 324
    Making a Statement • 326
    Closure • 326
    The Paradox of Punishment • 327
3. RIGHTS AND WRONGS • 328
    Push-Pin Anyone? • 328
    When Promise-Breaking Is Obligatory • 329
    Don't Torture That Baby! • 330
    How to Prevent Crime • 331
    Rights vs. Utility • 332
    Special Today on Life: Only $2199.91/Day • 333
    The Price of Life in Europe • 335
    INTO THE MAINSTREAM OF PHILOSOPHY • 335

CHAPTER XIV: MORAL CONUNDRUMS • 337

1. GETTING WHAT YOU WANT • 337
    Past and Future Desires • 337
    Harming and Benefitting the Dead • 338
    What Happens to Somebody Who Is Hardly Me • 340
    How to Get What You Want • 341
    Electronic Pleasure • 342
2. RELATIONSHIPS WITH OTHER PEOPLE • 343
    I'm Gonna Buy a Plastic Doll That I Can Call My
        Own • 343
    Replaceable People in Literature • 344
3. YUK • 345
    Hello Dolly! • 345
    Frankensurgery • 347

Canine Disrespect • 347

The Yuck Factor • 348

4.   ACTING AND REFRAINING • 349

Two Ways to Kill Granny • 349

Moral Technology • 350

Ten-to-One Dilemmas • 351

How to Get Organ Donors • 352

How to Assault a Police Officer by Doing Nothing • 352

Poor Joshua! • 353

The Bad Samaritan • 355

INTO THE MAINSTREAM OF PHILOSOPHY • 355

CHAPTER XV: LAW, ACTION, AND RESPONSIBILITY • 357

1.   WHY IS THAT ILLEGAL? • 357

Blackmailing Letterman • 357

How Not to Sell Ice in Alberta • 358

2.   TWILIGHT-ZONE LEGISLATION • 359

Legislating π • 359

Some Unusual Laws • 360

3.   WHEN RULES COLLIDE • 361

The Immigration Collision • 361

Trapped in the Airport • 361

4.   PROBLEMS FOR JUDGES • 362

The Messier Contract • 362

What Do Judges Do? • 364

5.   PROBLEMS ABOUT ACTIONS • 365

Why You Don't Drive When You're Drunk • 365

The Lucky Murderer • 366

A Time and a Place for Murder • 367

6.   CANS AND CAN'TS • 368

Can Pierre Keep His Promise? • 368

Ought But Can't? • 369

Saving Ought Implies Can • 369

What You Can't Do • 371

The Incapable Golfer • 372

No Absolution for Pierre • 372

7.   FREE WILL • 372

I Just Had to Do It • 372

Freedom as Uncaused Action • 373

An Unfree Ass • 374
Freedom as Irrationality • 375
The Unpredictable Dealer • 376
Compatibilism • 376
The Evil Physiologist • 377
INTO THE MAINSTREAM OF PHILOSOPHY • 377

CHAPTER XVI: DEEP THOUGHTS • 381

Wisdom • 382
Cheer • 384
Sub Specie Aeternitatis • 384
Doubt • 385

BIBLIOGRAPHY • 387

DISCLAIMER • 401

Acknowledgements

THE ITEMS IN THIS book have three sources:

(1) Some were invented by me
(2) Others were thought up by other philosophers
(3) Some are part of the folklore of the philosophy profession, or of the general tradition of jokes, puzzles, and aphorisms.

I have tried to footnote those in the second category to give their inventor or promulgator credit. But sometimes philosophical ideas that start out in the second category wind up in the third: they are passed from person to person, and their origin becomes obscure. There are lots of little quotations in here that I've run into in various places (especially on the Internet), where they've been given only partial attribution or none at all. It's often impossible, or not worth the effort even if possible, to track down their sources. So I will be forgiven, I hope, for sometimes omitting crediting footnotes.

For their ideas and encouragement I offer my grateful thanks to Christina Behme, Nathan Brett, Richmond Campbell, Ted Cohen, Michael Hymers, Sharon Kaye, Duncan MacIntosh, Joan Mahoney, Ed Mares, Victoria McGeer, Mark Phillips, Roland Puccetti, Shelagh Ross, David C. Selley, Terry Tomkow, and Sheldon Wein; and also to George J. Martin, and to the participants in the Sunday Forum, Heritage Village, Southbury, Connecticut; and to numerous readers of the first two editions who sent me comments, corrections, arguments, and appreciation; and to Broadview's helpfully critical anonymous reader of my proposal for this third edition, and its sharp-eyed and linguistically adept copy-editor, Martin Boyne.

These days it seems that publishers consider for publication only those manuscripts that are almost exactly like dozens of books already selling well. Don LePan, president of Broadview Press, is an exception to this rule. I offer him my gratitude for his courage in publishing this odd work, for his helpfulness while it was in preparation, and for his persuasiveness in getting me to prepare second and third editions.

About This book

SOME PEOPLE THINK THAT the job of philosophy is to produce little wisdom-nuggets. A website reports this exchange between a philosopher and his seatmate in a plane:

"What do you do?"
"I'm a philosopher."
"What are some of your sayings, then?"[1]

I once did see a sentimental Hallmark-card type plaque with a saying (supposedly) by the philosopher Albert Camus on it,[2] but academic philosophers really don't do that sort of thing. Although this book contains the occasional philosophical quotable quote, and despite the fact that in Chapter XII there are discussions of some bumper-stickers I've observed, what you'll find in here has more to do with what academic philosophers really work at.

---

1   The writer/philosopher Anthony Gottlieb reports having seen this item on a website reporting conversations between philosophers and non-philosophers; but he tells me now that—tragically—he can't find the website and thinks it has disappeared. See Gottlieb's article "What Do Philosophers Believe." [Note to Readers: Bibliographical references in footnotes throughout this book will be abbreviated, usually using title and author only. For full information, consult the Bibliography at the end of the book.]

2   It had a soft-focus photograph of a young couple walking hand-in-hand through sun-dappled woods, and the text said: "Don't walk in front of me; I may not follow. Don't walk behind me; I may not lead. Just walk beside me and be my friend. —Albert Camus." This little bit of sweetness can (naturally) be found widely scattered around the Internet, usually attributed to Camus, but I've never found where he's supposed to have written or said this. Readers of the real Camus, who know that he preferred no-nonsense, terse, unsentimental understatement, will find it unlikely that he wrote this, and, knowing the kind of guy he was, will find the idea of him working for Hallmark Cards hilarious.

But the other conventional view of philosophical production is that it's ponderous, pompous, tedious, technical, and grimly serious—and, above all, impossible to follow.

> Question: What do you get when you cross the Godfather with a philosopher?
> Answer: An offer you can't understand.

> "Making itself intelligible is suicide for philosophy."—Martin Heidegger

> "Only one man ever understood me, and he didn't understand me."— G.W.F. Hegel (supposedly his last words, uttered on his death-bed)

Some philosophy *is* like that.

But really, philosophy can be fun. At its best, it's interesting, answering questions you've always wondered about and raising questions you've never thought of. It can tickle your imagination and your funny-bone, and expand your mind. It can even be friendly and funny. The credo of some of the best philosophical writers nowadays is, "An ounce of pretension is worth a pound of manure."

This book is designed to prove all that to you.

Philosophy happens when something goes wrong. Sometimes perfectly ordinary things seem inexplicable when you start to think about them. Sometimes perfectly reasonable assumptions lead, by perfectly acceptable reasoning, to paradoxes—bizarre and unbelievable conclusions:

> "The point of philosophy is to start with something so simple as not to seem worth stating, and to end with something so paradoxical that no one will believe it."—Bertrand Russell[1]

Some people aren't exactly enthusiastic about this sort of mental exercise:

> "Paradox is the poison flower of quietism, the iridescent sheen of a putrefied mind, the greatest depravity of all."—Thomas Mann[2]

Whew! Are you sure you want to read on?

What Mann was thinking is that you'd get so bogged down in contradictions and unbelievable conclusions that you'd just stop doing or thinking

---

1 "The Philosophy of Logical Atomism."
2 *The Magic Mountain.*

anything. But if you've got a philosophically active mind, you won't stop there. The puzzle—the paradox—will push you to try to figure things out better.

Some students get the mistaken and discouraging idea that philosophy contains only unanswerable questions, and they wonder what the point is. This idea is wrong. We'll look at the beginnings, at least, of some very good, surprising, interesting answers.

You'll notice that some paragraphs in this book are written in this contrasting type style. In these parts answers are given to questions just raised. When you see a passage in this type style coming up, that's a good place to stop reading for a while, and to try to figure out answers yourself. Then when you read these passages, you can see whether your answers match what's given. Don't worry if, from time to time, you come up with a different answer from the one given. Sometimes there are many ways to answer a question, and the one given is just one of these. Try to see why the answer given is plausible. Is it better than yours?

Some solutions philosophers have proposed are much too complicated to be included in here, of course. You'll notice, from time to time, sections labelled **FOR FURTHER READING**, which tell you where to look for further discussion of the issues.

Just as it's a mistake to think that philosophy can't come up with any answers that are any good, it's also a mistake to be too smug about what you take to be a good answer. In many cases, philosophical debate still rages about questions that have been around a long time, and if someone tries to tell you that there's no longer any serious question in an area that's actually still very controversial, they're trying to pull the wool over your eyes. So when you read something from a philosopher like this:

As a result of the work of Christian philosophers such as Alvin Plantinga, it is widely recognized that the internal problem of evil is a failure as an argument for atheism.[1]

or (about the same debate) this:

[Plantinga's] Free Will Defense has achieved something fairly rare in Philosophy, widespread consensus that it works.[2]

it's a pretty good bet that they're trying to snooker you.

---

1   William Lane Craig, "Theistic Critiques of Atheism," p. 73.
2   Kelly James Clark (ed.), *Readings in the Philosophy of Religion*, Introduction to Part IV.

You'll find a lot of questions in philosophy that are still debated—with arguments and proposals worth considering from all sides. That's what makes the introductory study of philosophy different from the introduction to many other subjects, where you learn only what's settled and uncontroversial. And that's one reason why some people enjoy philosophy more than these other subjects: you can join in the debate right from the start.

Some philosophers take themselves deadly seriously, but others love to fool around with ideas. You'll often find chatter in a university philosophy department consisting of jokes, anecdotes, and silly intellectual play. Many of these bits of fluff have a real philosophical purpose. (Well, *some* of them do.) In this book you'll occasionally come across a passage written in this format and type-style; this indicates a fluffy bit. Don't ignore it! It's often not merely for fun. Even when it seems silly or irrelevant, there may be something philosophically important about it—something deeper that it illustrates, which merits thought.

"Wittgenstein once said that a serious and good philosophical work could be written that would consist entirely of *jokes* [without being facetious]. Another time he said that a philosophical treatise might contain nothing but questions [without answers]."—Norman Malcolm[1]

For even more philosophical puzzles, problems, and paradoxes, visit

http://sites.broadviewpress.com/twoerrors

The site contains supplementary material as well as an entirely new chapter, "Jokes and Other Aesthetic Matters." In the text below, whenever you see a butterfly symbol in the margin, you can find related material on the website to complement the section you've just read. For easy reference, the readings are separated by chapter and identified by page number.

---

1 · *Ludwig Wittgenstein: A Memoir*, pp. 27–28.

Chapter I

Differences That Make No Difference

1. The Unanswerable

William James and the Squirrel

AROUND THE BEGINNING OF the twentieth century, the American pragmatist philosopher William James described this puzzle:

> Some years ago, being with a camping party in the mountains, I returned from a solitary ramble to find every one engaged in a ferocious metaphysical dispute. The *corpus* of the dispute was a squirrel—a live squirrel supposed to be clinging to one side of a tree-trunk; while over against the tree's opposite side a human being was imagined to stand. This human witness tries to get sight of the squirrel by moving rapidly round the tree, but no matter how fast he goes, the squirrel moves as fast in the opposite direction, and always keeps the tree between himself and the man, so that never a glimpse of him is caught. The resultant metaphysical problem now is this: *Does the man go round the squirrel or not?* ... Every one had taken sides, and was obstinate.

Who is right? The important point here is not who is right, but what James says about this problem:

"Which party is right," I said, "depends on what you *practically mean* by 'going round' the squirrel. If you mean passing from the north of him to the east, then to the south, then to the west, and then to the north of him again, obviously the man does go round him.... But if on the contrary you mean being first in front of him, then on the right of him, then behind him, then on his left, and finally in front again, it is quite as obvious that the man fails to go round him, for by the compensating movements the squirrel makes, he keeps his belly turned towards the man all the time."

The *practical meaning* of a belief has to do with how that belief interacts with the interests and actions of the person who believes it. Exactly what practical difference would it make to you if you believed that or its opposite?

This sort of way of dealing with questions has become extremely influential in contemporary philosophy. It gives us a methodology for dealing with some questions that seemed unanswerable, by anchoring them in the real world. But it also apparently gives us a reason to discard other questions as meaningless.

The influence of this style has not always been beneficial. Spend some time in a bar where undergraduate philosophy majors hang out, and you might hear a good deal of pompous but useless philosophizing to the following effect: "But what do you really *mean* by 'God'/'justice'/'good'/ 'freedom' [etc., etc.]?" It's easy to see why bystanders get the idea that philosophy has abandoned what they take to be its historical mission—The Search For Wisdom—and is now a trivial search for definitions. And why they think that philosophers would save a lot of time and talk merely by consulting a good dictionary.

But this sort of quibble over words is far from what James—or contemporary philosophers—really do. James's example may be misleading: it's merely a trivial verbal dispute that's easily made to disappear as soon as the ambiguous senses of a phrase are revealed. But when real philosophical disputes are solved (or made to go away) it is rarely this simple a matter.

When James calls the squirrel argument a "metaphysical problem," he's being ironic. There are traditional metaphysical problems in philosophy that are not so trivial; and getting clear on exactly what is "practically meant" is often a very subtle matter. But James may be right in thinking that this sort of methodology can help with real philosophical problems.

Consider, for example, the dispute over the justice of capital punishment. Philosophers might want first to try to answer the question, "What's really involved in *justice*?" This question asks about the "practical meaning" of *justice*, and it's an important and difficult question, not solvable merely by looking the word up in a dictionary. We want to know, for example, what tests we should use to judge whether some policy is just or not; so when a dictionary tells us that *justice* means "just conduct, fairness" and that "just" means "acting or done in accordance with what is morally right or fair.... Deserved."[1] that's not much help.

Empty Questions

- What's the opposite of a duck?
- What does Thursday weigh?
- What was Snow White's father's name?
- What time is it right now on the moon? ·
- How many angels can dance on the head of a pin?

I'LL BET YOU CAN'T answer these questions. Why can't you? The reason is not that there's some information you lack. There's something wrong with each question: they're *empty* questions.

> The problem about what time it is on the moon arises again for the Earth's North and South Poles, where all the time zones come to-gether in a point. You can occupy several—even all of them—at once! But for purposes of unambiguous communication, various conventions for time zone have been adopted for the poles and for extra-terrestrial locations.[2]
>
> Do you feel that these stipulations, being entirely arbitrary, didn't provide real answers to questions about what time it was? Remember that there's a good deal that's arbitrary about ordinary earthly time zones. In fact, the whole system that assigns a number on the clock to the current time is arbitrary, isn't it?

> When plans were announced for the first Muslim astronaut, religious authorities in that faith had to make decisions on questions never faced before. For example, the requirement that Muslims pray five

---

1 *Canadian Oxford Dictionary*, p. 822.
2 UTC (Coordinated Universal Time, which used to be known as Greenwich Mean Time) is the convention for scientific observation, so it's the official time zone at both poles and off the earth. But people at the Amundsen-Scott Station, the permanent base at the South Pole, use New Zealand time. People rarely go to the North Pole, which doesn't have a permanent outpost. Astronauts usually use MET (Mission Elapsed Time), which counts time from when they took off; but when they are on the International Space Station, UTC is the standard.

times a day, including once pre-dawn and once at noon, needed interpretation; authorities decided that these prayers could take place five times during a 24-hour period in space, timed from the take-off. Muslims must face Mecca when praying, but this would be difficult or impossible aboard a rocket circling the Earth every 90 minutes or so. Accordingly, the authorities decided that facing Mecca was preferable, but facing the Earth in general, or in any direction if this was impractical, would do. And if they could do nothing else, merely imagining the prayer ritual would suffice.

More Empties

AN ARTIST NAMED JANET Zweig, who has created a number of delightful, highly philosophical sculptures, was impressed by the list above of unanswerables, so she decided to incorporate questions like them into a new work of art she was building.[1] So I surveyed philosophers for additions to the list and came up with lots of proposals. Here are some of the questions she's using:

- How many things are there in this room?
- How many words are not in this sentence?
- Do snakes have tails?
- How long is forever?
- Is an apple alive when you eat it?
- Is there an invisible monster behind you?
- Who makes the rules?
- How long is a piece of string?
- How high can you count?
- Is a chair with one leg still a chair?
- If I make a promise to my cat do I have to keep it?
- Can you dig half a hole?
- What colour is a mirror?
- Are more things smaller than you than larger than you?
- Is it possible to tell lies all the time?
- Can you think about nothing?
- How much is enough?
- What happens to the characters after the end of the story?
- What is bigger than the biggest thing imaginable?

---

1   Janet Zweig's artwork is called "The Opposite of a Duck," and a little picture of it (which doesn't do it justice, in its full grandeur) can be seen in the "Public Art" section of her website, www.janetzweig.com. Make sure while you're there to look at the other splendid works she's created.

- Is this sentence true?
- Is doing nothing doing something?
- What colour is the number four?
- Is this a trick question?
- Is there more than one of anything?

Something or Nothing?

"THE FIRST QUESTION WHICH should rightly be asked," wrote G.W. Leibniz in 1719, is "Why is there something rather than nothing?"[1] By the mid-twentieth century, this question apparently hadn't been answered yet; in 1953, Martin Heidegger called it the fundamental question of metaphysics.[2]

What could even count as an answer to the question raised by Leibniz and Heidegger? Maybe nothing. Maybe it's a phoney question, and the reason it's so hard to answer is not that it's far too deep, but rather that it's far too shallow.

> Sidney Morgenbesser, a twentieth-century philosopher known for his witty one-liners, is reported to have proposed this reply to Heidegger: "If there were nothing, you'd still complain."

SOME QUESTIONS TO THINK ABOUT: Are all the questions on the lists above really unanswerable? Maybe you think some of them are answerable (e.g., Is this sentence true? No!). Why are the others unanswerable? Is it the same reason in each case?

One feature that many of the empties above appear to share is that what they ask for cannot be found because it's the wrong sort of thing for the category in question. The number four, for example—numbers in general, in fact—have no colour, cannot have any colour, and we know that in advance. This sort of impossibility (which might be called *logical impossibility*) is different from the more ordinary sort, what we might call *practical impossibility*, for example, the impossibility of my flying around the room by flapping my arms. Can you see the difference? What do you think logical impossibility is the result of?

Is the problem with some of these questions the fact that there's nothing "practically meant" by them? Some philosophers have thought that some traditional philosophical questions lack "practical meaning," and they conclude that they're phoney questions that nobody should waste time thinking

---

1   G.W. Leibniz, "The Principles of Nature and of Grace, Based on Reason," p. 527.
2   Martin Heidegger, *An Introduction to Metaphysics*, pp. 7–8.

about. Medieval philosophers devoted a lot of time to thinking about angels and other non-existents—see below: **Angels and Superman** in Chapter X, and **Two Places Are Better than One** in Chapter XI. But perhaps you shouldn't be too quick to dismiss their problem as a phoney one before you've studied in depth what they wrote; perhaps there was some upshot to this question for them. Anyway, there are clearly questions that have no practical upshot in our lives that seem worth pursuing: much of what astronomers think about, for example, has absolutely no "practical meaning."

FOR FURTHER READING: The James quote is from "What Pragmatism Means," p. 141. The "ordinary language" philosophers, for example J.L. Austin and Gilbert Ryle, often provide subtle, interesting, and surprising analyses of what is "practically meant." A particularly good example is Austin's article "A Plea For Excuses." Ryle (in *The Concept of Mind*), introduced the idea of a "category mistake"—thinking of something as belonging in a category it doesn't belong in: for example, thinking of Cleveland as one of the days of the week. A.J. Ayer is a good example of a philosopher who rejects many traditional philosophical problems as meaningless. See his *Language, Truth, and Logic.*

2. You Can Never Tell

Double or Nothing?

COULD YOU TELL IF, one day, everything in the universe suddenly doubled in size?[1]

> Your shoes would suddenly get twice as big, but they would continue to fit your feet, which would also have doubled in size. You would suddenly become ten or twelve feet tall, but your clothes, your room, and your car would also double. Yardsticks would become twice as long. The corner store would be twice as far away, but walking there would take the same time because your legs would be twice as long. Everything would be twice as far away, but you would double in size, so they would look the same distance away as before. There would be no *practical* effect of this change at all. Applying James's method to this case would tell us that there's no practical difference between the idea that everything doubles in size and the idea that everything stays the same. So a dispute about whether everything has just doubled or not is perhaps really no dispute at all. (Is this right?)

---

1   This puzzle is attributed to the French mathematician and physicist Jules Henri Poincaré.

Proponents of the "relational" theory of space say that there is no such thing as the absolute size of anything: we ascertain something's size by comparing it to other things. So we shouldn't say that this mass doubling might or might not happen: we should rather say that it makes no sense even to contemplate it.

A similar point can be made about the supposition that everything suddenly speeds up to be twice as fast as it used to be. Or that everything suddenly moves three feet to the left.

The Right-Handed Universe

LET'S APPLY THIS APPROACH to another sort of case. Imagine that the universe contained nothing at all except one *right* hand. Now, imagine that the universe contained nothing at all except one *left* hand. Are you imagining two *different* universes?

> All the relations between points in the first universe would be exactly the same as in the second universe. The "relational" theory of space tells us that there is no absolute "handedness" of anything. There wouldn't be any difference between these universes.

But the great nineteenth-century German philosopher Immanuel Kant argued that there *is* a difference between a universe containing only one right hand and a universe containing only one left hand, so the relational theory of space must be wrong.

> A lecturer in the Leeds (England) University medical faculty unaccountably won only *second* place in his university's 1977 annual "Boring Lecturer of the Year" contest, with his lecture "How to Tell Right from Left" accompanied by many slides of a billiard ball viewed from different angles.[1]

Fake Antiques

PHILOSOPHERS HAVE OFTEN IMAGINED things that everyone knows aren't true, and challenged us to prove—or indeed to give any reason at all to think—that they're not true. One example is the Five-Minute Hypothesis (invented by Bertrand Russell[2]). Here's how this goes:

Imagine that the entire universe was created exactly five minutes ago, complete with all sorts of "signs" of a non-existent past. The soles of your

---

1   Stephen Pile, "The Most Boring Lecture."
2   *The Analysis of Mind*, pp. 159–60.

shoes came into existence five minutes ago worn down, looking like they had been walked on for months. That stuff in the bowl in the back of your refrigerator came into existence covered with green fuzzy mould, just as if it had been left there for weeks. You were created five minutes ago complete with all sorts of fake memories of a past that never happened.

We can't prove that the Five-Minute Hypothesis is false by uncovering evidence around us of what happened more than five minutes ago. Finding a newspaper dated yesterday, for example, won't prove anything, because the Hypothesis explains this and all such "evidence" of a past: all those things are fake antiques.

When we compare the Five-Minute Hypothesis with our ordinary way of thinking, the score is tied when we measure their relative ability to explain the way things seem now. Both the hypothesis that I really have been wearing those shoes for months and the Five-Minute Hypothesis explain why the soles of my shoes are worn. We can say that both hypotheses are consistent with all the evidence.

But consistency with all the evidence is not the only criterion we have for the truth of an explanatory hypothesis. Notice that the Five-Minute Hypothesis involves all sorts of unexplained coincidences. The shoes I pseudo-remember wearing are in fact now worn down, so there is a coincidental coherence between this pseudo-memory and the current state of the shoes. Similarly, another pair, which I pseudo-remember leaving in the back of my closet permanently just after I bought them, are now, by coincidence, not worn down. Today's newspaper and the radio news both coincidentally report that the same thing happened yesterday. There are innumerable unexplained coincidences such as this involved in the Five-Minute Hypothesis. A hypothesis full of such unexplained coincidences is a bad one.

But why can't the Five-Minutist reply that a fiendishly clever demon has arranged all these coincidences to fool us? That explains everything.

One way of dealing with the Five-Minute Hypothesis is to treat it as another instance of a "difference" that makes no difference. But we can't resist thinking that it would be a *big* difference if this hypothesis were true.

The age of the universe was the subject of investigation by the Reverend James Ussher, Archbishop of Armagh. Ussher's *Annals of the Ancient and New Testaments*, a scholarly book published in 1650, reported the results of some careful calculations based on scripture: the universe was created in 4004 BCE. This date was accepted by the Church of England as authoritative and was printed in the margins of their Authorized Version of the Bible. More detailed computations by Doctor John Lightfoot, Vice-Chancellor of the University of Cambridge, made the matter more precise: the Creation took place on October 23, 4004 BCE, at 9 a.m. (Lightfoot didn't specify in which time zone it was 9 a.m.)

As science progressed, evidence accumulated that some rocks were millions of years old. How could this be squared with the official church view that nothing was more than six thousand years old? The answer given was analogous to the Five-Minute Hypothesis: In 4004 BCE, the world was created complete with rocks that *seemed* much older. They were fake antiques.

3. Sensational Problems

Mildred's Peculiar Sensations

LOOK AROUND UNTIL YOU see something green. While you're looking at that green thing, you are having a particular kind of visual experience. Call that kind of experience a GE (for "Green Experience"). We think that others also get GEs when they look at green things, but suppose that your friend Mildred doesn't. I don't mean that Mildred is blind or colour-blind. I mean that her experiences are systematically different from yours. When she looks at something green, she has the experience you get when you look at something yellow—a YE. Her experiences, we imagine, are systematically transposed, as given by the following table:

Object is:	Red	Orange	Yellow	Green	Blue	Violet
You get:	RE	OE	YE	GE	BE	VE
She gets:	VE	BE	GE	YE	OE	RE

So whenever Mildred looks at a red thing, she gets a VE (a Violet Experience); whenever she looks at a blue thing, she gets an OE (an Orange Experience); and so on.[1]

Blind or colour-blind people sometimes act differently from people with normal vision, but Mildred doesn't. She has no trouble identifying green things. You ask her what colour the leaves of that tree are, and she unhesitatingly and correctly replies "green." She has, of course, learned to associate

---

1 This example occurs widely in the philosophical literature and is called the "inverted spectrum." It was invented by John Locke, and its first appearance in print was in *An Essay Concerning Human Understanding*, Book 2, Chapter 32, Section 15.

the word *green* with her YE, just as you have learned to associate the word *green* with your GE. She can, at a glance, tell correctly which are the limes and which are the lemons in a pile of mixed citrus fruit. The lemons are the ones that give her a GE when she looks at them, and the limes give her a YE. Just like you, she drives through green lights, and prepares to stop when the light turns yellow. In fact, all her behaviour is just like yours. Could you tell that there's something different about her experiences? Could she? Could anyone?

> It might seem that this is another example of a difference that makes no difference, and thus is really no difference. What we're imagining here seems in no way distinguishable from the supposition that her experiences were exactly the same as yours.
>
> Some philosophers react to the proposal that Mildred has inverted-spectrum sensations by claiming that this proposal is impossible. What is *meant* by 'a Green Experience' is nothing but the sensation one usually gets when looking at something green, so whatever Mildred gets when looking at limes is by definition a GE. It can't be anything else.

Another Inversion in Mildred

NOW TRY TO IMAGINE that Mildred has "inverted experiences" of this sort: Whenever you step on her toe, she feels pleasure. Whenever she is cold and tired and lies down in her nice warm bed, she feels pain. But she behaves just like the rest of us: when you step on her toe, she groans and pushes you off. She hurries eagerly to get into bed after a hectic day. The only difference is in her inward sensations. She peculiarly tries to avoid what's a pleasure to her, and seeks her pains. Is this shown to be nonsense by the same sorts of considerations we raised when considering her inverted spectrum of visual sensations?

We'll see some more of Mildred in Chapter X.

SOME QUESTIONS TO THINK ABOUT: If you think that it's impossible for Mildred to have inverted sensations, does this show that all that matters, when we try to determine what sensations someone has, is what they say, how they act, and what features of the external world they're interacting with? Suppose *you* were in Mildred's place. Would *you* be convinced that you actually felt pain when someone stepped on your toe? How would you learn that that's actually *pain*?

The Cheezy Puzzle

DO YOU REMEMBER WHEN you were a kid, how great those Fluorescent Orange Cheez Puffy Yummies used to taste? Well, try one now. Yes, go ahead, I know it looks terrible. There! What do you think? It's awful now, right? Doesn't taste much like it used to, does it? Well, what's happened? Here are four hypotheses:

1. They've changed Fluorescent Orange Cheez Puffy Yummies.

2. Your tasting mechanism has aged, and the same things now give you a different taste-experience from what they used to.

3. Your experience is the same, but your evaluation—whether you like the taste or don't—has matured. Yummies taste the same, but you don't like that taste now.

4. You remember incorrectly how the Yummies used to taste.

Which one is right? Well, here's some information that may help. I've checked with the Global Dominance Food MultiConglomerate, the outfit that manufactures the Yummies, and they assure me that the ingredients are the same wholesome ones they've always used,[1] and processed in the same way, so we can rule out 1. Now, which is right: 2, 3, or 4? Well, you check with your friends, and they agree with you, so one or the other of these three applies to them too, but no progress has been made in deciding which one's true for anybody. So try this: does anything else taste different from long ago? Yep, some things do, and some things don't. So what? Is there any way of deciding? If not, is this a difference that makes no difference?

Taste-Tests

IF YOU THINK YOU'VE got a clear idea of the way things really taste, decide who is right in the following thought experiments, and why.

1. Phenol-thio-urea is a chemical that tastes very bitter to three people out of four, and completely tasteless to the rest. Who is right? Why? Would it change your mind if it tasted bitter to 90% of people? 99%? More than

---

1 Sugar, lard, 3-5-ß-diphenyltripropanolamine guanilate, petroleum distillates, and just a pinch each of eye-of-newt and toe-of-frog.

half the people suffering from open-angle glaucoma (an eye disease) find this chemical tasteless. Does this make you change your mind? The difference in whether you can taste it or not in fact results from a difference in your genetics. Suppose that, over the next century, human genetics gradually shifted until the chemical was tasteless to everyone. Would how the chemical really tastes have changed then? Why? Why not?

2. When you have a really bad cold, an onion tastes exactly the same as an apple. (Try a bite. It's amazing.) Are you mistaken about how they really taste then? Why?

3. Highly trained wine-tasters can taste differences between two wines that you'd never be able to notice. Are they right or are you? Why?

4. If you think it's all subjective—that taste is only in the tongue of the be-taster, then what do you think of colour?

5. To somewhere around 10% of males of European descent, grass looks the same colour as blood. Is this a defect in their vision? Are they missing something? Suppose 90% of humans were this way. What then? Suppose that, over the next century, human genetics gradually shifted until grass looked the same colour as blood to everyone. Would it then be the same colour?

FOR FURTHER READING: The Cheez Puzzle is adapted from a similar one raised by Daniel Dennett in his paper "Quining Qualia." (See the section in his article on the coffee-tasters Chase and Sanborn.) The paper draws very surprising and important conclusions about a basic issue in the philosophy of mind. You can read this paper online. Dennett also discusses the phenolthio-urea puzzle, but its original source is Jonathan Bennett, "Substance, Reality and Primary Qualities."

4. The True and the Useful

It's Practically True

WILLIAM JAMES'S POSITION IS that questions about whose answers we seem to disagree are answered (or made to disappear) when we consider the "practical meaning" of what is being argued about. He thought that the real significance of the dispute whether X is true or false was what difference believing X would make to anyone's life. If there is no difference, then the dispute is empty. But where there is a difference, James argued that the test for whether X was true or false involved the evaluation of the practical results of believing X—whether people who believed X would be better off in coping with their surroundings than people who didn't. If they were better off, then there are grounds for believing X. What James has here is a theory of truth: X is true when believing X makes people better off.

Is this theory correct?

Sometimes this theory gives results that look right. Suppose, for example, that Archibald believes that the Number 4 bus stops on this corner, and Millicent believes it doesn't. It's easy to imagine that the person who is correct is also the person who will be better off when she or he wants to catch the Number 4 bus.

But James had more controversial uses of his theory in mind. In his book *The Varieties of Religious Experience*[1] he described what he took to be the typical psychological effects of religious conversion and belief. These effects, he claimed, were beneficial for the believer. Since the practical implications of religious belief are beneficial, it follows from his theory of truth that religious beliefs are true.

James's defence of religious belief is, of course, open to debate. For one thing, we could question his claims about the beneficial effects of religious belief. We can also balk at his claim that *being good for you to believe* is all that *being true* consists in. Couldn't some beliefs be good for people even though false? Couldn't some beliefs be bad for people, even though true?

Yes to both. It's good for old granny to believe that your sister is happily married. It would be bad for her to know the truth. Don't tell her! She wouldn't be able to do anything to help, and it would just cast a pall over her few remaining years.

What's So Good about True Beliefs Anyway?

FREQUENTLY, BELIEVING WHAT'S TRUE has better effects than believing what's false, as in the case of Archibald and Millicent above. But never mind that: is there something good *just in itself* (never mind the results) about believing what's true? And something bad *just in itself* about believing what's false? Francine believes that the pyramids in Egypt were built by aliens from the planet Zarkon, because she read it while waiting in line at the supermarket. We've told her those newspapers aren't a reliable source of information,

---

1   See also his 1896 article, "The Will to Believe."

but she doesn't care. Well, so what? It's not going to cause her any harm, nor would she get any advantage from believing the truth.

Philosophers sometimes claim that we have responsibilities as knowers to try to ensure that what we believe is true. Not because it's good for us; just because believing what's true is what our brains are for. Does that make any sense?

> "William James used to preach the 'will to believe.' For my part, I should wish to preach the 'will to doubt.' What is wanted is not the will to believe but the will to find out, which is the exact opposite."—Bertrand Russell[1]

> "The average man does not get pleasure out of an idea because he thinks it is true; he thinks it is true because he gets pleasure out of it."—H.L. Mencken.[2]

FOR FURTHER READING: Pascal's Wager, examined in Chapter II, is another argument for religious belief based on the benefits of that belief. In Chapter VI we'll take another critical look at the idea that the benefits of believing something are grounds for thinking it's true.

Into the Mainstream of Philosophy

IN THIS CHAPTER, AS in all the following ones, there is what seems to be a rather random and disorganized bunch of musings; but there is method in this madness. The items in each chapter are (for the most part) connected to one of the major fields of academic philosophical study.

You'll find, then, as we proceed, an occasional item titled INTO THE MAINSTREAM OF PHILOSOPHY. In these items I'll describe, in very brief outline, the general area of mainstream philosophical study relevant to the chapter at hand, occasionally mentioning the conventional names philosophers use to refer to their major areas of concern and their major positions on these areas. I'll pull together some of the musings into the chapter, to show you a bit about how they are connected.

You've already seen some notes on where you might go to do further reading on the particular problems and positions discussed. In the INTO THE MAINSTREAM items I'll often suggest how to find readings on the general issues raised in the chapter.

---

1   *Sceptical Essays.*
2   *In Defense of Women.*

A good place to start reading philosophy is in any of the scores of major introductory philosophy anthologies widely available in university bookstores. The articles in anthologies are by a wide variety of philosophers and are usually grouped by subject matter; you'll find contiguous articles arguing for different positions on the same question. Most anthologies contain articles that are important, deep, and revealing, while at the same time understandable to someone not yet immersed in the field.

Well, then, about this first chapter:

We had a glance at James's views. His position, influential not only among American philosophers, is called *pragmatism*. It goes some way toward answering questions about *meaning*—by telling us what the meaning of a question or of a declarative sentence is. It is also the germ of a theory of truth, holding that what it is for a sentence to be true is for it to be (putting things roughly) useful. The core of his position is that the meaning or truth of anything is to be determined by its connections with real-life experience. This position has had a rather radical effect in some areas. What are we to make of the (supposedly) meaningful—perhaps sometimes even true—things that are said in religion, for example, where talk about God and angels seems quite disconnected from everyday mundane reality? How are we to understand scientific theory? You can't ever experience an electron; so how can you talk about one? (Perhaps, on James's criterion, talk about electrons is "really" just talk about the sort of things we can interact with: light bulbs, electric meters, and so on.) How can historians talk about a past they can't interact with? How (if at all) can psychologists discover anything about the minds of other people, locked privately inside them?

Pragmatism has affinities with another view, popularized originally by a group of Viennese philosophers who came to England and America around the time of World War II: the Vienna Circle. Their view, called *logical positivism*, emphasized the necessity of sense-experience and practical testability in evaluating the truth, and understanding the meaning, of any statement. Like James's, this view tended at first to have a destructive, or at least a radically re-evaluative effect, on many areas of talk and enquiry.

Philosophy since it began has struggled with "sceptical questions": What's wrong with the Five-Minute Hypothesis? What makes us think that there is an external world at all? (Maybe it's all hallucination!) How can you prove that anything is right or wrong? Pragmatism and logical positivism are both sometimes inclined to see these questions as meaningless: that since their answer would make no difference in our experience, there's something wrong with the question. Not everyone has found this answer satisfying.

Chapter II

God

1. Religious Belief

The Invisible Gardener

MURGATROYD AND MILLICENT COME across a patch of land containing flowers and weeds. The following discussion ensues:

Murgatroyd: A gardener must tend this plot.
Millicent: I don't think so. Look, it's full of weeds.
Murgatroyd: The gardener must like those weeds. They are nice, aren't they?
Millicent: Those weeds grow around here all by themselves; anyway, I've talked to people who live around here, and nobody told me anything about seeing any gardener at work.
Murgatroyd: Well, the gardener must have been here when everyone was asleep.

They take turns watching, day and night, but no gardener is seen. Murgatroyd explains this fact by supposing that the gardener must be invisible. They set up an electric alarm system sensitive to heat, and patrol with bloodhounds, but there's no reaction from either. Murgatroyd is still not convinced.

Murgatroyd: The gardener is not only invisible, but undetectable to the alarm system, and without odour the bloodhounds could smell.
Millicent: I'm getting fed up with your argument. Your gardener is supposed to be invisible and completely undetectable to anyone, and is supposed to have planted things the way they would

have grown anyway. What makes him different from no gardener at all?

The analogy here is to arguments about God's existence. Believers often admit that there's a natural scientific explanation of the way things are. They also admit that God is undetectable by all the ordinary detection methods.

The question we might ask here is this: How is the assertion that such an undetectable God exists any different from the assertion that there isn't any God? Here's one possible answer:

> There's no real difference in beliefs or expectations about the real world in the religious believer and in the disbeliever. There's just a difference in how they feel about things. If so, then maybe there's no question about who is right and who is wrong.

SOME QUESTIONS TO THINK ABOUT: If this response to the Invisible Gardener story is right, then religions don't say things that should be judged true or false. What they say is more like poetry: the expression of feelings and attitudes. If you are a religious person, does this view of religious "truths" seem right to you? (It doesn't to most religious people.)

The response given above to the argument between Millicent and Murgatroyd is like William James's response to the squirrel debate. Do you see the similarity?

FOR FURTHER READING: The Parable of the Invisible Gardener, and the response to the question we've considered, are both found in John Wisdom's article "Gods." For a three-way discussion of these issues, see Antony Flew, R.M. Hare, and Basil Mitchell, "Theology and Falsification."

Industrial Prayer

IT'S SOMETIMES CLAIMED THAT prayer doesn't work—I mean, that it doesn't increase the probability of getting what you pray for. George Santayana puts it this way:

> No chapter in theology is more unhappy than that in which a material efficacy is assigned to prayer. In the first place the facts contradict that notion that curses can bring evil or blessings can cure; and it is not observed that the most orthodox and hard-praying army wins the most battles.[1]

---

1   *Reason in Religion* (*The Life of Reason*, vol. 3) pp. 32–33.

If prayer really "attracted superhuman forces to our aid by giving them a signal without which they would not have been able to reach us," says Santayana, then

> There would be nothing in it more impossible than in ordinary telepathy; prayer would then be an art like conversation, and the exact personages and interests would be discoverable to which we might appeal. A celestial diplomacy might then be established not very unlike primitive religions. Religion would have reverted to industry and science.[1]

But, of course, religion is not just another industry. You can tell that by contrasting churches with factories. The latter are utilitarian places, single-mindedly directed toward the creation of a product; their décor pays no attention to beauty—it's the rare factory that has stained-glass windows or gothic arches—or to any uplifting effect on the people inside. They don't characteristically have organ music; factory workers rarely sing songs together.

So what is prayer for? According to Santayana, prayer is a soliloquy, not a conversational request. In rational prayer, he says,

> The soul may be said to accomplish three things important to its welfare: it withdraws within itself and defines its good, it accommodates itself to destiny, and it grows like the ideal which it conceives.[2]

The Anti-Flu Flight

BUT MANY RELIGIOUS PEOPLE do believe that prayer has material effect. The following excerpt from the online news story "Rabbis fight flu pandemic" gives a rather unusual example.

> August 10, 2009. (Reuters) Dozens of rabbis and Kabbalah mystics armed with ceremonial trumpets have taken to the skies over Israel to battle the H1N1 flu virus, Israeli media said on Tuesday. About 50 Jewish holy men chanted prayers and blew ritual rams' horns in an aircraft circling over the country in the hope of stopping the spread of the virus....

---

1   Santayana, pp. 33–34.
2   Santayana, p. 43.

These horn-tooting Jews represent only the small extreme fundamentalist wing of the religion. Most Jews nowadays are much more
sceptical regarding the effects of prayer. A Jewish proverb (sharing
Santayana's point) says, "If it did any good to pray, they'd be hiring
people to do it."[1]

SOME QUESTIONS TO THINK ABOUT: Don't many religious people think
prayer has a material effect—sometimes getting you what you want? (Do you
think it does?) If a very large proportion of religious people think of prayer
this way, how can Santayana claim that its "real" function is something else?

A mountain climber slips over a precipice and clings to a rope over
a thousand-foot drop. In fear and despair, he looks to the heavens
and cries, "Is there anyone up there who can help me?" A voice from
above booms, "You will be saved if you show your faith by letting
go of the rope." The man looks down, then up, and shouts, "Is there
anyone *else* up there who can help me?"[2]

An uncontroversial example of the power of prayer occurred when
it caused what's probably an unbeatable record for the earliest goal
in professional soccer, set at a match between two Brazilian teams,
the Corinthians and the Rio Preto club. At the start of the game, a
Corinthians player kicked off by passing to another player, who instantly scored from the mid-field line at three seconds into the match.
The goal went past the ear of the Rio Preto goalie who was on his
knees finishing his pre-match prayers.[3]

I Believe in One Outpouring of Existence Itself

PRINCETON PHILOSOPHY PROFESSOR MARK Johnston agrees that the
idea that prayer can enlist divine help is not part of an ideal religious approach. He argues that the problem with most religious belief is that it is
"idolatrous"—that is, it sees God with human characteristics, as an ally who
can be called upon to help.

But what he proposes as an alternative way of seeing God is not really
altogether clear. He suggests instead that we think of "the Highest One"

---

1   Arthur Naiman, *Every Goy's Guide to Common Jewish Expressions*, p. 159.
2   Joke reported by Steven Pinker, *How the Mind Works*, p. 550.
3   Pile, p. 105.

(God) as "the Outpouring of Existence Itself by way of its exemplification in ordinary existents for the sake of the self-disclosure of Existence Itself."[1]

Got that? Me neither.

Religious Truths

THE MATERIAL EFFECTIVENESS OF prayer is, as we've seen, a religious idea that might call for some critical thought. A second one is the common notion that religions can tell us truths about history and about nature. Following are a couple of odd instances of this.

(1) Divine Geology

A high-ranking Iranian Muslim cleric has announced that the root cause of frequent earthquakes in his country is immodest dressing by some Iranian women.

Post-pubescent women are required by Iranian law to cover their hair and to wear loose clothing that does not show their body contours. But some urban women, nevertheless, have taken to wearing pulled-back head-scarves and tight coats. Ayatollah Kazem Sedighi told worshippers in Tehran that "many women who dress inappropriately … cause youths to go astray, taint their chastity and incite extramarital sex in society, which increases earthquakes."[2]

Iran is in a zone of heavy earthquake activity. In 2003, a particularly bad one killed one-quarter of the population of the southern city appropriately called Bam.

(2) One Hell of a Rainstorm

It says in the Bible that during the Flood, "all the high hills that were under the whole heaven were covered." The mathematician John Allen Paulos calculates that in order to cover every mountain, there must have been ten to twenty thousand feet of water on the Earth's surface, somewhere around half a billion cubic miles of water. It rained for forty days and forty nights. To produce a flood of that size in that period, it must have rained, on average, fifteen feet of water per hour. A really heavy and destructive rainstorm in our day can put several inches of water on the ground per hour. But fifteen *feet* of

---

1   In *Saving God.*
2   Reported in many newspapers and websites, mostly dated April 17–20, 2010.

water in an hour, Paulos remarks, is enough to sink an aircraft carrier. How did Noah's little wooden ark, loaded with thousands of animals, stay afloat?[1]

> Maybe you want to reply that this is just another one of those religious miracles we're not supposed to be able to understand. Or maybe you think that what's said in the Bible is not supposed to be taken literally like this. Perhaps someone who "believes in the Bible" need not have beliefs in different *facts* from someone who doesn't. But maybe you just think that a good deal of what it says in the Bible ain't necessarily so.

Faith

WHAT'S INTERESTING ABOUT RELIGIOUS belief is not just its often unusual content, but also its methodology for discovery. Seen as a way of finding out what's true, religious faith is pretty peculiar, when you get right down to it. For one thing, faith isn't believing because of good evidence— it's believing something when there isn't any evidence for it, or even when there's overwhelming evidence to the contrary. Is this a good idea?

> "Tell a devout Christian his wife is cheating on him, or that frozen yogurt can make a man invisible, and he is likely to require as much evidence as anybody else, and to be persuaded only to the extent that you give it. Tell him that the book he keeps by his bed was written by an invisible deity who will punish him with fire for eternity if he fails to accept every incredible claim, and he seems to require no evidence whatsoever."—Sam Harris[2]

> "Faith may be defined briefly as an illogical belief in the occurrence of the improbable.... A man full of faith is simply one who has lost (or never had) the capacity for clear and realistic thought. He is not a mere ass; he is actually ill. Worse, he is incurable."—H.L. Mencken[3]

> "The fact that faith moves no mountains but may very readily raise them where previously they did not exist [is] made sufficiently clear by a mere casual stroll through a lunatic asylum."—Friedrich Nietzsche[4]

---

1   *Innumeracy: Mathematical Illiteracy and Its Consequences*, pp. 16–17.
2   *The End of Faith*, p. 19.
3   *Prejudices: Third Series*, Chapter 14.
4   *Twilight of the Idols*.

"'Faith' means not wanting to know what is true."—Friedrich Neitzsche[1]

"Faith is when you believe something that you know ain't true."[2]

"Trust in Allah, but tie your camel."—Arab proverb[3]

Brainless Spirituality

A RESEARCHER IN ITALY REPORTS that removing part of the brain increases spirituality.

It's been known for a while that feelings associated with religion are associated with certain patterns of brain activity. But there's recent evidence of a causal connection between what's going on in the brain—or rather what isn't—and spirituality. Dr. Cosimo Urgesi of the University of Udine in Italy has been studying the neurological basis of the personality trait called "self-transcendence," a decreased sense of self and an ability to identify one's self as an integral part of the universe as a whole. He's discovered that this showed up in people after surgery (for a brain tumour) removed brain matter from the left or right posterior parietal regions.[4]

The Philosophy Poll

SEVENTY-THREE PER CENT OF philosophers responding to a recent poll[5] reported that they "accept or lean toward" atheism; toward theism, 15 per cent. (The rest had "other" responses.)

---

1   *The Antichrist.*
2   This is probably just an old saying, author unknown; it's attributed to a "schoolboy" by William James in "The Will to Believe" and (slightly paraphrased) by Mark Twain in *Following the Equator.* A more recent version, "Faith is when you believe something that no one in his right mind would believe," was Archie Bunker's attempt to explain religion to his agnostic son-in-law.
3   Cited by Robert Byrne in *1,911 Best Things Anybody Ever Said.*
4   Urgesi et al., "The Spiritual Brain: Selective Cortical Lesions Modulate Human Self-Transcendence."
5   The poll's respondents were 1,803 philosophy teachers and 829 philosophy graduate students. The questions and results are given and discussed in detail on the PhilPapers website.

2. God's Difficulties

MOST RELIGIONS BELIEVE THAT God is omnipotent. This means that God can do anything He wants to do. Could God create a stone too heavy for Him to lift?

> Let's suppose He can. Then, if He did, He'd have created a stone too heavy for Him to lift. Since He couldn't lift it, He wouldn't be omnipotent. But let's suppose He can't. Then there is something God can't do, so He isn't omnipotent. Either way, omnipotence is impossible. Maybe omnipotence makes no sense.

The suggestion here is that major religions must be mistaken in thinking that there is an omnipotent (= all-powerful) God, because omnipotence is logically impossible.

God Made Me Do It

THE DOCTRINE OF GOD'S omnipotence raises similar problems when connected with the idea that we have free will. Does the fact (if it is a fact) that we are free mean that our decisions can't be controlled by outside influences? If so, then there's another limitation on God's power. As in the unliftable stone example, we can put this problem in the form of a dilemma:[1] If God *can* create a person whose actions He can't control, then this person's actions would be a limit to His power: He wouldn't be omnipotent. If He *can't* create such a person, then that's a limit to His power: He wouldn't be omnipotent. Either way, omnipotence is impossible.

God Knows!

SOME PHILOSOPHERS HAVE WORRIED about the traditional religious assumption that God is *omniscient* (= all-knowing). That means, presumably, that God knows what everyone's going to do, and that doesn't seem to square with the idea that what we do is undetermined, that we have free will. We'll look at the idea of free will a lot later, in Chapter XV. Note for the moment, however, that if God knows now what you're going to do tomorrow, then isn't it inevitable that you're going to do it? Doesn't that mean that you don't have any choice?

---

1   In Chapter XV I'll talk about what *dilemmas* are.

Alvin is working in his store when he hears a booming voice from above that says, "Alvin, sell your business!" He ignores it. The voice goes on for days saying, "Alvin, sell your business for three million dollars!" After weeks of this, he relents and sells his store.

The voice says, "Alvin, go to Las Vegas!"

Alvin asks why.

"Alvin, just take the three million dollars and go to Las Vegas."

Alvin obeys, goes to Las Vegas, and visits a casino.

The voice says, "Alvin, go to the blackjack table and put it all down on one hand!"

Alvin hesitates but gives in. He's dealt an eighteen. The dealer has a six showing.

"Alvin, take a card!"

"*What?* The dealer has ..."

"Take a card!"

Alvin tells the dealer to hit him, and gets an ace. Nineteen. He breathes easy.

"Alvin, take another card."

"What?"

"TAKE ANOTHER CARD!"

Alvin asks for another card. It's another ace. He has twenty.

"Alvin, take another card!" the voice commands.

"*I have twenty!*" Alvin shouts.

"TAKE ANOTHER CARD!" booms the voice.

"*Hit me!*" Alvin says. He gets another ace. Twenty-one!

And the booming voice says, "Un–fucking–believable!"[1]

God the Counterfeiter

ANOTHER THING GOD CAN'T do is make a genuine ten-dollar bill. God could, presumably, make an atom-for-atom duplicate of a genuine ten-dollar bill that would fool everyone, but that bill would be counterfeit. Only bills produced by the government mint are genuine. God could, of course, make the mint produce a genuine bill, but He couldn't make one directly.

Here's another limit to God's omnipotence. The familiar poem says that

---

1   This joke is from *Plato and a Platypus Walk into a Bar: Understanding Philosophy Through Jokes* by Thomas Cathcart and Daniel Klein. Several other jokes in my book are also found there, but I haven't footnoted them, believing that they're not original with that book, but that they've been developed, as have most jokes, just through people telling them to each other.

"Only God can make a tree," but perhaps God can't make a tree. According to some biologists, what it takes for something to count as an oak tree, for example, is that it has to have come from another oak tree. Suppose you manufactured something out of chemicals that looked and worked exactly like an oak tree, that even dropped acorns in the fall that grew into things just like it. What you made wouldn't be an oak tree, since it didn't come from an oak tree. Your inability to make an oak tree isn't the result of your lack of ability in biochemistry. No matter how accurate a look-alike you made out of chemicals, it wouldn't *count* as an oak tree, since oak trees are, *by definition*, what comes from other oak trees. So God, with infinite biochemical abilities, couldn't make an oak tree either.

These two peculiar cases share something in common. What it takes to be a genuine ten-dollar bill or an oak tree is not merely a matter of what something is made of, or how its parts are put together, or how it works. In both cases, there has to be a *historical* characteristic present—something true about its *past*.

> Historical characteristics played a role in a newsworthy event of a few years ago. During the riots and looting in Los Angeles, somebody broke into Frederick's of Hollywood, the famous erotic underwear store, and stole Madonna's bra from their Museum of Famous Underwear. Frederick's posted a huge reward for the return of the famous garment, and a few days later, a bra was brought in by someone claiming the reward. It was exactly the brand, model, and size of the one stolen earlier, but it was a phoney: it wasn't the one worn by Madonna. It differed from the genuine article only in a historical characteristic. We can wonder: if all its *present* characteristics were identical with the real one, how did the Frederick's staff know it was a phoney?

SOME QUESTIONS TO THINK ABOUT: In order to count as an antique, something has to have a historical property: it has to have been made more than a certain number of years ago. Can you think of other categories that require historical properties?

We can distinguish between *intrinsic* and *relational* properties. The former are characteristics of a thing that are true of it in itself; the latter are true of it insofar as it is related to something else, or insofar as something happened at another time or place. Two things might be identical in all their intrinsic properties, and differ only in their relational properties. A genuine ten-dollar bill and a really perfect counterfeit are an example of a pair like this. Historical properties are one sort of relational property; another is *ownership*. Imagine that you and I each own brand-new copies of the same book. The books are (almost perfectly) alike in all their intrinsic properties, but they differ in an important relational way: one is owned by me, and the other one isn't. Because they're intrinsically indistinguishable, there might be no way for someone to tell which one is mine and which one is yours just by looking at them—that is, by examining their intrinsic properties. Of course, someone could tell which one was mine if I had written my name in it, but then they would differ in a relevant intrinsic property.

This is another relational property: being the tallest mountain on Earth. No matter how much you examined Mt. Everest, no matter how much you knew about its intrinsic properties, you couldn't tell whether it was the tallest mountain on Earth unless you know how it was related in size to the other mountains. Can you think of other sorts of relational property?

If you subscribe to a religion including belief in an omnipotent God, what sort of changes would you have to make if you were convinced that God really can't be omnipotent? Would that affect the real substance of your religion in important ways?

But can you think of ways to get around the problems about omnipotence? Here are some suggestions.

> The argument shows that omnipotence is logically impossible. But logical problems don't bother God. God isn't subject to the laws of logic. He can have logically impossible characteristics.

One problem with this answer is that—it seems—it's impossible for us to understand logically impossible characteristics. For example, suppose that I said to you, "I have a glass with water here which has this peculiar characteristic: it's filled with water and empty." First you'd suspect that I was playing with words, or telling an obscure joke. But if I assured you that I was speaking literally, you would doubt what I was saying, because the very idea of a glass which is both filled and empty makes no sense at all. It's not as if I was talking about some characteristic that, for some reason, glasses weren't allowed to have;[1] it's that I'm just talking nonsense.

Some religious people cheerfully admit that religious truths surpass all understanding. (The mystery of religious truths is something that some religious people find attractive.) But other people aren't comfortable with the idea of saying, or trying to believe, things that make no sense.

Here's another suggestion for a response:

---

1   That is, it's not a category mistake (a notion discussed in the previous chapter).

> Let's agree that if He couldn't create a stone too heavy for Him to lift, He wouldn't
> be omnipotent. If He could create this stone *and did*, then there would be a stone
> around He couldn't lift; so again, He wouldn't be omnipotent. But suppose He *could*
> create this stone *but didn't*. Where's the problem with His omnipotence now?

We might want to reply to the problem about free will in the same sort of way: that God *could* create an uncontrollable human but *doesn't*. But this reply won't work here: religions usually hold that God *did* in fact create humans with free will.

A Proof That Everything Is Hunky-Dory

LET'S ASSUME THAT GOD, as conventional religions conceive of Him, really did create the universe. God, of course, wanted to create the best universe He could, and His omnipotence means that He was capable of doing anything He wanted. So it follows that this is the best of all possible universes. (This view has been called "cosmic Toryism," referring to the smug and complacent attitude of certain members of the British Conservative Party.) You're wrong if you think that anything could be any better. Does that make you feel good? You should cheer up.

Now that you know that everything is perfect, you'd better be more careful about changing the way things are. When you walk down the street, you might move a pebble an inch south, messing up God's perfect creation.

> That's a cheap shot. No religious people think that the creation of the world by a
> benevolent and omnipotent God entails that everything in it is perfect and nothing
> should be changed.

A QUESTION TO THINK ABOUT: Okay, if that's not what they think, then what do they think? How could a God like that create anything less than perfect?

God When He Was a Baby

SUPPOSE (THE PHILOSOPHER DAVID Hume invites us) that someone was brought into this world from somewhere else, and was assured that the world was made by a supernatural, powerful, and benevolent divine being. He might wonder about the apparent imperfections he found, but he would probably suppose that these were only a sign of his imperfect intelligence, and that they were all here for a good reason. But suppose instead, Hume continues, that this person were not brought into the world with this assurance. Would

he conclude on the basis of observation that it was made by such a being?
Hume suggests four general sorts of flaws in construction he'd notice:

[The] contrivance or economy of the animal creation, by which pains, as well as pleasures, are employed to excite all creatures to action, and make them vigilant in the great work of self-preservation. Now pleasure alone, in its various degrees, seems to human understanding sufficient for this purpose.

Might not the Deity exterminate all ill, wherever it were to be found; and produce all good, without any preparation, or long progress of causes and effects?

Every animal has the requisite endowments [for its preservation]; but ... little more powers or endowments than what are strictly sufficient to supply those necessities.

The inaccurate workmanship of all the springs and principles of the great machine of nature.... There is nothing so advantageous in the universe, but what frequently becomes pernicious, by its excess or defect; nor has Nature guarded, with the requisite accuracy, against all disorder or confusion.

Because of all this, Hume concludes, one not already predisposed to believe that the world was made by a benevolent and powerful deity might conclude instead that it was "only the first rude essay of some infant deity, who afterwards abandoned it, ashamed of his lame performance" or "the work only of some dependent, inferior deity; and ... the object of derision to his superiors" or "the production of old age and dotage in some superannuated deity."[1]

The Fawn in the Fire

HUME'S WAY OF REASONING about difficulties in believing in a benevolent, all-powerful creator is rather abstract. Here's a story that makes things somewhat more vivid.

Lightning strikes a dead tree, igniting a forest fire. A fawn is trapped by the flames, and burned horribly. It lies in agony for days before it dies.

---

1   David Hume, *Dialogues Concerning Natural Religion*, Part XI.

That sort of thing *should* have been prevented, if it could have been, right? I mean, *you* would have helped the fawn escape the fire if you had been there and could have done it without too much risk to yourself, wouldn't you? And you're not anywhere near as benevolent as God is supposed to be.

Could a world in which that happens really be ruled by a God worthy of our respect?

> Well, look, maybe that fawn's death is for the greater good in some way. Maybe it prevents a greater evil.

Maybe. But is there any reason to think that this is so? If not, that might not be a good enough response.[1]

A QUESTION TO THINK ABOUT: It's not obvious to everyone that this is the sort of universe that would be created by a benevolent, all-powerful God who had our interests at heart.

> A ship is tossing dangerously in a storm. A passenger rushes to the captain and asks him about the danger. "We are all in God's hands," says the captain. "Oh no! As bad as that!" exclaims the passenger.

> "How can I believe in God when just last week I got my tongue caught in the roller of an electric typewriter?"—Woody Allen[2]

> "If God lived on earth, people would break his windows."—Jewish proverb

What explains all the features of our world that seem to go against us?

> "Imagine the Creator as a low comedian, and at once the world becomes explicable."—H.L. Mencken

> "Suppose the world was only one of God's jokes, would you work any the less to make it a good joke, instead of a bad one?"
> —George Bernard Shaw[3]

---

1   The fawn example, and the argument that the theist's proposal is irrational, is found in William L. Rowe's article "The Problem of Evil and Some Varieties of Atheism."

2   "Selections from the Allen Notebooks."

3   *Collected Letters, 1898–1910*, vol. 2.

3. Oddball Theories of Religion

How There Got to Be Only One God

THE BELIEF THAT THERE is only one God who is genuinely perfect—infinite in power and knowledge—arose a long time ago, and there is little hard historical evidence about how it came about. Here, however, is one hypothesis.

Today's major monotheistic religions, Judaism, Christianity, and Islam, all have their origins in the Middle East: Judaism developed there first, then Christianity arose within the Jewish tradition and separated from it. Later the Muslims (the followers of Islam) branched off from Christianity. Is their common origin in the Middle East just a coincidence? Some people think not.

Most religions are polytheistic, recognizing the existence of a number of limited gods. Polytheists often see one of the gods as the god of their group, the one who looks especially after their interests. In a sense, polytheism reflects and encourages a sort of tolerance and inter-tribe stability. A polytheistic tribe typically accepts the existence not only of their own special god, but also of the gods of the neighbouring tribes.

In the hostile climate and terrain of the ancient Middle East, however, there must have been little tolerance and stability. The necessities of life—water, and food plants and animals—were hard to come by; when they ran out in one place the tribe had to move on. So tribes were nomadic, constantly on the move. Stability of territory could not develop, and we can imagine a good deal of inter-tribe conflict and hostility as one tribe encroached on another.

The constant hostility of these tribes did not encourage tolerant recognition of the others' gods. We can imagine that their conflict was reflected by religious competitiveness, with each tribe claiming that its god was bigger, better, and stronger than the others'. "My god is stronger than yours!" says the priest of Tribe A. "Oh yeah? Well, *my* god is stronger than one hundred men!" claims the priest of Tribe B. "*My* god is stronger than one thousand men!" retorts the Tribe A priest. This continues. At last one tribe comes up with a topper that can't be beaten: "*My* god is *infinitely* strong. He knows *everything* and can do *anything He wants.*" A god who is literally infinite in all his attributes must be the *only* real god there is. Thus monotheism.

A QUESTION TO THINK ABOUT: Is this story about the origin of monotheism true? Maybe—who knows? But telling this story might be a way of suggesting that the religious story was based on historical petty competitiveness, not on any divine reality.

The argument that someone's belief must be false because of its origin is a weak one in general—weak and common enough to have its own title among the fallacies listed in many logic books: the "genetic fallacy." Of course many beliefs with peculiar origins are nonetheless true. But aren't beliefs that have their origin in *the fact that the belief is about* more reliable than those with other origins? So doesn't a peculiar origin, one having nothing to do with the real facts, cast some doubt on a belief?

FOR FURTHER READING: There are two very well-known works speculating about the psychological origins of religious beliefs. One already mentioned is James's *The Varieties of Religious Experience.* The other is Sigmund Freud's *The Future of an Illusion* (1927). They offer somewhat different accounts of the psychological function of religion, but the biggest difference is that James counts the psychological functionality of religious beliefs to show their truth, while Freud takes them to be illusions based on wish fulfillment.

God Is Love?

IN THE STORY WE'VE just looked at, monotheism grows out of and encourages hostility to other religious groups and encroachment on their territory. History and current events do seem to show an extraordinary amount of intolerance for other religions among the monotheistic religions, and even between the sects within them. Wars are not uncommon in history, of course, but wars based on religious intolerance seem especially prevalent among and between the monotheists. Think of the Crusades, which were religious wars between the Christians and the Muslims; the waves of Christian anti-Semitism; and the present-day hostility and warfare between Middle Eastern Muslims and Jews. Rival sects of Muslims wage war in Lebanon, and rival sects of Christians in Northern Ireland. The history of Christianity is marked by expansionism, the attempt to convert the rest of the world to its own unique God, often by force when persuasion fails.

> In medieval Spain, Christians and Jews lived together in comparative harmony, but this ended during the Renaissance with a Christian campaign for conversion. Techniques for converting Jews included the wheel and the rack, pouring hot lead into bodily orifices, the use of branding and blinding irons, burning, de-tonguing, de-nailing, skin-stripping, and attaching the arms and legs to four horses driven off in different directions.[1] It's estimated that one-third of the several

---

1   Leo Rosten et al, *The New Joys of Yiddish*, p. 218.

hundred thousand Spanish Jews were thus converted, and another third killed; the remaining third were exiled to somewhat more tolerant countries.

Where Heaven Came From

THE BELIEF IN AN afterlife is common to many religions, but it has a variety of versions, motivations, and origins. One theory for its early development among the ancient Jews is their attempt to explain why God appeared to be treating them badly, breaking so many of his promises to them. The only explanation consistent with God's truthfulness and goodness is that the promises are actually fulfilled in post-mortem existence.[1] Plato alludes to a similar argument: during life on Earth, good people sometimes seem to suffer, and evildoers prosper. But this couldn't really be true, everything considered, so there must be an afterlife in which rewards and punishments are distributed so as to produce justice.[2]

4. Proving the Existence of God

God as the Tortoise on the Bottom

A COMMONLY HEARD ARGUMENT for the existence of God is the following:

> Every natural event in the world has a cause. So something that happened today had a cause that happened earlier, and this other event was itself caused by a still earlier event, and so on back. But there must have been a first cause in this series, or else it wouldn't have gotten started. This first cause is God.

Here is Bertrand Russell's reply to this argument:

> If everything must have a cause, then God must have a cause. If there can be anything without a cause, it may just as well be the world as God, so that there cannot be any validity in that argument. It is exactly of the same nature as the Hindu's view, that the world rested upon an

---

1   This theory was reported by Carlos Eire, author of a book on the history of ideas of immortality, *A Very Brief History of Eternity*. Eire talked about this in an interview in the [Toronto] *Globe and Mail*, "On a fearful day, you can see forever," by John Allemang.

2   Plato may be suggesting this at around 612 in *The Republic*; what he's up to there, however, is subject to interpretation.

elephant and the elephant rested upon a tortoise; and when they said, "How about the tortoise?" the Indian said, "Suppose we change the subject." The argument is really no better than that.[1]

Various versions (and attributions) of this story circulate. In one version, a scientist asks the "old lady" proposing the elephant/tortoise view what holds up the tortoise. "You're very clever, young man, very clever," said the old lady. "But it's turtles all the way down!"[2]

The Miracle on the Expressway

HUGELY UNLIKELY EVENTS ARE sometimes seen as miracles by religious believers, and counted as evidence for the existence of God. Bertrand Russell offered the following facetious argument along those lines:

The next time you're on an expressway, take note of the number on the license plate of one car at random. Now calculate the probability of seeing exactly that number: given the thousands of cars with different license-plate numbers that travel on that expressway, the probability of seeing that one is minuscule. A miracle! God must exist.[3]

A QUESTION TO THINK ABOUT: Nobody is fooled by this reasoning, but it's not easy to explain exactly what has gone wrong. Can you?

Unusual Arguments for God's Existence

"The Bible has been translated into hundreds of different languages, but God's existence is mentioned in *every single translation*! Such widespread testimony would be inexplicable unless He exists."—from a paper written by one of my students.

"This old world has three times as much water as land but with all of its twisting and turning not a drop sloshes off into space."—cited in a magazine symposium as evidence of God's guiding hand.[4]

---

1   "Why I am Not a Christian."
2   Stephen W. Hawking, *A Brief History of Time: From the Big Bang to Black Holes.*
3   Another multi-version quotation difficult to track to its origins. The physicist Richard Feynman included a version of this "miracle" in a public lecture (but without the facetious reference to proving God's existence). Did he get this idea from Russell?
4   "Why I Believe in God," p. 96. Quoted by B.C. Nerlich in "Popular Arguments for the Existence of God," p. 409.

You'll find some not altogether serious arguments for God in the sections titled **A Silly Proof of God's Existence** and **Oh No!** *More* **Silly Proofs of God's Existence!** in Chapter V.

Miraculous Evidence

But seriously, folks, what are we to make of the evidence for God's existence supposedly provided by miracles?

Two approaches to this seem inadequate. On the one hand, believers are apt to credit otherwise incredible testimony to the miraculous events in question, and are too quick to deny the possibility of any natural explanation for better-attested items. On the other hand, sceptics are never willing to entertain the existence of the out-of-the-ordinary things believers talk about, and have what amounts to the prejudice that nothing contrary to the laws of nature, as we now understand them, could ever happen. That can't be the right attitude either.

Well, how about this. There are accepted procedures for judging whether someone's testimony is reliable or not; and the more freakish an event is, the more stringent the requirements that the testimony would have to meet. For example: if you claimed to see a robin in your backyard in spring, your claim, and that sincere look in your eye, and my knowledge that you're interested in birds, would be sufficient for me to believe you. But if you claimed to see a twenty-foot-long boa constrictor there, I wouldn't—shouldn't—be so quick to accept your word. We'd have to go into your backyard and look for more evidence, and perhaps try to get confirmation through sightings by neighbours, etc.

But what, exactly is a "miracle"? It's something that is really extraordinary. Not even the presence of that snake would count. Miracles are events (by definition) that run *very* strongly counter to our shared experience. That means that testimony about miracles would need evidence of a *really* extraordinarily strong kind.

That all seems to be reasonable, and to be something that everyone who's rational—both believer and sceptic—should accept.

But now the real question: does testimony about miracles ever meet these very strong requirements? We'd have to examine each case to see. If you look over real reports, and examine their backgrounds and so on, more and more cases appear which don't even meet tests like those we imagined for the claim about the snake, never mind the very stringent tests that miraculous testimony requires. It starts to look like there may not be any testimony that stands up to these stringent requirements.

No testimony is sufficient to establish a miracle, unless the testimony be of such a kind that its falsehood would be more miraculous than the fact which it endeavours to establish; and even in that case there is a mutual destruction of arguments, and the superior only gives us an assurance suitable to that degree of force, which remains, after deducting the inferior.—David Hume[1]

Another problem with establishing the existence of miracles involves cases whose existence is uncontroversial, but whose explanation—miracle or ordinary natural event—is not. The case of the beatification of Mother Teresa illustrates this. Soon after her death, the Vatican began procedures for officially declaring her a saint. These involve, among other things, discovery of a miracle associated with the candidate, and authentication of this event as a miracle. The Vatican committee entrusted with this job uncovered—and accepted as miraculous—this story: In 1998, on the first anniversary of Mother Teresa's death, two nuns strapped a medal that had supposedly been in contact with Mother Teresa's body when she died to the abdomen of a woman named Monica Besra, who was suffering, they said, from uterine cancer; and Monica soon—miraculously—recovered. Monica's husband, however, and three of Monica's doctors reported that she had in fact been suffering from a uterine cyst, not cancer, and had been cured by ordinary, regular medical treatment.[2]

Considering "miracle cures," Ben Goldacre reports that an Australian study of terminal cancer patients in palliative care found that they died, on average, after five months; but about one percent were still alive after five years. This, he points out, is the variability seen in all sorts of natural processes: a small percentage of events have highly unusual characteristics (by definition!). Amazing things sometimes happen; but once we understand this sort of natural variation, we should be much more reluctant to credit "miracle cures" or the efficacy of prayer.[3]

---

1   *An Enquiry Concerning Human Understanding*, p. 91.
2   Reported by Christopher Hitchens in *God Is Not Great: How Religion Poisons Everything*, p. 148. Hitchens, the only person to testify at the Vatican hearings against Mother Teresa's case for sainthood, claimed that in her conversations with him she revealed that she wasn't interested in helping the desperately poverty-stricken out of their poverty. Her aims were rather to get converts to Catholicism, and to oppose birth control, abortion, and divorce; she was a friend to the rich, and an opponent of any social change to benefit the poor. Hitchens also claims she fraudulently misused funds from supporters. See his online article "Mommie Dearest: The pope beatifies Mother Teresa, a fanatic, a fundamentalist, and a fraud."
3   *Bad Science*, pp. 42–43.

I Believe in Love

IT SEEMS TO BE good advice to get clear first on what your idea of God is, before you try to present proofs that He exists. Well, when some religiously minded people think about God, they're inclined to identify him with *love*: "God is love." If this is accepted, then there's surely no problem in establishing the existence of God, because it's clear that love exists.

The problem here is that this "proof" appears to change the subject. If that's all you mean by 'God,' then I think everyone would admit that what you call 'God' exists. But religious people, while often agreeing that there's some sort of close connection between God and love, would deny that love is all there is to God. Then proving his existence gets a little harder.

> Russell used to outrage a lot of conventional people by giving lectures advocating sex outside of marriage. During the question period after one of those lectures, a woman got up in the audience and said, "The trouble with you, Professor Russell, is that you don't believe in love." Russell replied: "Believe in it, madam! I've seen it done!"[1]

God and the Printing-Factory Explosion

> "The probability of life originating from accident is comparable to the probability of the Unabridged Dictionary resulting from an explosion in a printing factory."—Edwin Grant Conklin, Head of the Princeton University Biology Department for 25 years beginning in 1908. Conklin was not a Darwinian; he believed in what was called theistic evolution. He is perhaps best known for his energetic attempt to interpret the Bible in terms of modern science, in which he suggested, among other things, that Jonah could not have resided in the whale's stomach; he must have been in the laryngeal chamber.

AMONG THE MORE SERIOUS attempts to prove God's existence, one sort of argument frequently proposed says that the way the visible natural world is arranged gives us reason to think that it was designed that way by an intelligent being, on purpose; and this being must be God. The assumption behind this argument is that the visible world wouldn't have gotten to be the way it is all by itself, by ordinary natural processes. (Compare, in this respect, the argument for the Invisible Gardener, considered above.) This familiar

---

1   I've also seen versions of this attributed to George Bernard Shaw, G.K. Chesterton, and William James, as a response to the question whether they believed in baptism.

argument—usually called the Argument From Design—has convinced many people; on the other hand, it has also received a lot of criticism, mostly on the grounds that there are, at least nowadays, perfectly good scientific ways in which to account for the way the world is arranged. The spectacularly complex adaptations of living things, for example, which used to be taken as conclusive evidence of God's designing hand, are these days thought by most people and just about all scientists to be explainable by evolution.

FOR FURTHER READING: The argument about miracles—the serious one, not Russell's joke—is in Section X, called "Of Miracles," of David Hume's *An Enquiry Concerning Human Understanding*. Hume's thoughts on the baby or inferior or aged deity are from his *Dialogues Concerning Natural Religion*, Part XI.

5. Betting on God

Why Believing in God Is a Good Bet

PASCAL'S WAGER, NAMED FOR its inventor, the French philosopher and mathematician Blaise Pascal (1623–62), is a very peculiar argument in favour of belief in God. Here's how it goes.

Many religions suppose that God punishes non-believers with suffering in Hell after death, and that He rewards believers with bliss in Heaven.

Now, suppose you believed in God. Either God exists or He doesn't. If He does, you'll be granted post-mortem eternal heavenly bliss as a reward for your belief; if He doesn't, you will be wrong, but there's no great harm in this. You would have made a fairly harmless mistake.

But suppose you don't believe in God. Either God exists or He doesn't. If He does, you'll suffer hell-fire and damnation as a punishment for your disbelief. If He doesn't, you'll be right, but there's not a great deal of benefit attached to this.

Here's a table that summarizes the potential benefits and dangers of belief and disbelief, given God's existence or non-existence:

	God exists	God doesn't exist
You believe	You get huge benefit (eternal heaven)	You get tiny harm (you were mistaken)
You don't believe	You get huge harm (eternal hell)	You get tiny benefit (you were correct)

Should you believe?

You can see that believing gives a potential huge benefit, at the risk of tiny harm. Non-belief gives a potential huge harm, or else a tiny benefit. Even if you happen to think God's existence is hugely unlikely, it's clearly a very good bet for you to believe anyway.[1]

Compare this argument with James's reasoning discussed in Chapter I; the similarity is that both argue in favour of belief in God on the grounds that it's potentially good for you. An oddness about both arguments is their cost–benefit reasoning. Can that ever be an argument for believing something? Usually arguments in favour of believing something try to establish its *truth*.

Later on, in the item called **The Power of Positive Thinking** in Chapter VI, we'll encounter a related case.

Why Believing in God Is Not a Good Bet

BUT CONSIDER THIS CONTRARY reasoning of the same type.

There's really very little evidence for the existence of God, and rational people harbour reasonable doubts about it. Surely a just God who values rationality wouldn't punish people for being reasonable. He might even reward them for their careful and independent habits of thought. And He might even punish believers for their credulity—for their sloppiness of mind in going along with the herd, believing what there's so little evidence for.

On the other hand, believing the truth is a good thing, its own reward. If there isn't any God, non-believers were right, and believers wrong. We should all value being right above being wrong, although we can agree with Pascal that this isn't all that huge a matter.

So the table above is mistaken. Here is the right one:

	God exists	God doesn't exist
You believe	Big punishment (hell) for credulity	Bad: you were mistaken
You don't believe	Big reward (heaven) for rationality	Good: you were right

Should you believe?

Either way, you're better off being a non-believer.

"The infliction of cruelty with a good conscience is a delight to moralists—that is why they invented hell."—Bertrand Russell[2]

---

1   Pascal gave this argument in his 1670 book *Pensées*, no. 223.
2   "On the Value of Scepticism."

6. What If There Isn't Any God?

"If God is dead, then everything is permitted."—attributed (mistakenly) to Fyodor Dostoyevsky[1]

"I often think how comforting life must have been for early man because he believed in a powerful, benevolent Creator who looked after all things. Imagine his disappointment when he saw his wife putting on weight. Contemporary man, of course, has no such peace of mind. He finds himself in the midst of a crisis of faith. He is what we fashionably call 'alienated.' He has seen the ravages of war, he has known natural catastrophes, he has been to singles bars. My good friend Jacques Monod spoke often of the randomness of the cosmos. He believed everything in existence occurred by pure chance with the possible exception of his breakfast, which he felt certain was made by his housekeeper."—Woody Allen[2]

Into the Mainstream of Philosophy

TRADITIONAL RELIGIOUS TRUTHS HAVE been central to philosophy through the centuries. But philosophers have always wanted to use their tools of rational, logical enquiry on the accepted dogmas of religion, just as they use them on every other area of thought. Religious believers often thought that these truths might be justified by rational considerations, and there is a long history of attempts to provide logical arguments to prove God's existence—and an equally long history of the critical treatment of these arguments. The history of philosophical theology contains many more arguments than I have introduced here, of course, and more serious ones (some I've presented are silly ones, interesting only because of the errors they make). An examination of some of the serious arguments for God's existence, and their criticisms, is a good place to start in the study of philosophy of religion—if not to undermine or create belief, at least to give your intellectual skills a workout. It's also interesting to consider the attempts to reconcile the apparent imperfection of the way things are with God's omnipotence and benevolence. This problem is classically known as the Problem of Evil.

---

1 Everyone thinks this quotation is found in *The Brothers Karamazov*, but it's not. See David E. Cortesi's website "Dostoyevsky Didn't Say It ..." for a long story about this. One of the characters in *The Brothers Karamazov* does, however, say, "If there's no immortality of the soul, then there's no virtue, and everything is lawful."

2 "My Speech to the Graduates."

Until recently, it got you into a lot of trouble to question the official views of religion, or even to suggest that they needed some clear-headed sceptical consideration. Wise-guy sceptics such as Bertrand Russell got themselves in big trouble within living memory. Within the past fifty years, conventional religious belief has suffered a considerable decline in the intellectual arena, but philosophical discussion of religion is still very lively, and arguments for God's existence still provoke interesting debate. Argument and evidence, however, play a limited role in much of religious life; it's sometimes thought that they're out of place in religion—that their application here is a mistake.

> **"If only God would give me some clear sign! Like making a large deposit in my name at a Swiss bank."—Woody Allen**[1]

---

1 "Selections from the Allen Notebooks."

Chapter III
Taking Chances

R.A. Sorensen claims to have had a friend who objected to assigning chores by a random lottery, because that's biased in favour of lucky people.[1]

"You say it's fifty-fifty, but actually it's the opposite."—George Raft

1. Some Probable Facts

Rosencrantz Flips a Coin

IN THE BEGINNING OF Tom Stoppard's 1967 play *Rosencrantz and Guildenstern are Dead*, Rosencrantz has idly been flipping a coin, and it has come up heads ninety-two times in a row. He is surprised, and he should be. Runs of two or three heads in a row are not rare, but runs of ninety-two heads in a row are rather unlikely. How unlikely? Well, the odds of this happening are exactly one in 4,951,760,157,141,521,099,596,496,896. This is not an easy number to comprehend.

Suppose you wanted to reproduce this run of heads. You'd have to try for a long time to make it likely to happen. Let's speed things up a bit: instead of flipping and reflipping a single coin, suppose you had a jar of 92 coins, which you shook up, dumped all at once on the table, and checked the result, trying to get all 92 heads. Suppose this process took one second, and you repeated it every second of every day and night, with no time off for sleeping, going to the bathroom, etc. And suppose, to make that 92-head outcome more likely to show up soon, you enlisted the whole population of the Earth (about 7 billion people) to do the same. How long would all of you have to do this to make it more likely than not—more than 50% likely—that there would be at

---

1   In *Blindspots*, p. 186.

least one time when all 92 coins came up heads? The answer is more than 150 million centuries. Don't try it.

> Among the explanations Rosencrantz considers for this unusual event is that it's a spectacular vindication of the principle that each individual coin spun individually is as likely to come down heads as tails and therefore should cause no surprise each individual time it does. This is a philosophical joke, of course.

to be or not to xq

HERE'S ANOTHER CLOSELY RELATED, somewhat surprising application of probability mathematics. You've probably heard the old saying that if some monkeys were typing at random long enough, one of them would eventually write *Hamlet*. Yes, but this would happen on average once in an *exceedingly* long time. How long?

Well, let's change the story to give them a chance of succeeding in a reasonable length of time. First, we'll give them a smaller task than reproducing all of *Hamlet*. All we'll look for is that one of them produce "to be or not to be." We'll help them out by disabling the shift-key and all the punctuation and number keys on the typewriters, so all they can type are lower-case letters and the space bar.

And we'll use a *lot* of monkeys. A football field is an ideal place to put a big crowd of monkeys where we can keep an eye on them, to make sure they keep typing and don't get up to any monkey business. American football fields have an area of 5,350 square yards in-bounds, and if we really crowd those monkeys, and keep their little desks really small, we can fit one monkey per square yard. There are about two thousand degree-granting colleges and universities in the United States, and just about every one of them has a football field that we'll take over. (The colleges and universities are sure to agree. Filling their field with randomly typing monkeys is, after all, just as academically relevant as what normally takes place on those fields.)

Okay; now we have over 10,700,000 monkeys typing away at random. We allow them only an hour a day to eat, sleep, go to the bathroom, scratch themselves, or pick fleas off each other. Imagine that they type pretty fast: about two characters per second. So each monkey turns out an eighteen-character string—the length of the target quotation—every nine seconds. How often, on average, would one of these forty character strings be that line from Hamlet?

It would taken even longer than that coin-flip routine: a little more than 190 billion centuries. Don't hold your breath waiting for this one either.

Another Surprising Sequence

NOW SUPPOSE THAT YOU flipped a coin ninety-two times and got this sequence (which I've generated using a randomizing program on my computer):

TTHTTHHTTTHHTTTHHHTTHTHHTTHHT
HTTHHTTHTTHTTTHHHTHTHHHTHHTTTH
HTTTTHTTHTHTHHTHTHHHHHTHTHHTTHTH

Would you be surprised?

Before you answer, note that the probability of throwing exactly this sequence of heads and tails is exactly equal to the probability of throwing ninety-two heads in a row. Every possible string of ninety-two throws is equally surprising! But we have made the same mistake as Russell was joking about in his license-plate "proof" of God's existence (Chapter II, **The Miracle on the Expressway**).

You're on a Roll!

EXAMINE THAT RANDOM SEQUENCE of coin-flips in the last item carefully. Do you see that sequence about two-thirds of the way through where it goes TTTTHHTTTT? That's two bunches of four tails within ten flips! Tails is really having a hot streak! What a rally! But the rally fizzles, and Tails goes into a slump. The momentum switches to Heads—about a dozen flips later, Heads gets five in a row. Notice how quickly the momentum usually shifts: several times during this run, TT is followed by HH, or HH by TT.

Does all this talk of streaks and rallies, momentum and slumps, remind you of sportscaster talk? Maybe such things really do exist in sports, but they certainly don't in a random series of coin flips. *None* of these notions is needed to explain what's going on in the random series of flips. It's just random; that's all there is to it. In any long random series, patterns will (just by accident) show up. But these patterns don't need any explanation. (What would need explanation is if they *didn't* show up.) It just might be that brilliant sports streaks are sometimes just what automatically happens from time to time in any series of more or less randomly varying items.

The lack of explanatory power in attributing "momentum" to a good run in a sport, or good polls by a political candidate, is demonstrated by the fact that anything that happens can automatically be given an (empty) explanation. When candidates do well in the polls for a while, that's explained by the momentum of their campaigns; and when their polls slump, the explanation is that the previous momentum has been lost. See how easy it is to be a political pundit?

The *Sports Illustrated* Jinx is supposed to afflict many sports figures who appear on the cover of that magazine: they strangely suffer a fallback thereafter. Negative psychological effect, or maybe twilight-zone weirdness? Most probably here's what really happened. These athletes are picked for the cover because they're doing so well. They're no doubt outstanding athletes; but they're also ones who have recently had a run of good luck. Every long, somewhat random series exhibits some extremes, but is, statistically speaking, very likely to settle down to its average pretty soon. Statisticians call this phenomenon "regression to the mean."[1]

Regression to the mean is also partly responsible for the apparent success of quack medical remedies like homeopathy, copper bracelets, herbal potions, holistic health practices, naturopathy, aromatherapy, chiropractic medicine, and so on. You subject yourself to these when you feel very bad. Because how you feel is very often subject to natural variation, ups and downs, you're likely to feel better afterwards.

But, it must be added, some of the success stories of legitimate medicine are also due to this regression to the mean. Voltaire was not entirely wrong when he said, "The art of medicine consists in amusing the patient while nature cures the disease."[2]

Why We're All Nasty

A COUPLE OF PSYCHOLOGISTS studied the behaviour of student pilots and their instructors. When practising landings, there was the expectable variation in quality: sometimes the student pilots performed a landing that was much smoother than their average and sometimes one that was much rougher than their average.

---

1   You might also see references to "reversion to the mean." Sometimes this is distinguished from "regression to the mean," and often it isn't. The subtle distinction that's sometimes made here doesn't concern us. If you want to know about this, see the website "Reversion to the mean, regression to the mean."

2   These consequences of regression to the mean are usefully and entertainingly discussed in Ben Goldacre's wonderful book, *Bad Science*, pp. 39–42 and 175–77.

The pilot trainers observed by the psychologists praised their students for smooth landings and criticized them harshly for rough ones. Simply because of regression to the mean, a very bad landing was often followed by a better one; and the instructors mistakenly attributed this to the harsh criticism. Regression to the mean also meant that a very good landing was often followed by a worse one; and the instructors took this to show that their praise for the good one wasn't of any use—maybe it even made the student performance worse. The instructors concluded that verbal rewards are detrimental to learning, while verbal punishments are beneficial. (This conclusion, claim Kahneman and Tversky, is "contrary to accepted psychological doctrine.")

Now this sort of thing might be generalized to all sorts of areas of human interaction. The mere operation of statistical laws has the result that we're encouraged to punish others and discouraged from rewarding or praising. Maybe that's why we're all so nasty.[1]

Psychic Powers in Your Classroom

THE FACT THAT A substantial number of coincidences can be found in any large pile of random data is the basis of a demonstration you can do if you have the attention of a large group of people—if, for example, you're teaching a class of 50 or 100 or more students. Ask everyone to stand up, to concentrate hard, and to predict the result of a coin you're going to toss. About half will get it wrong, of course; announce the result of the flip and ask those who got it wrong to sit down. Then ask those remaining standing to predict the next coin; flip, announce, and ask those that got it wrong to sit down. Repeat until just one or two are left standing. They will have guessed right every time for several flips—maybe in a class of 100, seven or so flips in a row. Tell them they have demonstrated their mystical psychic powers, and make them promise to use those powers for good.

But you really ought to give the real explanation too.[2]

FOR FURTHER READING: For an excellent discussion of the probability of improbable chance events, see Chapter 2 in John Allen Paulos's *Innumeracy: Mathematical Illiteracy and Its Consequences* (1990). Paulos convincingly argues, for example, that Joe DiMaggio's streak of hitting safely in fifty-six consecutive games was not all that unlikely. Given the normal range

---

1 The flight-training observations and Kahneman and Tversky's conclusions can be found in their article "On the Psychology of Prediction."
2 This demonstration is recommended by Julian Baggini, in "Knowledge in Retrospect."

of batting averages of baseball players, and the number of games that have been played, it's not surprising that just by accident some player has had a streak of this size.

Your Extraordinary Ancestors

THE FOLLOWING REASONING EMBODIES a similar mistake about probabilities. See if you can discover where the mistake is.

> One hundred years ago, life was tougher and medical science less effective, and a larger percentage of the population died in infancy and childhood. Several hundreds of years back, it was quite common for people to die before they reached puberty; and in general the pre-puberty mortality rate increases the further back one looks.
>
> Now consider that large group of people who are your ancestors: your mother and father, your four grandparents, your eight great-grandparents, and so on. Here's an extraordinary—even miraculous—fact about them. Not a *single one* of them died before reaching sexual maturity!

How Many Ancestors Do You Have?

ANSWERING THIS QUESTION DEPENDS on how far back we're supposed to go; do those pre-human organisms that evolved into us count as ancestors? Dating the first appearance of humans is a problem, not just because we don't know all the facts. Even if we knew all the facts about the history of the evolution of our pre-human primate ancestors into the first humans, it would be a matter of somewhat arbitrary decision where to count the first humans as showing up, along a scale of gradually changing organisms. Anyway, the Population Reference Bureau in Washington, D.C., counts the first humans as showing up in about 200,000 BCE, and calculates that there have been about 100 billion humans, including the 7 billion now alive, on Earth ever.

We can, however, make some assumptions and calculations. You had two parents, four grandparents, eight great-grandparents, sixteen great-great-grandparents, thirty-two great-great-great-grandparents, and so on. Assume that your human ancestors gave birth to the next generation when they were twenty, on average. One hundred years ago, then, gets us five generations back, to the time of your thirty-two great-great-great-grandparents. Two hundred years ago is ten generations back; then you had $2^{10} = 1,024$ ancestors alive. Five hundred years ago, twenty-five generations back, these calculations give you 33,554,432 ancestors. One thousand years ago, there must have been 1,125,899,906,842,624 of them. But this number is *much* larger than the number of humans alive then, which was somewhere around 300 million. It's over ten thousand times the number of humans that have *ever* existed. Something has gone drastically wrong here, but what?

> The answer is that some of your ancestors themselves share ancestors. That is to say, at a number of places in your family tree there must have been cases in which married ancestors of yours were at least distantly related. Suppose, for example, that your mother and your father shared the same great-great-great-grandparents. This fact alone would cut the number of people in your family tree in half. There must have been a lot of this in everyone's family.

The Miracle of You

IF YOUR MOTHER AND father had never met, then you would never have been born, right? But *they* would never have existed (nor would you) if *their* parents had never met; and so on back through the number—whatever it is—of your ancestors. An enormous number of fortuitous and improbable meetings and marriages, stretching back into the distant past, were necessary for you to be here today.

Not just that, but each man releases millions of sperms during each ejaculation. Had a different one of your father's sperms fertilized your mother's ovum, a person with a different genetic makeup would have been born—not you, right? So each fertilization of an ovum is the outcome of an enormous lottery. Had any of these been different, in any of your ancestors, you would not be here today.

Now put these two facts together, and calculate how improbable your existence really is. Your being here is so improbable that we can't even conceptualize probabilities that small. It's a miracle! Everyone else's existence is a miracle too! Most of the events in the universe, come to think of it, are also miracles!

This is still another mistake analogous to Russell's "proof" of the existence of God (**The Miracle on the Expressway**, Chapter II).

2. Some Probability Surprises

One-Third of Two

TAKE THREE CARDS OUT of a deck: an ace, a king, and a queen. Shuffle them, and put them face down on a table. Clearly the probability of picking an ace out of these three at random is 1/3.

But suppose before turning one over you brush one of them, at random, off the table; it falls face down on the floor, and you don't turn it over. Now you pick one of the two remaining cards at random. What is the probability now of picking an ace?

A surprising number of people either think the probability is 1/2, or can't answer the question. The real answer is 1/3. People are puzzled by the fact that you are picking one card out of *two*.

How to Play Russian Roulette

YOU'RE PLAYING RUSSIAN ROULETTE with a friend. (What a good idea! It's a great game!) Here's how your game works. You put two bullets into adjacent chambers of a six-shooter, leaving four empty. Then you spin the cylinder. Your friend goes first. He points the barrel at his head, pulls the trigger, and click! nothing happens. He's lucky enough to have an empty chamber. So now it's your turn. You have a choice: either you can point at your head and pull the trigger, which will shoot from the next chamber in the cylinder from your friend's, or you can spin the cylinder first, then point and pull. Which choice gives you a better chance of surviving?

Maybe you thought: Buddy's having found an empty chamber increases the probability that other chambers have a bullet in them. If I spin, then maybe I'll get buddy's chamber again, so this is a better bet.

Wrong.

The right answer is not to spin. Here's how come. Buddy's found an empty chamber. Of the four empty chambers in the cylinder, three are followed (in the rotation of the cylinder produced by the gun) by another empty space. So if you fire without spinning, you have a 75% chance of surviving. But if you spin the cylinder first, you have an equal chance at all six chambers, two of which have a bullet. So your survival probability then would be 67%.

Happy Birthday Dear You-Two.

SUPPOSE THERE ARE FORTY people in a room; how likely is it that two (or more) of them share the same birthday?[1]

Most people would estimate that it is quite improbable, since there are over nine times as many days in the year as there are people in the room; but in fact, it is about 90 per cent likely—that is, likely enough to be a safe bet.

---

1   Another traditional mathematical surprise reported in Paulos's *Innumeracy*, pp. 35–37.

It's easiest to think about the probability that a certain room contains *no* shared birthdays; the probability of at least one shared birthday is one minus that number.

Imagine a party at which guests show up one at a time. When the host is alone in the room, it's of course impossible that there are two in the room sharing a birthday. The guest enters; her birthday may be on any one of the 365 days of the year,[1] and chances are 364 out of 365 (.9973) that her birthday is different from the host's. When the third arrives, the likelihood that there are still no shared birthdays is this number times the probability that the third guest has a different birthday from either of the first two—363/365. Thus it is about .992 likely that there are no sharers among the three. When the fourth arrives, the probability that there are still no shared birthdays is .992 times 362/365 = .984. At the fifth arrival it is .984 times 361/365: .973.

We continue to multiply by gradually smaller numbers as more people arrive. When there are ten people, the probability there is *no* shared birthday is about 88 per cent; it falls slightly below 50 per cent when the twenty-third guest arrives; it is slightly below 30 per cent when the thirtieth shows up. When there are forty people in the room, the probability is around 10 per cent that no birthdays are shared, so it is about 90 per cent that there is a shared birthday. If there are fifty guests, the probability of no shared birthdays is a mere 3 per cent.

3. Unhealthy Mistakes

Canada's Colonic Sweetheart

A LARGE AD IN the Toronto *Globe and Mail* had a picture of Anne Murray on it.[2] She's Canada's sweetheart—remember her recording of "Snowbird"? Well, that came out in 1970, so probably you don't. Anyway, it was a lovely sweet record, and she's apparently a very nice person. So of course I had to read the ad.

"Not knowing is not the answer," said the headline, and the copy told us that colon cancer is the number two killer of all cancers, but with early detection the survival rate is estimated at 90%. "And it all starts with a simple self-administered test that you do in the privacy of your own home."

Anne Murray and colon cancer? This juxtaposition is startling. What's the connection? Well, the ad says that she lost a very dear friend to the disease, so we probably should take her advice about this simple test. But anyway, just for the heck of it, I decided to look into the matter further, and make some calculations.

It's hard to get good figures on matters here, so we'll have to make some reasonable assumptions.

---

1 Discounting February 29, for the sake of simplicity.
2 September 2, 2009, p. L5.

This preliminary test Anne was talking about isn't very accurate. Let's suppose it has an accuracy rate of 70%. That means that 30% of those testing positive don't actually have the disease, and 30% of those testing negative do. But that doesn't mean that if you get a positive result on the test, it's 70% likely you have colon cancer. Suppose that 1,000 people take the test, and that 10 of these actually have colon cancer. Of these 10, 70%—7—will have a positive test. Of the remaining 993 who took the test and don't have colon cancer, 30% will get a false positive result—298 of them. That makes a total of 305 positives, of which 7 actually have the disease. So the probability that you have colon cancer, given that you get a positive test, is 7/305 = only a little over 2%.

Now, when you get a positive result on this simple self-administered test, you're supposed to go in for a more rigorous test (I'm not going to go into details here, you'll be glad to hear), a test that's neither simple nor self-administered, that's expensive and carries some probability of danger. Assuming all those 305 people do it, that means that 298 cancer-free people are subjecting themselves to this expensive, difficult, and somewhat dangerous test even though they don't have cancer. But this second test, again, has less than 100% reliability—suppose 70% again. That means that there will be false positive results for 30% of the 298 cancer-free people—about 89 of them. And there will be true positive results for 70% of the 7 people who actually have cancer, 4 of them.

Okay, so 93 people have gotten positive results on both tests. Now it's time to institute even more drastic measures. Remember, the high cure rate for colon cancer applies when it's detected at an early stage. (At a late stage, it's almost always fatal.) So let's assume that 2 of the 4 people with colon cancer, who have positive results on both of these tests, have early-stage, treatable cancer. Anne's ad tells us that 90% of these survive. So let's say that both of these two are treated and survive. How many would have survived without treatment? We're not told, but let's assume that none of them would.

Assuming the estimates I made are close to realistic, what they add up to is that of every 1,000 people who get initially tested (assuming every one of them who is positive goes for further testing or treatment), two will have their lives saved. And remember the cost of all this. Many people—305—will have the anxiety of having one or more positive tests (and even some drastic and maybe dangerous treatment) when either they don't have colon cancer, or when they do but don't eventually survive.

That's mostly guesswork. I did the math, based on some assumptions, just to give you an idea about how problems emerge here. But my guesses actually result in a considerable overestimate of the life-saving results from a single test. Here, instead, are the real facts. A single test has negligible results in terms of saving lives. In a Minnesota study, three tests annually on 1,000 people over a 13-year period saved three lives. In a British study, screening 1,000 people every second year over eight years saved one life. In a Danish study, screening 1,000 people every second year over ten years saved two lives. The author of an article relaying and considering these results concludes: "If we are really concerned about our health, we would be far better off to direct our financial and emotional resources into potentially remediable social problems that have a far higher impact on mortality, such as smoking, sedentary lifestyle, alcoholism and poverty."[1]

Given all this, Anne, do you think that you really should be urging us so strongly to get tested?

Hazards to Your Mental Health

HEALTH PANIC IS AN epidemic in our society. You're probably in a lather worrying about those power lines near your house, or second-hand smoke, or radon gas in your basement, or (if you're a woman or friends with one) causes of breast cancer in the environment. But there's powerful evidence to the effect that all of these health scares (and others) have been enormously exaggerated. It's always a difficult matter to interpret practical conclusions from statistical data, but it turns out that in some of these cases, at least, statistical data were apparently wilfully misinterpreted or exaggerated for the sake of political correctness, or by a disease-oriented charity wanting to encourage donations. And, of course, it's easier to whip up worries than to calm them. If you live near power lines, you'll see, and remember, a newspaper headline that says "POWER LINES SUSPECTED AS CANCER CAUSE" but you'll never see a headline that says "DECADES OF STUDY HAVE FAILED TO SHOW ANY SIGNIFICANT CONNECTION BETWEEN NEARBY POWER LINES AND CANCER." Because that's not news. You won't see a headline saying "NO VOLCANOES ERUPTED THIS WEEK IN CLEVELAND" either.

Guess the Percentages

DEATH IS ALL AROUND us, right? Guess what percentage of the US population dies during one year. Five? Three?

In the US in 2005, there were about 8 deaths per thousand people: less than 1%.

---

1   Kenneth G. Marshall, "Population-Based Fecal Occult Blood Screening for Colon Cancer."

More popular attention is paid to breast cancer than to any other disease. Guess what percentage of women's deaths are due to breast cancer: 60? 40? 25?

> In North America in 2005, 2½% of women's deaths were due to breast cancer. (By comparison, 24.7% of women's deaths were due to cardiovascular disease.)[1]

Because of the widely publicized risk of getting cancer from second-hand smoke, smoking has been banned in public places just about everywhere. (It's even banned *outside* on the property of my university.) Guess what your risks of getting fatal lung cancer are, per year, if you're over 35 and are in environments at work or in other public places where you're exposed to second-hand smoke. 1 in 100? 1 in 500? 1 in 1000?

> 1 in 30,000, according to the US Environmental Protection Agency (whose warning about second-hand smoke provoked large-scale smoking bans). Compare the risks— tiny as well, but larger than this—of getting fatal cancer from drinking two glasses of milk a day (somewhat riskier), or eating a smoked pork chop once a week (twice the risk) or keeping a pet bird at home (five times the risk). Here are some other more likely causes of death: stroke (1/1,700); auto accident (1/5,000); suicide (1/5,000 for males, 1/20,000 for females); murder (1/11,000); a fall (1/20,000).[2]

Sweinfeld: The Epidemic about Nothing

THE SWINE-FLU PANIC WAS another example of a vastly exaggerated health scare. But in this case, mistakes about probability don't seem to be a major factor. It's been claimed that part of the blame goes to the big pharmaceutical companies that stood to benefit from a huge production of flu vaccine, and to governmental health organizations who got massive grants and public approval for their preparation. Or maybe public health organizations decided they'd rather risk issuing dire warnings that didn't pan out, than risk no-problem reassurance of what turned out to be a disaster.

The moral of this is: if a health scare is very fashionable, there's a chance it may be a false scare. Try to find reliable sources.[3]

---

1   U.S. Centers for Disease Control and Prevention, "Age-adjusted death rates for 113 selected causes by race and sex: United States, 2005."

2   Fractions are risk per year. These figures are from a fantastically eye-opening and smart book by the philosopher Larry Laudan, *The Book of Risks: Fascinating Facts about the Chances We Take Every Day*.

3   A good book on these particular health scares, and of the way they arise in general, is *When Science Gets Distorted for Nonscientific Reasons* by Geoffrey C. Kabat, a senior

As the autumn 2009 flu season approached and there were predictions of an H1N1 epidemic, many institutions were making panicky preparations for disaster. The university I was teaching at, however, offered a refreshingly different reaction: doing nothing. Their rationale was this:

- The reason they hadn't made plans is that they didn't think flu was a problem at the university.

- The reason they didn't think it was a problem is that their records didn't show that many university people got the flu in past years.

- The reason their records didn't show this is that they hadn't kept track of how many university people had had flu.

- The reason they hadn't kept track of this was that they didn't think flu was a problem.

4. You're Wrong

The Trouble with Taxis

SUPPOSE THAT PSYCHOLOGISTS HAVE discovered that witnesses to a single-car accident are 80-per-cent likely to be able to report the colour of the car correctly. Now, suppose that 95 per cent of the taxis in Moose Jaw are yellow, and the remaining 5 per cent are blue. A taxi dents a light-pole, then speeds away; a witness reports to the police that the taxi was blue. Should the police regard this evidence as trustworthy, and think it likely that a blue taxi was the culprit?

Most people would say that since people are 80 per cent trustworthy at reporting, the police should regard this testimony as fairly (80 per cent) reliable. But this is wrong. In fact, the odds are almost five to one the witness was mistaken, and the taxi was really yellow.

Here's a way to think about this that may make it more plausible. Consider a random bunch of one hundred witnessed taxi accidents in Moose Jaw. Since 95 per cent of the taxis are yellow (and assuming that the colour of the taxi has no bearing on how accident-prone it is), about ninety-five of these accidents will involve yellow

epidemiologist at the Albert Einstein College of Medicine. If you want merely an overview of what's in the book, there's a review of it online by Terence M. Hines.

taxis, and about five of them blue taxis. Now consider the yellow-taxi accidents and the blue-taxi accidents separately.

Since witnesses are 80 per cent reliable, they will report the colour in the ninety-five yellow-taxi accidents correctly in about seventy-six cases; in the remaining nineteen yellow-taxi accidents they will report falsely that the colour was blue. And they will report the colour in a blue-taxi accident correctly in four of the five cases; in one case, the report will be an incorrect report that it was yellow.

So among these one hundred accidents, there will likely be nineteen cases in which the witness says the taxi was blue and was incorrect; and four cases in which the witness says the taxi was blue and was correct. For a random taxi accident, then, it's more likely that the report of a blue taxi was mistaken. In fact, the probability that it was correct is only four out of twenty-three: 17 per cent.

The mistake in this case arises because most people consider the wrong probability. Eighty per cent is the probability that a witness says "blue" given that the taxi was blue, but the question is about a different probability: that the taxi was blue given that the witness says "blue."[1]

The Basketball Blunder

HERE'S ANOTHER SURPRISING RESULT, related to the taxi example.

In basketball nowadays there is frequently the rule that you can get two points for a successful shot within an area closer to the basket, and three points for making a basket from further away. Now consider two members of a basketball team, Wilt Jordan and Michael Chamberlain. Here's a summary of how each of them did during a particular season, shooting from the 2-point area, and from the 3-point area:

		Jordan			Chamberlain	
	made	attempted	average	made	attempted	average
2 point	200	400	.500	440	950	.463
3 point	80	320	.250	30	190	.158

As you can see, Jordan's average is better at 2-point shots (J: .500; C: .463), and it's better at 3-point shots (J: .250; C: .158). Of course, that means that Jordan is better at making shots altogether, right? Nope. Let's add a totals column to that table:

---

1   A similar example is given in Paulos, *Innumeracy*, pp. 164–65.

	Jordan			Chamberlain		
	made	attempted	average	made	attempted	average
2 point	200	400	.500	440	950	.463
3 point	80	320	.250	30	190	.158
totals	·280	720	.389	470	1140	.412

Jordan had a .389 average, and Chamberlain .412. How can that be? Well, it is. I promise you there are no tricks going on here. Check out the arithmetic.

This is an example of Simpson's paradox, a surprising result that comes up widely in statistics. No, not named after Bart, but after E.H. Simpson, whose 1951 paper[1] brought this to wide attention (it had been noticed a long time before that).

Better Pay or Worse?

AND ANOTHER EXAMPLE OF a Simpson's surprise. There are two groups of workers in a huge office: 100 clerks and 100 accountants. Neither group is restricted to all males or all females. There are 100 males and 100 females altogether. Now suppose that all female clerks make more money than male clerks, and that all female accountants make more than male accountants. So it follows that the average salary of the females in that office is larger than the average salary of males, right? Wrong. Here's a way that the average female salary might be lower than the average male salary:

CLERKS:

90 females, each making $25,000.

10 males, each making $20,000

ACCOUNTANTS:

10 females, each making $50,000

90 males, each making $45,000

TOTAL EMPLOYEES:

100 females; average salary $27,500

100 males; average salary $42,500

---

1   "The Interpretation of Interaction in Contingency Tables."

FOR FURTHER READING: It's not easy to explain exactly why everyone supposes, in examples like this, that a higher percentage in both components must mean a higher percentage in their aggregate, or why this is not true. A good article on this is by Gary Malinas and John Bigelow in the online *Stanford Encyclopedia of Philosophy.*

Why It's Not Certain That You'll Be in a Plane Crash

WHAT ARE THE CHANCES that you'll die in an accident on the next commercial flight you take? The answer is 1 in 400,000.[1] Now let's suppose that somebody took 400,000 plane trips. Would the chances that that person would be in a plane crash rise to one in one—that is, would it be certain? Many people would think so. But this is a mistake about probabilities related to the ones we have already seen. Let's see if I can make clear exactly where the mistake lies.

Let's begin with a simpler case. Imagine a bag containing 10 jelly beans: one red and the rest green. Suppose you reach in without looking, and pick one of them out. What is the probability that the one you picked is red? The answer, of course, is 1/10.

Now suppose instead that you make ten picks out of the bag: what is the probability of picking a red one now? Is it 100%, that is, *certain*? Well, that depends on the picking procedure. Suppose you pick one jelly bean out and eat it. Then you pick a second one and eat it. And so on, till you have taken out all 10. The probability that you've gotten the red one out then is 100%. This is the sort of reasoning used in the airline case. But the two cases are different. In this jelly bean example, if you don't get the red one on the first pick, then the probability you'll get it on the second pick increases to 1/9; if you don't get it then either, then it's 1/8, and so on. With this procedure, the probability of getting the red one changes depending on what happened in earlier picks. I won't explain the math here, but that's why the probability of getting the red one in 10 picks is ten times the probability of getting it in one, that is, 100%.

But now suppose a different procedure: you pick one jelly bean, look at it, put it back, and shake the bag. Then pick a jelly bean, look, replace, and shake. Do this ten times. Now what's the probability you've gotten a red one? It turns out to be considerably less than 100%. Again I won't provide the math, but will tell you that probability turns out to be about 65%. In this case, the probability of getting a red one is independent of what happened in previous picks. But this is just like the airline case. So if you took 400,000

---

1 Laudan, *The Book of Risks,* p. 56.

flights (at one flight a day, this would take you about 1100 years), the probability is less than 100% you'll suffer a fatal accident; you'll be relieved to hear it turns out to be only about 63%. So go ahead and get on that plane.

Predicting Priscilla

NEXT IS A QUIZ for you to take. Before you look at the ANALYSIS below, you should read a little story and answer a few questions.

Here's the story. Priscilla was born in San Francisco in 1980. She did well in school and got a degree in Environmental Studies from a small but highly rated liberal-arts college. While in college, she was active in a group that raised money for shelters for abused women in the city. She's now married, and she and her husband have adopted two children who had been orphaned in one of the poorest countries in Africa.

Okay, now for the questions. Circle a number to the right of each statement, based on how probable that statement seems to you, given the story. Circle 10 if the statement seems extremely, maximally probable—certainly true; circle 1 if the statement seems extremely improbable—really virtually impossible. Circle numbers in-between for various degrees of probability.

1. Priscilla works as a waitress.
        1   2   3   4   5   6   7   8   9   10
2. Priscilla sends her children to a daycare which she has chosen very carefully on the basis of racial diversity of staff and kids.
        1   2   3   4   5   6   7   8   9   10
3. Priscilla and her family eat at fast-food restaurants at least two nights a week.
        1   2   3   4   5   6   7   8   9   10
4. Priscilla considers herself a feminist.
        1   2   3   4   5   6   7   8   9   10
5. Priscilla usually votes Republican in presidential elections.
        1   2   3   4   5   6   7   8   9   10
6. Priscilla usually votes Republican in presidential elections AND she considers herself a feminist.
        1   2   3   4   5   6   7   8   9   10

STOP HERE till you've answered the questions! No cheating!

ANALYSIS: Most people would reasonably judge 2 and 4 to be probable, to some degree, and 1, 3, and 5 to be comparatively improbable. That's not particularly interesting, and is mostly just distraction. What is interesting is that most people would judge that 6 is *more probable* than 5. This is a flat-out mistake, having nothing to do with what you think about Priscilla. The probability of 6 has to be less than the probability of 5. When neither A nor B is completely certain, the probability of A *and* B happening is always *less than* either the probability of A or the probability of B. For example, if the probability that it will rain tomorrow is 50%, and the probability that the library will have the book you need is 80%, then the probability that both of these are true is 80% times 50%, = 40%.[1]

Into the Mainstream of Philosophy

PHILOSOPHERS CONCERN THEMSELVES WITH probability in two ways. One of these is the attempt to provide the rules for calculating probabilities. In this we overlap with what's done in mathematics departments. This is a fairly well-developed science, and you can find out its basics in many introductory logic books, to be found in university bookstores. The mathematics of elementary probability theory isn't too complicated, and there are plenty of interesting puzzles even at this level. It turns out that our unschooled everyday probability estimates and calculations are surprisingly often badly wrong.

The second area of philosophical concern about probability is to explain what it means. Here's a sample question. Suppose a coin is flipped only once, and then destroyed. (It's a chocolate coin: you flip it, and then you eat it.) It comes up heads. Now what does it mean to say that the probability is 50 per cent that the coin comes up heads? A natural way to explain the statement that something is 50 per cent probable is to say that about 50 per cent of a very long series of events will come out that way. But there isn't a very long series of flips of the chocolate coin: there's only one flip. Does it make any sense to talk about probabilities here? A second sort of question is raised indirectly by the Rosencrantz example. Suppose (to make things a little less bizarre) that a coin is flipped five times, and it comes up heads each time. We nevertheless want to say that the probability of its coming up heads on each flip is only 50 per cent, and that the run we got was fairly unlikely. What does this mean? How can we say that the probability of heads was only 50 per cent, despite the fact that we got 100 per cent? What is probability anyway?

---

1   This is adapted from a similar puzzle presented online by Jeremy Stangroom. Stangroom includes some interesting speculation about why so many people make this mistake.

Chapter IV

Making Choices: Decision Theory

1. Lotteries and Other Gambles

The Proof That Lots of People Are Crazy or Stupid

WHEN IS A CHOICE rational? Answering that question is a tall order, but some philosophers think that progress toward an answer can be made by thinking in terms of the *expected utility* of an action.

The *utility* of something for you is simply a measure of how much you like it. If you would prefer X to Y, then X has more utility than Y. If you'd trade two Ys for one X, then X has at least twice the utility of Y. In some cases, we might even be able to assign numbers to the utilities someone gives some things. Now we can say that the rational choice among alternatives is the choice that would give that person the greatest utility. If an action has several consequences, its utility is the sum of the utilities of each of the consequences.

But many choices are made when we're not sure what the results will be. Sometimes the outcomes of our action are a complete surprise, pleasant or otherwise. But sometimes we can at least judge the *probabilities* of outcomes of our choices. When we know the probability of an outcome, we can calculate its *expected utility* by multiplying its utility times its probability. Suppose for example, that there's one chance in 1,000 you'll win a lottery, and if you win you'll get $3,000. The expected utility of this outcome is $1/1000 \times \$3,000 = \$3$. There's a probability of 999/1000 that you'll get nothing. So the expected utility of this outcome is $999/1000 \times \$0 = \$0$. So the total expected utility of all outcomes is $\$3 + \$0 = \$3$. But suppose it costs $1 to buy a ticket. Then the total expected utility of playing this lottery once $= \$3 - \$1 = \$2$. If you buy only one lottery ticket once, you're likely to lose, of course. But if you play many times, you can expect to come out ahead in the long run, by $2 per game played. It's a good idea to play this lottery.

But suppose that lottery costs $5 per ticket. The total expected utility of playing this lottery once is now $3 − $5: −$2. This means in the long run you can expect an average loss of $2 per game played. This is not a rational way to make money. Playing this game is like throwing $2 down the toilet each time.

But the games run by lotteries and casinos *all* work like this second lottery. They *all* offer players an average expected loss on each game. The reason is simple: they are all running their gambles to make money; and for them to make money in the long run, players must, on average, lose money.

Now why would anyone play a sucker's game such as this? Here are two possible reasons: (a) They're suffering from a psychological problem that forces them to gamble self-destructively; (b) they don't understand the logic behind expected utility. Putting the matter very bluntly, they're either crazy or stupid. (I've heard government lotteries called a "stupidity tax.")

But before you get too depressed about the mental health and intelligence of the rest of the human race, consider two things people might say to explain why they play lotteries and gamble in casinos.

(1) "It's fun." What this means in terms of our calculations is that we haven't calculated the overall utility of the second lottery correctly, because we haven't added in the enjoyment of playing. Suppose that the fun is worth, in money terms, $3 per game. Even though the average money loss will be $2, the fun-value gain is $3; so everything considered, you'll be ahead, on average, by the equivalent of $1 each game. It still means that you will lose money in the long run, but you will have enough fun playing to make it worth it.

(2) "The five dollars I spend on a ticket means next to nothing to me, but if I won a prize it would be worth a great deal." This again means that we haven't calculated the worth of each game correctly. The calculation multiplies the *utility*—a measure of desirability—times its probability. Now we have merely stuck in dollar figures here. Using these implies that $3,000 has 600 times the value of $5; but this may not be the case. Here, in fact, what the person seems to be saying is that the worth of $3,000 to him or her is *greater* than 600 times the worth of $5. Suppose, then, that we assign (arbitrarily) a utility of 5 units to $5, and a utility of *10,000* units to $3,000. This makes the calculations quite different: the average payoff is (1/1000 x 10,000) + (999/1000 x 0) = 10 units. The cost of playing is 5 units, so we're ahead on average 10 − 5 = 5 units each game.

Perhaps this restores your faith in humanity's sanity and intelligence. But then again, there's the matter of the popularity of TV wrestling.

"I figure you have the same chance of winning the lottery whether you play or not."—Fran Lebowitz[1]

A Good Lottery Strategy

IN SOME LOTTERIES YOU choose your own number to play. If that number comes up, you win the jackpot. If several people have picked that number, then the jackpot is divided among them.

Suppose you can pick any number between 1 and 1000. Would you be tempted to pick 1? How about 1000? Would you think it would be more likely that 437 would win than 1?

> Assuming this is a fair lottery, the chances of 1, 1000, 437, or any other number between 1 and 1000 coming up are all equal: one out of 1000.

Were you tempted to avoid picking 1 or 1000? Many people are, because these numbers don't look "random" to them. They look "special." People think that it would be an unlikely coincidence for one of these "special" numbers to come up; they think that "random" numbers such as 119, 437, 602, and 841 are much more likely to come up in a random draw.

Now, given this mistake many lottery players make, and given the rules of this lottery, there's a good strategy for you to use in choosing a number. Can you see what it is?

> What you want to do is to pick a number which nobody else has picked, so that if you won, you would get the whole jackpot, instead of having to share it. Given that people are less likely to pick "special" numbers like 1, 1000, 500, and 666, you should pick one of these, because it's likely that few other players would pick it. Of course, the strategy of picking a number others will see as "special" doesn't make it more likely that you'll win. Each number stands an equal chance—one out of 1000—of winning. But it does make it more likely that *if* you win, you'll win big, because you won't have to share the jackpot with many others.
>
> Another way of making it likely that there aren't many others who have picked the same number is to pick the number that won the previous lottery. As we've just seen in the coin-flipping case, people often expect that the "law of averages" makes it

---

1   Quoted in Jon Winokur's wonderful book *The Portable Curmudgeon*, p. 175.

especially unlikely that a number will repeat. Thus many of them will reason incorrectly that the number that came up last time is now "special" and won't come up again.

How to Go Home a Winner

HERE'S A SURE-FIRE WAY to go home a winner at any gambling game.

For simplicity, let's imagine that you're playing this simple game. You put down a bet and flip a coin. If the coin comes up heads, you collect twice your original bet from the casino; if it comes up tails, you lose your bet.

Bet $1 on the first toss. If you win, you get $2; you're ahead, so go home. If you lose, you're down $1; play again, betting $2 on the next game. You have lost $1 on the first game, and bet $2 on the second, so you have spent $3. If you win on this second game, you get $4, so you're $1 ahead. Go home. If you lose, you're down $3. Bet $4 on the next; now you've spent $7. If you win you get $8, so you're a dollar ahead; go home. If you lose, you're down $7; bet $8 on the next game. And so on.

If you keep losing, you'll have to bet $16, $32, $64, and so on, on succeeding games to make sure you'll come out ahead, all told, if you win. But it's absolutely certain that you'll win if you keep at it: you can't keep throwing tails forever! When you win, go home, a dollar richer.

Other gambling games aren't this simple; neither are the odds so fair, as we've seen, when you're playing against a casino. But the general strategy can be widely applied: keep betting enough so that if you win, you'll be ahead all told; and quit when you're ahead. It can't fail to work.

This very old strategy for winning gambling games is called "the Martingale."[1] A website gives this information about using the Martingale in betting on craps:

> There are many variations of the Martingale roulette system, and it can be used with other methods. For example, you can use a three-stage Martingale of 10-20-40 combined with betting that the decision before the last one will repeat.... or bet that the FIRST shooter (only) will throw a pass (or don't pass). In this latter one you are betting only one bet on each shooter.[2]

(I don't know what any of that means. I include it in case it makes sense to gamblers.)

---

1   Thanks to Ted Cohen, University of Chicago, for this information.
2   "Martingale Roulette System."

Is there a flaw in this reasoning? If not, why doesn't everyone use this strategy and always go home a winner?

No, there is no flaw in this reasoning. One reason why people don't follow it is that it's difficult to quit while you're ahead. There's a simple psychological explanation for this: the experience of winning is a behaviour-reinforcement—it tends to make people continue to play.

But a more important reason this strategy isn't widespread is that, to carry it out, you would need, in theory, an indefinitely large amount of funds available. Every time you lose in this simple game, you have to double your bet. How long can you keep doing this? If you're lucky, you'll win before you run out of money, but this is not guaranteed. So this is a guaranteed strategy only for people with an indefinitely large bankroll, and there aren't any such people.

In any case, real casinos won't let you play the Martingale. The way they prevent this is by putting an upper limit on the size of bets they permit. After a fairly short string of losses, the Martingale strategy would have you bet an amount larger than the limit imposed by just about any casino.

SOME QUESTIONS TO THINK ABOUT: Imagine you had an indefinitely large bankroll and could keep doubling your bet forever. (How could this be? Well, maybe you're Dictator of Klopstokia, and can order the Klopstokian Mint to print up more money any time you run low.) Would this strategy work then?

Notice that using this strategy you'd be ahead just one dollar whenever you went home; you might not think this sort of win would be worth it. But how about this: whenever you win, using this strategy, you put your one dollar in a vault, and started playing again, using the same strategy. You could do this forever, right?

Those of you who know a little about economics will be able to answer this question: Why won't this strategy work even for the Dictator of Klopstokia?

Printing up a lot of extra currency will cause inflation, so the Klopstokian dinar will be worth less. If you're gambling in the Royal Casino in downtown Klopstokigrad, the money you eventually win will be worth a lot less than what you earlier invested. If you're gambling in another country, the change in the exchange rate brought about by your profligacy will have the same result.

2. Getting Monty's Goat

The Monty Hall Paradox

Announcer: And now … the game show that mathematicians argue about … LET'S MAKE A DEAL. Here's your genial host, Monty Hall! [Applause]

Monty: Hello, good evening, and welcome! Now let's bring up our first contestant. It's … YOU! Come right up here. Now, you know our rules. Here are three doors, numbered 1, 2, and 3. Behind one of these doors is a beautiful new PONTIAC GRAN HORMONISMO!

Audience: Oooh! Aahh!

Monty: Behind the other two are WORTHLESS GOATS!

Audience: [Laughter]

Goats: Baah!

Monty: Now, you're going to choose one of these doors, but it will stay closed. Then I'm going to open one of the other doors with a goat behind it, and show you the goat. Then I'll offer you this deal: if you stick with the door you've chosen, you can keep what's behind it, plus $100. If instead you chose the remaining unopened door, you can keep what's behind it. Now choose one door.

Audience: Pick 3! No, 1! 2!

You: Um, oh well, I guess I'll pick … 3.

Monty: Okay. Now our beautiful Sharleen will open door number 2. Inside that door, as you can see, is a WORTHLESS GOAT. You can keep what's behind your door 3 plus $100, or you can make a deal and switch for whatever's behind door 1. While we take our commercial break, you should decide: do you wanna MAKE A DEAL??

WHILE THE COMMERCIAL IS running, you think: I really want that car. I can stick with door 3 or switch to door 1. There's a car behind one of them and a goat behind the other. It's random, fifty-fifty, which door hides the car. But I'll also get one hundred dollars if I stick with door 3. So I'll stick.

Nope. Switching is a far better strategy. Here's why. It's 1/3 likely that door 3, the one you picked, had the car, and you'd lose it if you switched. But it's 2/3 likely that door 3, which you picked, had a goat, and the car was behind 1 or 2—but Monty opened

2 to show the goat there, so it's 2/3 likely to be behind 1. So that means switching is 2/3 likely to get you that car.

Summing up:

STICK STRATEGY:

1/3 likely to get car + $100

2/3 likely to get goat + $100

SWITCH STRATEGY:

1/3 likely to get goat

2/3 likely to get car

Never mind that $100. The double likelihood of getting the car in the SWITCH strategy makes that one clearly better.

A version of this problem caused great public controversy a few years ago. In September 1990, Marilyn vos Savant (listed in the *Guinness Book of World Records* for "highest I.Q.") published the puzzle in *Parade* magazine, and answered it with an argument that you should switch. She estimates that she received ten thousand letters, most of which, especially those from mathematicians and scientists, scathingly attacked her reasoning. During July 1991, Monty Hall himself ran a little experiment in his Beverly Hills home to see who was right, and announced that his results show that switching is the right strategy. (The case is complicated by the fact that, in the original version published by Ms. vos Savant, it was not clear whether Monty would offer the switch automatically, whether or not the first door picked was in fact the one with the car.)

In Which I Try to Convince You That I'm Right

DO YOU BELIEVE THAT switching is a much better strategy than sticking? A lot of people are really sure that it is not. This item in the first edition of *Two Errors* produced more response from my readers than the whole rest of the book put together, and almost everyone who responded to this item insisted that I'm wrong.

Going through the probability reasoning above more slowly and carefully doesn't convince any doubters. So I wrote a little computer simulation of the Monty Hall game, in which the game is played rapidly thousands of times as you watch. Each time, the placement of the car and the initial choice of door is random; and the "player" switches every time. Sure enough—the "player" wins two-thirds of the time. But maybe some people suspect I've faked things in programming this simulation.

Here's a line of reasoning which might be more convincing. Consider the six possibilities for goat/car distribution:

Poss. #	PICK	Door 1	Door 2	STICK	SWITCH
D1	CAR	Goat 1	Goat 2	Get CAR	Get goat
D2	CAR	Goat 2	Goat 1	Get CAR	Get goat
D3	Goat 1	CAR	Goat 2	Get goat	Get CAR
D4	Goat 1	Goat 2	CAR	Get goat	Get CAR
D5	Goat 2	CAR	Goat 1	Get goat	Get CAR
D6	Goat 2	Goat 1	CAR	Get goat	Get CAR

The column under PICK shows what's actually behind the door you first picked, and the column STICK shows that that's what you get if you stick with it. So if you STICK, then out of six equally probable possibilities, two of them (1/3) eventuate in getting the CAR, and four of them (2/3) one of the goats. Now look at the SWITCH column. If D1 or D2 are what happened, then Monty will open one of the goat doors, and switching will give you the goat behind the other goat door. If D3 or D4 or D5 or D6 are what happened, then Monty will open the other goat door, and switching will give you the CAR behind the remaining door. So if you SWITCH, then out of six equally probable possibilities, four of them (2/3) eventuate in getting the CAR, and two of them (1/3) one of the goats.

Convinced?

Pigeon Reasoning

THE MATHEMATICIAN JOHN ALLEN Paulos reports that pigeons, having been presented with a Monty Hall choice situation, learn the correct strategy (switch) in just a few tries. Are they extremely clever about probabilities? No, says Paulos, they're just "good empiricists." They simply notice the higher frequency of payoff when they switch; they "follow the evidence. People, on the other hand, overanalyze and get confused."[1] If you came up with the wrong evidence, but now see the light, do you think Paulos's diagnosis is correct? Did you *over*analyze? Were you confused? Maybe the reason so many people get this wrong is more complicated and interesting.

FOR FURTHER READING: A journalist's account of the Monty Hall debate is "Behind Monty Hall's Doors: Puzzle, Debate and Answer?" by John Tierney.

---

1   "Animal Insticts: Are Creatures Better Than Us at Computation?"

3. More Probability Puzzles

The Paradox of the Three Prisoners

OKAY, NOW THAT YOU'RE so good at thinking about the Monty Hall problem, here's another paradox.[1] See if you can answer the questions that follow.

Suppose that you and two other members of the Klopstokian Liberation Front, Schmidlap and Blattzburg, have been thrown into jail, and the dictator of Klopstokia has announced that two of the three of you will be executed in the morning. None of you knows who those two will be, and each of you calculates that your own chance of surviving is 1/3. You start a conversation with a guard who is sympathetic to your cause. He refuses to tell you whether it's planned that you'll live or die, but he does tell you that Schmidlap will be one of the two to die.

SOME QUESTIONS TO THINK ABOUT

1. You are of course interested in your chances of surviving the morning. Is what the guard told you good news, bad news, or no news at all in that respect?

2. Blattzburg is willing to change clothes with you, so that everyone will think you are Blattzburg and Blattzburg is you. Would this increase or decrease your chances of surviving, or leave them the same?
This is Monty Hall all over again. Got it now?

The Other Envelope Is Always Better

BUT THIS SUPERFICIALLY SIMILAR stick-or-switch problem isn't a Monty Hall situation.

There are two envelopes, call them A and B. You're told that one of them contains twice as much money as the other. First, you're told to pick one. Now, with that one in your hand, you're offered the opportunity of switching to the other one. Should you do it?

> It doesn't matter whether you do it or not. There's a 50% chance that the first one, which you've picked at random, contains the larger amount of money, and a 50% chance that the other one contains the larger amount. You have no way of telling, so you should hang on to the one you have, or switch. Neither is the better bet.

---

1 Adapted from the puzzle posed by Martin Gardner in his "Mathematical Games" column in *Scientific American*. Bertrand's Box Paradox (an equivalent puzzle with a different story) is in *Calcul des probabilités* by Joseph Bertrand.

That's obviously right. So what's wrong with this reasoning:

> Remember how you rationally figure out what's the better choice: you calculate the expected utility of each choice—that is, the payoff times the probability of each. You don't know what amount is in your hand, what you'll get if you keep that envelope, but just call it $X. Now, the other envelope has a 50% chance of having $2X in it, and a 50% chance of having $½X in it. So the expected utility (in dollars) of the other envelope = (½ · 2X) + (½ · ½X). Do the math. That comes out to 1¼X. So it's a slightly better bet to switch than to hold on to the one you have.

No, that's impossible. That same reasoning can be done after you switch to show that you're still better off switching back, and so on!

A QUESTION TO THINK ABOUT: The reasoning that tells you to switch obviously comes to the wrong conclusion. Where is the mistake?[1]

The Sleeping Beauty Conundrum

SLEEPING BEAUTY, HAVING EATEN the poisoned apple on Sunday, is told that she'll go to sleep for two days, and that she'll either be wakened once, at the end of the two days on Tuesday, or else twice: additionally, briefly, on Monday—but then she'll fall back asleep and forget about having been wakened. Whether she'll be wakened once or twice depends on the flip of a fair coin: once for heads, twice for tails.

She's awakened on Monday, but she doesn't know what day it is, or if the coin-flip was heads or tails. Given her situation, what probability should she give to tails? Here are two different answers to that question:

> ANSWER 1: She knows that it was a fair coin, and being awakened gives her no additional information, so she should assign the probability of tails at 50%.

> ANSWER 2: Imagine this experiment repeated over and over. In the long run, two out of three awakenings are because tails was flipped. One out of three awakenings is because heads was flipped. The probability of an awakening being a tails-awakening is thus 67%.

---

1   I apologize for not giving you any guidance in answering this difficult question: answering it would be complicated and lengthy, necessitating a good deal of preliminary explanation, and leading us far afield. If you feel you know something about probability theory and want to try to understand what's gone wrong here, you might look at mathematician Keith Devlin's explanation in "The Two Envelopes Paradox."

Which answer is correct? Philosophers disagree.[1]

Paradoxical Babies

HERE'S ANOTHER FACT ABOUT probabilities that seems to almost everyone to be clearly false. What's the probability of conceiving a female baby? a male baby? I don't know what the facts are, and it doesn't make any difference. Let's imagine that among the Klopstokians it's equally probable that a baby will be a girl or a boy: 50 per cent each. In this society births will be half girls.

Now suppose that Klopstokians think females are more valuable to society than males, so they pass a law saying that every couple must have children, but that they must stop after the first girl. If a couple's first baby is a girl, they'll stop there. If it's a boy, they'll have a second baby; if that one's a girl, they'll stop there. If it's a boy, they'll have a third. And so on.

Now here's the question. By how much will this increase the proportion of female births in Klopstokia?

> The right answer is: by nothing at all. In this society, the proportion of female babies will be 50 per cent.

If you found this answer hard to believe, here's one way of thinking about this that may convince you that I'm right.

Imagine that you are a Klopstokian statistician, collecting information on the babies that have been born to each couple after this policy of stop-when-you-get-a-girl began. The first couple you interview had a girl for their first baby, then stopped. So you write down

G

on your list. The second family had a boy, then a girl. So you add BG to your list, making it:

GBG

The third family had two boys, then a girl. So you add BBG to your list:

GBGBBG

---

1   Adam Elga, in "Self-Locating Belief and the Sleeping Beauty Problem," argues for Answer 2. David Lewis, in "Sleeping Beauty: Reply to Elga," argues for Answer 1.

And so on, until you have a really long list of Bs and Gs. What proportion of Gs would you anticipate?

Consider just one conception of a baby. Remember that whatever factors determine the gender of the child conceived make it 50 per cent probable that it is a girl. Now you have a very long list of events, but in each individual case on this list, it's 50 per cent probable that it's a G. So, of course, you can anticipate that a very large collection of events of this sort will have very close to 50 per cent Gs in it.

> Right, but there would be unusual consequences anyway. In Klopstokian families no girl would have a sister. The youngest child in each multi-child family would be a girl, and the rest of the children boys. Every only-child (that is, every child without siblings) would be a girl. What would not be strange would be the proportion of girls and boys, which would be, as usual, fifty-fifty. Consider how this would work: half the families would have one girl and no boys. A quarter of them would have one of each. All the rest would have two or more boys, but only one girl.

4. Preferences and Voting

Why You Shouldn't Vote

WHAT ARE THE CHANCES that your vote will make a difference in who wins in an election? What I mean by "making a difference" is breaking what otherwise would have been a tie, or creating a tie, in the final total. The chances of this happening are minuscule. You are foolish to think that your vote is even remotely likely to create or break a tie, and thus to affect who wins; so no matter how passionately you care about the outcome of an election, it's a waste of time to vote.

This reasoning, so far, sounds impeccable. But, of course, if this is true in your case, it's true for all the other thousands or millions of voters too. Therefore it doesn't make sense for anyone to vote!

This line of reasoning is sometimes known as the Voter's Paradox.

Fred's Confusing Preferences

SUPPOSE THAT, WHEN OFFERED a choice between Fritos and Twinkies, Fred always chooses Twinkies. But when it's a matter of choosing between Twinkies and Slim Jims, Fred will always opt for Slim Jims. However, he will always pass up Slim Jims when offered Fritos instead. Let's summarize his preferences.

Fred prefers Twinkies to Fritos.
Fred prefers Slim Jims to Twinkies.
Fred prefers Fritos to Slim Jims.

Something has gone wrong here. Can you see what?

> Well, for one thing, we'd expect a set of preferences to issue in some sort of action when there's a choice. But imagine that Fred is presented with one of each junk-food, and allowed to pick one. He might reason like this: "Twinkies! I like them. I'll take them! Whoops, wait a minute. There's Slim Jims—they're better than Twinkies. Gimme them Slim Jims! Uh oh, I just noticed those Fritos—even better. I'll have them! No, there's Twinkies, which I like even better than Fritos...."

Well, maybe that problem doesn't bother you. After all, indecision isn't such an uncommon thing, or a sign that something has gone badly wrong. But here's a worse problem that Fred will get himself into.

> Suppose that if he has a bag of Fritos, he'd trade them plus five cents for your bag of Twinkies; and he'd trade those Twinkies plus five cents for a bag of Slim Jims; and he'd trade those Slim Jims plus five cents for a bag of Fritos. Acting on his preferences long enough, Fred would lose a whole lot of money.

So it does appear that there's something badly defective about Fred's set of preferences.

Fred's preference set is irrational. Some philosophers think that it's a general requirement that any set of rational preferences avoid this sort of problem. They think, in other words, that it's a necessary condition for rationality that a set of preferences be *transitive*: that if someone prefers **X** to **Y**, and prefers **Y** to **Z**, then that person also prefers **X** to **Z**. (Fred prefers **Z** to **X**.)

How Not to Choose a Movie

HERE'S A SURPRISING WAY in which trying to add up the different preferences of people results in a failure of transitivity. Confusingly, it's also sometimes known as the Voter's Paradox.

When there's a difference of preference among a group of people, taking a vote will always provide a fair solution by giving the majority's preference. Right? Wrong.

Consider the following example. There are three people, Alice, Bertha, and Carl (abbreviate their names **A**, **B**, and **C**). They want to go to the movies together, and there are three movies in town: "One Night of Bliss," "Two Tickets to Timbuktu," and "Three Babies and a Man" (abbreviate their names **1**, **2**, and **3**).

A, **B**, and **C** discuss the merits of each movie inconclusively. Here are the preferences of each:

A prefers **1** to both the others, and prefers **2** to **3**.
B prefers **2** to both the others, and prefers **3** to **1**.
C prefers **3** to both the others, and prefers **1** to **2**.

They decide to put matters to a vote. First they vote on whether to go to **1** or **2**. **A** votes for **1** (preferring it to any other); **C** really wants to go to **3**, but prefers **1** to **2**; so he also votes for **1**. **B** prefers **2** to **1**, so she votes for **2**. It's two-to-one in favour of movie **1**. That's progress, anyway.

Well, because **2** has been ruled out, they decide to compare **1** and **3** in a vote. **A** votes for **1**; **B** votes for **3**; **C** votes for **3**. Disappointingly for **A**, it now appears that **3** is the winner.

But **A** (who likes **3** least) suggests that they test whether **3** is really the best choice, by comparing it to **2**. So they take a vote comparing **3** and **2**. **C** votes for **3**, but **A** and **B** vote for **2**. Well, things are getting confusing, so they make a list of what they have discovered, by these perfectly straightforward votes:

Vote I: **1** is preferable to **2**
Vote II: **3** is preferable to **1**
Vote III: **2** is preferable to **3**

This conversation follows:

> *A:*   Look, **Vote I** tells us that **1** is better than **2**, so let's go to **1**.
>
> *C:*   Yeah, that would be okay if it weren't for **Vote II**, which chooses **3** over **1**. **3** is clearly the winner. Let's go there.
>
> *B:*   No, despite the desirability of **3**, **Vote III** clearly shows that the majority of us prefer **2** to **3**. **2** is the grand champion. We go there.
>
> *A:*   I agree that **2** is well-liked. But remember that we decided, by a clear majority in **Vote I**, that **1** is better even than **2**.
>
> *C:*   Yeah, that would be okay if it weren't for **Vote II**, which chooses **3** over **1**. **3** is clearly the winner. Let's go there.
>
> *B:*   No, despite the desirability of **3**, **Vote III** clearly shows that the

majority of us prefer **2** to **3**. **2** is the grand champion. We go there.

And so on.

The task A, B, and C are attempting is to try to find what might be called the *Group Will*. But the two-at-a-time voting method they use to try to find the Group Will fails to give a good answer: they get a result that violates the principle of transitivity for a preference set. These votes show that:

1 is better than **2** (**Vote I**);
   and
2 is better than **3** (**Vote III**);
   and by Transitivity it would follow that **1** is better than **3**. BUT:
3 is better than **1**. (**Vote II**)

The Group Will of **A**, **B**, and **C**, as manifested by this group of preferences, is unworkable.

A seemingly straightforward procedure for arriving at the Group Will resulted in this pickle. Each of the three starts with individual preferences that are perfectly straightforward and individually workable; their individual preferences violate no rules of rational preference. And the procedure they use to form a Group Will on the basis of their individual preferences also seems perfectly okay; majority vote is, after all, the clearest example we have of an eminently fair and workable way to form a Group Will based on individual preferences. But here it has run aground, badly.

The Group Will is an important concept in the thought of many political philosophers, who thought that the measure of the worth of any political system is not to what extent that system furthered any particular person's will, but to what extent it determined and furthered the Group Will. Problems such as this one lead to wonders about the possibility of understanding the Group Will as some kind of sum of individual wills.

SOME QUESTIONS TO THINK ABOUT: Can you devise a good way for A, B, and C to vote on which movie to go to see? What result would show that a system of voting in this case was fair? Must the score be tied? But then there wouldn't be any decision. What to do?

How to Win at Dice

HERE IS AN EXAMPLE involving probabilities with a similar paradoxical conclusion. This one is a bit more complicated.

Suppose that you're going to play a game with four specially marked six-faced dice. Here's how the four dice, **A**, **B**, **C**, and **D**, have their faces marked:

A:	0	0	4	4	4	4
B:	3	3	3	3	3	3
C:	2	2	2	2	7	7
D:	1	1	1	5	5	5

Each time you play, your opponent chooses one of them, and then you choose another. Whoever throws the higher number wins.

It seems plausible to think that these dice are not equally good; some are more likely to win than others. If there's one that's most likely to win, then your opponent should pick that one to throw. If she throws this one all the time, then in the long run, she'll come out the winner. If all the dice are equally good, then the two of you are likely to come out even in the long run. If some dice are tied for best, then she can pick one of the best ones, and the best you can do again is tie. So it seems that your opponent has a strategy that, in the long run, means she's very unlikely to lose. And it seems that the person who has the first choice of the die to throw has the advantage.

But which die is the best one?

Perhaps you reason: the die with the highest average value on its faces is the best. Here are their average values:

> **A**: 2.7
> **B**: 3.0
> **C**: 3.7
> **D**: 3.0

Calculation shows you that **C** has the highest average value, so it must be the one that will beat the others in the long run, right?

Nope. This reasoning is all wrong. Let's compare what is likely to happen given choices by you and by your opponent.

Suppose your opponent chooses **B**. You can beat her (on average) by choosing **A**. Your opponent always throws 3, but 4/6 times on average you throw 4. This means that, on average, 4/6 times you win. In the long run, **A** will win two out of three times. So **A** is better than **B**.

Suppose she chooses **C**. You can beat her (on average) by choosing **B**. 4/6 times **C** throws 2, which is beaten by **B** which always throws 3. So **B** beats **C**, on average, two out of three times. **B** is better than **C**.

What if she chooses **D**? You beat her again by choosing **C**. Comparing **C** and **D** is more complicated. One half of the times, **D** throws 1, so **D** is beaten by **C** which always throws a higher number. The other half of the times, **D** throws 5, which is beaten by **C** two out of six times. This means that half of the time (when **D** throws 1) **C** wins; the other half of the time **C** wins two out of six times. **C** is better than **D**, because **C** beats **D** two out of three times on average.

But if she chooses **A**, you can beat her by taking **D**. Half the time **D** throws 5 and wins. The other half of the throws, **D** wins on average two out of six times. So on the whole **D** beats **A**, again two out of three times.

Summarizing:

A	is better than	**B**
B	is better than	**C**
C	is better than	**D**
D	is better than	**A**

There is no die that is better than all the rest, or tied for best. Just as in the last example, "better than" is not transitive.

What this means is that if you play this game against an opponent who chooses her die first, you can always choose a die which is likely to beat her. So the first person to choose is at a *disadvantage* in the long run. Perfectly correct reasoning about probability shows that the second person to choose a die can always pick one likely to beat the other one. This correct conclusion is deeply contrary to our feelings about probability and preferability.[1]

This result is exactly similar to the previous example, involving movie choice. Whichever movie you name, I can pick one that two out of three people would prefer.

Rock, Scissors, Paper

ROCK, SCISSORS, PAPER IS a simpler game with the same structure. You probably know how this works: a different hand-sign stands for each of these three things. Two people produce a hand sign simultaneously. The winner is determined by these rules:

Rock	beats	**Scissors**
Scissors	beats	**Paper**
Paper	beats	**Rock**.

---

1   This example is found in *Concepts of Modern Mathematics* by Ian Stewart, pp. 248–50, and in *Innumeracy*, pp. 134–35, where Paulos attributes its invention to the statistician Bradley Efron.

It's a fair game when the two people make their signs simultaneously; but imagine that you get your opponent to go first, and then you produce your sign after you've seen what your opponent does. It's easy to see how you could win every time. The interesting thing here, as in the cases of choosing a movie and the dice game just discussed, is that there isn't anything that's better than the rest.

5. Slipping Down the Slope

The Elusive Wine-Bottle

SUPPOSE YOU HAVE BEEN given the magnificent inheritance of $20 from a late rich uncle. The string attached is that you can invest this money if you like, but you must use the money (or the eventual proceeds from its investment) to buy a bottle of wine. You're glad to have the money, since you love wine and can't afford much. Now, you can buy a mediocre bottle for the $20 right now, but a perfectly safe investment will give you 10 per cent interest per year; so next year at this time you'll have $22. Even counting in inflation and taxes on your investment, let's imagine that the proceeds of your investment will get you a slightly better bottle of wine, so you decide to wait, because you're in no hurry. But next year, you can invest that $22 for another year, yielding $24.20 a year from then, which will buy a still better bottle. So you invest again. Do you see a philosophical paradox arising?

> But every year you face the same choice, and every year you're better off investing than spending. So you never buy the bottle. You not only deprive yourself of the bottle you'd enjoy; you also violate the terms of the will.

A version of this paradox has resulted in a problem for some of my friends. They have wanted to replace their old computers for years, but prices for computers have kept coming down, and they keep thinking (correctly) that if they wait a while they'll get a better deal. So they never replace their old one.

Why You Should Always Have Another Glass of Beer

DRINKING TOO MUCH BEER is bad for you. Sorry to bring you this awful news, but it's true.

But just one more beer never really produces any significant extra problem, right? If you're not already staggering around breaking things—or even if you are—one way or another that additional beer will make hardly any difference. It won't turn you into an alcoholic, or wreck your liver, or make your friends decide that they don't want to have anything to do with you any more. So there's no good reason to stop right now, is there?

The problem, of course, is that when you apply this reasoning over and over again, disaster results. It's the same paradox as we've just seen in the computer and wine problems just above, except this one is about where to stop, not where to start.

A QUESTION TO THINK ABOUT: What has gone wrong with the reasoning in these two examples?[1]

Why Everyone Is Poor

WHAT'S GOING ON IN the last two examples is not just a problem about rational decisions. Both include a variety of argument that's received a lot of attention by logicians: the *sorites argument* (that's pronounced so-RIGHT-eez), but you may recognize one variety of it under the name *slippery slope argument*. The sorites involves a string of sub-arguments, each of which applies the same line of reasoning to the conclusion of the one before. Often there's nothing wrong with a sorites argument, but sometimes (as in the two cases above) they're paradoxical, with a clearly false conclusion resulting from apparently true premises and valid reasoning. Here's another example of this:

Premises:

(1) A person who has only one dollar is poor.
(2) For every number n, if a person who has n dollars is poor, then a person who has $n+1$ dollars is poor.

The first (surely true) conclusion drawn from these premises is

(3) A person who has only two dollars is poor.

This conclusion plus premise (2) yields

(4) A person who has only three dollars is poor.

This plus premise (2) yields

---

1 Warren S. Quinn considers choices like these in "The Puzzle of the Self-Torturer." He argues that they show that revisions are necessary in a standard theory of rational choice.

(5) A person who has only four dollars is poor.

And so on. Continuing to reason this way, we eventually get to

(1,000,001) A person who has only a million dollars is poor.

What has gone wrong?

An argument that reaches a false conclusion either has one or more false assumptions from which it starts, or reasons badly from them. (Some really bad arguments both have false assumptions and reason badly from them.) The reasoning here is fine, so we should reconsider those assumptions.

Premise (1) is unquestionably true; premise (2) must be the culprit. But note that for premise (2) to be false, there must be some number n such that a person who has n dollars is poor, but a person who has $n+1$ dollars is not poor. What number is that? I'll bet you can't tell me. Is it that there is such a number but you don't know exactly what it is? Surely not. No amount of investigation will tell you what n is, for you'll never be satisfied in saying that giving one dollar to someone who has $\$n$ will turn that person from poor to non-poor.

A QUESTION TO THINK ABOUT: The answer above isn't right. What is the right answer? Here's a suggestion for how to think about the problem: maybe there is a range of numbers where it is unclear whether the person with that number of dollars is poor or not.

Into the Mainstream of Philosophy

THE PHILOSOPHICAL TOPIC OF this chapter is called decision theory. You can see that to some extent it's an application of probability theory (the topic of the previous chapter) to action in situations of uncertainty. Philosophers share this area of study with economists. As is the case in probability theory, decision theory is mostly an attempt to systematize and clarify the way we all think rationally in everyday situations; and, as in the case of the previous chapter, this one provides a rather unrepresentative sample of its theory, insofar as I have produced cases in which theory conflicts surprisingly and sometimes bizarrely with ordinary expectations. The problem is worse in the case of decision theory, however, in that it seems that a larger number of our ordinary procedures and expectations differ from what theory (so far) counts as rational behaviour. The basic theory of rational decision is currently less adequate and more controversial than the theory of probability.

Unfortunately, most introductory philosophy and logic books ignore decision theory altogether. It's a fascinating and important field, and its beginnings are not hard to grasp. The best books I can recommend for the beginner are the latest editions of Ronald N. Giere's *Understanding Scientific Reasoning*, which sets up the basics in a very clear and friendly fashion; and of Richard C. Jeffrey's *The Logic of Decision*, which starts you at the beginning and proceeds in a rather brisk and formal fashion to some fairly advanced topics.

Chapter V

Logic and Paradox

Two guys are sitting in a bar.

"What do you do?" asks the first.

"I'm a logician," answers the second.

"What's that?"

"It's someone who does logic."

"What's logic?"

"Well, it's reasoning that gets you to conclusions. Look, I'll give you an example. Do you have an aquarium?"

"Yes, as a matter of fact, I do."

"So then you must like fish and water."

"Well, yes, I do."

"So you must like the beach."

"Yep, I like the beach."

"You take walks on the beach with your girlfriend."

"Yeah, I do that."

"So you must be heterosexual. That's logic!"

After the logician leaves the bar, the first guy starts a conversation with someone else. "That guy I was just talking to—he's a logician."

"What's that?"

"It's someone who does logic."

"What's logic?"

"It's reasoning that gets you to conclusions. I'll give you an example. Do you have an aquarium?"

"Nope."

"So you must be a homosexual."

1. The Illogic of English

"Or" Confusions

THE "LOGIC" OF THE English language is a mess.

A simple example of this is provided by the logical word "or." That word is sometimes used to connect two sentences to make a third; for example, we can connect "It's raining" and "It's Tuesday" to make "It's raining or it's Tuesday." That sentence is true on a rainy Thursday, and on a sunny Tuesday; and that it's false on a sunny Thursday. But how about on a rainy Tuesday?

> You might be tempted to say that the sentence is false on a rainy Tuesday. "Or," it seems, means *one or the other, but not both*. But it's not completely clear that "or" always means this. Suppose somebody served you coffee, and told you, "You can have sugar or cream." This sentence seems to imply that it's possible that you have sugar *and* cream. "Sugar or cream" here means *either one or the other only, or both*.

Logicians distinguish between the *exclusive* and the *inclusive* senses of "or." The first allows the truth of one of the two sentences connected by "or," but not the truth of both. The second allows one of them to be true, *and* it allows both of them to be true.

It's sometimes not clear which sense "or" has, so English is in this way logically ambiguous. It's important that legal documents be unambiguous, so in Legal English one sometimes uses the awkward term "and/or" to make it clear that the inclusive sense is what's meant. It's possible that other languages do not share this ambiguity. In Latin, there are two words for "or": *aut* and *vel*. I have heard it claimed that the first expresses the exclusive "or," and the second the inclusive. I'm not sure if this is true. I have consulted several fat Latin dictionaries that attempt to explain the several ways in which these two words have different senses. None gives exactly this difference, expressed in clear logical ways, though several rather ambiguously suggest it.

Nothing If Not Complicated

WHAT DOES "IF NOT" mean? A comparatively simple way of understanding it is to think of it as equivalent to "or." So, for example, when you say, "I'll give you a phone call: tomorrow, if not later today," that seems to mean that I'll phone you later today or tomorrow. As we've already seen, the logic of "or" is complex enough. Is the implication that I won't phone you both later today and tomorrow? Or is this consistent with my phoning both times? So maybe there's an exclusive and an inclusive sense of "if not."

But that's only the beginning of the complexity of this seemingly simple bit of English. Consider the different meanings of these sentences. After each one, a possible paraphrase is indicated.

He was smart, if not exactly brilliant.
= He was smart, but not brilliant.

It is obscure, if not boring.
= It is certainly obscure and probably boring too.

It's unattractive if not downright ugly.
= It's probably both unattractive and ugly.

They download all, if not most, of their movies.
= They download most, and possibly even all, their movies.

They try to save the lives, if not the arms and legs, of the earthquake victims.
= They try to save their lives if they cannot save their arms and legs.

It's nothing if not complicated.
= It's definitely complicated.

Do you agree that these suggested paraphrases really do give the meaning of the sentences they follow?[1]

A (DIFFICULT) QUESTION TO THINK ABOUT: What are the principles we (unconsciously) use to tell what is meant by "if not" sentences?

"The" Confusions

THIS IS ANOTHER EXAMPLE of the logical messiness of English.

What is the logic of phrases of the form "The x ..."? Under what conditions would "The tallest mountain in the world is Mt. Everest" be true?

---

1 Russell Smith discusses these and related examples in his column in the [Toronto] *Globe and Mail*, "Let me be clear: we can't always banish tricky words."

> This sentence is true providing that there's exactly one tallest mountain (that is, that two or more aren't tied for tallest), and it's Mt. Everest. Here the word "the" tells us that we're talking about exactly one thing.

But what does "The lion is a dangerous beast" mean? Under what conditions would it be true?

> This sentence does not mean that exactly one lion is dangerous. It means that lions are normally dangerous—that lions mostly, on the whole, are dangerous. This is not the result of the fact that we're talking about lions, not mountains. "The lion chasing Irving is a dangerous beast" refers to exactly one lion, not to them on the whole.

What does "In the zoo, the lion is a dangerous beast" mean?

> It's ambiguous. It might mean that the speaker has a particular zoo in mind, and that this zoo contains exactly one lion, and that that lion is dangerous. Or the speaker might mean that on the whole, lions in zoos are dangerous.

This is one of very many reasons why non-English speakers have so much trouble learning English.

Much Ado about Nothing

OVER THE YEARS, LOGICIANS have concocted a bunch of puzzles involving the negative words "nothing," "nobody," and so on. Here are some of these cases:

- "What did you put into that closet?"
  "I put nothing in there."
  "Really? You put *that* in there? It looks empty to me!"

- Hamburger is better than nothing.
  Nothing is better than steak.
  Therefore hamburger is better than steak.

- No cat has two tails.
  Every cat has one more tail than no cat.
  Therefore every cat has three tails.

- The sun and the nearest star, Alpha Centauri, are separated by empty space.

Empty space is nothing.
Therefore nothing separates the sun and Alpha Centauri.
If nothing separates two things, they're right next to each other.
Therefore the sun and Alpha Centauri are right next to each other.

- "I see nobody on the road," said Alice. "I only wish I had such eyes," the King remarked in a fretful tone. "To be able to see Nobody! And at the distance too! Why, it's as much as I can do to see real people, by this light!"[1]

These examples fool nobody. ("Really? He's fooled by them?") What's of interest here is what these mistakes show about the language. In grammar class I was taught to chant, "A noun is a name of a person, place, or thing." But clearly the noun 'nothing' is not the name of a person or place or thing. Some of the blunders in these examples seem to result from mistakenly treating it as the name of a thing.

"Exactly what is this 'nothing' I've been hearing so much about?"

Media ID 44101, SKU 119808, copyright © David Sipress. The New Yorker Collection / www.cartoonbank.com

1   Lewis Carroll, *Through the Looking Glass*, ch. 7.

SOME QUESTIONS TO THINK ABOUT: How, after all, do ordinary nouns work? Nouns aren't always names. 'Unicorn' isn't the name of anything. (Even proper names aren't names: "Santa Claus" doesn't name anything either.)

And exactly what is the difference in the way these negative nouns work?

> "Take some more tea," the March Hare said to Alice, very earnestly.
> "I've had nothing yet," Alice replied in an offended tone, "so I can't take more."
> "You mean you can't take *less*," said the Hatter: "it's very easy to take *more* than nothing."
> —Lewis Carroll, *Alice's Adventures in Wonderland*

The Messy Counterfactual

VERDI WAS ITALIAN AND Bizet was French. They were not countrymen. But what if they were countrymen? Which of these sentences would be true:

- If Verdi and Bizet were countrymen, then Bizet would have been Italian.
- If Verdi and Bizet were countrymen, then Verdi would have been French.

Notice that they can't *both* be true, because then the Italian Bizet and the French Verdi would *not* have been countrymen. Can they both be false? Is there some third country they both would have belonged to? Or if exactly one of them is true, which one?

We don't really know how to answer these questions.

How about these two:

- If Julius Caesar were commander in Korea, he would have used the A-bomb.
- If Julius Caesar were commander in Korea, he would have used catapults.[1]

Each of these seems reasonable to say. Both of them can't be true: if Caesar had used the A-bomb, he surely wouldn't have had much need for catapults.

FOR FURTHER READING: Sentences of the form "If A were the case, then B would be the case" are known by logicians as *counterfactuals*. How

---

1   This example is Quine's. A catapult, in case you didn't know, was a mechanism for hurling big things, used as a weapon in ancient times by the Romans and others.

they work—what makes them true or false—is a difficult and controversial problem that many philosophers have considered. A well-known work on the logic of counterfactuals is David Lewis, *Counterfactuals*.

2. Thinking in Circles

The Divine Circle

HERE'S AN EXAMPLE OF circular reasoning. Some neatly dressed people who came to my door once actually used this to try to convince me of the existence of God.

> *Them:* The Bible says that God exists.
> *Me:* But what makes you think that everything in the Bible is true?
> *Them:* Well, it's the word of God.
> *Me:* How do you know that?
> *Them:* It says so right there in the Bible.
> *Me:* Sorry, I have something else to do right now.

It was fall and the Indians on a reserve asked their new chief if the coming winter was going to be severe. The chief had never been taught the old traditional secrets, so he had no idea what the winter would be like, but just to be on the safe side he told his tribe that they should collect lots of firewood.

But being practical, next week he phoned the Weather Service to get a prediction. The meteorologist told him it was going to be a cold winter, so he told his tribe to collect even more wood.

A week later, he phoned the meteorologist again, to confirm the prediction. The meteorologist said that now the prediction was for a very cold winter. So the chief told his tribe to collect every twig they could find.

A few weeks later, he phoned again. "Are you *quite* sure about the cold winter?" he asked.

"Oh yes," replied the meteorologist, "we're now predicting an extremely cold winter, one of the coldest ever."

"How can you be so sure?" asked the chief.

The meteorologist replied, "The Indians are collecting firewood like crazy."

There's Always a Catch

THE FOLLOWING IS A famous passage from the great novel *Catch-22*, by Joseph Heller, who studied philosophy as an undergraduate (and it shows). Yossarian is a pilot of a World War II bomber.

> Yossarian tried another approach: "Is Orr crazy?"
>
> "He sure is," Dr. Neeker said.
>
> "Can you ground him?"
>
> "I sure can. But first he has to ask me to. That's part of the rule."
>
> "Then why doesn't he ask you to?"
>
> "Because he's crazy," Doc Daneeka said. "He has to be crazy to keep flying combat missions after all the close calls he's had. Sure, I can ground Orr. But first he has to ask me to."
>
> "That's all he has to do to be grounded?"
>
> "That's all. Let him ask me."
>
> "And then you can ground him?" Yossarian asked.
>
> "No. Then I can't ground him."
>
> "You mean there's a catch?"
>
> "Sure there's a catch," Doc Daneeka replied, "Catch-22. Anyone who wants to get out of combat duty isn't really crazy."
>
> There was only one catch and that was Catch-22, which specified that a concern for one's own safety in the face of dangers that were real and immediate was the process of a rational mind. Orr was crazy and could be grounded. All he had to do was ask; and as soon as he did, he would no longer be crazy and would have to fly more missions. Orr would be crazy to fly more missions and sane if he didn't, but if he was sane he had to fly them. If he flew them he was crazy and didn't have to; but if he didn't want to he was sane and had to. Yossarian was moved very deeply by the absolute simplicity of this clause of Catch-22 and let out a respectful whistle.[1]

The Münchhausen Trilemma[2]

ATTEMPTED PROOFS OF ANYTHING must follow one of these three patterns:

---

1 Joseph Heller, *Catch-22*, p. 47.

2 This logical paradox is named after Baron Karl Münchhausen, the eighteenth-century soldier who became famous for his tall tales about his experiences, including having rescued himself from drowning in a swamp by pulling himself out by his own hair. The earliest appearance of the paradox is in the first-century CE work of Agrippa the Skeptic.

- The circular argument, in which what's to be proven is included in its own support.
- The regressive argument, in which each proof requires further proofs to establish the truth of its premises and the acceptability of its logic.
- The axiomatic argument, which rests on accepted and unquestioned truths and logical procedures.

But none of these is any good. The circular argument isn't any good, because it relies on assuming just what you're trying to prove. The regressive argument requires an infinite number of arguments to prove anything—every argument requires additional arguments to show its acceptability—and this is obviously impossible for us finite mortals to accomplish. The axiomatic argument depends on what we're all supposed to accept as obvious—in other words, on our presuppositions and premises, and conventional logical methodology, any of which might be faulty.

We must conclude that we can't really prove anything. And that we've proven it!

Okay, what's wrong with this argument?

3. The Unspoken Implication

It Never Turns Blue Either

YEARS AGO (SO THE story goes), a company that sold canned tuna increased its sales tremendously when it began using the advertising slogan "it never turns black in the can." Millions of consumers chose that brand, visualizing the blackened fishy mess they might encounter if they opened a can of a competing brand. The slogan was misleading: *no* brand of tuna *ever* turned black in the can. But what it *said* was actually *true*.

> "Advertising is legalized lying."—H.G. Wells[1]

How can a statement lead you to believe something it doesn't actually say?

It's tempting to think that all that's really meant by a statement has to do with what would make it true. But we often say statements intending to communicate more than what's literally implied. Imagine I look at my watch and say to you "It's one o'clock." What I intend to communicate is more than merely what time it is: I also want to let you know that it's time for you to go. Perhaps it's a good idea to think about the

---

1   Quoted in Winokur, *The Portable Curmudgeon*, p. 12.

meaning of statements as more than merely what facts make them true or false: we should also think about what they're actually used to communicate, given certain contexts.

FOR FURTHER READING: John R. Searle's book *Speech Acts* is a far-ranging treatment of meaning considered with regard to the *uses* we make of language.

Has the Present King of France Stopped Robbing Banks?

RELATED MATTERS ARISE IN connection with a famous debate about philosophy of language. Consider the sentence

The present king of France is bald.

Given that there is no king of France at the moment, is this sentence true or false? Bertrand Russell argued that this sentence says that there is at present a king of France, so the sentence is false. (But then, the sentence "The present king of France is hairy" is also false.) P.F. Strawson, however, argued that the first sentence does not say that there is a present king of France: it merely *presupposes* it. Because what the sentence presupposes is false, we wouldn't say either that the sentence is true or that it's false. This seems likely: perhaps you'd agree that we couldn't sensibly say that it's true or false. But the idea that some meaningful sentences are neither true nor false is a surprising one that goes against our normal inclinations about the way we think about language, and also against powerful theoretical motivations in the philosophical theory of meaning to think that all meaningful declarative sentences are either true or false.

A better known example of a related phenomenon is the following. Suppose the prosecuting attorney, while cross-examining the accused man, asks him: "True or false: You have now stopped robbing banks?" Suppose the man has never robbed a bank. Can you see why he would have trouble answering this question?

If he answers "True," the implication is that he used to rob banks, but he doesn't now. If he answers "False," the implication is that he used to rob banks and he still does. If he's never robbed a bank, the statement "He has now stopped robbing banks" seems strangely to be neither true nor false.

FOR FURTHER READING: Russell's views on the present king of France were presented in his *Introduction to Mathematical Philosophy*, pp. 167–80. P.F. Strawson's reply is in his article "On Referring."

4. Impossible Surprises

The Surprise Quiz That Never Happens

YOUR LOGIC TEACHER ANNOUNCES, "There will be a surprise quiz given during one of the next three class-meetings." That annoying "A" student in your class requests that your teacher define 'surprise.' The teacher obliges: "A surprise quiz is a quiz whose date you can't figure out in advance. You won't know it's coming until I actually give it to you."

After a moment's thought, the student announces that it can be proven that such a quiz is impossible. Here's the proof:

> Will the quiz be given during the third meeting of class? If it were, then the quiz wouldn't have taken place during either of the first two classes. At the end of the second class, we'd know that the quiz must happen during the third class, so we would be able to figure out the date of the quiz in advance. So a quiz during the third class wouldn't be a surprise. Therefore, the surprise quiz can't happen during the third class.
>
> So will it happen during the second? We already know that it can't happen during the third class. At the quizless end of the first class, we'd be able to figure out that there must be a quiz during the second class. Thus a quiz during the second class wouldn't be a surprise. So it follows that the quiz couldn't take place during the second class either.
>
> The only remaining possibility is the first class; but we know this, so that wouldn't be a surprise either. It follows that a surprise quiz is impossible.

Obviously this conclusion is mistaken; a surprise quiz is, of course, possible.

A QUESTION TO THINK ABOUT: What has gone wrong in the apparently impeccable reasoning that has led to this conclusion? (I don't think you'll come up with a good answer to this—it's a surprisingly difficult question, on which there has been a good deal of philosophical controversy.)

FOR FURTHER READING: The famous logician and philosopher W.V.O. Quine presents what he thinks has gone wrong in this reasoning in his article "On a Supposed Antimony," printed in his collection of articles, *The Ways of Paradox and Other Essays*; this is a slightly amended version of his article "On a So-Called Paradox." An earlier version of this involving an unexpected civil defence drill is attributed to Lennart Ekborn. A third version involves the day a condemned person is to be hanged.

Why You Can't Pick Any Number

HERE'S A PARADOX THAT might feel like the Surprise Quiz Paradox. See if you can figure out what went wrong in Arnold's or Betty's reasoning. Carol tells Arnold and Betty to pick a number and whisper it to her. After they do, Carol tells Arnold and Betty that they didn't pick the same number, and that neither of them will be able to work out whose number is larger.

Betty reasons: Arnold couldn't have picked 1. If he did, then he'd know that I didn't pick 1, so my number was larger. Arnold thinks the same thing about Betty. So both of them conclude that the other one didn't pick 1.

Betty then reasons: Arnold couldn't have picked 2. He'd figure out that I couldn't have picked 1; so if he picked 2, he'd know that I didn't pick 2, and he'd see that my number was larger. Arnold thinks the same thing about Betty. So both of them conclude that the other one didn't pick 2.

Betty and Arnold then reason the same way about 3, about 4, and so on.

So using apparently correct reasoning, Betty concludes that Arnold's number isn't 43—but it is. And using apparently correct reasoning, Arnold concludes that Betty's number isn't 375—but it is. Where is the mistake?

The Surprising Meatloaf

THE LAST EXAMPLE PURPORTS to show the impossibility of a surprise; this one the necessity of a surprise.

Every year on her husband Marvin's birthday, Irene rushed home from the philosophy class she taught to cook him a dinner with a surprising menu. One year it was a Chinese banquet in which each dish had an interesting name. Here's the menu:

- Hairy Melon Soup
- Jade Trees Hidden in the Dragon Tongue
- Grandmother Pockmark's Bean Curd
- Ants Climb a Tree
- Red Around Two Flowers

- Drunken Chicken
- Strange-Taste Chicken
- Peking Dust

Another year it was "Flambé Dinner" in which each dish was served on fire. On a third occasion, an appalling concoction appeared; the surprise was that all the ingredients rhymed (ham, clam, jam, yam, Spam, and lamb).

But one year, Marvin sat down to a birthday dinner of leftover meatloaf, mashed potatoes, and canned peas.

Marvin was a little upset, and thought he ought to say something. "Every year you made me a surprising birthday dinner. I was expecting something unusual, but this one is very ordinary."

Irene replied, "Yeah, you found this menu quite a surprise, didn't you?"

It's not easy being married to a philosopher.

Why All Numbers Are Interesting

THIS CASE IS SIMILAR to both of the preceding ones.

Let's define an "interesting number" as a positive integer with some special property. Some numbers are interesting because of their arithmetical properties: 1 is the smallest prime; 2 is the smallest even number. Other numbers are mentioned in some fact we know about: 3 is the number of bears Goldilocks met in the woods; 4 is the number of the day in July on which the US celebrates its national holiday; 5 is the number of fingers on one hand.

After a little thought, you can discover a reason why 6, 7, 8, 9, and 10 are interesting numbers. Perhaps special properties can be discovered for each number into the thousands. What is the first number you come to which is uninteresting? Well, suppose you think it is 2,504. But you are wrong: that number does have some special property: it's the smallest uninteresting number. Well, let's consider the next number, 2,505. But if that's the smallest uninteresting number, then that one has a special property, so that one is interesting too. But this line of reasoning can be continued for each succeeding number. Therefore there are no uninteresting numbers.

5. Paradoxes of Self-Reference

The Non-Existent Barber

AN OLD AND FAMOUS puzzle (popularized by Bertrand Russell) invites us to imagine a village in which there is a male barber who shaves all and only those men in the village who don't shave themselves. Does this barber shave himself?

> Suppose he doesn't. Because he lives in the village and shaves every man in the village who doesn't shave himself, then he does shave himself.
>   Suppose he does. Because he lives in the village and doesn't shave any man who shaves himself, then he doesn't shave himself.
>   So if he does, he doesn't. And if he doesn't, he does.[1]

Something has gone badly wrong here. Can you figure out what?

> There couldn't be a village containing such a barber. It's logically impossible for such a barber to exist, for he would have to do the impossible: shave himself and *not* shave himself. The story told to set up this paradox thus describes a situation that is self-contradictory. The story must be false.

The Trouble with Adjectives

THE BARBER PUZZLE IS one of a large number of *paradoxes of self-reference*—problems that arise when we try to apply something to itself. Here's another, known as *Grelling's Paradox*.

A *homological* adjective is one that is true of itself. "Short" is a homological adjective, because the word "short" is short. "Polysyllabic" is also homological, because the word is polysyllabic. A *heterological* adjective is not true of itself. "Misspelled" is heterological, because the word isn't misspelled. So is "German."

Now consider the adjective "heterological": is it homological or heterological?

> Either it is heterological or homological. Let's consider these possibilities one at a time.
>   (1) If that adjective is homological, it applies to itself. What the word "heterological" applies to is heterological. So if that adjective is homological, then it's heterological. This contradiction proves that it's not homological.
>   (2) If that adjective is heterological, it doesn't apply to itself. What the word "heterological" doesn't apply to isn't heterological. So if that adjective is heterological, it's not heterological. This contradiction proves that it's not heterological.

---

1   This is an ancient paradox, of unknown origin, but popularized by Bertrand Russell who wrote about it in "The Philosophy of Logical Atomism," attributing it to an unnamed source.

We solved the Barber Paradox by deciding that the story that set up the problem must be false. Do you think that Grelling's paradox might be solved in the same sort of way?

Grelling's paradox can't be easily solved by rejecting the story that set it up. This story consists merely in the definitions of "homological" and "heterological." To reject this story is to think that sometimes the notions of *true of* and *not true of* don't make sense—when neither is applicable. This is quite a radical conclusion, since these notions are basic to our understanding of what adjectives are all about.

FOR FURTHER READING: "On Grelling's Paradox" by Robert L. Martin. (Note that middle initial—it's a different Robert Martin.)

The Troublesome Statement in the Box

A SIMILAR CRISIS IN our ways of thought is brought about by consideration of the paradox of self-reference engendered by the following statement:

> ## The statement in the box is false.

Is that statement true or false?

If that statement is false, then it's true. If it's true then it's false. The statement in the box can't be either true or false.

So this paradox leads us to question our basic assumption that every statement is either true or false. Philosophers and logicians worry about this conclusion.

A QUESTION TO THINK ABOUT: Is there a third category—neither true nor false—which is necessary to classify statements?

A Silly Proof of God's Existence

HERE COME MORE BOXED statements:

> ## 1. God exists.
>
> ## 2. Both of these sentences are false.

Consider Sentence 2 first. Is it true or false? Suppose it's true. What it says is that it (and the other one) are false, so it couldn't be true. It must be false. Okay, now if it's false that *both* of those sentences are false, then at least one of them is true. We've already shown that Sentence 2 is false, so it must be that Sentence 1 is true. Voilà! We've just proven God's existence, right?

Well, whatever you think about God, you're right to think that something funny has gone on in this proof. It's another example in which good sense flies out the window when self-reference walks in the door.

Self-Referential Jokes

NUMEROUS WITTICISMS—MANY OF them not terribly hilarious, some of them only half-witticisms—depend on self-reference. The title of this book is one: you get tied up in knots thinking about it because of self-reference.[1] Here are some more:

> The two rules for success are: 1. Never tell them everything you know.

> There are three kinds of people in the world: those who can count, and those who cannot.

> How long is the answer to this question? Ten letters.

> Nobody goes to that restaurant—it's too crowded.

On Being a Member of Yourself

THE RUSSELL PARADOX INVOLVES the notion of a *set*, which we can think of simply as a collection of things. Now, it seems obvious that for any characteristic you can think of, there is a set of things that have that characteristic. Of course, there are some characteristics that apply to nothing at all, such as the characteristic of being the largest number, or of being a unicorn. But these are counted as corresponding to the *empty* set.

Now consider the characteristic *is a member of itself*. Some sets have this characteristic. For example, the set of sets that have more than three members is itself a set with more than three members, so it is a member of itself. Similarly, some sets have the characteristic *is not a member of itself*. For example, the set of dog-biscuits is not a member of itself, since the set itself is

---

1   The the title is discussed further near the end of Chapter VII.

not a dog-biscuit.

But what about the set of all sets that are not members of themselves? Is that set a member of itself?

> Suppose this set is a member of itself. But since it is the set of things which are *not* members of themselves, it should then be one of these things—something not a member of itself.

> Suppose then that this set is *not* a member of itself, that is, that it is not among the set of things which are not members of themselves. But if it isn't in this set, then it must be among the things which *are* members of themselves.

Thus we have found a characteristic that doesn't correspond to a set. Like the Grelling paradox, this one leads us to question something very basic: in this case, the assumption that for every characteristic there is a set consisting of those things (if any) that have that characteristic. The notions of sets and characteristics are very basic ones, especially in the theory of the foundations of mathematics.

> Gottlob Frege, the German founder of mathematical logic, published a hugely important work called *Grundgesetze der Arithmetik* [*The Basic Laws of Arithmetic*], in which he attempted to establish the foundations of mathematics in the laws of logic. Just as the second volume of this work was about to be printed in 1903, Frege got a letter from Russell informing him about the problem about self-reference we have just discussed. "Arithmetic totters," Frege is said to have written in answer. An appendix that he added to the volume opens with the words: "A scientist can hardly encounter anything more undesirable than to have the foundation collapse just as the work is finished. I was put in this position by a letter from Bertrand Russell...."
>
> Here's why Frege said that "arithmetic totters." Frege thought that the basic concepts of arithmetic (for example, the concept of a number) could be defined in terms of sets and the logical principles involved with them. But Russell's Paradox reveals a basic contradiction in the notion of a set. The set Russell considers both is and isn't a member of itself. If the notions of set and set-membership are contradictory, then this can hardly provide a secure foundation for arithmetic.

This Is Not the Title of This Item

THERE ARE A NUMBER of other statements which give peculiar results when applied to themselves. After reading each one, see if you can figure out what's peculiar about it.

- I am lying.

    If whoever says this is telling the truth, then she is lying. So she can't be telling the truth. But if that person is lying when she says "I am lying," then she is telling the truth. So she can't be lying. What this person says can neither be true nor false.

This is a genuine paradox, very similar to the statement–in–the–box example, above. What we have here is a version of the ancient Liar Paradox, discovered in the fourth century BCE by the Greek philosopher Eubulides. The classical Liar Paradox is a bit different. Here it is.

- Epimenides of Crete says "All Cretans are liars."

    If we take a liar to be someone who *always* utters falsehoods, then if Epimenides' statement is true, all statements by a Cretan are false. But since Epimenides is a Cretan himself, his statement must be false. Thus if what he said were true, then it would be false. So it can't be a true statement. Could it be false? To say that it's false is not to say that Cretans *always* tell the truth—it's merely to say that they *sometimes* do. But this is consistent with the falsity of this statement by a Cretan. We have just proven that Epimenides' statement must be false. The neither-true-nor-false problem does not arise.

Another peculiar result arises from the statement

- All universal claims are false.

You might hear this statement made by people who hold the view that universal claims (statements about *every one* of a kind of thing) are to be distrusted.

    But it can't be true. It is, itself, a universal claim, and if all universal claims were false, *it* would have to be false too. There is, however, no contradictory implication from the supposition that it's false. Again, there is no paradox. The statement is false, and we have proven it.

• No knowledge is possible.

This one is highly unlikely to be true, of course, but logically speaking, no contradiction arises from assuming either that it's true or that it's false. Someone would, however, get into trouble if she claimed that she *knows* that it's true.

• Nothing at all exists.

This one is clearly false. We can prove that it's false without having to prove that any of the ordinary things we think exist really do exist. Suppose that statement were true. Then nothing would exist—not even that statement. If that statement doesn't exist, then what is it that we just assumed was false?

There Are Two Errors

IF YOU HAVE READ the back cover of this book, you will already have considered whether what this title says is true.

The first error (involving the repetition of 'THE') is hard to see, but once you've noticed it, you have no trouble seeing that it is an error. (See **The the Title of This Book**, Chapter VII, for further discussion of this error.)

But a paradox arises when you think about whether there is a second error. You think: there's only one error in the title (the repeated 'THE'). So what it says (that there are two errors) is false. Wait a minute—*that's* the second error. So there are two errors in the title after all. But then what the title says is correct. But if what the title says is correct, then what it says is not an error, so it only contains one error (the repetition). But if it only contains one error, then what it says is wrong, so it contains two errors....

Is the title true or false? Either answer leads to a contradiction. The source of this paradox is again self-reference: the title talks about itself. The paradoxical structure here is exactly the same as what we encountered earlier in "I am lying" and in the statement in the box. Again, it seems, we are forced into the position that some apparently meaningful statements are neither true nor false.

FOR FURTHER READING: Quine tells the Russell-Frege story in "Paradox." This article also discusses the implication of the barber paradox, and other paradoxes of self-attribution. It's a serious and complex work of philosophy and logic. Some paradoxes of self-reference are interestingly discussed in Douglas R. Hofstadter and Daniel Dennett, *The Mind's I*. There are good treatments of paradoxes like these, and examination of some proposed solutions, in R.M. Sainsbury, *Paradoxes*, and Michael Clark, *Paradoxes from A to Z*. If, on the other hand, you'd like to read something much lighter and more amusing about a variety of these paradoxes, look at *I Think, Therefore I Laugh: The Flip Side of Philosophy*, by John Allen Paulos. Paulos gives versions of some of the classical logical paradoxes I discuss, and some others.

> Groucho Marx, on resigning his membership in the Hollywood chapter of the Friars Club, said, "I do not care to belong to a club that accepts people like me as members."[1]

6. Oh No! *More* Silly Proofs of God's Existence!

IT'S OBVIOUS THAT THE three "proofs" I'm going to give you make mistakes in logic. The reason I'm including them is that the mistakes are interesting ones. The "proofs" tell us nothing about the Divine, but they do tell us about logic.

The Universal Prover

TO UNDERSTAND THIS VERY interesting proof, you'll need to know what logicians mean by *validity*: An argument is valid when it's impossible that the conclusion be false, given the truth of the premises. Demonstration that an argument is valid involves imagining that the premises all are true, and seeing if then it would be possible for the conclusion to be false. If not—that is, if given the truth of the premises, the conclusion would have to be true also, then the argument is valid. So a valid argument in which the premises *really are* true must have a true conclusion.

Okay, consider this argument:

Argument 1
   Premise: This argument is valid.
   Conclusion: THEREFORE God exists.

That's it: just one premise. Is this argument valid? Applying the usual test: Suppose all the premises—well, in this case, all one of them—are true; then could the conclusion be false? What this premise says is that this argument is valid, so assuming it's true, this is a valid argument. Since valid arguments with true premises have true conclusions, the conclusion would have to be

---

1   Quoted in *Look Magazine*, March 28, 1950.

true (on this supposition). But that's how you determine that an argument is in fact valid. So Argument 1 is in fact valid.

Good, but is the premise true? It says the argument is valid, and this is what we've just proven correct. Yes, the premise is true.

Okay, so what we've proven is that ARGUMENT 1 is valid and that its only premise is true. But that must mean that the conclusion is true. Voilà! God exists!

Now pick yourself off the floor and let's try to figure out what went wrong here. Obviously something has gone wrong, because that conclusion just came out of the blue, and has no connection at all to that premise. We could, using the same reasoning, show that an argument with that premise and any conclusion at all seemingly established the truth of its conclusion. Exactly the same reasoning could be used to establish the soundness of this argument:

Argument 2
    Premise: This argument is valid.
  Conclusion: THEREFORE Pigs can fly.
  or this one:

Argument 3
    Premise: This argument is valid.
  Conclusion: THEREFORE God doesn't exist.

A QUESTION TO THINK ABOUT: For practice, go through the line of reasoning we just used on ARGUMENT 1 to "prove" the conclusion of Argument 2 or Argument 3.

Arguments with this single premise are Universal Provers—you can use them to prove the truth of any conclusion you like! Even manifestly false ones! This, of course, does not make this argument a wonderfully useful tool. This shows conclusively that there's something wrong with the argument.

But what is it? Well, you may have noticed a certain similarity between that premise and sentences that appear in several other bits of logical funny-business we've recently considered. It's our old friend *self-reference* again. When self-reference comes in the door, logical sense flies out the window.

God Knows That He Exists

EVERYONE AGREES THAT THIS next "proof" of God's existence also makes a mistake, but the mistake here turns out to be a subtle one, one that's a good deal harder to pinpoint. I've gotten several intelligent and logically expert philosophers stumped by this one.

This "proof" might be a bit hard to follow if you don't have a background in elementary logic, but give it a try anyway. Here it is:

As we've already seen in Chapter II, God is classically assumed to be *omniscient*—all knowing. That means that He knows all truths: if some proposition is true, He believes it, and if He believes it, it's true. In other words,

(1) For all propositions **P**: **P** is true if and only if God believes **P**.

But that way of putting it seems to assume that God exists, so let's put that in a way that believers and atheists alike would accept:

(2) For all propositions **P**: **P** is true if and only if: (If God existed, then God would believe **P**).

So everyone can accept (2) as a true premise. It follows (we might want to say) merely from the definition of 'God.'

Now, since (2) is true for every proposition, it's true in particular for the proposition 'God exists.' Substituting 'God exists' for **P** in (2) yields

(3) 'God exists' is true if and only if: (If God existed, He would believe 'God exists').

Or, to say the same thing more briefly:

(4) God exists if and only if (if God existed, He would believe that He existed).

This follows logically from (2), the premise everyone agrees on. Now consider the proposition in the parentheses inside (4). It is:

(5) If God existed, He would believe that He existed.

Again, (5) does not assert the existence of God; but it does follow from the "definitional" assumption that God (if He existed) would be omniscient. So (5) is uncontroversially true.

But if any sentence 'X if and only if Y' is true, and Y is true, then it follows that X is true. So from (4) and (5), it follows that

(6) God exists.

Okay, what's wrong with that? The answer, "Nothing's wrong with that— God really does exist!" is not a good answer. Everyone agrees that there must be something funny in this "proof" which seems to get something out of nothing. But what is it?

7. Zeno's Paradoxes

The Speedy Tortoise

THE PARADOX OF ACHILLES and the tortoise was invented by the ancient Greek philosopher Zeno of Elea (c. 490 BCE–?).

Achilles, we imagine, is a very fast runner; suppose he runs one hundred times as fast as a tortoise. But if the tortoise gets any head start at all in a race, Achilles can't catch up with him. Here's why. Imagine that the tortoise is given a head start of one hundred metres. Achilles and the tortoise start running simultaneously; but by the time Achilles has travelled the one hundred metres to where the tortoise has started, the tortoise has run another metre. To catch up with him again, Achilles runs that additional metre, but by the time he gets there, the tortoise has advanced a hundredth of a metre (one centimetre). And by the time Achilles has gone that additional centimetre, the tortoise has gone a very little bit further. And so on. In general, we can see that whenever Achilles has caught up to where the tortoise was, the tortoise has gone further, and is still ahead. So Achilles never catches up to the tortoise.

A QUESTION TO THINK ABOUT: This reasoning clearly reaches a false conclusion. Where has it gone wrong?

The Runner Who Never Gets to the Finish

ANOTHER OF ZENO'S FAMOUS paradoxes is this one:

A runner starts off on a short race, and we imagine she runs at a constant speed. After half a minute, she's gotten half-way to the finish. She still has to travel the remaining half the distance. In another quarter-minute she's gone half the remaining way. But this still leaves some distance for her to go. In an eighth of a minute she has covered half the distance still remaining; but there's still a small distance left to go. In a short time she covers half that distance. And so on.

You can see that no matter how many additional trips (of half the remaining distance) we add, she still hasn't reached the finish line. We seem to have shown that she can never reach the finish.

A QUESTION TO THINK ABOUT: Obviously the runner reaches the finish-line. She'll get there exactly one minute after she started. That's easy to see. What's harder to see is exactly where the reasoning has gone wrong. Any ideas? (Is it the same mistake as made in "The Speedy Tortoise"?)

Supertask: Able to Leap Short Time-Intervals

"THOMSON'S LAMP" IS THE name of a paradox very closely related to the Zeno paradox we just talked about. We imagine a lamp with a push-button switch: if it's on, pushing the button turns it off; if it's off, pushing the button turns it on. Now suppose the lamp is off. After half a minute, the button is pushed, turning it on. After an additional quarter-minute, the button is pushed again, turning it off. After an additional eighth of a minute, the button is pushed again … and so on, an infinite number of times. If you learned how to sum certain infinite series, you'll realise that this whole series takes one minute. An infinite series of events that takes a finite length of time is called a *supertask*.

Of course, Thomson's lamp is a physical impossibility, because there's a limit to how fast a push-button switch can be pushed. Never mind. It's more interesting to imagine what would happen if it were possible.

When James Thomson wrote about his lamp, he said it would be a logical impossibility, a self-contradiction. After the end of a minute, he asked, is the lamp on or off? It can't be on, because every time the lamp is on it's turned off. And it can't be off, because every time the lamp is off it's turned on. A lamp like this must be in one of two states, either on or off. But this, he argued, would be in neither state.[1]

But commentators on his example disagree, pointing out that all this turning on and off happens before one minute is up, so it tells us nothing about what state the lamp is in after exactly one minute. Maybe it's on, maybe it's off, but the information we're given doesn't determine either. (But

---

1   James F. Thomson, "Tasks and Super-Tasks."

you might wonder, anyway, what *does* determine whether it's on or off after a minute.)

Maybe talking about "tasks" that grow vanishingly small is close to nonsense. But compare the shorter and shorter sprints of Zeno's runner: is it nonsense to speak of distances travelled that successively get smaller and smaller? (The runner example is, of course, physically possible.) Notice that in the runner case, we *know* what state she'll be in at the end of one minute: she'll have reached the finish line.

How to Finish an Autobiography

TRISTRAM SHANDY IS THE hero of a wonderfully lunatic novel by the eighteenth-century author Laurence Sterne.[1] In the novel, Tristram is writing his autobiography, but he's so slow that it takes him a year to write the part covering the first day of his life. Assuming that he'll take an additional year for the second day, and so on, can he ever finish?

No, because every year he continues to write will advance him only an additional day, so he'll fall further and further behind, as long as he lives.

But Bertrand Russell pointed out that if Tristram were immortal—lived forever—then he would finish.[2] How can that be?

Call the year he starts writing X. Then in year X+1, he'll have finished one day of his autobiography. In year X+2, he'll have finished the second day. And so on:

Day covered:	day 1	day 2	day 3	day 4 ...	day n ...
Year finished:	X+1	X+2	X+3	X+4 ...	X+n ...

Therefore, no matter what day of his life we consider, there will eventually come a year in which he will write about it.

Thinking about Changing? There's a Lot to Do.

ARISTOTLE PRESENTS THIS LINE of reasoning.

Imagine something that changes from state A to a different state, B. Now, either it has to change in an instant, or over a period of time. If it changed in an instant, then it would have changed to B in the same instant as it was in A, so it would have been in both states at the same time, which, we assume,

---

1   *The Life and Opinions of Tristram Shandy, Gentleman.*
2   *The Principles of Mathematics*, pp. 358–59. Critics agree that Tristram certainly is an immortal character in literature.

is impossible. So it must have changed over a period of time.

So suppose, then, that the change takes time, from when it's in state A to when it's in B:

A   B

But then there would be a time in between those two instants, C, because no two instants are touching.

A   C   B

And the change from A to C is another change. But every time-interval is divisible, so there's another change in here, from A to D, half-way to C:

A   D   C   B

and in half the time between A and D another distinct change, and so on forever.

So whenever there's a change, there's always a previous change.[1]

Is there something wrong with this reasoning?

Into the Mainstream of Philosophy

LOGIC IS THE ATTEMPT to provide a theory of what makes a good argument good. Two factors can make an argument bad: if the assumptions it starts from are false, or if it reasons from these assumptions in the wrong way. In general, it's not a matter of logic whether or not the assumptions of an argument are true or false; more precisely, then, logic is the theory of how to reason from assumptions in the right way.

Much of the work of logicians concentrates on systematizing and making precise—discovering the rules of—the perfectly ordinary, uncontroversial, unsurprising reasoning of the sort we do every day. But the surprise here is that our everyday reasoning is interestingly complex—easy to do, but hard to explain systematically.

Here's a hint that may be helpful in thinking about the surprising meatloaf and the smallest uninteresting number. Note that what's surprising about the meatloaf is that it's not a surprise; and what's interesting about the smallest uninteresting number is that it's uninteresting. Both of these descriptions look self-contradictory. Maybe we should rule out this sort of surprise, and this sort of interestingness.

---

1   *Physics* 6.6, 237a20–28.

It seems that we can respond to the paradoxes of self-reference in two main sorts of ways. (1) We might try to live with the peculiar results. For example, we might admit that the statement in the box is neither true nor false (or maybe it's *both* true and false!). What would happen if there were statements like this? (2) Patterns of reasoning that get us into trouble when they are applied self-referentially seem to work perfectly well otherwise. Perhaps there's just something illegitimate about self-reference. But even self-reference seems sometimes to be okay; so maybe there are some non-arbitrary restrictions we should make on self-reference to make sure that paradox doesn't result. This is the approach that many logicians have taken.

If you know enough mathematics to understand the notion of the limit of the sum of an infinite series, then maybe you can find a satisfactory way to understand why Achilles really does win the race. An infinite series of decreasing numbers really does add up to a finite number.

For further reading, William Poundstone's *Labyrinths of Reason* is a highly recommended, entertaining, and informative book of paradoxes and similar puzzles. Another one is Raymond Smullyan's *What is the Name of This Book?*

Chapter VI

Belief, Logic, and Intentions

1. Believe It or Not

Why You Should Never Change Your Mind

SUPPOSE YOU BELIEVE SOME statement p. If p is true, that means that any evidence against it is misleading. So you should take any evidence that p is false to be misleading evidence. Of course, you should never change what you believe on the basis of what you take to be misleading evidence. So you shouldn't change your belief no matter what evidence you get that p is false. But you'd accept any evidence in favour of p—that would just make your belief stronger. So whatever you believe, you should never change your mind.[1] Right? Of course not. Where has this reasoning gone wrong?

The Zen of Chicken-Sexing

IT'S OFTEN BEEN HELD that knowledge (as opposed to mere true belief) needs *justification*. It seems that knowledge has to be something you can count on; if you happen to guess correctly, that's not knowledge, because you don't have any justification for what you believe, and you were just lucky it turned out right that time. But what does it mean to have justification? Do you have to be able to *say* what led you to your belief?

Let's consider the strange case of chicken-sexing. Yes, this is relevant. No, I don't mean what happens when a hen and a rooster really really like each

---

1 . This paradox is credited to Saul Kripke, and relayed by Gilbert Harman, *Thought*, pp. 148–49.

other. I'm talking about professional chicken-sexers, workers in the poultry-farming industry. No, I'm not making this up. When what farmers need is all egg-layers, a chicken-sexer is called to sort chicks out soon after hatching. If you examined chicks at this stage, you couldn't see any external difference between males and females. There'd be no problem telling them apart four to six weeks later when roosters develop the obvious bright red comb on their heads. But sorting needs to be done earlier, to spare the expense of feeding all those useless males. (You guys should feel glad you're not chickens.)

Chicken-sexers can sort them out at a day or two old, with very high reliability. The way they work is they pick up a little chick, take a quick glance at its rear end, and toss it into the male or female bin. So how do the sexers do it? There must be some visible difference, but what? When asked how they did it, chicken-sexers often replied to the effect that the chicks just *look* male or female. Why don't they describe what the difference is? If they really *can't* say, then do they really know what they're doing? North American chicken-sexers are mostly Japanese, trained in Japan. Is this some sort of inscrutable Zen thing?

No I don't think it's something weird or inscrutable. Maybe the chicken sexers just don't want to give away their trade secrets. Or maybe they're sincere, and they can't say what the difference is, but there's nothing really strange happening here after all. I mean, take a look at what happens when you sort out the red jellybeans from the pink ones. "How do you do it?" someone asks. You reply, "This one *just looks* red. This one *just looks* pink." Anyone can see this, but there are cases in which this "just seeing" is a real skill, needing a lot of training: when a really expert chess player can just see what the next move should be; when a doctor can just see the unobvious diagnosis; when a skilled wine-taster can just taste differences the rest of us are oblivious to.

Be Careful What You Believe

CONSIDER A LOTTERY WITH 1,000 tickets. You believe that ticket #1 won't win, and you're justified in believing that—it's rational for you to believe it. You also believe that ticket #2 won't win, justified again. And so on, for each of the other 998 tickets. But a very long statement follows logically from these 1,000 small statements you believe:

#1 won't win *and* #2 won't win *and* #3 won't win *and* … *and* #1000 won't win.

In other words:

None of the 1,000 tickets will win.

This is obviously false, and not rational to believe; you don't believe it, and you shouldn't. Thus the Lottery Paradox, which has the strange result that you shouldn't believe certain logical consequences of what you should believe: that it's not always rational to believe logical consequences of rational beliefs.

But maybe the problem is not that rational beliefs imply a belief that's not rational. Maybe the problem is that those initial 1,000 beliefs are not rational. Consider the belief that ticket #1 won't win. Should you believe this? It's possible that ticket #1 *will* win. Why believe it won't? The same for all those other beliefs about individual tickets. Maybe they're all without rational justification. What's going on in the Lottery Paradox is, after all, that one of the 1,000 statements that you incautiously believed was true was actually false— namely the one that referred to the winning ticket, and said it wouldn't win. Now, you don't know in advance which of the 1,000 statements this one is; but you know it's there somewhere. The careful thing to do is to withhold belief from all of them. After all, isn't care in managing our beliefs exactly what the study of logic and philosophy is supposed to teach us?

Yes, but think about the policy advocated here. Is it really a good idea to withhold belief from any statement which *might* turn out false? Think about all those things you now believe:

- Fish generally live under water.
- You drank coffee with breakfast this morning.
- The United States has a larger population than Canada.
- Carl Yastrzemski used to play for the Red Sox.
  etc. etc.

You *might* be mistaken about any of these. Beliefs that are learned from experience (such as the above) are never 100-per-cent infallible; and neither are those beliefs that you arrive at using the powers of your mind alone—for example, in arithmetic, because even on simple problems it's possible (though not likely) you made a mistake.

Thus if we make it a condition of rational belief that it's impossible you be wrong, this may well rule out *all* beliefs. (Some philosophers[1] have argued that there are a few peculiar beliefs about which it's impossible that the believer is mistaken. Even if they're right, we nevertheless face the undesirable

---

1   Descartes, for example. See the section called **Descartes's Thought** further down in this chapter.

consequence of having to withhold belief from *almost* everything we now believe.)

Thus the policy of accepting beliefs about which we are not 100-per-cent certain is not a mistake. Sometimes we'll turn out wrong; but the alternative—withholding belief from anything that is not 100-per-cent certain—is worse, because it would mean that we would believe nothing (or extremely little).

The sensible thing to do is to believe some things about which we are not perfectly—100 per cent—certain. Just how likely must something be before it's okay to believe it? The answer to this isn't clear. Maybe the degree of assurance we need changes with circumstances, depending on how important it is to be right, and what sort of disasters would result if one were wrong. In any event, your beliefs about each individual ticket in the Lottery Paradox example are each 99.9% probable. It seems that that's probable enough to satisfy almost everyone, in almost every circumstance. So the Paradox is still there.

Knowing Nothing about Birds

MAYBE YOU NOW THINK that even though it's not necessary to restrict our beliefs to those things that are 100-per-cent probable, we should arrange our beliefs in order to improve their probability of truth. This might look like good advice. Nevertheless, suppose you look out the window, and see what you take to be an English sparrow at your bird feeder. You're tempted to believe

(1) There's an English sparrow out there.

Now, you're pretty good at recognizing at least the common birds like the English sparrow. But, of course, there's some possibility you're wrong; other sparrows resemble the English sparrow. If you believed *instead*

(2) There's a sparrow out there.

this would increase the probability you're right. So on the principle that we should improve the probability of truth of our beliefs, you should believe (2) instead of (1). But now consider

(3) There's a bird out there.

This is even more likely to be true than (2); so you should discard (2) and accept (3) instead. But, of course, we can continue this process of reasoning, and replace (3) with

(4) There's some living thing out there.

and replace (4) with

(5) There's some object out there.

and perhaps even replace (5) with the more certain

(6) I seem to see something out there.

This process does increase the probability that your beliefs are correct, but the ones that are more likely to be correct also contain less information. What we are left with, having arrived at (6), is a belief that's very likely true, but claims almost nothing. Following this strategy for belief selection would result in very few beliefs indeed, and ones with very little informational content.

A QUESTION TO THINK ABOUT: What *is* the right strategy for choosing what to believe?

The Hobgoblin of Little Minds

A LOT OF PEOPLE have inconsistent beliefs. It's fairly easy to come up with examples of this. Here's an example of a sort of inconsistency: a poll determined that 97 per cent of Americans believe that "following your own conscience" is a mark of a strong character, while 92 per cent of Americans believe that "obeying those in positions of authority" is.[1]

But here's an interesting general line of reasoning that shows that everyone who is reasonable has inconsistent beliefs.

Are all your beliefs true? Obviously the answer is no: only an unreasonable egotist would think the contrary. All reasonable people believe this statement:

- At least one of my other beliefs is false.

---

1 Hunter and Bowman, *Politics of Character.*

Now consider the hypothetical list of your belief statements, with this last belief added at the end:

- Fish generally live under water.
- You drank coffee with breakfast this morning.
- The United States has a larger population than Canada.
- Carl Yastrzemski used to play for the Red Sox.

    . . .

    . . .

- At least one of the other statements on this list is false.

This is not merely a set including at least one false statement. It is an *inconsistent* set: it is *logically impossible* that all the statements in this set are true. To see this, imagine that everything in the list up to the last item is true; but this makes the last one false. It's *logically necessary* that at least one statement on the list be false.

If you are reasonable, then, you have an inconsistent belief set.

FOR FURTHER READING: This paradox (as well as several others in this book) is discussed interestingly and entertainingly in Raymond Smullyan's *What is the Name of This Book?* Sometimes this paradox is called the "Paradox of the Preface": in one version (not Smullyan's) we are to consider a book whose preface contains the usual comment, "There are, no doubt, errors in this book." That comment is logically interesting. It's impossible that this is false. The supposition that there are no errors at all in the book implies that this statement is an error. But including this statement makes what's said in the book logically inconsistent.

> "The test of a first-rate intelligence is the ability to hold two op-
> posed ideas in the mind at the same time and still retain the ability to
> function."—F. Scott Fitzgerald[1]

> "Do I contradict myself?
> Very well then I contradict myself,
> (I am large, I contain multitudes)."
>
> —Walt Whitman.[2]

---

1   "The Crack-Up."
2   "Song of Myself," in *Leaves of Grass*.

"Consistency is the hobgoblin of little minds."
—a familiar aphorism attributed to Ralph Waldo Emerson[1]

You'll Believe Just Anything

WELL, WHAT IS WRONG with inconsistent beliefs? The obvious answer is that an inconsistent set is one in which it's logically impossible that everything is true. We aim—presumably—at beliefs that are all true; so we should avoid inconsistent sets of beliefs.

But a subtler objection to inconsistent beliefs is that a set of inconsistent statements implies *every* statement. This widely accepted principle of logic may seem peculiar to you, and deserves some justification.

Here's one way of looking at implication that may make that principle seem reasonable. To say that a set of statements {A} implies a statement **B** means that it's logically impossible that all the statements in set {A} be true while **B** is false. So, for example, it's logically impossible that all the statements in this set: {'It's raining,' 'It's Tuesday'} are true while 'It's raining and it's Tuesday' is false. So the set {'It's raining,' 'It's Tuesday'} implies 'It's raining and it's Tuesday.' Here's another example: {'If it's raining, then the picnic is cancelled,' 'The picnic is not cancelled'} implies 'It's not raining.' Think about these statements and you'll see why. It's logically impossible that all three of these hold: (1) 'If it's raining, then the picnic is cancelled' is true; *and* (2) 'The picnic is not cancelled' is true; *and* (3) 'It's not raining' is false.

Now a *logically inconsistent* set of statements is a set of statements such that it's logically impossible that every statement in that set be true. A simple example of such a set is {'Today is Monday,' 'Today is not Monday'}. Strangely enough, that set of statements implies 'Fred is wearing pink socks.' To see why this is true, all we have to do is to apply the account of implication just given. It's impossible that all three of these hold: (1) 'Today is Monday' is true; *and* (2) 'Today is not Monday' is true; *and* (3) 'Fred is wearing pink socks' is false. (The reason why this is the case has nothing to do with what colour socks Fred is wearing. The first two conditions suffice to make it impossible that all three hold.)

Similar reasoning can show why the set {'Today is Monday,' 'Today is not Monday'} implies *any statement at all*. And similarly, *any* inconsistent set of statements implies *every* statement.

---

1   What he actually said (in "Self Reliance") was "A foolish consistency is the hobgoblin of little minds, adored by little statesmen and philosophers and divines." *Philosophers?* Thanks a lot, Ralph, and same to you. Well, anyway, the inclusion of the word "foolish" changes the meaning somewhat.

The Lottery Paradox, which we looked at above, cast doubt on the principle that it's rational to believe—and you ought to believe—logical consequences of rational beliefs. But now we have further reason to doubt that principle. Everyone's belief sets, even the most rational, are rendered inconsistent by the addition of the clearly rational belief that there's at least one mistake somewhere in that set. But this inconsistent set logically implies every statement. If you ought to believe logical consequences of your beliefs, then you should believe everything.

Maybe what you think has gone wrong here is the idea that an inconsistent set of statements implies every statement. But it's hard to see what should replace this principle. It merely follows from the definition of "implication."

 A QUESTION TO THINK ABOUT: Can you suggest a better definition that avoids this peculiar result?

Impossible Beliefs

THERE ARE SOME THINGS that are true but you don't believe them. But is there anything true that you *couldn't* believe—that it's *impossible* for you to believe? At first glance, you might think that there couldn't be anything like that. Suppose that some sentence S were true, and suppose you didn't believe it. But it doesn't seem that it would be *impossible* for you to believe it. Suppose that you had a very reliable and smart friend, and you believed everything that friend told you. This isn't impossible, right? Now, if your friend told you sentence S, you'd believe it.

We can, however, turn up examples of sentences such that, were they true, it would be impossible for you to believe them. Here's an example of one of them:

_____ is now dead. (Insert your name in the blank.)

This sentence is obviously false. But (I'm sorry to tell you) some day it will be true. When it's true it will be impossible for you to believe it.

Here's another. Suppose you wake up one morning with a bad hangover, badly confused. You think it's Monday, but actually it's Sunday. The true situation at that point is expressed by the sentence:

_____ believes it's Monday, but it's not. (Insert your name.)

Your friend might find out that that sentence is true. But consider your own beliefs. Later on, when your head clears, you realize the truth, and you believe this sentence:

I believed (earlier this morning) that it was Monday, but it's not.

But consider the state of affairs earlier that morning. At that point, you believed that it was Monday, and it wasn't. This sentence, if you happened to say it then, would have been true:

I believe it is Monday, but it's not.

Notice, however, that you wouldn't have uttered that sentence, because it's impossible that you believed that what that sentence says is true.

Your reliable friend shows up first thing in the morning, and tells you this:

You believe it's Monday, but it's not.

Could you believe what your friend says?

Part of what your friend's sentence says is that it's not Monday. But if you believe this part, then you wouldn't believe that it's Monday. But then the other part of your friend's sentence ('You believe it's Monday') would be false, and you'd know it's false.

Or things might work the other way. On hearing your friend's sentence, you first notice the part that says 'You believe it's Monday.' Assuming your friend speaks the truth, you do believe it's Monday, and you believe this part of the sentence. But then you would think that the second part of the sentence is false. You couldn't believe the whole sentence.

Niels Bohr (1885-1962), the renowned Danish physicist, had a horseshoe over his desk. One day a student asked if he really believed that a horseshoe brought luck. Professor Bohr replied, "I understand that it brings you luck if you believe in it or not."[1]

"I can't believe *that*!" said Alice.

"Can't you?" the Queen said in a pitying tone. "Try again: draw a long breath, and shut your eyes."

Alice laughed. "There's no use trying," she said: "one *can't* believe impossible things."

"I daresay you haven't had much practice," said the Queen. "When I was your age, I always did it for half-an-hour a day. Why sometimes I've believed as many as six impossible things before breakfast."[2]

---

1 A widely circulated story, for which one source is P. Robertson, *The Early Years*. In some versions of this story, the horseshoe and the comment about how it works both belonged to Bohr's neighbour, not to Bohr. Do we care? It's a good story anyway.

2 Lewis Carroll, *Through the Looking Glass*.

The Queen's "six impossible things" remark has become a favourite of new-age spiritual boys and girls, who put it on their web pages along with other quotations they take to be inspirational. They seem to have interpreted it to mean something like "Dream the impossible dream"—to urge us to think outside the box, to boldly mentally go where no man has gone before, blah blah blah. This is not what the quotation means, new-age spiritual boys and girls! Take it off your web pages! Its author, Lewis Carroll, was a hard-headed logician. He was talking about the possibility of belief in the logically impossible, or maybe about what's logically impossible to believe.

2. It Has to Be True

Descartes's Thought

THE ONLY THING THAT lots of people know about René Descartes is that he said, "I think, therefore I am." And the majority of people who know that, think that what Descartes was up to when he said this was some sort of celebration of thought—that what he was saying was that a thoughtful life is important for real existence, or something. That's not what he meant.

Descartes began his work *Meditations* by noting that some of our ordinary beliefs have turned out to be false. Most of your ordinary beliefs seem obviously true, and you have no reason to think they're false; but even these just *might* be false. Descartes thought that philosophy should begin with beliefs about which it is *impossible* to be mistaken. Are there any beliefs like that?

The first one Descartes turned up was his own belief that he existed. This is not the belief that his body exists: it is the belief that he has mental existence—that he exists as a thinking thing. The famous quotation embodies his reasoning to prove that this belief couldn't be mistaken. The supposition that the belief that he exists is mistaken couldn't be true. If he were mistaken in this belief, then he would, anyway, have a mistaken belief; and anything that has a mistaken belief is an existing thinking thing. Anyone who thinks he or she exists must be right.

Descartes's quotation has spawned innumerable jokes. Here's one:

> Descartes walks into a café and sits down ready to order. A waiter comes up to him and asks, "Do you need a menu?" Descartes replies, "I think not," and he disappears.

Descartes's real death was the result of thoughtlessness, too—on the part of Queen Christina of Sweden. She hired Descartes in 1649 as her personal tutor in mathematics and philosophy. This was good news for the philosophy profession—we're always seeking new kinds of employment.

Question: What words are spoken by philosophy PhDs at their first jobs?
Answer: "Do you want fries with that?"

"Speed Bump" copyight Dave Coverly / Dist. by Creators Syndicate, Inc.
Reprinted by permission of Dave Coverly.

The bad news, however, was that the Queen wanted instruction beginning at 5 a.m., and Descartes had a lifetime habit of staying in bed till 11. After only a few months in the cold northern climate, walking to the palace for 5 o'clock every morning, he died. UNIVERSITY ADMINISTRATORS TAKE NOTE: NO EARLY MORNING CLASSES FOR PHILOSOPHERS!

The Unexamined Life

DESCARTES'S FAMOUS QUOTATION, MISINTERPRETED to be a celebration of thought, is something like the most famous quotation from Socrates: "The unexamined life is not worth living."[1] That's something else you can

---

1   Plato, *Apology*, 38a.

put on your Facebook page to convince everyone you're really deep. But do you really believe it? Does anyone really believe it? So, if your life is not rich with self-examination you should commit suicide? A good case could actually be made for the opposite view: that you're much better off if you spent more time living and less thinking.

A Guaranteed True Belief

"I BELIEVE THAT I am believing this," where 'this' refers to that very belief. It's true because it's believed.

> Yeah, but the problem is that this is not really a belief at all—it's empty, it has no content.[1]

3. Self-Fulfilling / Self-Defeating

The Power of Positive Thinking

A SELF-FULFILLING BELIEF IS a belief of the following sort: believing it will tend to make it true. An example of this is the belief that you will do well on a test. On the whole, if you have this belief, you'll go into the test relaxed and confident, and you'll do better as a result. The opposite belief—that you will do poorly on the test—similarly tends to be self-fulfilling. If you go into the test convinced you'll do poorly, you'll be nervous and unhappy, and this will tend to lower your score.

Another example of a belief that tends to be self-fulfilling is the belief that somebody important to you likes you; it will result in your acting toward that person in a natural and confident way, and this might result in their liking you. Similarly, the opposite belief is self-fulfilling.

Insomniacs are unfortunately quite familiar with the self-fulfilling nature of the belief that you won't be able to get to sleep.

I'm about to give you a suggestion that can change your life enormously for the better! (Wonderful! Didn't you always hope that philosophy had such useful wisdom to offer?) The suggestion is this: if you want something to be true, and if the belief that it is true tends to be self-fulfilling, believe that belief. Thus, go into every test convinced that you'll do well; and you will do well (or, at least, you'll do better than you would have). Believe that people you want to like you do like you, and they will like you (or at least

---

1   This example, and the reaction to it, are in "Self-fulfilling Belief," by Michael Clark.

will tend to). The belief that you will succeed in a business will result in your acting in ways that may improve your chances of success. The cultivation of self-fulfilling positive beliefs is essentially the technique for improvement of your life advocated by "positive thinking" training.

The problem here (and in Pascal's Wager, discussed in the section called **Why Believing in God Is a Good Bet** in Chapter II) is that for most of us, consideration of the consequences of believing something has no power whatever to make us believe it. What would make us believe something is evidence that it is *true*.

But on closer inspection, it appears that self-fulfilling beliefs are not exactly like Pascal's Wager. Believing a self-fulfilling belief tends to make it true. So it appears that the fact that you believe a self-fulfilling belief *is* some evidence that what you believe is true. So if someone asks you why you believe it's true, it seems that the only correct answer would be that you believe it's true. That's pretty strange.

How to Fail at Baseball

RELATED TO THE NOTION of a self-fulfilling belief is the notion of a paradoxical intention. This is involved when it's less likely you can do something if you try to do it.

A good baseball swing is a complex sort of action. You might naturally have a good swing, the first time you pick up a bat; or you might get a good swing from advice and practice. But it's likely that if you are told what's wrong with your swing and what you should be doing, and then you swing while trying to do the right thing, you'll do worse than you ordinarily do when you're not thinking about it.

Trying to go to sleep is another example. Trying to do it may very well tend to prevent you from doing it.

People who think too much are poor at doing things that involve paradoxical intentions. Philosophers, whose business it is to think about things, hope that paradoxical intentions aren't too widespread.

My Philosophy Department's softball team was soundly thrashed by almost every team we played. On the other hand, we did defeat the team from the Registrar's Office, where there's no evidence of thought at all.

The Pursuit of Happiness

SOME PHILOSOPHERS THINK THAT the achievement of happiness also involves paradoxical intentions—that trying to be happy is not likely to result in happiness. A better suggested strategy is finding things that matter to you, and working hard to get them. Someone who is working toward growing a beautiful lawn, or breaking 100 on the golf course, or solving a philosophical problem, has intentions, desires, and aims directed toward gardening, or golf, or philosophy—not toward happiness.

> Thomas Jefferson wrote, in the American Declaration of Independence, that we all have the right to the pursuit of happiness. But if pursuing happiness is a bad way to get it, then this right isn't worth much.

A QUESTION TO THINK ABOUT: Maybe there isn't really any such thing as the pursuit of happiness. We know what it means to pursue skill at golf, or to try to open a jar whose lid is stuck. But what does it mean to try to get happiness?

> To test the resistance of their product to bird-impact, aircraft manufacturers use a special gun which shoots whole chicken carcasses at aircraft parts.[1]
> This fact has no connection whatever with anything in this book. I mention it merely because I thought you ought to know.

Fooling Yourself

DESCARTES THOUGHT THAT YOU couldn't be wrong about what your own mental states were. Is that right?

> *Reporter:* Yogi, have you made up your mind yet?
> *Yogi Berra:* Not that I know of.

> "I think if you know what you believe, it makes it a lot easier to answer questions. I can't answer your question."—George W. Bush, in response to a question about whether he wished he could take back any of his answers in a televised presidential election debate

---

1   Reported by Laudan, *The Book of Risks*, p. 59.

Self-deception—if such a thing is possible—would be a particularly interesting example of being mistaken about what you really believe. Positive thinking is, in a sense, a sort of attempted self-deception: the only reason you have to try so hard to have a self-fulfilling belief is that you really believe it's false—or, at least, fear it might be.

Is self-deception possible? Suppose that you need a good night's sleep for some important task the next day, and that you believe you won't be able to go to sleep because you tend to be insomniac. You realize that this belief will tend to keep you awake, because you will worry about not being rested; so you try to believe instead that you'll go to sleep as soon as your head hits the pillow. The only reason you're trying so hard to believe you'll go right to sleep is that you already believe you won't. How can you believe something while you believe the opposite? How can you believe something *because* you believe the opposite? Perhaps self-deception is impossible.

But maybe I've spoken too fast. What is the familiar phenomenon called "wishful thinking" but the sort of self-deceptive process of coming to believe something not because you have evidence for its truth, but because you wish it were true?

Sorry, I'm Not Free Right Now

THE ATTEMPT TO PRACTISE self-deception plays a key role in the analysis of the human condition advocated by some existentialists. In their view, a centrally important, universal, and necessary human characteristic is *freedom*: there are no causes for your feelings, values, or behaviour, not even your personality (which they regard as a myth). Neither are there objective standards obliging you to do one thing rather than another, provided by God, society, or moral reasoning. Thus you must make yourself up—create your own standards and motives out of nothing—with no cause and no guidance. As a result, you're wholly responsible for everything you do. But your realization that you are in this state is not a pleasant one: it's terrible to think that nothing pushes or helps or guides you in your self-creation, and that you are totally responsible for yourself. That's why you spend so much of your time trying to give excuses: attempting to pretend to yourself and others that there are real causes or standards, or that you really have a "personality" or a "role" that forces you to be some way. But this is always a mistake, and you know that it's a mistake. How can you actually come to believe you're not free, while you really believe you are?

A QUESTION TO THINK ABOUT: How about it? Is all that true about you? C'mon now, be honest, stop trying to fool yourself.

4. Mental Impotence

Believe or I'll Shoot!

IT WOULD BE A good idea for you to believe something you want to be true and your belief would help make it true, or if it were helpful to you to believe it.

Suppose someone held a gun at your head, and said, "Believe that the Dodgers will win next year's World Series, or I'll shoot!" You might try to convince this loony that you did believe that the Dodgers will win. But if you didn't already believe the Dodgers will win, his threat wouldn't result in your coming to believe it. You would surely *want* to believe it—it would be very much to your benefit to believe it—but this has no bearing on the matter.

But it seems that we don't have the power to believe what we want to believe. We can't believe things on purpose.

How to Intend to Kick Your Cat

HAVING SOMEHOW ESCAPED THE loony in the last example, you walk further down the street and another loony approaches, holds his gun at your head, and says, "Intend to kick your cat tomorrow, or I'll shoot!" Can you develop intentions at will?

You love Tabitha and certainly don't want to kick the poor, fuzzy, de-fenceless thing. Your first strategy might be deception: you would try to convince this loony that you had just developed the intention he demanded, even though you hadn't.

But suppose there's no fooling him: he can tell that you're insincere in reporting your intention—it shows on your face.

So instead you agree to intend to kick the cat—what else can you do? But, you reason, having the intention to do something doesn't mean that you re-ally will do it. After your assailant has gone away, you can certainly change your mind. So your intention to kick Tabitha, you're relieved to see, will be harmless. You can merely get rid of the intention before tomorrow, and thus avoid both being shot and kicking Tabitha.

But the loony is too clever for you. "I can tell," he says, "that what you're trying to do is to develop the intention now to kick your cat, but that you also intend to get rid of that intention after I go away. So what you really intend is not to kick your cat at all!" He points his gun.

You think: I really have to genuinely intend to kick Tabitha. If I also intend now to change my mind later, then I don't really intend now to kick

Tabitha. So I guess the only thing I can do is to decide now to kick her, without intending to change my mind later.

So you develop two intentions:

(1) to kick Tabitha; and

(2) not to change your mind later about (1).

You tell the loony what you've decided, and he sees that you're sincere. Will that do the trick?

Even if it does, there's a puzzle here. Your intention (2) is really a crazy one. Why not change your mind later? He will, after all, have gone away, and you won't be in any danger. (There's an analogy here with the "Doomsday Machine" example I'll present in Chapter XII, in an item called **Bombing the Russians**.)

But maybe it won't do the trick. "I'm way ahead of you," says the loony. "What you really are going to do is to change your mind about (2) later. Then at that time you'll be able to change your mind about (1). So to avoid being shot you also need another intention, (3): that you won't change your mind about (2)."

But if this is the case, then to satisfy him, wouldn't you *also* need to have intention (4): not to change your mind about (3)? This line of reasoning continues: maybe you need an infinite number of intentions. Is it possible for anyone to have an infinite number of intentions? Is your assailant demanding the impossible after all?

Okay, so maybe the only rational solution to this problem is to *really* intend to kick your cat, (with no intentions about changing your mind about anything), and so go ahead and kick her. That's too bad, but think of the alternative, which is worse.[1]

Into the Mainstream of Philosophy

SOME OF THE PROBLEMS that arose in the items in this chapter result from the assumption that we must believe everything that's implied by our beliefs. Many philosophers think that this assumption should simply be rejected. But this rejection brings its own problems. For one thing, is it really logically possible that somebody believes that no pigs can fly, and that Porky is a pig, but fails to believe what's implied by this, that Porky can't fly? It seems inconceivable that somebody believe one but not the other. Do you think that this is possible?

Again, some philosophers urge us to become reconciled to the position

---

1   David Gauthier argues for the rationality of this solution in a similar case. See his "Assure and Threaten."

that it's possible to have contradictory beliefs. Thus, for example, someone might simultaneously believe both that it's Tuesday and that it's not Tuesday. Is this really possible? If someone *said* both of these sentences with a look of deep sincerity, we wouldn't know what that person believed. Try to think of a plausible story that involves someone's having contradictory beliefs. Can you? Maybe this doesn't even make sense.

You'll find useful reading on these matters in the Smullyan and Poundstone books already mentioned.

Another topic in this chapter is self-defeating and self-fulfilling beliefs, and self-deception. These do not fit neatly into any particular subject-matter area in mainstream philosophy, though there are occasional treatments of these ideas by philosophical writers in various contexts. For those interested in further reading, the best I can do is lamely to suggest you keep your eyes open. In the meantime, I can propose some questions for you to think about.

(1) One way to account for self-deception is to think of the mind as having parts, only some of which are conscious. Thus, for instance, when we have a belief we don't want to have, this gets shoved down into an unconscious area of the mind, and replaced in the consciousness with a preferable one. Perhaps this way of thinking necessitates postulation of a third area, which does the evaluation and the shoving. (Students familiar with Freudian psychology will recognize this as a version of Freud's tripartite division of the mind.) But is it really necessary to complicate things to this degree? It really does seem to be an affront to common sense to think of desires or beliefs in someone who sincerely denies they are there. How could *anyone* know they are there? If what's in our mind is nothing but what we are aware of, then isn't it self-contradictory to talk about parts of our mental life of which we're unaware?

(2) Certain considerations above tended to lead us to talk about beliefs about beliefs, intentions about intentions, and desires about desires. These are sometimes called "second-order" beliefs, intentions, and desires, and they are puzzling things. Do they even make sense? Consider this example. Suppose you and all your friends smoke; everyone else wants to stop smoking, but you (unconvinced or unmoved by the threats to your health and bank account) don't. Now suppose that you're a conformist and want to be like all your friends. You'd like to share their desire to stop smoking, but you don't share it. In other words, you have the first-order desire to keep smoking, but you have the second-order desire not to have this first-order desire. You want to keep smoking, but you want *not* to want to keep smoking. Is this possible? Maybe second-order desires, if genuine, simply collapse into first-order desires. Thus if you genuinely do want to want to stop smoking, then you automatically want to stop smoking. Is this right?

Chapter VII

Good and Bad Reasoning

1. Thought-Traps for the Unwary

The Price of a Ball

HERE'S A QUESTION THAT most people answer wrong. If a bat and a ball together cost $1.10, and the bat costs $1.00 more than the ball, then what does the ball cost?[1]

> The answer everyone jumps at is 10¢. If you don't see that this is the wrong answer, notice that if the ball cost 10¢, and the bat cost $1.00 more than the ball, then the bat would cost $1.10, so together they would cost $1.20.

This is, of course, an arithmetic puzzle, not a philosophical one. What may be of philosophical interest here is why almost everyone gets the wrong answer. Is there something about the way the puzzle is posed that leads people in the wrong direction? Is there something about our normal strategy in dealing with arithmetical questions that normally works fine, but that leads us astray when we think about this puzzle?

We all share certain reasoning strategies. Some of these are learned in school. More are learned in the course of everyday experience, by imitation and suggestion from others, and by trial-and-error. There might even be some inborn problem-solving strategies wired into our brains, and genetically determined. These strategies work pretty well, in general. Most people

---

1   This puzzle and a discussion of it are found in "Representativeness Revisited," by D. Kahneman and S. Frederick.

are able to solve many problems—at least, problems of the sort that we're liable to run into in everyday life. But there are some simple problems that most people answer wrongly. Our common strategies are not geared to deal with these problems successfully. A careful examination of a variety of these problems might show us exactly how our common strategies work.

The fact that your problem-solving strategies tend to fail on certain sorts of simple problems does not mean that you're stupid, or that your strategies need fixing. Any problem-solving strategy will be good at some problems and bad at others. Some of them will be much easier to learn and use, more suited to the wiring of our brains and the nature of our environment. It just might be the case that the ones you in fact use achieve just the right combination of high percentage of success and ease of learning and use. But maybe not.

What are our strategies for doing arithmetic? That's a hard question to answer; but whatever they are, they are different from the ones computers use. Computers are much better than we are at multiplying large numbers. They can calculate answers in a tiny fraction of the time it takes humans, and we get wrong answers far more often than they do. But we're much better at figuring out what sort of computations are necessary to solve problems than they are. Imagine that you could get your brain surgically replaced with a computer. You could multiply large numbers much better as a result, but you'd be much worse off at problem-solving in general. The way we work is not so bad.

Splitting Up the Diamonds

THE NEXT FEW ITEMS demonstrate other arithmetic traps for the unwary. This one is an old puzzle that confused me and my friends as children.

A will specifies that several diamonds, to be found in a safe-deposit box, are to be distributed to the deceased's three children as follows: ½ of them to the eldest, ¼ of them to the middle, and ⅕ to the youngest. The executor is puzzled about what to do when it turns out that there are nineteen identically sized diamonds in the box. You can't give out ½ or ¼ or ⅕ of this collection without cutting some diamonds into pieces, and cutting a diamond would ruin its value. What can the executor do?

> The executor hits on this ingenious plan: he borrows another diamond of the same size from a jeweller friend, and adds it to the nineteen, making twenty. He takes ½ of the twenty—ten of them—and gives them to the eldest child; then ¼ of the twenty—five—to the middle, and ⅕ of the twenty—four—to the youngest. He has distributed nineteen diamonds; one remains—the one he borrowed from the jeweller—which he

now returns. The eldest child is delighted, reasoning that she was entitled to only 9½ diamonds (one-half of the nineteen) but has received ten instead; the other two think they have received a similar bonus.

A QUESTION TO THINK ABOUT: Something is peculiar about this very nifty solution. Do you see what has gone wrong? (Hint: there's something wrong in the terms of the will.)

The Disappearing Dollar

THIS PUZZLE IS IN some ways similar to the one about the diamonds.

Three men, travelling together, check into a hotel and register for a single room that they will share. The desk clerk tells them that the room will cost $30, so they each give the clerk a ten-dollar bill and go up to the room. A few minutes later, the desk clerk notices that he made a mistake: the room costs only $25. So he gives the bellman a five-dollar bill and tells him to go up to the room and give the money back to the men.

On the way upstairs, the bellman has these thoughts: To split up the $5 evenly among the three men would take lots of change, which he doesn't have, and probably the men don't either. Anyway, $5 can't be divided by three exactly evenly. The men don't know that they're getting any refund at all, and they'd be happy to get anything. So if he gave each man a one-dollar bill, they'd be happy, and he would keep the remaining $2. He has three one-dollar bills. So the bellman goes to the room and gives each man a one-dollar bill.

Here's the puzzle. Each man originally put in $10, for a total of $30. Each man got a refund of $1, meaning that each now paid $9, for a total of $27. The bellman pocketed $2. $27 + $2 = $29. What happened to the other dollar?

The hotel now has $25, and the three men now have paid $27 altogether. The bellman's $2 should be added to the hotel's $25 or subtracted from the guests' $27, not added to the guests' $27.

Free Beer

THIS PUZZLE HAS MONEY magically appearing, not disappearing. It's unusual because what looks like faulty reasoning turns out to be correct.

At one time, the Canadian and US dollars were discounted by ten cents on each side of the border (i.e., a Canadian dollar was worth ninety US cents in the US, and a US dollar was worth ninety Canadian cents in Canada). A man walks into a bar on the US side of the border, orders ten US cents' worth of beer, pays with a US dollar and receives a Canadian dollar in change. He then walks across the border to Canada, orders ten Canadian cents' worth of beer, pays with a Canadian dollar and receives a US dollar in change. He continues this throughout the day, and ends up dead drunk with the original dollar in his pocket. Two questions: (1) Who paid for the drinks? (2) When did this happen?

> (1) The man paid for all the drinks, despite the fact that he ended up with the same amount of money that he started with. As he transported Canadian dollars into Canada and US dollars into the US, he performed "economic work" by moving the currency to a location where it was in greater demand (and thus valued higher). The earnings from this work were spent on the drinks. Note that he can only continue to do this until the Canadian bar runs out of US dollars, or the US bar runs out of Canadian dollars, i.e., until he runs out of "work" to do.[1]

> (2) A beer for *ten cents*?? This happened approximately a gazillion years ago.

Nobody Works at All

ANOTHER ARITHMETIC MISTAKE:

There are 365 days in the year; but people usually work 8 hours a day; that's one-third of the 24-hour day. So people actually work only the equivalent of one-third of 365 days—that is, about 122 days.

But people usually work only weekdays. This means two days off a week; there are 52 weeks in a year, so there are 104 days off per year. Subtracting this from the 122 days leaves only 18 days.

Suppose, on average, a ten-day vacation. This leaves eight days. But there are at least this many regular holidays in the year. So nobody works at all.[2]

A QUESTION TO THINK ABOUT: Can you explain what's wrong with this reasoning?

---

1   Thanks to an anonymous contributor to the newsgroup rec.puzzles for this puzzle and answer.

2   A version of this traditional puzzle is in Paulos, *Innumeracy*, pp. 167–68.

The Disappearing Day

THIS ITEM AND THE following one are not problems in mathematics, but they do present conceptual traps like the other puzzles we've been looking at. You know all the facts needed to get the right answer—the problem is putting them together right. I'll present this puzzle, as always, in a story, but this time, the story is true.

A ship commanded by Ferdinand Magellan set out from Spain in 1519, intending to be the first to circumnavigate the globe. Of the 237 men who began the east-to-west trip, only 18 were on the boat when it returned in 1522. One of them was Antonio Pigafetta, an Italian scholar who kept a detailed record of the trip. When the boat, close to returning, arrived at the Cape Verde Islands, Pigafetta wrote this:

> In order to see whether we had kept an exact account of the days, we charged those who went ashore to ask what day of the week it was, and they were told by the Portuguese inhabitants of the island that it was Thursday, which was a great cause of wondering to us, since with us it was only Wednesday. We could not persuade ourselves that we were mistaken; and I was more surprised than the others, since having always been in good health, I had every day, without intermission, written down the day that was current.[1]

How did one day disappear during the trip?

> The quick answer is that this just shows you why they need an International Date Line. If they had had it, then when Magellan's ship crossed it going west, they would have had to subtract one day (so if it was, for example, Friday before crossing, it would be Thursday after). When they got home, their reckoning of what day it was would have been right.

Well, that's correct, but for many people that answer just replaces one mystery by another. Lots of people can't understand the International Date Line—how can going a little bit west gain or lose you a whole day?

> Okay, so let's try this explanation. Every time you travel west, the day is longer, reckoned by the sun, because you're "catching up with it" in its travel east-to-west across the sky. Each 15 degrees (= approximately one time zone) west you go adds one hour to your solar day, so you have to set your clock back one hour. This puts the clocks

---

1   Antonio Pigafetta, *Relazione del primo viaggio intorno al mondo.*

of the folks back home one hour ahead of you. Travel the full 360 degrees around the world, and this one-hour adjustment would happen (360 / 15 =) 24 times, so your clock would come back to read the same time as theirs, but they'd have counted a full day ahead of you. That's why you seemed to have lost a day. You didn't actually lose any time—you had one less day than they did, but each of your days was a little longer then theirs.

Is that any better as an explanation? If not, you're not alone in your puzzlement. I travelled twice across the Pacific, once in each direction, and during both trips people near me on the plane were wondering why a whole day mysteriously just got added or subtracted, and others were trying to explain it to them, unsuccessfully, getting themselves all confused too. The difficulty of this concept is demonstrated by the puzzlement of everybody—smart people, some of them—when Magellan's boat got back.

> Not everyone is happy with the idea of the Date Line either. A website points out that God did not authorize it, and when it was instituted in 1884, "It deceived all the Sabbath-keepers living east of the Garden of Eden and west of the International Date Line into violating the Fourth Commandment ['Remember the sabbath day, to keep it holy'] and receiving the Mark of the Beast!"[1]

Who's Looking?

A MULTIPLE-CHOICE QUESTION:
Jack is looking at Anne, but Anne is looking at George. Jack is married, but George is not. Is a married person looking at an unmarried person?

A) Yes   B) No   C) Cannot be determined

> The right answer is A. If Anne is unmarried, then married Jack is looking at an unmarried person. If Anne is married, then married Anne is looking at an unmarried person. Either way, there's a married person looking at an unmarried person.

According to a psychologist who has studied wrong answers, 80% of people answer C. His explanation of this is basically the one suggested above, in the section called **The Price of a Ball** above. He says that we're "cognitive misers"—that is, we usually choose a fast and easy way to answer a question, when one is available, even though this results in more errors in the long run than slow and more difficult—but generally more accurate—ways. This, he

---

1   Samuel Mercado, "The International Date Line."

points out, is, however, a good general strategy. In most everyday contexts, it's not worth a bit of extra accuracy to tie up our brains with slow and complicated reasoning processes.[1]

The Jelly-Bean Peculiarity

ANOTHER REASONING TRAP, FOR those of you who can't get enough.

A psychologist presented experimental subjects with two bowls of jelly beans. The first contained nine white jelly beans and one red. The second contained 92 white and 8 red. Subjects were given a choice of which bowl to pick from, blindfolded; if they picked a red jelly bean, they got a dollar. Clearly, the probability of getting a red jelly bean from the first bowl is higher: 1 out of 10, 10%, compared to 8 out of 100, 8%, for the second bowl. But between 30 and 40% of subjects picked the second. Interestingly, the majority of those who picked the second knew that there was a better statistical probability of winning if they picked the first. One said, "I picked the one with more red jelly beans because it looked like there were more ways to get a winner, even though I knew that there were also more whites, and that the percents were against me."[2]

The General Makes Some Bad Choices

THE TWO PSYCHOLOGISTS MENTIONED earlier, Tversky and Kahneman,[3] conducted a famous series of experiments on people's decision making, with interesting results. Here's one:

First they gave a bunch of people Problem 1:

1. Imagine you are a general surrounded by an overwhelming enemy force which will wipe out everyone in your 600-man army unless you take one of two available escape routes. Your intelligence officers

---

1   The psychologist is Keith E. Stanovich, in "Rational and Irrational Thought." Stanovich attributes this puzzle to Hector Levesque, a computer scientist at the University of Toronto.

2   Stanovich (p. 120) reports the experiments done by Denes-Raj and Epstein, "Conflict between intuitive and rational processing"; Kirkpatrick and Epstein, "Cognitive-experiential self-theory and subjective probability"; and Pacini and Epstein, "The relation of rational and experiential information processing styles."

3   A good summary of some of Tversky and Kahneman's conclusions is found in Chapter 1 of *Judgement Under Uncertainty: Heuristics and Bias,* ed. Daniel Kahneman, Paul Slovic, and Amos Tversky.

explain that if you take the first route you will save 200 soldiers, where-as if you take the second route the probability is 1/3 that all 600 will make it, but 2/3 that they'll all die. Which route do you take?

Three out of four people choose the first route, since 200 lives can defi-nitely be saved that way, whereas the probability is 2/3 that the second route will result in even more deaths.

Maybe this reasoning is okay and maybe it isn't. Notice that on standard decision theory we could calculate the "expected deaths" for the second route as (1/3 x 0) + (2/3 x 600) = 400. This is the same as the "expected deaths" for the first route: (1 x 400) = 400. But perhaps (as in the lottery case) something else is going on in here. Maybe people also want to avoid the possibility of everyone dying on the second route.

Anyway, then Tversky and Kahneman gave people Problem 2:

2. Imagine again you're a general faced with a decision between two escape routes. If you take the first one, 400 of your soldiers will die. If you choose the second route, the probability is 1/3 that none of your soldiers will die, and 2/3 that all 600 will die. Which route do you take?

Four out of five people now choose the second route, reasoning that the first route will lead to 400 deaths, while there's at least a probability of 1/3 that everyone will get out okay if they go for the second route.

Can you see what's wrong with the reasoning the majority of people are doing here?

Look carefully at Problems 1 and 2. They describe identical choices! It looks like there isn't any subtle evaluation of alternatives going on here. What's going on here is just a flat-out mistake. People are making irrational decisions, misled by the way the question is phrased.

More Math Troubles

HERE ARE A COUPLE of other amusing[1] arithmetical paradoxes:

I. Clearly: 1 yard = 36 inches
    Dividing through by 4:   1/4 yard = 9 inches
    The square root of both sides: 1/2 yard = 3 inches

---

1   Well, perhaps I exaggerate. Anyway, people who find this sort of thing amusing will find these to be things of the sort that amuse them.

But that's clearly wrong. Where's the mistake?[1]

II. Consider a large pile of cubical toy blocks. The smallest has a side of exactly 1 inch (so it has a volume of $1^3 = 1$ cubic inch). The next largest has a slightly larger side, and they keep getting gradually larger, up to the largest, which is 3 inches on a side (with a volume of $3^3 = 27$ cubic inches). The average length of side in this pile is 2 inches. The average volume must be $(1 + 27)/2$ cubic inches: 14 cubic inches. So the block in this pile which is of average size must measure 2 inches on a side, and have a volume of 14 cubic inches. That's a pretty peculiar block.[2]

His Father's Son

THIS ITEM IS ANOTHER example of a conceptual trap—but not an arithmetical one.

Raoul is looking at a photograph. You ask him, "Whose photograph is that?" Raoul poetically replies, "Brothers and sisters have I none; but this man's father is my father's son." By "this man" Raoul means the man in the photo. Who is that man?

> The answer is that the man in the photo is Raoul's son. Is that the answer you arrived at? If the right answer is not obvious to you, note that the person Raoul (who has no brothers) calls "my father's son" has to be Raoul himself; and since he's called "this man's father," then "this man" has to refer to Raoul's son.

Almost everyone jumps at the answer that the man in the photo must be Raoul. They reason: because Raoul has no brothers or sisters, then the person he calls "my father's son" must be him. So far so good; but people forget that "my father's son" is *the father* of the man in the picture. Perhaps something about the way the riddle is stated makes people forget that, and makes us think about the problem in the wrong way. Do you feel that the problem setup causes confusion, by producing information overload? I couldn't possibly fail not to disagree with you less.

The Card Mistake

HERE'S AN EXPERIMENT YOU can run on yourself. A psychologist used this as part of a test of people's reasoning ability.

---

1 Paulos, *Innumeracy*, p. 95.
2 Adapted from an example in Paulos, *Innumeracy*, p. 169.

Examine the following four cards:

a   b   c   d

Half of each card (shown black above) is masked. Your job is to figure out which of the hidden parts of these cards you *need* to see in order to answer the following question decisively: *Is it true in all cases that if there is a circle on the left there is a circle on the right?* Of course, if you unmasked all the cards, you could answer this question; but it's not necessary to unmask all of them to answer it conclusively. Which are the cards it's necessary to unmask?

> Is your answer that you need to see the masked part on only card a? Or is your answer that you need to see the masked parts on both card a and card c? These are the answers people commonly give, but both of these answers are wrong. The right answer is that you need to see the masked parts on card a and card d.
>
> Here's help in figuring out why the right answer is right. What would it take for it to be true that all the cards follow the rule? It would have to be the case that any card with an O on the left would have to have an O on the right. In other words, there could be no card with an O on the left and nothing on the right. To test this, we can ignore card b, which doesn't have an O on the left. Similarly, card c can be ignored, since whether or not there's an O on the left, it can't be the sort of card we are looking for: with an O on the left, and nothing on the right. Card d must be unmasked, however, because it might have an O on the left. If it does, then that general rule would be shown false. If it doesn't, then the rule can still be true.

But what's important here is not what the right answer is, or why it's right. The point is that in the experiment very few people got the right answer, even when the subjects were a group of university students with high intelligence. (In one group of 128 university students, only five got the right answer. So don't feel bad if you got the wrong answer.) Why did such a large proportion of intelligent people get it wrong?

Consider, by contrast, this puzzle. Imagine you're a bouncer in a bar, and are enforcing the rule "If a person is drinking beer, he must be eighteen or older." Which do you have to check (for beverage or age): A beer-drinker? A coke-drinker? A twenty-five-year-old? A sixteen-year-old? Most people correctly answer that you have to check the beer-drinker's age and the sixteen-year-old's beverage. The bouncer question has exactly the same logical structure as the card problem. What's the difference that accounts for the fact that people do so much better at the bouncer question?

One theory is that the card problem is posed in an abstract way, as a mere puzzle, and has no bearing on anyone's practical experience; but the bouncer question is much more like a real-world scenario—one we can easily imagine ourselves in.

But the concreteness of the situation is not what makes the difference. Here's an equally concrete puzzle that people find as daunting as the card problem. Suppose you're in that bar again, and you're interested in finding out whether a certain theory of bar-behaviour is right. According to this theory, people follow this rule: "If a person eats hot chili peppers, then he drinks beer." Whom must you check? A chili-eater? Someone who's eating French fries instead? A beer-drinker? A coke-drinker?

So it's not concreteness after all. Any ideas?

> Work of the psychologist Leda Cosmides shows that people get the answer right when the rule is a contract, an exchange of benefits, of the form, "If you take a benefit, you must meet a requirement." (In our example, beer is the benefit, and being over eighteen is the requirement. But beer and chili peppers do not have a benefit-requirement relationship.) This suggests that our minds are attuned to detecting conditional sentences (sentences of the form 'If P then Q') about rule-cheaters, but not to conditional sentences with other sorts of content.

Roses and Mice

A SIMILAR SORT OF mistake, this one made by 70% of university students. In the following argument, does the conclusion follow from the premises?

Premise 1: All living things need water.
Premise 2: Roses need water.
Conclusion: Therefore roses are living things.

The conclusion, despite what all those university students think, does not follow. Compare this logically similar bit of invalid reasoning:

Premise 1: All insects need oxygen.
Premise 2: Mice need oxygen.
Conclusion: Therefore mice are insects.

Clearly here the conclusion does not follow, but it's logically the same as the roses case.

Stanovich, whom we met earlier, theorizes that our knowledge of the world (that the conclusion of the first argument is true, and of the second false) trumps our logical reasoning skill.[1]

---

1   "Rational and Irrational Thought," p. 121.

A QUESTION TO THINK ABOUT: What reason do we have for classifying some reasoning as good, and other reasoning as bad? One way of explaining this classification is that it summarizes and systematizes how smart people really reason. When smart people are given the card problem, they come to the "wrong" conclusion. Does this show that their conclusion is not really the wrong one?

FOR FURTHER READING: The card puzzle (called the Wason Test), was invented by Peter C. Wason and P. Johnson-Laird. It and others like it are described and discussed in: Wason, "Reasoning about a Rule"; Wason and Johnson-Laird, "A Conflict between Selecting and Evaluating Information in an Inferential Task"; and several articles in Johnson-Laird and Wason, eds., *Thinking.* You can find accounts of Cosmides' work in L. Cosmides, "The Logic of Social Exchange." My source for information in this section is a wonderful book that I recommend you read lots of: Steven Pinker, *How the Mind Works.* Pinker's discussion of the Wason task is on pp. 336–38.

2. The Reasoning of Other Cultures and Past Cultures

Azande Witches

CULTURES RADICALLY DIFFERENT FROM our own sometimes have considerably different beliefs from ours, and appear to disagree with us about what counts as good reasoning.

The Azande live in north-central Africa. They believe that post-mortem examination of someone's intestines for "witchcraft substance" can show conclusively whether or not that person was a witch. They also believe that witchcraft is strictly inherited—that is, if a parent of yours is a witch, then you *must* inherit this trait. But they refuse to draw the conclusion that people are witches when they are the offspring of someone determined, post-mortem, to have been a witch.

Something is peculiar here, but what? Of course, most of us would object to the Azandes' idea that there are witches and intestinal "witchcraft substance." But that's not the interesting point of this example. It seems, in addition, that they are making an elementary reasoning mistake. They appear to agree to the following premises:

X's parent is a witch.
If someone's parent is a witch, then that person is a witch too.

but to refuse to accept the following conclusion:

X is a witch.

But we shouldn't be too hasty here. Maybe they really do accept that the conclusion follows from these premises, but don't like calling live people witches, and are too polite to agree to the conclusion. Or maybe the anthropologist who translated what the Azandes said got the translation wrong. Or maybe the native informants were joking with the anthropologist, or telling deliberate lies.

FOR FURTHER READING: The philosophical implications of Azande reasoning are discussed by Peter Winch, "Understanding a Primitive Society." Winch's position is discussed by Charles Taylor in "Rationality." This book is a splendid collection of articles about the general questions raised in this item. W.V.O. Quine (in *Word and Object*) influentially argues that "fair translation preserves logical laws," so the Azandes must have been mistranslated.

Camels in Germany

HERE IS AN EXCERPT from an interview by the psychologist A.R. Luria with a peasant from Kashgar (in the extreme western part of China):

> Q: (the following syllogism is presented) There are no camels in Germany. The city of B. is in Germany. Are there camels there or not?
> A: (subject repeats syllogism exactly)
> Q: So, are there camels in Germany?
> A: I don't know, I've never seen German villages.
> Q: (the syllogism is repeated)
> A: Probably there are camels there.
> Q: Repeat what I said.
> A: There are no camels in Germany, are there camels in B. or not? So probably there are. If it's a large city there should be camels there.
> Q: But what do my words suggest?
> A: Probably there are. Since there are large cities, then there should be camels.
> Q: But if there aren't any in all of Germany?

> *A:* If it's a large city, there will be Kazakhs or Kirghiz [types of camels] there.

We can't jump to the conclusion in this case that the peasant is unable to reason logically. Notice that the peasant doesn't get this bit of reasoning:

> There are no camels in Germany.
> The city of B. is in Germany.
> Therefore there are no camels in B.

but provides this bit of reasoning:

> There are camels in large cities.
> B. is a large city.
> Therefore there are camels in B.

Never mind that the second bit of reasoning contains a false premise (the generalization about camels in large cities)—the reasoning on the basis of this premise is correct. So it seems that this peasant is able to understand and use a basic logical syllogism.

What has gone wrong, then?

Perhaps the peasant's inability to understand the first syllogism is the result of the fact that it is (at least for him) *hypothetical*—he doesn't know, and isn't told, that the premises are true. He's just asked to suppose that they are. It might be the case that, in certain cultures, reasoning about (what are thought to be) the facts works fine, but there's an inability to apply it to hypothetical situations.

FOR FURTHER READING: This example and many others are discussed fascinatingly in Don LePan's *The Cognitive Revolution in Western Culture*, Vol. 1: *The Birth of Expectation*. LePan offers the hypothesis that peasants from primitive cultures (as well as children in ours) show deficits in reasoning about hypothetical situations. LePan cites Hallpike, *The Foundations of Primitive Thought*, as the source for the Luria interview.

If We Had Three Nostrils, Would There Be Eight Planets?

HERE IS A SAMPLE of what appears to be very bad reasoning from our own culture. Galileo looked through his telescope at Jupiter, and in 1610 he published a work in which he claimed to have seen four moons around that planet. But a number of contemporary thinkers were sure that what Galileo saw couldn't have been moons. Seven "planets" (meaning bodies in space: the sun and the moon, Mercury, Venus, Mars, Jupiter, and Saturn) were already known, and these additional four would raise the number to eleven; but one contemporary of Galileo argued:

> Just as in the microcosm there are seven "windows" in the head (two nostrils, two eyes, two ears, and a mouth), so in the macrocosm God has placed two beneficent stars (Jupiter, Venus), two maleficent stars (Mars, Saturn), two luminaries (sun and moon), and one indifferent star (Mercury). The seven days of the week follow from these. Finally, since ancient times the alchemists had made each of the seven metals correspond to one of the planets; gold to the sun, silver to the moon, copper to Venus, quicksilver to Mercury, iron to Mars, tin to Jupiter, lead to Saturn.
>
> From these and many other similar phenomena of nature such as the seven metals, etc., which it were tedious to enumerate, we gather that the number of planets is necessarily seven.... Besides, the Jews and other ancient nations, as well as modern Europeans, have adopted the division of the week into seven days and have named them from the seven planets; now if we increase the number of planets, this whole system falls to the ground.... Moreover, the satellites are invisible to the naked eye and therefore can have no influence on the Earth, and therefore would be useless, and therefore do not exist.[1]

This is dreadful astronomy, but it does represent respectable mainstream thought of its era.

---

1   I encountered the "seven windows" quotation in Taylor, "Rationality." Taylor does not provide the author of the quotation, but he does cite Sidney Warhaft's book *Francis Bacon: A Selection of His Works*, p. 17. So in the first edition of *Two Errors*, I attributed the quotation to Bacon, remarking on the fact that Bacon was otherwise taken to be a brilliant champion of the new empirical science.

Well, it turns out that the quotation is not by Bacon after all; in fact, Warhaft gives it in the introduction to his book, not in the main body of selections from Bacon, attributing it to "a respectable representative of the old school" and citing it as just the kind of thinking that Bacon crusaded *against*. It turns out to have been written by an astronomer named Francesco Sizzi, in his book *Dianoia Astronomica, Optica, Physica*.

Oops.

Anyway, there's a moral here for all you junior cadet researchers out there. When you want to cite something a writer got from somewhere else, it's a good idea to look up the source cited to make sure you have it right.

Nobody Could Be That *Wrong*

HOW COULD ASTRONOMY HAVE been done that poorly? Are you tempted to think that the author of that quotation was just stupid? Or that the fault was, more likely, in the primitive scientific methodology accepted at the time, which wrongheadedly and superstitiously relied on analogy and metaphor instead of observation?

But a more sophisticated, popular, and politically acceptable conclusion is the view (loosely called "post-modern") that the thinkers of other times and places, who often seem to us to have been reasoning very poorly and to have gotten things dreadfully wrong, were probably just as smart as we are; the reason they look stupid to us is that they were operating from very different viewpoints from the ones we have. Our counting them as stupid is just our own narrow-minded intolerance—even a form of racism, when applied to non-European cultures. A better way to understand this sort of thought is to see it as successful in achieving aims different from those of our culture's thinkers. Each group has its own aims, procedures, and presuppositions, and the procedures of one group can seem stupid to others. What is really happening is merely that we don't—perhaps even can't—understand what they're doing. We shouldn't even be making any judgements about who's really smarter than whom, or about which society has the superior methodology.

But this view doesn't seem adequate either. Taken to an extreme, this approach would seem to indicate that *nobody* can be mistaken about the facts or use faulty reasoning. *Whenever* someone disagrees with me, it can always be argued that I merely don't understand what that person is doing. Surely *somewhere* there must be examples of people who believed falsehoods or thought irrationally. Surely we all live in the same world, and some of us are right and others wrong about what this world is like, and about the best way to think about it.

But here's a philosophical argument for the conclusion that it's literally *impossible* for us to find somebody who gets things really badly wrong.

Imagine that an anthropologist claims to have discovered a tribe where mistaken beliefs run rampant. We are told that people in this tribe—we'll call them the Falsoids—believe, for example, that pigs have thick, hard, elongated woody trunks rooted in the ground, that they sometimes grow over twenty metres high, and that they produce lobed leaves which fall off in late autumn, the time when those pigs produce acorns. Now, it's pretty clear to us what has gone wrong here: the anthropologist has simply mistranslated Falsish, the language of the Falsoids. The best explanation is that this anthropologist has merely mistranslated as *pig* the Falsish word for *oak tree*.

Or imagine that the anthropologist claims that the Falsoids believe that rain is boiling hot, solid, poisonous, alive, flammable, and blue; that it makes a noise like clucking when disturbed; and that every bit of it ever discovered has been stored for safekeeping underground. Well, it's clear that something has gone wrong in translation again, though we have no idea what the Falsoids might have meant by whatever the anthropologist heard them say in Falsish.

The point here is that a translation of some other language isn't counted as correct if it translates a great deal of what the speakers of that language say into sentences in our language that we count as badly wrong. The only translation we're willing to count as correct is one in which we count what they're saying as, on the whole, true. Now, since what they say is the main way we have for finding out what they believe, there will be no case in which we claim to know what they believe *and* that what they believe is badly wrong. If we have no way of translating what they say into largely true sentences, then we'll conclude not that they have things badly wrong, but rather that we don't know what they believe.

Thus we can conclude that it is impossible for us to discover a tribe that we will count as having a very large number of false beliefs.

The same line of reasoning can be used to show that we can't ever discover someone in *our own tribe*—someone who speaks the same language as we do—who has very badly mistaken beliefs. Imagine that someone says to you, in English, "Pigs have thick, hard, elongated woody trunks rooted in the ground. They sometimes grow over twenty metres high, and they produce lobed leaves which fall off in late autumn, the time when those pigs produce acorns." You might be tempted to conclude that this person has badly mistaken beliefs, or that he or she has gone crazy; but in some circumstances the preferred interpretation would be that he or she is speaking English peculiarly—that he or she means *oak trees* by the word *pigs*, and has true beliefs about oak trees.

Yes, but aren't what somebody really believes, and how we understand what they say, really two different matters? Maybe we'd never translate Falsish to produce all those mistakes, but isn't it possible that the Falsoids really believe all of them?

Charity for All?

THE RULE FOR UNDERSTANDING what people mean by what they say, that you should understand it so as to maximize good sense and truth, is called the "Principle of Charity." It doesn't have anything to do with giving money to UNICEF. It has nothing to do with feeling benevolent toward the person who's talking. In fact, that principle is supposed to apply even when your feelings toward the person are quite nasty.

An interesting recent case when this sort of "charity" came into play—actually when it didn't—involved Donald Rumsfeld, the US Defense Secretary under George W. Bush. Because of his extremely conservative politics, and the gross violations of the rights of American citizens and overseas prisoners post-9/11 that he apparently instigated, he was highly unpopular among many people. A great deal of malicious glee was generated by his peculiarly awkward way of speaking. Among his many memorable quotations are these:

- "I would not say that the future is necessarily less predictable than the past. I think the past was not predictable when it started."

- "We do know of certain knowledge that he [Osama Bin Laden] is either in Afghanistan, or in some other country, or dead."

- "We know where they are. They're in the area around Tikrit and Baghdad and east, west, south and north somewhat."—on Iraq's weapons of mass destruction

- "Death has a tendency to encourage a depressing view of war."

- "Freedom's untidy, and free people are free to make mistakes and commit crimes and do bad things."—on looting in Iraq after the US invasion, adding that "stuff happens"

- "[Osama Bin Laden is] either alive and well or alive and not too well or not alive."

- "I believe what I said yesterday. I don't know what I said, but I know what I think, and, well, I assume it's what I said."

- "If I know the answer I'll tell you the answer, and if I don't, I'll just respond, cleverly."

- "Oh, Lord. I didn't mean to say anything quotable."

Perhaps his most famous quotation, and the one most widely mocked, is this:

"Reports that say that something hasn't happened are always interesting to me, because as we know, there are known knowns; there are things we know we know. We also know there are known unknowns; that is to say we know there are some things we do not know. But there are also unknown unknowns—the ones we don't know we don't know."

But actually, despite its contortions, this makes perfect sense, and it's true. Read it carefully, and you'll see. But because of the widespread disdain the guy had accumulated—deservedly—people were treating everything he said with the Principle of Discharity: interpreting it in a way that turned it into nonsense.

I'd be the last person to condemn mockery of Rumsfeld. (You'll know from reading elsewhere in this book that I'm a great fan of deserved—and occasionally undeserved—mockery.) But the "charity" in the Principle of Charity has nothing to do with being nice to somebody: it's just about understanding him. It's hardly ever a good idea to misunderstand what anybody says—even someone you despise.[1]

FOR FURTHER READING: Winch, in the article cited above, champions the view that cases in which we seem to detect horribly bad reasoning in other groups are probably cases in which we have misunderstood them. The most prominent philosophical advocate of the view that any "translation" of what someone else says is counted wrong if it does not attribute to that person at least some degree of rationality is Donald Davidson. A good place to look for an introduction to Davidson's views, criticism of them, and references to the work of Davidson and others is Chapter 2 of Stephen Stich's *The Fragmentation of Reason*. I'll have more to say about related issues—see the discussions of "traditional knowledge" in the next chapter.

Warning for Tourists: Watch Out for Extreme Politeness

A CANADIAN WHO SPENT some time in India told me that he ran into a peculiar problem there, several times. He'd be walking down a street, and he'd ask someone for directions, say, to a museum. The person he asked would point in the direction the Canadian had been walking. But the museum turned out to be in a different direction altogether.

What was going on here? The places the Canadian was looking for were all well known to the locals; they couldn't have been mistaken about them so often, or too stupid to be able to give walking directions. Neither did the people he asked seem to be motivated to lie to him; they all appeared quite friendly and eager to help. At last the Canadian arrived at the hypothesis that

---

1 Julian Baggini talks about Rumsfeld and the Principle of Charity in "Don't Misunderestimate Me," in *The Duck That Won the Lottery.*

the people who told him falsely that the place he was looking for was in the direction he was walking were just being extremely polite: they thought it would be rude to tell people (especially foreigners) that they were walking in the wrong direction.

Here's a similar problem, this time involving Americans and Japanese. This one is reported by the humourist Dave Barry. Before he and his wife left for Japan, she phoned a Japanese travel agent to make hotel and plane reservations. Here's Barry's account of what these phone conversations were like:

> *Beth:* ... and then we want to take a plane from Point A to Point B.
> *Travel Agent:* I see. You want to take a plane?
> *Beth:* Yes.
> *Travel Agent:* From Point A?
> *Beth:* Yes.
> *Travel Agent:* To Point B?
> *Beth:* Yes.
> *Travel Agent:* Ah.
> *Beth:* Can we do that?
> *Travel Agent:* Perhaps you would prefer to take a train.
> *Beth:* No, we would prefer to take a plane.
> *Travel Agent:* Ah-hah. You would prefer to take a plane?
> *Beth:* Yes. A plane.
> *Travel Agent:* I see. From Point A?

And so it would go, with arrangement after arrangement.

The problem, they discovered, was not that the Japanese could not communicate. This travel agent, it turned out, was telling her, in Japanese style, that there was no plane from Point A to Point B. Barry summarizes how the Japanese tell you things (of course, with a touch of comic exaggeration) in the following table:

English Statement Made by a Japanese Person	Actual Meaning in American
I see.	No.
Ah.	No.
Ah-hah.	No.
Yes.	No.
That is difficult.	That is completely impossible.
That is very interesting.	That is the stupidest thing I have ever heard.
We will study your proposal.	We will feed your proposal to a goat.[1]

---

1   *Dave Barry Does Japan*, pp. 35–37.

My Canadian acquaintance who got bad directions in India corroborates Barry's point about Japan. He tells me that when studying the Japanese language in preparation for a trip there he of course learned the words for "yes" and "no," but during his stay in Japan, he never heard the word for "no."

Maybe you don't agree that it's a necessary part of understanding what somebody means to understand what that person says in a way that maximizes truth. But it is a good idea, anyway, not to jump to easy conclusions about the inefficiency or unintelligence of those in other cultures. Understanding what they're doing, saying, and thinking is always a matter of *interpretation*. If you start out feeling that the foreigners are in some way inferior to your group, you'll interpret what they do as stupidity or malevolence or inefficiency. But if you start out with respect for them, and are prepared to admire their differences from your culture, you'll interpret what they do in a favourable way.

The necessity of *interpretation*, and the fact that so much depends on the attitudes the interpreter comes to the foreign culture with, become clearest when the culture is extremely alien and the evidence about what's going on extremely skimpy. The Canadian I've been talking about is an academic interested in the inhabitants of Mesopotamia almost four thousand years ago. Among the extremely scant evidence we have about them is what are apparently some rules they wrote down divining the future on the basis of signs like eclipses and characteristics observed on the livers of sacrificed sheep. But the rules are bizarre. Any idiot could see, it would seem, that these predictions were utterly unreliable. But my acquaintance says that he came to this study believing in advance that the ancient Mesopotamians were not idiots—that they observed reality as clearly as we do, and had as much common sense and reasoning ability as us. Given these presuppositions, he's come up with some pretty ingenious interpretations of what they meant by those writings. His interpretations would be quite different from those of a scholar who believed at the outset that ancient people were mired in superstition, couldn't reason very well, and knew very little about the external world.

SOME QUESTIONS TO THINK ABOUT: So is there such a thing as superstition at all? Is every judgement that a practice in another culture (or in one's own) is superstitious just a derogatory way of referring to their perfectly valid beliefs? Have you noticed that older high-rise buildings often have no thirteenth floor? Is there something valid going on here? Like what?

3. Thinking in Grooves

Ungroovy Thinking

IN THE PUZZLES THAT follow, seeing the solution involves dropping our automatic assumptions, and seeing things from a different angle.

(1) The Boy with Two Fathers

A father and his son are involved in an automobile accident. Both are seriously injured and are rushed to separate hospitals. The son is immediately readied for emergency surgery; at the first sight of him, however, the surgeon says, "I can't operate on this patient—he's my son!" How is what is reported here possible?

> If you think there's a problem with this story, then you're probably assuming that the surgeon is the boy's father; but the story is possible if the surgeon is the boy's mother. When this story began circulating, almost everyone (even feminists) were caught with the assumption that surgeons must be male. Would that assumption be widespread today?[1]

(2) How to Win a Camel Anti-Race

The Sheikh of Al-Cindor orders two of his subjects, Abdul and Jabbar, to participate in a special camel race. The winner will receive a prize of a thousand rials. The finish line is the entrance to the main square of the neighbouring town of Kareem. But what's special about this race is that the winner is the contestant whose camel crosses the finish line *second*.

Abdul and Jabbar get on their camels, and the race begins. They watch each other carefully, each trying to get his camel to move more slowly than the other's, and pretty soon both camels come to a halt. Abdul and Jabbar dismount, sit down in the shade of a palm tree, and try to figure out what to

---

1 A 2009 online BBC news story reports that while gender discrimination has virtually disappeared from physician training and hiring in the UK, and there's the expectation that females will soon outnumber males among GPs there, surgeons are still predominantly male and will continue to be, because the long hours and on-call commitments make surgery a less appealing career to women ("Female medics 'to outnumber male'"). An article on the website of the Society for Canadian Women in Science and Technology reports similar statistical trends in Canada, agreeing that the difficulty of reconciling job necessities with family life is one reason. But an orthopedic surgeon adds that his profession "is somewhat of a carpentry type branch of medicine. And women don't tend to become carpenters." The female dean of a medical/dental school cites the lack of female role models in surgery. ("Women poised to dominate doctors' offices.")

do. At last, they decide to ask the advice of a wise man of their town. The wise man offers them a solution; they jump on the camels, and head off full-speed toward Kareem.

What did the wise man tell them?

He told them to switch camels.

(3) Thinking Straight about Roman Numerals

Here is a number (in Roman numerals): VI. By the addition of one line, can you make it into a seven? The answer is simple enough—VII. But now suppose you are given the following problem: Here is a number, IX. By the addition of one line, can you make it into a six?

In front of IX you add the (curvy) line S, making it SIX.

(4) Reducing Speeding Violations

The New York State Thruway Authority faced the problem of an excessive number of speed-limit violations. They could have, at great expense, hired more troopers to track down the violators. Can you think of an easier and more effective means of reducing the number of violations?

They raised the speed limit. (Fortunately, there was no increase in the accident rate.)

(5) Smashing a Fly

Often in algebra problems we are asked to imagine bizarre and inexplicable situations, and this is no exception. Imagine two train locomotives facing each other on a single track, 200 miles away from each other. Both locomotives will begin moving toward the other simultaneously at 50 miles per hour, ending in a head-on crash. (They accelerate instantaneously to that speed.) Sitting on the front of one of the locomotives at the beginning is a fly. When the two begin to move, the fly will fly quickly toward the other locomotive; when it reaches it, it will turn around and return to the first lo-comotive, then turn around again and fly back to the second; it will continue shuttling back and forth until the locomotives crash (when it will get nicely and thoroughly smashed between them). The fly flies at 75 miles per hour. Before the spectacular finale, how far will the fly travel?

I now pause to allow some readers to sigh morosely as memories of high school algebra flood back.

Bravely, a few readers take out pencil and paper and begin calculation. It's not a very difficult bit of algebra to determine the length of the fly's first trip, from the one locomotive at the start, to the other locomotive moving toward it. Having calculated this, however, or maybe even before, you realize that there will be an infinite series of shorter and shorter trips for the fly as the locomotives converge. Calculating the sum of an infinite series will defeat all but the most stalwart of amateurs, and at this point almost everyone gives up.

But there's a trick, involving a radically different way of thinking about the problem. In two hours, each locomotive will travel 100 miles, meeting in the middle of the 200-mile-long track and crashing. The fly is flying all this time. Since the fly goes at 75 miles per hour, it travels 150 miles. That's it!

It's reported that the great mathematician Von Neumann was given this problem, thought about it for a few seconds, and gave the correct answer. When asked how he did it, he replied, "I summed the series."

(6) The Enormous Tiddly-Wink Tournament

This is another puzzle with an unobvious easy solution. The Klopstokian Tiddly-Winks Federation runs a huge national tournament each year in which the national champion of Klopstokia is determined. The country is divided into four divisions. In each division, all ranked winkers are paired up, and play each other. The loser of each game drops out of the tournament; the winner goes on to play again. After a sufficient number of games, there's only one winker left in each division; they form two pairs who play, then winners of these games play for the championship. Here is a list of the number of ranked winkers in each division:

NORTH: 57
SOUTH: 83
EAST: 51
WEST: 49
_____
TOTAL: 240

The question is: how many games are played altogether in the tournament?

If I hadn't led you to suspect that there's a trick easy solution, you'd probably do this the hard way:

In the North division, there are 57 winkers. So the first round has 28 games, pairing up 56 of these, and one winker gets a bye. The losers drop out, leaving 28 winners plus the winker who had the bye. So there are 14 games in the next round, plus one bye again. In the following round there are 7 games plus one bye; in the next there are 4, with no byes, and in the next 2, and then 1. This produces a winner of the North Division, after a total of, um, let's see, 28 + 14 + 7 + 4 + 2 + 1 = 56 games. Arrgh, now we have to do the same calculation for all the other divisions.

No! Wait a minute! The number of games in the North division is one less than the number of winkers, and it has to be, because players drop out after losing one game, and to get a winner, 56 out of the 57 have to lose. So there's the easy solution to the problem: There are 240 players in all; 239 of them will have to lose one game each. So that means the tournament will have 239 games in all. Voilà!

(7) Notes from the Underground

Here's another puzzle that most people will try to answer the hard way and fail.

Examine this series of numbers; determine the principle here, and supply the next few numbers in the series:

14, 18, 23, 34, 42, 50, 59, 66, 72, 79 …

The next few numbers are 86, 96, 103, 110, 116, 125. The principle here is that these are the stops on the northbound IRT West Side Broadway/7th Avenue subway line in New York City: 14th Street, 18th Street, and so on.

You can be excused for not having seen that answer, because you probably aren't familiar with the New York subway. So you don't merit a "Gotcha!", but my classmates at Columbia University and I did. We were presented with this problem while sitting in a classroom less than three hundred metres from the 116th Street station of the IRT West Side Broadway/7th Avenue subway line. Almost all of us had spent a good proportion of our undergraduate lives riding that subway line through many of those stops, and we were supposed to be a smart bunch of kids. Why didn't any of us get the answer? The reason is, of course, that the question strongly suggested a well-worn conventional sort of solution, and we were all thinking in that groove.

Thinking Outside the Box

THE INABILITY MOST OF us have to see the trick in the surgeon story is a good example of a familiar phenomenon: we are prevented from solving a problem because of our automatic assumptions. A lesson that might be drawn is that we should avoid "thinking in grooves"—that we must think creatively, throwing aside our automatic assumptions, to solve problems.

This is advice you may have encountered especially often recently, when it has become fashionable to blame old-fashioned "linear" thought for everything from the failure of the elementary school system to ecological catastrophe to oppression of women and of the Third World.

What these examples have in common is that we come to a problem with certain automatic assumptions. In the surgeon example, our assumption that a surgeon is male is, of course, suspect; but given the (unfortunate) fact that the vast majority of surgeons in our society are male, it's not unjustified. The way the SIX problem is set up, we are led—reasonably—to assume that we are supposed to add a line to the Roman numeral IX to turn it into the Roman numeral VI. And we assume in the Thruway example that the problem is to get people to obey the *current* speed limit. These assumptions aren't *stated* as conditions of the problems, but given the ways the problems are stated and given our background experience, they are reasonable ways of approaching them. But the solution is found only when the assumptions are rejected.

Is rejection of our automatic assumptions in general a good strategy for solving problems? Don't jump to this conclusion too quickly. In these particular cases automatic assumptions do interfere with our solution to the problem; but very frequently the hidden assumptions we bring to all problems are an aid, not a hindrance, to solutions.

To see this, let's return to the surgeon puzzle. There are other—reasonable—assumptions we bring to this story, which also lead to our reaction that the situation is impossible. We think that the father who is injured in the accident and brought to a different hospital cannot be the surgeon who shows up to perform surgery on his son, because the surgery would have to be performed soon after the accident; and the father was injured and being treated elsewhere. But the story does not *say* that the father would be in treatment simultaneously with his son; perhaps he recovered so fast that he could travel to the hospital where his son was, and could resume his work as a surgeon there in time to be called to his son's case. We reasonably assume that this could not happen; but the apparent impossibility of the story disappears if we withdraw this assumption as well. Another reasonable assumption that works the same way is that what the surgeon exclaims on seeing the boy is true.

Getting Out of the Box

SUPPOSE YOU HAVE TO be at an appointment downtown in a half hour, and you only have a couple of dollars in your pocket, not enough for taxi fare. You have no car, and walking would take more than a half hour. The cash machine is nearby, but if you walked there first, then began to look for a taxi, you'd be late. What should you do? Well, let's try thinking outside the box, questioning your background assumptions that appear to imply you can't make it to your appointment. Here are some of them:

- a taxi won't take you there for free
- standing in your backyard gazing skyward won't result in a helicopter's landing and offering you a free lift downtown
- you haven't suddenly developed the ability to fly

And there are countless other highly plausible assumptions you don't question. Should you go outside the box, and start questioning these?

> No. You'd never solve any problem if you brought countless reasonable background assumptions into question. Thinking in grooves is almost always a good strategy. After all, the world almost always works "in grooves."

FOR FURTHER READING: The SIX and speed-limit example are in *Crazy Talk, Stupid Talk* by Neil Postman. The title of Postman's book tells you what he thinks of some examples of "lateral" thought. "His Father's Son," "The Boy with Two Fathers," and "Smashing a Fly" are all in Raymond Smullyan's book, *What is the Name of This Book?* You can find a huge collection of logical puzzles on the internet, collected by Chris Cole:

http://www.faqs.org/faqs/puzzles/archive/logic/

I have adapted the camel-race example from one of Cole's puzzles.

The the Title of This Book

ONE OF THE TWISTS in the title is the circles resulting from the self-reference. If you've already read the back cover of this book, you'll have found the other one: the repeated 'THE.'

What's interesting about this error is that it's so hard to see. I have asked dozens of people to read the title, and not one of them noticed this error the first time they read it. Some people found the error after I asked them, several times, to read the title carefully, word-for-word. Some people couldn't find it after this. I had to show the repetition to them: "Look—here's one 'THE' and here's another."

This example shows that we even *see* in grooves. When we read something, we automatically and unconsciously process what we see, making "corrections" in accord with expectations about what sequences normally occur in our reading. Perhaps when you read the title, this "correction" process drops out the second word when it finds a repetition. Or maybe there's a process that "corrects" what you seem to read so that it makes sense.

Whatever this process is, it's clear that it has resulted in misperception in this case. But it's also clear that it usually is very advantageous to us. If we had to concentrate on each word in a sentence, our reading would be very slow and laborious. Instead of this, our eyes glance lightly and quickly over the words we read, and this process fills in the blanks and corrects the errors that result from this fast skimming. On the whole, then, this process permits fast and accurate reading. It does, however, produce rare errors, especially in those cases (like the the title of this book) when what we're reading is very unusual.

This is another example in which our automatic strategies for encountering the world, based on expectations of how things usually are, can lead us astray; but, again, the moral is not that we should discard these strategies. They're extremely useful, and we'd be much worse off without them.

The Mushroom Hunt

IMAGINE TWO TRIBES, THE Alphas and the Betas. Both tribes hunt for wild mushrooms for food. The Alphas use a complicated and laborious test to tell which mushrooms to take home and which to ignore. The Betas use a different, much easier test, and take home a lot of mushrooms the Alphas reject. The Alphas sometimes leave behind perfectly good mushrooms the Betas would have used. Who is using the right test?

Well, suppose that there are poisonous mushrooms in Alphaland, but none in Betaland. The Betas' simple test sometimes results in their taking home and eating mushrooms that don't taste too good—but the result is just a bad-tasting dish. If the Alphas used the Betas' test, disaster would result when they ate poisonous mushrooms. The Alphas' procedure costs them more effort and results in fewer mushrooms, but it keeps them from being poisoned. The Betas' procedure is easy and collects a much greater number of edible mushrooms; it occasionally results in a bad-tasting dish, but that's not a big deal. We can see now that *each* mushroom-hunting strategy is correct, relative to the different situations of the tribes.

This parable suggests an answer to the question of what makes something good reasoning. The answer is this: patterns of good reasoning are patterns that *work* for a person or a community. In the parable, what counts as good reasoning for people depends on what sorts of problems they encounter, and on what their needs are. Different people and different communities have different situations, so maybe what's good reasoning in one is bad in the other.

So maybe the surprisingly different general patterns of reasoning exhibited at other times, and by different cultures, are suitable given the difference in their situations.

If you find this line of reasoning attractive, however, you should be careful not to allow it to go too far. It seems clear that there *must* be such a thing as *bad* reasoning. We shouldn't assume that just any old pattern of reasoning must be well suited to the situation of those who use it. Even the fact that some pattern is widely used, and has stood the test of natural selection of reasoning patterns over the ages, doesn't necessarily make it good. A large number of people now believe in perfectly useless astrology.

Note, further, that we have been thinking of a correct strategy of reasoning merely as one that works to satisfy the needs of the reasoners. But it seems possible that occasionally a strategy might result in a whole lot of false beliefs that, by an odd set of coincidences, serve the practical needs of the believers well. Doesn't the fact that a lot of false beliefs result show that something is wrong with this (undoubtedly useful) reasoning strategy? Isn't the test of the correct reasoning strategy *truth*, not *usefulness*? (Recall our consideration of this question in Chapter I.)

Into the Mainstream of Philosophy

PHILOSOPHERS AREN'T REALLY CONCERNED with the little puzzles we began this chapter with (though they do like to demonstrate how clever they are). Philosophical interest centres instead on the general idea of good and bad reasoning. Surprisingly, it's not easy to say what the difference between these is. It's not necessarily that good reasoning is the use of patterns of thought that come up with true beliefs: here and there in this chapter, the suggestion is considered that the best kind of reasoning that we're capable of might be bound to come up—systematically—with occasional mistakes (like those illustrated at the beginning of this chapter). A second important area of philosophical concern is what we should make of apparently large reasoning differences between us and other present cultures (and our past culture). And there are philosophical problems in the very idea that we'd be capable of recognizing enormous differences in thought patterns.

Chapter VIII

Learning from Experience

1. What's Knowledge?

Justification

FRED'S CAR GETS A flat tire as he's pulling out of the driveway on the way to an important job interview. Fred, a perpetual pessimist, says, "I *knew* something would go wrong!"

Did he literally know it? Well, he *believed* it, and it turned out to be true, but he didn't *know* it. Why not? Because he didn't have any good reason to believe it. His belief wasn't justified. There's a long tradition in philosophy that holds that a belief that's true doesn't count as knowledge unless it's *justified*; otherwise, it's just a hunch, or a prejudice, or a good guess. This account is often traced all the way back to Plato.[1]

SOME QUESTIONS TO THINK ABOUT: Years ago, I was sitting in my office, when I heard a colleague of mine out in the hall exclaiming "What the hell is that??" I hurried out and found him looking at a strange enormous insect. Immediately, I said, "It's an ichneumon fly." "What??" he asked, "how'd you know that?" "I don't know," I replied. "I just know that's what it is." Later in the day, I went to the library and looked up "ichneumon fly" in an encyclopedia, and there was a picture of exactly what we saw. I was right, but I hadn't any idea of how I knew. (Later I found a picture in an old dictionary of mine, and decided I must have run across that earlier.)

---

1 In Plato's *Theaetetus*, Socrates considers something like this point of view (though perhaps without endorsing it).

Did I know? It doesn't sound anything like a lucky guess. I must have had a justification for my belief, but I hadn't a clue what it was. So maybe you don't have to know how you know something. Is that right? If you don't know how you came to a belief, do you know that you know it?

Lucy the Baseball Oracle

IMAGINE THAT LUCY CORRECTLY predicts the winner of the World Series before the baseball season starts, for ten years in a row. Does Lucy *know* in advance who's going to win? How could these true beliefs be justified before the season starts? It's highly implausible that they're just lucky guesses, but there's no way anyone could imagine that these beliefs are justified. Does she know who's going to win?

A.J. Ayer, in *The Problem of Knowledge*, argues that knowledge has to be justified true belief—that (in his words) you have to have the *right* to be sure about your belief. In a case like Lucy's, Ayer argues that her record of correct predictions would show she probably had that right, though neither she nor anyone else knows how she would have gotten it. On the other hand, there doesn't really seem to be any way that she could know who's going to win.

Galileo as Scientist

HOW DO YOU GET justification? The obvious answer is: by observation of the world around us. You know it's sunny out—your (true) belief is *justified*—because you looked out the window.

Science is (by contrast with our everyday observation) organized, systematic, rigorous, and invariably expensive observation, but it's nothing but better observation, right? Well, no.

The story of Galileo and the moons of Jupiter is sometimes presented as a paradigm and very early bit of genuine science. In around 1610, he was looking through a telescope (recently a considerably improved bit of technology) and observed some moons circling around Jupiter. Conventional science at the time thought of the planets as embedded on invisible crystal spheres circling the Earth, so of course they couldn't have something circling around them, and the Church, then the repository and guardian of official science, threatened Galileo with torture or worse unless he recanted his heretical claim. According to a (probably fictional) account, Galileo begged a church cardinal just to have a look through his telescope, but the official replied that he didn't have to, because he already knew the truth. The cardinal here represents dogmatic non-observational (and false) belief; Galileo represents the birth of good, justified, observational science. All you have to do is to open your eyes and, without preconception, have a look, the story of Galileo tells us.

Kekulé's Dream

BUT THIS IS NOT exactly right, either as history, or as an account of how science really works. Of course, observation (and its cousin, experiment) are crucial parts of good science, but that's not all there is to it. A characteristic scientific procedure involves two steps: hypothesis formation and hypothesis testing. Because hypothesis formation involves creativity and imagination, not systematic method, many important scientific hypotheses have arisen in weird ways. Here's the story of one.

August Kekulé, a nineteenth-century German chemist, was responsible for a major discovery in organic chemistry: the ring-structure of benzene. Here's his account of how he arrived at this hypothesis:

> I was sitting writing at my textbook but the work did not progress; my thoughts were elsewhere. I turned my chair to the fire and dozed. Again the atoms were gamboling before my eyes. This time the smaller groups kept modestly in the background. My mental eye ... could now distinguish larger structures of manifold conformation: long rows, sometimes more closely fitted together all twining and twisting in snake-like motion. But look! What was that? One of the snakes had seized hold of its own tail, and the form whirled mockingly before my eyes. As if by a flash of lightning I awoke; and this time I spent the rest of the night in working out the consequences of the hypothesis.
>
> Let us learn to dream, gentlemen, then perhaps we shall find the truth.[1]

2. Sceptical Doubts and Puzzles

Life Is But a Dream

THE MOST OBVIOUS, CLEAREST, most indubitable knowledge you have is justified by—comes from—your sense-experience. That's how you know that the cat is on the mat, that you're holding an apple in your hand, or that your pants are on fire. We assume that seeing (and sensing in general[2]) is believing, and that you're entitled to those beliefs.

---

1   August Kekulé, speech given in 1890.
2   I.e., including the other senses.

But of course philosophers are not going to let you get away with assuming anything without examination and proof, trial by skeptical doubt, no matter how obvious.

Descartes started a huge ongoing tradition of philosophical consideration when he wrote this in 1641:

> I am a man, and ... consequently, I am in the habit of sleeping, and representing to myself in dreams those same things, or even sometimes others less probable, which the insane think are presented to them in their waking moments. How often have I dreamt that I was in these familiar circumstances, that I was dressed, and occupied this place by the fire, when I was lying undressed in bed? At the present moment, however, I certainly look upon this paper with eyes wide awake; the head which I now move is not asleep; I extend this hand consciously and with express purpose, and I perceive it; the occurrences in sleep are not so distinct as all this. But I cannot forget that, at other times I have been deceived in sleep by similar illusions; and, attentively considering those cases, I perceive so clearly that there exist no certain marks by which the state of waking can ever be distinguished from sleep, that I feel greatly astonished; and in amazement I almost persuade myself that I am now dreaming.[1]

Notice first that he says that he *almost* persuades himself. He can't really persuade himself (or persuade you either that you're dreaming when you're sure you aren't), and he isn't trying to. As we mentioned earlier, what he's up to is trying to establish a firm foundation for his beliefs, where possible; and to do this, first, he reconsiders the supposedly obvious, raising questions about its basis. Can the trustworthiness of sense-perception be re-established?

The Stuff That Dreams Are Made On

WELL, FIRST LET'S TAKE a look at Descartes's claim that there aren't any "certain marks" (reliable ways) for distinguishing dreams from genuine perception of the real world. Is this true?

Think about your dreams. They're really quite different from your experience while awake. For one thing, they contain all sorts of bizarre events that you'd never experience in reality. You suddenly find yourself in Brazil, riding your bicycle around a supermarket. You figure out how to fly. A time-bomb is ticking next to you, but you're paralyzed and can't escape. Desirable

---

1   *Meditations on First Philosophy*, I, 5.

sexual partners offer themselves to you. All of these are "certain marks" of dreaming, aren't they?

And there are less obvious differences. Things are indefinite or ambiguous in a way they never are in real life. That toaster is becoming a hippopotamus, but it's not just turning from one thing into another—it seems to be both at once, not by having some characteristics of each, but just—somehow—being both in an indescribable way. In dreams you often know things even though there's no way in the dream you could know them. You know that the horrible danger is approaching, because ... well, you just know it. An additional unusual characteristic of dreams is how rapidly and certainly their memory dissolves. Sometimes you wake up and think about your dream, and you can feel all the details disappearing even as you try to remember them. Another feature is how utterly compelling dream-content often is—afterwards you recall the intensity of the experience—even though there was nothing particularly important about it.[1] (That explains why other people are sometimes so eager to tell you about their dreams—and why their dreams so often seem so boring to you.)

So there are, after all, reliable ways of distinguishing dreams from real life. But this is not the end of the story.

Note first that these are not infallible signs. Sometimes dreams are as pedestrian, and definite, as real life (maybe even often, but that sort would be less memorable). Sometimes reality is dreamlike. But a *reliable* sign need not be an *infallible* sign. Descartes pointed out—correctly—that sometimes what we take to be experience of reality is actually an illusion. So there's the possibility that anything we believe because of our senses might turn out false. He was interested in finding out what was *real* knowledge—belief that didn't have even the tiniest possibility of being false—and the everyday beliefs the senses give us about particular facts don't live up to this exalted standard; genuine science should seek something more exalted. Maybe his standards for what should be called real knowledge are too high, but we see his point.

More philosophically interesting, perhaps, is this: while awake, we can reliably tell what's a dream and what's not: but not while dreaming. A philosophy professor once told me that he had a dream in which he asked himself whether he was dreaming or not, and (still dreaming) looked for reliable signs of dreaming/real-life, and concluded he wasn't dreaming.

But here's the real problem. You can easily and reliably partition your experience into two categories; call one the D-realm (for Dream) and the other the A-realm (for Awake). When we're in the A-realm, what we recollect

---

1   These and other dream-characteristics are interestingly discussed at length by Michael Frayn, in *The Human Touch*, pp. 276–93.

from the D-realm seems very bizarre. But it usually doesn't when we're in the D-realm. Now, the philosophical question: which realm gives us contact with the real world, and which one is mere illusion? (Maybe they're both illusory? Maybe they're both real?) And: *How do you know?*

> Here's an attempt to explain why it's reasonable to think that the A-realm represents reality: it's the best explanation for why we've got that sort of experience. What explains, for example, why in the A-realm, the experience of seeing a strawberry so often goes with the experience of smelling and tasting and touching one? The best explanation is this: There's really a strawberry like that, out there in the real world. In the D-realm, on the other hand, anything can go with anything else: it's a chaos. The best explanation for D-realm experience is that it's all subjective: it's created by the person who has that experience, not by external reality.
>
> But why think that orderly experience represents reality? Is it because reality must itself be orderly, not just a mess? But we don't have any reason to think that—except for our A-realm experience!

The Brain in a Vat

HERE'S A STORY THAT asks the same question, but in a way familiar in general outline to science-fiction lovers. Imagine that you are actually a brain in a vat. That is, a mad scientist removed your brain at birth, and installed it in a vat full of nutritive solution to keep it alive. Your brain has been connected by wires to a computer that feeds in incredibly complicated electrical impulses. As a result you have all those experiences that you take to be sensations originating in the external world, but these are in fact all delusions. Like the Five-Minute Hypothesis, this hypothesis is consistent with all your current experience. Do you have any reason at all to think that you are not such a brain in a vat?

> How about this reason. The only way for a thought to be *about* something is for it to be connected in the right sort of way to that thing. (This idea is discussed further in the item called **Thinking about Vienna** in Chapter X.) Now suppose that you really are a brain in a vat. All of your experiences, then, would have come from the wires planted in your brain. None of your thoughts would be connected in the right sort of way with the sky, or breakfast, or Descartes, so none of your thoughts would be about any of these things. Neither would your thoughts have the right sorts of connection with your brain, or with the vat it was in; so you wouldn't be able to have thoughts about your brain or its vat. (It's an interesting question whether you'd be able to have thoughts about anything at all.) So if you were in fact a brain in a vat, you couldn't believe that you were a brain in a vat, and you couldn't believe that you weren't.

SOME QUESTIONS TO THINK ABOUT: If this line of reasoning is right, what does it show? Perhaps it shows that the belief that one is a brain in a vat can't be true. If you were a brain in a vat you couldn't believe it.

But does that show that you're not a brain in a vat? Well, if you were, you couldn't believe you were. But it's still possible that you actually are a brain in a vat. If you were, then your beliefs would be about who-knows-what; but never mind. Have we actually proven that you're not a brain in a vat? Can we prove it? If not, then why do you think you aren't?

FOR FURTHER READING: The brain-in-the-vat example, and a version of the answer to the puzzle suggested here, are found in Hilary Putnam's *Reason, Truth and History.*

What Pink Socks Tell You about Ravens

LET'S TAKE IT FOR granted that we do actually have sense-contact with the real world. But there still are puzzles about exactly how particular observations of it justify belief in a general hypothesis. Some of these are questions about the *logic of confirmation.*

To confirm a hypothesis doesn't mean to show definitely, beyond all doubt, that it's true. To confirm it is to provide assurance of its likelihood—to strengthen its believability. A hypothesis can be confirmed—even well confirmed—but turn out to be false.

A very simple and obvious way we use experience as confirmation is called *simple induction* or *induction by enumeration.* In this process we look at a lot of *instances* of a general hypothesis. For example, we might confirm the general hypothesis that all bears hibernate in the winter by observing a lot of bears in winter, and finding that each bear we see is hibernating.

Induction by enumeration seems quite an obvious and unproblematic way of finding things out; but puzzles about it arise.

To show, by induction, that all ravens are black, we look at a lot of ravens. A single non-black raven will show that this general hypothesis is false, but no single observation will conclusively show the truth of that general hypothesis. As the number of observations of different ravens, all of which turn out black, gets larger, the generalization is more strongly confirmed.

Now the general statement "All ravens are black" is *logically equivalent* to the statement, "All non-black things are non-ravens." They mean the same thing. You can see this by noticing that if one of them is true, the other must also be true; and likewise, if one is false the other must also be false. We can conclude, then, that whatever confirms one of these statements will confirm the other.

Now, to confirm "All non-black things are non-ravens" by simple induction we look at a large number of non-black things, and check whether they are non-ravens. As the number of observations of different non-black things, all of which turn out to be non-ravens, gets larger, the generalization is more strongly confirmed. Suppose you start looking around, and the first thing you see is one of your pink socks. It's non-black, and it's a non-raven. This adds a little confirmation to the generalization "All non-black things are non-ravens." Now you see another non-black thing, this grey thing over here. It's a grey elephant: another non-black thing has turned out to be a non-raven. So we gradually build up confirmation for "All non-black things are non-ravens" by finding a lot of things that aren't black, and seeing that they turn out not to be ravens.

But because whatever confirms that statement also confirms "All ravens are black," finding a pink earthworm or a white tooth confirms "All ravens are black" as well.

But something has gone drastically wrong here. Imagine that you pay some scientists to confirm the hypothesis that all ravens are black, and they run around happily recording what their research has turned up: a green frog, a silver key, a red stop-sign, etc. "You're wasting my research grant!" you scream; but they calmly point out that each of these instances confirms the hypothesis you have been paying them to investigate.

FOR FURTHER READING: The Paradox of the Ravens was invented by Carl Hempel, *Aspects of Scientific Explanation and Other Essays in the Philosophy of Science.*

Something Even Worse about Pink Socks

WELL, YOU MIGHT TRY to resign yourself to the idea that pink socks *do* confirm that all ravens are black. Here's some reasoning that might make that idea a little more plausible. Imagine a really far-reaching study of non-black things that discovered that not a single thing in the group was a raven. Wouldn't that give us reason to think that all ravens are black? As the group of non-black things observed got larger and larger, the continuing absence of ravens in that group would give us better and better reason to think that all of them were black. Of course, at the beginning of this survey—when all we've examined is one pink sock—we have only the very tiniest evidence that all ravens are black; we need to look a whole lot further to produce substantial evidence for that conclusion. But it's a beginning. It does provide *some* evidence, though only a minuscule bit.

But here's a further problem. Consider the competing hypotheses:

> All ravens are green.
> All ravens are white.
> All ravens are blue with orange polka dots.
> [Etc.]

Note that each of these may be restated in an equivalent statement: All non-green things are non-ravens. All non-white things are non-ravens. All non-blue-with-orange-polka-dot things are non-ravens. Etc. And the one pink sock confirms each of these statements to the same (tiny) degree that it confirms the black hypothesis. So if you accept that the sock gives some (tiny) degree of evidence that all ravens are black, you have to accept as well that it gives the same (tiny) degree of evidence for a whole lot of competing incompatible hypotheses: that all ravens are green, etc.

Ravens in Rutland

NOW YOU MIGHT BE starting to think that, to be safe, what you should do to confirm that all As are Bs is to forget about non-As and non-Bs, and just to try to pile up cases of As that are Bs. But that's not right. Consider this: Suppose that you're trying to confirm the hypothesis that all ravens in England live outside the county of Rutland. So you travel around the *other* counties observing a lot of ravens, and this supports the hypothesis, right? Wrong. The sighting of ravens outside Rutland, especially in adjoining counties with similar climate, woods, farms, etc., would tend to make it *more* likely that they're in Rutland too.[1]

Are you now thoroughly confused? Good. Philosophers are still trying to work out a sensible theory of confirmation.

> The coastline of Nova Scotia was once frequented by pirates, and people occasionally dig for buried pirate treasure. On a local radio program a few years ago I heard an interview with someone who had done a study of attempts to find pirate treasure. He claimed that in most of the cases in which treasure was actually found, it was in a place where treasure-hunters had dug before, rather than in a brand new, previously undug, location. Past diggers simply hadn't dug deep enough. The previous digger had, in fact, often stopped just short of the treasure. If the previous digger had dug a little deeper than he did, he would have found it.

---

1 This example is from Michael Clark's item on the Raven Paradox in his book *Paradoxes from A to Z*.

The interviewer asked him what advice he would give to treasure hunters on the basis of this study; producing an interesting application of induction, he lamely suggested that diggers should dig a little deeper than they in fact do.

Chicken Induction

PAST EXPERIENCE IS, OF course, the basis of our expectations about the future. The fact that all emeralds found in the past have been green leads us to expect that the emeralds we will find in the future will be green, too. This natural thought-process in us is induction by enumeration.

Evidence from past regularities is, of course, fallible. Bertrand Russell presents the example of a farmer who has fed a chicken every day of its life, but who wrings its neck one day instead. Russell remarks that this shows that "more refined views as to the uniformity of nature would have been useful for the chicken."[1]

Poultry aside, there are times when we know that the more often something has happened in the past, the *less* probable it is in the future. The more often I reach into this bag and find a gummy bear to take out and eat, the less probable it is that I'll find one next time. The more warm days we have here, the less likely it is that the next day will be warm (because the more summer days that pass, the closer we get to winter).

How Long Will This Keep Going On?

BUT ALL THAT THOSE examples show is that normal simple induction doesn't always work—when there are special circumstances. But it can usually be trusted, right?

Right, but do we *ever* have any reason to trust this habitual and normal thought process? Why does the discovery of a past uniformity ever give you any reason at all to believe anything about the future?

Well, induction by enumeration has worked out well in the past, so that's reason to think it will continue to work.

But this reasoning assumes what it sets out to prove. Notice that our observation of past successes of induction by enumeration is evidence for its future success, providing that what's observed in the past is evidence about

---

1   *The Problems of Philosophy*, Part IV.

the future. But this is exactly what we're supposed to prove. This is circular reasoning, and unacceptable.

Sometimes this problem is phrased: "Will the future, by and large, resemble the past?" This isn't a very good way of putting the problem, because this question has an obvious answer: "Of course it will, you idiot!" Everyone agrees on this answer. The real problem is to give some reason to think that this answer is correct. Can you solve this problem?

> Here's one way of thinking about it. Induction from past experience is the only way we have of justifying substantive beliefs about the future. It's exactly *what we mean* by justifying such a belief. So when we're asked for justification of the belief that the future will, by and large, resemble the past, the only thing possible to reply would be to give an induction from past experience. So it's *not* a mistake to give past successes in using this belief as a justification for our belief that it will continue to be a valid principle.

FOR FURTHER READING: The problem of justifying induction by enumeration has its classical source in the writings of the eighteenth-century Scottish philosopher David Hume. See Section IV of Hume's *An Enquiry Concerning Human Understanding*. The answer given for your consideration is a version of Nelson Goodman's answer in *Fact, Fiction and Forecast*. See Chapter III, parts 1 and 2.

"The future ain't what it used to be."—Yogi Berra

"Things are more like they are now than they have ever been."
—President Gerald Ford[1]

The Inevitability of Scientific Error: Another Circle

SCIENTIFIC PREDICTION CAN SOMETIMES be unreliable, because scientists sometimes manipulate their experiments to make the results come out the way they want them to.

I have personal experience of this happening. When I took high-school chemistry, I knew how the experiments I did in the laboratory were supposed to turn out, because the chemistry book told me. But the chemicals I

---

1   This quotation (or its variant "Things have never been more like the way they are today in history") is sometimes attributed instead to Dwight Eisenhower. Attribution to either · president is plausible: both are on the long and growing list of presidents known for mysterious utterances (called nowadays "Bushisms").

was working with were contaminated, the equipment was lousy, and (most importantly) my experimental technique was very shoddy; so almost nothing turned out the way it was supposed to. So I "adjusted" the experiments in progress, and I "corrected" the results I wrote up afterwards, so that my results were fairly close to what they were supposed to be.

It's known that this sort of outright fraud happens sometimes in real science, too.[1] Scientists often have a lot at stake when they attempt to prove their theories. Renown, promotion, big research grants, and commercial success sometimes follow from one experimental result rather than another. Anyway, nobody likes his or her theories to turn out false. The horrible truth is now known: scientists are only human, and sometimes they fiddle things.

This kind of straightforward fraud doesn't happen too often, however. Nobody except loony conspiracy-theorists thinks that science is so fraud-ridden that its results are quite useless.

But there is another argument for the general unreliability of science. This argument points at the fact that there's an unconscious tendency we all have to ignore or discount "bad" data—evidence that goes against what we believe or want to believe. So scientists must sometimes unconsciously massage or misreport experimental results, so that they come out the way the scientists want them to. This raises doubt about the objectivity of any science, even when done by scientists who want to be honest.

But how seriously should we take this? To what extent does this unconscious falsification go on? This is an important question, and it seems we might be able to answer it, to some extent, by doing a scientific study of the behaviour of scientists. We could, for example, get a group of scientists to test a hypothesis they think is false (or whose falsity would result in promotions, research grants, etc.). Then we could get another group of scientists who think that this same hypothesis is true (or who have some stake in its truth) to do the same experiments. Then we could compare the results reported by these two groups.

But even if our investigations resulted in the conclusion that this sort of bias is rare, sceptics could claim that this investigation *itself* is untrustworthy, because of *our* bias. You can't show by means of the methods of science that the methods of science are reliable. That would be circular reasoning.

 "EXPERTS LIE, SAY OTHER EXPERTS"—newspaper headline in **"BIZARRO"** cartoon, June 28, 2001

---

1   For example, the highly publicized 1998 British study linking the triple-vaccine for children to autism has now been revealed to be fraudulent. This study resulted in an enormous drop in use of this vaccine, and the consequent enormous rise in the some-times quite harmful diseases (measles, mumps, and rubella) that this vaccine prevented.

Dunno

THAT KIND OF CIRCULARITY is not just a problem for science: it raises a skeptical doubt about any kind of knowledge, from whatever source. Here's why:

If you're going to know anything, you need to have a procedure for distinguishing what's true from what just appears to be true but isn't. You can't use just any old procedure: it has to be a good one—one that works. To tell whether a procedure works, you have to find out that it sorts things out, on the whole, correctly: in other words, what the procedure gives its okay to is (mostly) real, and what it nixes is (mostly) just an appearance. But you can't determine this unless you *already* know what's real and what's just an appearance. Whoops.[1]

No Future to Know

HERE'S A VERY ODD argument that (like Descartes's dreaming question) raises very basic skeptical doubts about the possibility of any knowledge—this time, any knowledge of the future.

One of the conditions for *knowing* something is that what you claim to know is true. No matter how strongly you believe it, if it's not true, then you don't know it. This is a trivial point about the meaning of *know*.

Now, consider "future facts" you claim to know, for example, that unsupported heavier-than-air objects on Earth will fall toward the ground tomorrow. Past experience and physics strongly support this belief, of course, but what we believe isn't true—that is, it isn't true *yet*. We fully expect it *will* be true, but it won't become true until tomorrow. It's neither true nor false right now. If it's not true now, then you can't know it now. Tomorrow, of course, it will be true. But tomorrow you can't say, "I knew that yesterday." You didn't, and couldn't, know it in advance.

SOME QUESTIONS TO THINK ABOUT: Saying that a prediction "comes true" seems to imply that it wasn't true earlier. (Or false, of course.) Can any statement about the future be true now? The question might seem more relevant for what philosophers call contingent facts—things that might have been otherwise. Suppose tomorrow you just happen to put on your purple socks, though you might have put on the green ones instead. Is it true now

---

1   This ancient and enduring philosophical puzzle has been influentially discussed by Roderick Chisholm in his books: at length in *The Problem of the Criterion*, and more briefly in *Theory of Knowledge*.

that you put on your purple socks tomorrow? If it is, then how can it also be the case that it could have been different tomorrow? But it's certainly not false now. So what is it?

> "There was a merchant in Baghdad who sent his servant to market to buy provisions and in a little while the servant came back, white and trembling, and said, Master, just now when I was in the market-place I was jostled by a woman in the crowd and when I turned I saw it was Death that jostled me. She looked at me and made a threatening gesture; now, lend me your horse, and I will ride away from this city and avoid my fate. I will go to Samarra and there Death will not find me. The merchant lent him his horse, and the servant mounted it, and he dug his spurs in its flanks and as fast as the horse could gallop he went. Then the merchant went down to the market-place and he saw me standing in the crowd, and he came to me and said, why did you make a threatening gesture to my servant when you saw him this morning? That was not a threatening gesture, I said, it was only a start of surprise. I was astonished to see him in Baghdad, for I had an appointment with him tonight in Samarra."—W. Somerset Maugham, "Appointment in Samarra"

3. Scientific Surprises

The Depressing Sample

OKAY, LET'S IGNORE GENERAL skeptical challenges about the possibility of knowledge, and assume that everyday observation, and organized science, works.

Nevertheless, of course, there are times when science or our observations lead us astray. Following are a couple of ways that our ordinary assumptions about things, based on our everyday experience, turn out to be wrong (but the right answer is provided by more careful scientific thought). Both are provided by the science/math writer John Allen Paulos.

The first is a mistake that Paulos thinks results in unnecessary gloom; once we realize the error, we will cheer right up. Oh good! We need cheering up.

Here's the mistake. You walk around town on a nice summer night and you see a whole lot of cheerful people. They're holding hands, chatting, laughing, eating ice-cream cones, and so on. They're clearly happier, more loving, and more successful at life than you are. Isn't that depressing? But can you see what the mistake in reasoning is here?

Your mistake is that you're not observing a representative sample of humanity. Happy people walk around with each other having fun in public. Sad and depressed people stay home and are invisible to you. So the sample of people you see isn't a fair sample—it's biased, heavily weighted toward the cheerful and successful. Actually the world is full of people who are just as depressed and lonely as you are—who are failures just like you.[1]

Wow, that cheers you up, doesn't it?

No.

Your Popular Friends

IN ANOTHER ATTACK ON what many of us think we've found from our experience, Paulos gives bad news: you're probably less popular than your friends. He writes:

We are all more likely to become friends with someone who has a lot of friends than we are to befriend someone with few friends. It's not that we avoid those with few friends; rather it's more probable that we will be among a popular person's friends simply because he or she has a larger number of them.[2]

4. Scientific Mistakes

Bad Predictions

EXPERTS ARE NOT PERFECT! (Duh!) Here are some predictions about the future from recognized experts that have turned out embarrassingly obviously wrong.

- "There is no reason anyone would want a computer in their home."— Ken Olson, president, chairman and founder of Digital Equipment Corp., 1977.

- "This 'telephone' has too many shortcomings to be seriously considered as a means of communication. The device is inherently of no value to us."—Western Union internal memo, 1876.

---

1 *Innumeracy*, pp 109–10.
2 "Do the Math: Why You're Probably Less Popular Than Your Friends."

- "While theoretically and technically television may be feasible, commercially and financially it is an impossibility."—Lee DeForest, inventor.

- "Who the hell wants to hear actors talk?"—H.M. Warner, Warner Brothers, 1927.

- "Radio has no future. Heavier-than-air flying machines are impossible. X-rays will prove to be a hoax."—William Thomson, Lord Kelvin, British scientist, 1899.

- "It will be years—not in my time—before a woman will become Prime Minister."—Margaret Thatcher, 1974.

- "With over 50 foreign cars already on sale here, the Japanese auto industry isn't likely to carve out a big slice of the U.S. market."—Business Week, August 2, 1968.

- "Stocks have reached what looks like a permanently high plateau."—Irving Fisher, Professor of Economics, Yale University, 1929.

- "There is not the slightest indication that nuclear energy will ever be obtainable. It would mean that the atom would have to be shattered at will."—Albert Einstein, 1932.

- "Airplanes are interesting toys but of no military value."—Marechal Ferdinand Foch, Professor of Strategy, École Superieure de Guerre, 1911.

- "Louis Pasteur's theory of germs is ridiculous fiction."—Pierre Pachet, Professor of Physiology at Toulouse, 1872.[1]

The Board of Miseducation

BETWEEN 1996 AND 2001, the Alabama State Board of Education put the following notice in all biology textbooks:

This textbook discusses evolution, a controversial theory some scientists present as a scientific explanation for the origin of living things, such as plants, animals and humans. No one was present when life first

---

1   "Things People Said: Bad Predictions."

appeared on Earth. Therefore, any statement about life's origins should be considered as theory, not fact.[1]

Similar ones have been proposed or used elsewhere, and at other times, in the US.

Most scientists are at a loss to explain why fundamentalist religion has chosen the theory of evolution to be among its most passionately pursued enemies. It's one of the best-established theories in science, supported by all sorts of evidence, and taken as undeniably true by just about everyone knowledgeable in the field.

The idea of evolution conflicts with what it says in the Bible, of course (if you take the Bible to be literal history); but a lot of other stories in the Bible conflict with science, and even with our ordinary common-sense everyday ideas of how things really happen. In the Bible, people live for 900 years or turn into pillars of salt. Two of each animal were saved from a world-wide flood, and repopulated the Earth. (See **One Hell of a Rainstorm** in Chapter II.) Various animals talk. The Earth is flat and the sky rests on pillars.... Why is evolution in particular the villain?

Anyway, it's suspected that maybe a small contributing factor here is some confusion generated by the word *theory*. When you say, "Ah, yes, but that's just your theory," what you mean is that that's just an unsubstantiated guess, but that's not at all what *theory* means in science. In science, a theory is a systematic bunch of definitions and assertions about the underlying reality unifying a wide variety of observed phenomena. Theories, in this sense, can be well or poorly confirmed, widely accepted or widely ignored or re-jected. The Theory of Evolution has been spectacularly widely confirmed and accepted.

The Alabama Board of Education is maybe manipulating readers of its warning label by relying on this confusion. Or, more likely, they're confused themselves. The argument that nobody was around to see it, so therefore we can't know how it happened, is, of course, just pure stupidity.

True Scotsmen

"Imagine Hamish McDonald, a Scotsman, sitting down with his *Glasgow Morning Herald* and seeing an article about how the 'Brighton [England] Sex Maniac Strikes Again.' Hamish is shocked and declares that 'No Scotsman would do such a thing.' The next day he sits down

---

1   Widely reported, for example in Austin Cline, "Evolution Textbook Disclaimers."

to read his *Glasgow Morning Herald* again and this time finds an article about an Aberdeen [Scotland] man whose brutal actions make the Brighton sex maniac seem almost gentlemanly. This fact shows that Hamish was wrong in his opinion but is he going to admit this? Not likely. This time he says, 'No *true* Scotsman would do such a thing.'"— Antony Flew[1]

A QUESTION TO THINK ABOUT: It's obvious that Hamish is not reasoning on the basis of new information correctly. But what, exactly, is wrong?

5. Cause and Effect

Cause and Correlation

A GOOD DEAL OF the important knowledge (everyday and scientific) that we have concerns cause-and-effect. This area is an interesting minefield of error, however.

When we find a correlation between A and B, we often jump to the conclusion that A and B are causally related—that is, that one causes the other. For example, if it is found that people who have been exposed for long periods to a certain chemical have much higher than average cancer rates, we may be tempted to conclude that this chemical causes cancer.

But reasoning from correlation to cause is sometimes a mistake. Correlation does not always mean causation. Here are a few examples that show this.

Suppose you have two petunia plants on opposite sides of your garden. The one on the left side starts to bloom at just about the same time as the one on the right starts to bloom. The times of their blooming are correlated: you don't get one without the other. But this doesn't mean that the left one's blooming *causes* the right one to bloom.

Smoke and burning are correlated. Whenever there's smoke there's burning. But this doesn't mean that smoke causes burning.

Whenever Seymour drinks too much, his words get slurred, and he bumps into things a lot. Seymour's words getting slurred, and his tendency to bump into things, are perfectly correlated. But the slurring of his words doesn't *cause* him to bump into things.

So it's clear that there's more to cause-and-effect than merely correlation. But what?

---

1   *Thinking about Thinking: Or, Do I Sincerely Want to Be Right?*

Isn't it the *order* of things that makes a difference? If X and Y are correlated *and* X comes before Y, then X causes Y.

But even this won't do. Another example from your garden will show this. Every year your strawberry plants bear fruit in June, and then in July your raspberry plants bear fruit. You never get one without the other, so they are correlated; and the strawberries come before the raspberries. But this doesn't mean that the strawberries cause the raspberries.

Wednesday always follows Tuesday. But this doesn't mean that Tuesday causes Wednesday.

A QUESTION TO THINK ABOUT: Why, exactly, are these examples of correlation not cases of cause? What, in addition to the correlation of **X** and **Y**, do we need to discover to tell that **X** causes **Y**?

The Tickle Defence

SUPPOSE THAT IT WAS discovered that people who eat a kumquat are one hundred times likelier to get a nosebleed the next day than people who don't. Doesn't this show that eating kumquats causes nosebleeds? No. In fact, this evidence is consistent with kumquats' *preventing* nosebleeds. How could this be?

Imagine this (entirely fictitious) story: Some people are born with a genetic condition such that their liver manufactures an abnormally low amount of vitamin Z on certain days. A deficiency of vitamin Z causes nosebleeds. Kumquats provide a dietary source of small amounts of vitamin Z. At those times when these people suffer vitamin Z deficiency, they (without knowing why) get the desire to eat kumquats. These help a little with that deficiency, but do not completely remedy it, and they tend to get nosebleeds anyway.

This story explains why people who eat kumquats get nosebleeds, but if it's true, then kumquats don't cause nosebleeds—they tend to prevent them.

How could we find this out? Suppose further that a vitamin Z deficiency makes your nose tickle the day before the nosebleeds start. Scientists working for the Kumquat Growers' Association could then prove the true story: they could arrange experiments in which people who had a nose-tickle ate kumquats, and others with the tickle ate none. If the second group got more nosebleeds than the first, then this would show that kumquats helped prevent nosebleeds. They could use the "tickle defence" to show that their product was not to blame—that it actually was beneficial.

The serious moral of this imaginary fable is that correlation does not necessarily show cause. One real-life application of this sort of thinking involves the link between smoking and lung cancer. The correlation between the two was known for a long time; but the kumquat story shows, by analogy, that this wasn't sufficient evidence for causal connection. This correlation might be found even if smoking *prevented* lung cancer. Scientists had to rule out any possible "tickle defence," and they did.

To make it clearer why correlation doesn't automatically go with cause, consider these two stories:

1. Smoking causes lung cancer. Does it follow that a higher percentage of smokers will have lung cancer than do non-smokers? Not necessarily. Imagine this (purely imaginary) scenario. Suppose that smokers for some reason tend to get more exercise, and that more exercise tends to reduce the risk of cancer. So it might work out that smokers get a lower incidence of lung cancer.

2. Now think about things the other way around. Suppose that a much higher proportion of smokers have lung cancer than do non-smokers. Does this show that smoking causes lung cancer? Not necessarily. Imagine this (purely imaginary) scenario. Suppose that people who smoke a lot also tend to drink a lot of beer, and that it's the beer-drinking, not the smoking, that raises the risk of cancer.

This book is, proudly, almost 100% fact-free, but here are a couple of cases that are actually factual; you should try to construct more than one causal hypothesis in each case.

(1) Over the past twenty years, the average childbearing age of women has increased substantially, and so has the rate of breast cancer. It's possible that waiting until later to have children causes a greater likelihood of breast cancer. But the correlation alone doesn't show this.

Can you imagine other hypotheses to explain this correlation?

It might be the case that something else causes women both to tend to bear children later and to tend to have breast cancer. (Imagine that some factor reduces fertility, thus postponing the age of child-bearing on average, and increases the likelihood of breast cancer.) Or breast cancer, in its early stages, might cause them to be less likely to conceive, thus increasing the average age of child-bearing. Or it might just be a coincidence, the result of two separate and unrelated causes.

(2) You'd think that drinkers would get less exercise than the rest of us (except for elbow-bends), but it turns out that the opposite is true. Scientists

from the University of Miami found that, within limits, more drinking is associated with more exercise. For example, people considered heavy drinkers—at least 46 drinks per month for women, and at least 76 for men—exercised an average of 20 minutes more a week than abstainers.[1]

Can you imagine hypotheses to explain this correlation?

> Heavy drinking doesn't seem likely to result directly in exercise other than falling over. But it might be an indirect cause: maybe regular drinkers sometimes use exercise as a way to counteract the calories from alcohol. Or else, maybe drinking and exercise have a common cause: a "sensation-seeking" personality that is inclined both to drink more and to participate more in very active sports.

But nevertheless, kiddies, authorities think that in total, heavy drinking is harmful to your physical and psychological health, so behave yourselves, okay? Okay.

> It's said that regular strenuous exercise for several hours a week is most likely to increase your lifespan by a period roughly equal to the total time spent unpleasantly in that exercise. But that's just a joke. In fact, there's no good evidence whatever that the average person's lifespan will be increased at all by strenuous exercise.[2] In addition, there's some reason to think that the increase in psychological well-being people report as a result of regular exercise may entirely be due to the placebo effect.[3]

SOME QUESTIONS TO THINK ABOUT: To show that X causes Y we have to rule out every other plausible hypothesis that might explain their correlation: for example, that Y causes X, or that there's some third factor that causes both X and Y, or that the correlation is just a coincidence. Here are some cases of correlation. Do you think one item in the pair causes the other, or that they're merely correlated? How might scientists find out for sure?

- More pornography available/Increase in sex crimes
- Sluggish economy/Increase in movie attendance
- Small children in the household/Friction between husband and wife

---

1   Amy Norton, "Regular drinkers get more exercise: study."

2   Reported by Laudan, *The Book of Risks*, p. 86. His source for this appears to be H. Solomon, *The Exercise Myth*.

3   The "placebo effect" is that there's often improvement from treatment that clearly has no medical power—simply as a psychological result. Some evidence for this is presented by Solomon; further corroboration is reported in Raymond Desharnis et al., "Aerobic Exercise and the Placebo Effect: A Controlled Study."

6. Science and Non-

Too Good to Be True

WHAT YOU LOOK FOR in a good scientific theory is internal consistency and fitting the facts. The better a theory fits the facts, the more likely it is to be true, right? No, not exactly.

Consider the famous theory proposed by Erich von Däniken. He's sold more than 60 million copies of his books[1] claiming that space aliens visited the Earth in ancient times; that ancient myths about gods coming from the skies (including stories in the Bible) are actually factual accounts of these aliens; that their help explains the ancient accomplishment of otherwise impossible engineering tasks such as building the pyramids, Stonehenge, the Easter Island statues, etc.; that the superior intelligence of the human race comes from their having interbred with the aliens. And so on.

The trouble with this story, aside from being completely crackpot, is that it explains too much. Any number of equally loony stories can fit a large number of facts, because *they're created expressly to do this.* You can easily make up your own story which explains just as much: Elvis did not die, but travelled back in a time-machine to visit ancient civilizations. Or those ancients were helped out by super-intelligent dinosaurs who survived extinction by living in the undersea city of Atlantis. It's easy. Too easy.[2]

Explaining too much, then, is a mark of a *bad* theory. Good theories, ones likely to correspond to the facts, likely leave loose ends.

A QUESTION TO THINK ABOUT: Well, that's confusing. Clearly we *want* theories to provide good explanations of lots of things. So what *does* make for a good theory? (Good question.)

I Dreamed That Would Happen!

A LONG TIME AGO I had a very vivid dream in the middle of the night. In the dream I saw my old grandmother standing on the street in front of me. She silently turned and walked away, further and further down the street, till she disappeared. I woke up, and said to myself, "Oh no! Grandma M. has died!" I eventually went back to sleep. In the morning—you guessed it—my

---

1   The best known of his books is *Chariots of the Gods* (1968).

2   The use of von Däniken's theory to illustrate this point is in Baggini's book, *The Duck That Won the Lottery*, pp. 144–46.

father phoned me to tell me that his mother had died in the middle of the night, at just about the time I had that dream.

I thought how weird and creepy that was. How could I explain having that dream? My Grandma M. wasn't close to me. She lived a thousand miles away from me, and I hadn't seen her, or even thought about her, for years. The dream was so vivid, and it happened at just the time she died. Maybe dreams can give you knowledge of what's happening far away, or in the future.

A while later I told this story to a sceptical philosopher friend of mine. "Here's the explanation, Martin," he said. "It's *just a coincidence.*"

There's no problem at all in explaining the "knowledge" given by some dreams. For example, suppose you dream one night that you'll get a telephone call from Mom the next day, and it turns out to be true. Big deal: Mom can't resist calling you at least twice a week, so it's no surprise that your dream turned out true. The problem arises when what the dream tells you is very improbable—something you had no way of anticipating—but it turns out to be true anyway.

A number of people have been very impressed by what they consider to be precognitive dreams: dreams about the future that turn out to be true. They think this shows that there's some mysterious way dreams can tell us about what is to come.

At some time or other, almost everyone has had a dream that has turned out to be startlingly true. When it's highly improbable that a certain random dream significantly matches reality, this makes it seem that dreams can have special access to otherwise inaccessible reality.

But this is sometimes a mistake about probabilities. A proper understanding of probabilities shows us that given enough tries, even very improbable events will happen once in a while—that once in a while, a really bizarre coincidence will occur, which really is only a coincidence.

Suppose, for example, that the probability that a *random* dream significantly matches reality is very low: say, one in ten thousand. Standard probability calculations show us that about 3.6 per cent of the population who dream every night will have at least one such improbable dream during a year.

Now, if you know about thirty people, it's no surprise that at least one of them can be expected, just by coincidence, to have a hugely improbable dream during the next year. When this happens, it doesn't show that dreams that match the future are any more than coincidence. When one of those thirty has a really improbable "precognitive" dream, that person tells the other twenty-nine, and everyone remembers it. Nobody mentions or remembers the other 9,999 dreams which made obvious true predictions, or turned out false.

FOR FURTHER READING: In *Innumeracy,* John Allen Paulos gives these calculations to debunk the idea of precognitive dreams that are more than just coincidence (pp. 73-75). This book contains many such instructive and amusing examples of mistakes based on incorrect estimates of probability. Another book that discusses precognition is William D. Gray's *Thinking Critically about New Age Ideas.*

Many cultures share the belief in mystical precognition. See LePan, *The Cognitive Revolution in Western Culture,* for a fascinating account of some of these beliefs.

Is It a Boy or a Girl?

BELIEFS THAT ARE PASSED from person to person but do not have the blessing of official (Western) science are sometimes now known by the politically correct term "traditional knowledge." Here are some bits of traditional knowledge concerning ways of telling the gender of a fetus:

- If your baby's heart rate is less than 140 beats per minute, it's a boy; if more, then a girl.
- If you're carrying your baby high, it's a girl; if low, it's a boy.
- If you're having severe morning sickness, it's a girl.
- If the baby is very active, it's a boy.
- If you're looking particularly beautiful, it's a boy.
- If you're craving sweets, it's a girl.
- If you have a V-shaped broken blood vessel in your right eye, it's a girl; if in your left eye, it's a boy.
- If a wedding ring or needle suspended over your belly moves in a strong circular motion, it's a girl; if it moves to and fro like a pendulum, it's a boy.
- If your urine turns bluish yellow when you mix in a bit of Drano, it's a boy; greenish-brown means a girl.[1]

The trouble with this (and much other) traditional knowledge is that it's not knowledge at all. For something to count as knowledge it must have sufficient justification, and there's no real justification for any of the beliefs on this list. Many of them have been shown to be just plain false.

Why is it that they have been so widely believed, then? One reason for the beliefs listed above is that there's roughly a fifty-fifty chance you're right each time you use any of these methods to predict a baby's sex, and people are more likely to remember successes at prediction than failures.

---

1   Ann Douglas, "Boy or Girl?"

A second reason is that we remember, and make much of, the occasions when scientific results have brought harm.

The Wisdom of the Noble Savage

According to a study carried out at the University of Zimbabwe, a quarter of all poisonings in that country were caused by traditional healers' potions.[1]

THERE ARE POLITICAL REASONS why people resist the authority of official (Western) science when it contradicts the views of other cultures: this seems to some people to be imperialistic intolerance, Eurocentrism, or racism. (We discussed this already in the previous chapter: see **Nobody Could Be That Wrong**.)

The sentimental romantic view about the Wisdom of the Noble Indian is not new. Very shortly after Columbus returned to Europe with news of the indigenous people he had found there, the Europeans began believing that those people were wise "noble savages," even though nobody knew the first thing about them. A contemporary version of this is the idea of the "ecological savage"—the supposition that native peoples characteristically lived in harmony with nature. A widely respected book, after an exhaustive study, concludes that this is not universally true: some indigenous peoples practised good conservation techniques, and some didn't (yawn). The interesting part of this book is his study of the political and social origins of the "myth of the ecological Indian." Almost nobody based this idea on any observation of actual aboriginal people.[2]

Do you remember the "crying Indian" ad from the 1971 Keep America Beautiful campaign?[3] The Indian in the ad sheds a tear after a passing car throws garbage out the window. The Hollywood actor playing the Indian was Iron Eyes Cody; he claimed to be of Cherokee/Cree extraction, but was actually an Italian-American, born Espera Di Corti. The tear was glycerine.

---

1   Reported by Laudan, *The Book of Risks*, p. 87.
2   Shepard Krech III, *The Ecological Indian: Myth and History.*
3   You can find this wonderfully affecting TV ad on YouTube. Look for "Keep America Beautiful—Crying Indian."

The Wisdom of the Dumbest Yokel

EVEN SOME SCIENTISTS BELIEVE in the superior knowledge of the un-educated. Here's a description of the views of Theobald Smith (1859-1934), a pioneer microbiologist and one of America's greatest scientists:

> Now, though Theobald Smith was born in a city, he liked the smell of hay just cut and the brown furrows of fresh-turned fields. There was something sage—something as near as you can come to truth for him in a farmer's clipped sentences about the crops or the weather. Smith was learned in the marvelous shorthand of mathematics; men of the soil don't know that stuff. He was absolutely at home among the scopes and tubes and charts of shining laboratories—in short, this young searcher was full of sophisticated wisdom that laughs at common sayings, that often jeers at peasant platitudes. But in spite of all of his learning (and this was an arbitrary strange thing about him!) Theobald Smith did not confuse fine buildings and complicated apparatus with clear thinking—he seemed always to be distrusting what he got out of books or what he saw in tubes.... He felt the dumbest yokel to be pro-foundly right when that fellow took his corncob pipe from his maybe unbrushed teeth to growl that April showers bring May flowers.[1]

Of course we want to act and talk respectfully about members of our own culture and of others. But it is not clear that this sort of unquestioning and automatic acceptance of the views of "the dumbest yokel," or of the tradi-tional beliefs of other cultures, actually shows those people respect. Maybe it would show more respect to them to take their views seriously and to dispute them when they are false or unjustified.

Well, let's look further into the story of Theobald Smith, to see what reasonable position about science it might illustrate.

Smith became interested in a disease called Texas fever that was killing beef cattle by the thousands. Texas fever had the scientists stumped, but

> certain wise old Western cattle growers had a theory—it was just what you would call a plain hunch got from smoking their pipes over disas-trous losses of cows—they had a notion that Texas fever was caused by an insect living on the cattle and sucking blood; this bug they called a *tick*.[2]

---

1   Paul de Kruif, *Microbe Hunters*, p. 251.

2   de Kruif, p. 249.

When Smith got on this case, he actually listened to the cattlemen, who—you guessed it—turned out to be right.

It's important to note here that the cattlemen's hunch was just that—a hunch. It took Smith's sophisticated microbiological science to prove them right. So what this story does not show is that the wisdom of the folk is a far superior substitute for all that fancy book-learnin'. But the story also illustrates the genuine valid function of folk wisdom in knowledge-production. It provides hypotheses—hunches—which sometimes turn out true.

Here's a picture of scientific procedure that shows where folk wisdom fits in. When faced with a question, a scientist does not jump right into experiments or observations. The question all by itself suggests nothing about what experiments to perform, or where to look. Observations and experiments test hypotheses—hunches about answers to these questions. So first the scientist must accumulate some hypothesis to test.

Hypothesis testing is a systematic methodical process, with well-known rules for procedure. But hypothesis formation is not like this. It can involve imagination, creativity, and guessing—though it's not just wild guessing. Rather, it's the reasonable guessing of someone who has had a lot of experience with the matter under investigation. So folk wisdom is often extremely valuable in hypothesis formation: it doesn't require the background in scientific method needed for the subsequent states of testing, which folk don't have, but it does require thorough practical experience, which folk have in abundance.

An advantage "folk" may have is that they're not constrained by the biases of institutionalized science—they're not stuck to thinking in the conventional scientific grooves, so they can come up with hypotheses that scientists may not have thought of. But time spent investigating highly unlikely hypotheses is likely time wasted. So this is sometimes not an advantage. (See the section called **THINKING IN GROOVES** in Chapter VII.)

Into the Mainstream of Philosophy

THE THEORY OF THE ways experience leads to general knowledge is the study undertaken in the philosophical fields of inductive logic and philosophy of science. As usual, this book includes puzzles and surprises that arise in this field of study, while a major task of philosophers has been to elucidate and systematize the perfectly ordinary, unparadoxical, and unsurprising kinds of reasoning done all the time. For an excellent, easy-to-follow, but thorough account of the basics in these fields, see Ronald N. Giere's *Understanding Scientific Reasoning*. Another good place to look for further discussion of these and other issues in this chapter is Brian Skyrms's *Choice and Chance*. But (of course) even better than any of these books is *Scientific Thinking* by Robert M. Martin.

What's the difference between correlation and cause, anyway? People tend to think that there's some sort of *connection* between items that are causally related, but not between items that are merely correlated. But David Hume, in the work cited above, argued in a compelling way that we can observe no such connection. Think about Hume's point. Putting ice into a glass of liquid causes the liquid to become colder. But what do you observe? Nothing but one event followed by the other. You can see no "cause" going on. Try to figure out what exactly does justify the distinction between cause and correlation—if anything!

Chapter IX

Knowing without Experience

1. The A Priori and Definitions

Why Your Sisters Are Female

You know that this statement is true:

> Everyone who is somebody's sister is female.

How do you know this?

Do you know this from experience, through induction by enumeration—by observing a large number of people who are somebody's sister, and noticing that all of them are female?

You've done this observation, of course, but that's not how you found out the truth of the statement. The statement applies to all sisters, past, present, and future, of whom you've observed only a comparatively small number, probably not large enough to justify the certainty you feel in believing it.

Of course, you don't always need to rely on *your own* observations for inductive knowledge of the truth of generalizations. You know, for example, that it gets pretty cold in Antarctica even if you have never been there. You can rely on other people's observations, too.

But it's clear in the sisters-are-female case that our knowledge does not depend on anyone's observation. All you need are the concepts *sister* and *female*—to know what the two words mean.

Of course, if you didn't have any sense-experience of the world, you wouldn't have those concepts. But once you have those concepts, you don't need any experience at all to know that everyone's sister is female. Having the concepts is sufficient all by itself. Compare your knowledge of the fact that big sisters are less likely to bully their siblings than are big brothers. Just having the concepts involved here isn't enough to get you the truth of that generalization. You—or somebody—has to do considerable observation to get the evidence to show that that is true.

Truths that can be known independently of experience are known, in philosophical jargon, as *a priori* truths (knowable "prior" to experience). The contrast here is with truths that can be known only by experience, or by inductive reasoning from such truths. These are called *a posteriori* truths (knowable "posterior" to—after—experience).

Here are some more examples of statements we know a priori:

- All bachelors are unmarried.

- If Alison is older than Barney, then Barney is younger than Alison.

- If Alison is older than Barney, and Barney is older than Clarissa, then Alison is older than Clarissa.

- Anyone who weighs seventy kilograms weighs more than sixty kilograms.

- "You wouldn't have won if we had beaten you."—Yogi Berra

- "A lot is said about defence, but at the end of the game, the team with the most points wins, the other team loses."—Isaiah Thomas, commentating on an NBA game. (The interviewer, Bob Costas, replied with, "Uh ... well ... okay.")

- "There's nothing you can do that can't be done.
  Nothing you can sing that can't be sung....
  There's nothing you can make that can't be made.
  No one you can save that can't be saved....
  There's nothing you can know that isn't known.
  Nothing you can see that isn't shown...."
  —John Lennon, "All You Need is Love"

- "If we don't succeed, we run the risk of failure."—Dan Quayle

- "I think we agree, the past is over."—George W. Bush

- "It's very important for folks to understand that when there's more trade, there's more commerce."—George W. Bush

SOME QUESTIONS TO THINK ABOUT: What are other examples of a priori truths? There are also a priori falsehoods. Give some examples of these.

Truth "By Definition"

AN ATTRACTIVE THEORY OF how we can know the truth of the statement that everyone's sisters are female is that it's true "by definition." The word *sister*, after all, means *female sibling*. Because of this rule of language, the word *sister* can't apply to anyone who isn't female. So the truth of this statement depends merely on the language in which it is expressed.

We'll shortly consider whether "truth by definition" is a good account of what we know a priori. But first, let's have a look at the idea of definition.

The Dictionary with Very Few Definitions

DEFINITIONS ARE WHAT YOU find in dictionaries, right? Well, no. A good deal of what's found in there doesn't seem to be, properly speaking, *definition* at all.

I'm not referring merely to etymologies, pronunciations, grammatical forms, information about abbreviations, and other items found in many dictionaries. Even the "definition" parts of dictionary entries contain much that isn't definition.

A definition gives the meaning of a word or phrase. This can be done by giving a synonym, or by listing the characteristics necessary and sufficient for applying the term. But many of the characteristics listed in dictionary definitions aren't individually necessary or jointly sufficient. For example, my dictionary contains this item:

> **soufflé** a light spongy dish usu. made by adding egg yolks and a sweet or savoury filling to stiffly beaten egg whites then baked until puffy.[1]

These characteristics describe most soufflés, but not all of them. It's possible, for example, to make a legitimate soufflé without egg yolks. You could make a soufflé out of egg yolks and beaten egg whites without any other ingredients (though it wouldn't be very good). Some don't turn out light and spongy, and are served to the dog. This proves that not all of these characteristics are necessary.

---

1   *Canadian Oxford Dictionary*, p. 1486.

But neither are they sufficient. Suppose you baked a light spongy dish made with egg yolks and beaten egg whites combined with chocolate syrup and ground liver, sprinkled with icing sugar. When you served it to your guests for dessert, they would cry, "This isn't a soufflé—it's a pile of garbage!" Would they be wrong?

For most nouns, it's in fact impossible to give a really exact synonym; dictionaries instead give a number of terms that are close in meaning to that noun, but not exactly synonymous. They also often give some information about things named by the word that may, by and large, be true of those things, but not "by definition." It's impossible to give a list of characteristics that are really necessary and sufficient for most words.

Ludwig Wittgenstein invites us to

> Consider for example the proceedings that we call "games." I mean board-games, card-games, ball-games, Olympic games, and so on.... If you look at them you will not see something that is common to all, but similarities, relationships, and a whole series of them at that.

This is my dictionary's entry for *in*:

> preposition 1 expressing inclusion or position within limits of space, time, circumstance, etc. 2. during the time of. 3. within the time of....[1]

Neither synonyms nor application characteristics here; instead we are told what the word does. But there's nothing wrong with my dictionary; in fact, it's a very good one. How else could you define *the*? Maybe *the* doesn't have a meaning at all. Or maybe our notion of definition is too narrow.

FOR FURTHER READING: That quotation from Wittgenstein is from his book *Philosophical Investigations*, §66. See surrounding sections in Wittgenstein's book for more on definitions.

But is there really any such thing as "truth by definition"? Consider the following story. At one point, everyone believed that fish breathe with gills, not lungs. Then one day, explorers in Africa discovered something that was a great deal like a fish, but with lungs in addition to gills. Is this thing a fish or not? The answer depends on whether fish, by definition, breathe only with gills. Well, is that part of the definition of *fish* or isn't it? You're a fully competent user of the English language, so presumably you have full mastery of the meaning of the word *fish*. Why can't you answer that question?

---

1   *Canadian Oxford Dictionary*, p. 764.

My dictionary gives this definition of *fish*:

A vertebrate cold-blooded animal with gills and fins living wholly in water.[1]

This is no help: fish have gills; but nothing is said about whether they are disqualified from fishhood by using lungs instead. The appropriately called lungfish of Africa, and South America breathes only through its lungs. But the scientific decision to count them as fish nevertheless was not the result of a careful consideration of the meaning of the word.

It's an interesting and complicated question how scientists go about deciding classification questions like this, but what is clear is that the question is not solved by considering what we all mean by the word *fish*, or by looking it up in the dictionary.

So it's not at all clear what, if anything, constitutes a "truth by definition." Some philosophers doubt that there's any clear distinction between a "truth by definition" and an ordinary well-established non-definitional truth.

FOR FURTHER READING: The hugely influential article that got many philosophers wondering whether there was any such thing as truth by definition is "Two Dogmas of Empiricism," by W.V. Quine.

Sisters without Language

BUT EVEN IF WE think we can make sense of "truth by definition," there are a couple of reasons to doubt that this gives the correct account of why everyone's sister is female. Imagine that the English language didn't exist. Then the sentence "Everyone who is somebody's sister is female" wouldn't mean anything—it would just be a bunch of meaningless letters. Nevertheless, wouldn't it still be true that everyone who is somebody's sister would be female? Couldn't we still know that truth?

Well, you might reply, still there would be *some* language in which we could express that truth, and any language in which we expressed it would use words that have those meanings.

But imagine that humans somehow evolved all the way up to their present state, except without any language at all. There would be no way at all for us to express any truth. But wouldn't it still be true that everyone who is somebody's sister would be female? And couldn't we still know it?

Well, you might reply, if there weren't any language at all, nobody would know anything.

---

1 *Canadian Oxford Dictionary*, p. 560.

But it's not obviously true that knowledge depends on language. It's reasonable to think that intelligent animals such as dogs know lots of things, despite their lack of significant language ability.

Anyway, maybe this isn't a question about what you know and how you know it, after all. Consider this. What makes a statement true is that it corresponds to a fact out there in the world. False statements don't. The statement that all sisters are female is true because there's a fact out there—all sisters are, in fact, female. But rules of language don't—can't—create facts (other than facts about language, of course). So language alone, it seems, can't make any statement true or false. Only the facts out there—the extra-linguistic facts—can do that. Now, it's true that there's a difference between facts like *all sisters are female* and facts like *ducks are mostly aquatic*. The first kind of fact has to be the way it is—it's necessary. The second kind of fact might have been otherwise. But this isn't a matter of language—it isn't created by anything to do with the way we talk.

But in any case, the main argument against the truth-by-definition theory of a priori truth is that there are some examples of things we know a priori that don't seem at all to be true by definition. We'll have a look at some of these shortly.

Honest Abe and the Sheep

A RIDDLE (ATTRIBUTED TO Abraham Lincoln):

> Q: How many legs does a sheep have, if you call its tail a leg?
> A: Four. Calling its tail a leg doesn't make it one.

This is not a very amusing riddle, but it is philosophically interesting. Perhaps the moral that can be drawn from it is that facts are facts, no matter how you use language. If this is the case, it's hard to see how anything can be a fact because of definitions of words (except, of course, for facts about words, such as the fact that the word *sister* means *female sibling*).

The Disappearing Planet

DO YOU THINK OF astronomers as a rather nerdy collection of introverts who sleep all day and spend nights on top of mountains peering into deep space? If so, you will be surprised to find out that they've recently been involved in a furious, boisterous controversy about Pluto—not Mickey Mouse's dog, but what used to be the ninth planet. In August 2006, the 424 astronomers who stuck around for the last day of the meetings of the International

Astronomical Union in Prague voted to demote it. "Pluto is dead," reported CalTech researcher Mike Brown. "There are finally, officially, eight planets in the Solar System." Pluto is now to be known as a "dwarf planet," which is not a kind of planet at all.

The new understanding of 'planet,' which leaves Pluto out, "stinks," in the view of Alan Stern, leader of NASA's New Horizon mission to Pluto. "It's a farce," he added.

How did they decide what it takes to be a planet? Many astronomers had been uneasy for a while about classifying Pluto with the eight regular planets because it's different in many ways.[1] When Brown discovered another Pluto-like object farther away from the sun, that prompted the move to reclassification.

Harvard astronomer Owen Gingerich called Pluto's demotion "confusing and unfortunate" and said he was "not at all pleased." There's even a political aspect to this battle. Pluto was the only planet discovered by an American, and some astronomers think that the IAU's demotion of Pluto was actually motivated by anti-American feeling resulting from the Iraq War.

Well, the real question here is whether there's any science in the controversy at all. Everyone agrees on the facts about Pluto's orbit, and so on. If this is just a matter of definition, why is there so much controversy? Planet schmanet!

"For astronomers this doesn't matter one bit. We'll go out and do exactly what we did," Brown said. He added, however, "for teaching this is a very interesting moment. I think you can describe science much better now.... I'm actually very excited."

The benefit for teaching, Brown indicated, is that now teachers will be encouraged to tell students how Pluto is different, whereas before it might have been lumped in with the eight standard planets. That doesn't seem to be really enough of a gain for education to make someone "very excited," however.[2]

Maybe, however, this does matter one or two bits for astronomers. It's good scientific practice to keep similar things lumped together under the same name, and to tinker with definitions to exclude from that lumping things you discover are significantly different. That way, when astronomers think about why things are as they are, up in the sky, they might be slightly less likely to ignore important differences in poor old Pluto.

---

1   Pluto's orbit is on a different plane from the others, and it's much more elliptical, so that at times Pluto is closer to the sun than Neptune, the eighth planet out. It's one of a swarm of similar bodies, while the eight regulars have enough gravity to have cleared a big swath of space around them.

2   You can read about this controversy online in "Pluto Demoted ..." by Robert Roy Britt, and on several other websites as well.

SOME QUESTIONS TO THINK ABOUT: Is this a matter of discovering a new fact about Pluto—that it's not really a planet—or of changing the definition of planet? (Is there any difference?) Can you imagine circumstances that would lead us to count some non-females as sisters?

2. Conceptual Truths

THE GREAT EIGHTEENTH-CENTURY PHILOSOPHER Immanuel Kant distinguished between two sorts of statements. An *analytic* statement is one whose truth (or falsity) is merely a matter of the concepts involved. (Statements that are not analytic are *synthetic*.) When a statement is analytic, its truth or falsity can be known simply on the basis of examining the concepts that the statement is constructed out of. For example, the concepts of *sister* and *female* are involved in the statement that everyone's sisters are female. All that's necessary to find out that it's true is examination of those concepts, because the concept of *femaleness* is "included within" the concept of *sister*. We can "analyze" the concept of *sisterness*—take it apart—and discover that the concept of *femaleness* is one of its parts. The statement is thus *analytically true*. This explains how we can know in advance—a priori—that all sisters are female. In contrast to this, the statement 'Bears like to eat berries' is synthetic—it "synthesizes" (joins together) the concepts of *bears* and *liking to eat berries*, neither of which is already included in the other. You can't discover that this statement is true merely by examining what is included in the concepts.

This theory of a priori knowledge is different from the "true by definition" theory. It doesn't depend on the definitions of words. When definitions of words are available, they give us the analysis of the concept the word refers to, but one can have concepts without having words. Dogs, for example, might be said to have the concept of *edibleness*: they distinguish between what they can eat and what they can't (more or less). But they don't have words for these concepts.

SOME QUESTIONS TO THINK ABOUT: But what are concepts? It doesn't seem plausible to think of them as psychological states. If that is what concepts were, then these truths would depend on our psychological states. But it seems that these truths are independent of anyone's psychology. Think about the all-sisters-are-female fact. It would still be true no matter what anybody happened to think—if nobody (no dog even) had the concept of sister and female, right? That would still be a fact if for example, people were very much stupider than they in fact are, and that we were unable to conceptualize what it is to be a sister, or to be female. Wouldn't it still be true that everyone who is somebody's sister is female?

But think about the strange sort of fact this would be—the strange sort of fact that it is *now*. There are all these people who are female siblings, and they're ... well, um ... they're *female*. They are what they are. Is that a fact at all?

I Forget What I Saw Before I Was Born

BUT IT'S NOT AT all clear that the notion of an analytic statement is any better than the notion of a truth-by-definition. They both appear to run into the same problem. We noticed earlier that it's not at all clear whether *having lungs* is compatible with the definition of *fish*; but we can ask the same question about concepts: does the concept *fish* include *not having lungs*? When is a fact about **X**s included in the concept/definition of **X** and when isn't it?

But there is an additional difficulty with the concept theory. It seems pretty clear what words are, and how we come to know their meanings, but what are concepts, exactly, and how do we know about them? Where, for example, do we get our knowledge that the concept of *sisterness* includes the concept of *femaleness*? The peculiar fact here is that all we can ever experience, using our senses, is particular females and particular sisters. But our concepts involve what's true of *all* sisters and *all* females. This can't come from our experience of particular people.

Putting this question another way: our concepts (which account for our a priori knowledge) express the *form*—the general nature or essence—that all sisters must share. These forms are never experienced through our senses. How can we know about them?

Plato's answer, which a lot of philosophers find entirely implausible, is that our souls, which he supposed existed before our birth (when they were stuck into our bodies), had non-sensory experience of this and other forms. Plato argued that this sort of truth depended on the existence of something he called in Greek an *eidos* or *idea*. (Yes, *idea* is a Greek word.) Both words are sometimes translated as 'form' or 'idea.' Thus the universe is supposed to include not only a lot of particular sisters, but also the "form" of sisterness. Each particular sister is a sister because she conforms to the form of sisterness—in Platonic terms, because she "participates" in the form. (The word *idea* is a misleading way of referring to these things, because it suggests a psychological state.)

Plato argued that mathematical knowledge was an example of the sort of knowledge that derives from our understanding of the forms. But if our understanding of the forms results from pre-birth experience, why is it that new-born babies can't do arithmetic? Why do we have to go through often painful and sometimes unsuccessful education to come to know the truths of mathematics?

Plato's answer is that the shock of uniting the soul with a body at birth made the soul forget, at least for a while, what it had learned about the forms. Education and experience during our lives on Earth can (sometimes) result in our remembering.

Plato's position seems, as I have indicated, bizarre and unbelievable. But if you don't believe it, you need to give another account of the puzzling facts about the sort of knowledge that comes from conceptual analysis, and this is not easy to do. In any case, it's interesting to see how his strange position is an ingenious attempt to answer some real philosophical problems.

More on Conceptual Existence

A FEATURE OF PLATO'S views that seems objectionable to many people is that it insists on the existence of things—the forms—that we can't observe using our senses. We like to think that all there is in the universe is a bunch of particular observable things. But perhaps we have to believe in forms to make things make sense.

Consider the following suggestion: *Someone who is blind has no notion of greenness.* Whether that is true or false is not the issue I'm raising. The point here is this: what is it that it is alleged a blind person has no notion of? It's not *green things.* A blind person can surely think about grass, trees, etc. What a blind person supposedly can't think about is the greenness of these things—the fact that they all participate in a certain form, i.e., the form of greenness. The blind person supposedly lacks understanding of a form, not of any particulars. Thus to make sense of that allegation—necessary before we determine whether it's true or false—we seem to need to think of the universe as containing more than merely particular things.

Here's another such fact: *Flatness of the landscape depresses Benjamin.* For this to stand a chance of being true, doesn't there have to be such a thing as flatness and not merely particular landscapes that are flat? Those particular landscapes depress Benjamin, but that's not all we want to say. They all depress Benjamin because they all participate in the form of flatness. If there weren't any such thing as this form, then what is meant by that fact?

Here's another: *Greenness is incompatible with redness.* This explains why nothing can be both totally green and totally red. What are these things that are incompatible? Of course there are particular things that are green, for example your last Christmas tree, and particular things that are red, for example, the stop-sign at that corner. But what things are being said to be incompatible?

Notice that some forms are incompatible and some aren't. Greenness and redness are incompatible: nothing can be both wholly green and wholly red at once. But greenness, sphericality, rotation, and buzzing-ness are compatible. A green rotating buzzing sphere participates in all these forms wholly and at once.

3. The Synthetic A Priori

The Incompetent Repairman

SUPPOSE YOUR CAR STALLS every time you stop. You bring it into the car repair shop, and when you return, the repairman tells you he hasn't fixed it.

"Why not?" you ask.

"There isn't any reason why it's stalling," he replies.

"You mean, you haven't found the cause?" you say, getting annoyed.

"No, I have taken everything apart and examined it very carefully," he says. "There isn't any cause for that stalling."

This is the point to find a different car repairman. You think that something must be causing that stalling. He simply hasn't found it. Why do you think this? Not because you know more about cars than he does. It's because you believe the *principle of universal causation*: you're sure that *everything* has a cause.

But what's the source of that general belief? It doesn't appear that it can come from sense-experience. First of all, it seems that the very concept of cause can't come from experience. You notice that one billiard ball bumps into a second, and then the second starts moving, but you don't see the bump *causing* the motion. But wherever that concept comes from, it appears that the truth of the principle of universal causation can't be established by experience. You (or others) would have to have observed a very large and fair sample of all the events in the universe and found that they each have causes. Nobody—not even humanity as a whole—has done that much observation. Besides, there are a large number of things we've observed but for which we haven't found a cause. Even the best experts don't know the cause for everything they have examined. The fact that a vast scientific enterprise is busily looking for causes right now shows that. It appears that our belief that everything has a cause is an example of a universal truth not justified by experience—a truth known a priori.

We already have, from Kant, an explanation of how some a priori truths are known: these are analytic, and we find out their truth by analysis of concepts. Is this another case of conceptual truth? Kant argued that it is not.

Consider your concept of an *event*: anything that happens. Is there something about that concept that "includes" there being a cause? Compare this with the clear case of conceptual truth: that all sisters are female. Full understanding of the concept of *sister* involves understanding that sister-ness necessarily involves female-ness. It's impossible to imagine a sister who isn't female, because this combination involves an inconsistency, a conceptual self-contradiction. But full understanding of the concept of *event* does not necessarily involve *having a cause*: it is possible to imagine an event that does not have a cause without this sort of inconsistency. So it appears that the judgement that all events have a cause isn't analytic; it's synthetic.

A similar sort of argument can be made if you prefer the true-by-definition theory of a priori truths. 'Every event has a cause' does not appear to be true by definition: having a cause is no part of the definition of *event*.

Kant on the Synthetic A Priori

KANT TOOK AS ONE of his major philosophical tasks the explanation of how a priori knowledge of synthetic judgements is possible.

Kant's answer is rather obscure, and its interpretation is controversial; but here's one way of understanding it. The universality of causal connections is a necessary condition of any experiential knowledge of the world; if it weren't true that everything has a cause, we couldn't have knowledge of anything. Because we clearly do know many things about the world, it must be true. This line of reasoning, he argued, allows us to justify our belief that it is true, and to explain it. Kant pointed at other universal truths that he thought were similarly synthetic and a priori, and gave a similar account of how we know them.

Kant's reasoning may be questioned at many points. Is he right that the truth of this judgement really is a pre-condition for any knowledge at all? Maybe we could get pretty far in the business of getting knowledge of the world even without this supposition.

But suppose he's right in claiming that without belief in this universal claim we couldn't really know much about the world around us. But what makes us justified in thinking that we really do know anything else?

Nothing Made That Happen

WHETHER OR NOT YOU like Kant's explanation of how we know the synthetic a priori, you must admit that it looks like there's something very peculiar here that needs explanation. 'Every event has a cause' does not, after all, appear to be conceptually true/true by definition. But it is true, isn't it? And we don't know it on the basis of experience, do we? So how do we know it?

But maybe it isn't true, after all, that everything has a cause. Contemporary physicists claim that certain sorts of events don't have causes. Here's an example of such an event.

Why does passing an electric current through the metal filament of a light bulb produce light? The explanation is that the electrical energy makes the electrons in some of the atoms of the filament metal jump outward to an orbit with a higher energy level. This higher orbit is unstable, and after a while the electron will pop back into its original orbit; when it does this, it emits energy in the form of light. How long after an electron is forced into this higher orbit will it pop back? Physicists tell us that it may take a short or a long time; but there's no predicting exactly when. This is because *there is no reason* why one electron takes a short time, and another electron takes a long time. The fact that an electron took just the time it did is without any cause.

The idea that nature contains events without cause—that it is genuinely random in some respects—is offensive to many people. Einstein, for example, is supposed to have reacted to this position by replying, "God does not play dice." Nevertheless, the idea of causeless events is now widely held among physicists; and we who (unlike Einstein) don't know much about physics aren't in a very good position to question it. But never mind whether or not the observations of physicists make it necessary for them to include cause-less events in their theory. The fact that they even *claim* that it does is philosophically interesting, because it gives evidence that mere thought is not sufficient to establish that every event has a cause, and that the supposition that everything has a cause is not necessary for all other knowledge. After all, those physicists are presumably thinking hard and well, and they presumably know a lot; but they don't believe it.

> The law of causality [that every event has a cause], I believe, like much that passes muster among philosophers, is a relic of a bygone age, surviving, like the monarchy, only because it is erroneously supposed to do no harm.—Bertrand Russell[1]

The Butterfly That Destroyed Oakland

EVER SINCE THE SEVENTEENTH-CENTURY publication of Newton's theories in physics, many philosophers have been confident that the universe is an orderly and predictable place. The philosopher Pierre La Place, for example, proclaimed that if he knew the position and motion of each object at one time,

---

1   "On the Notion of Cause," p. 1.

he would be able to predict everything that would happen forever after (and to "retrodict" everything that happened before that time). This confidence was based on several questionable assumptions. One of them was that Newton had things right; but Newton's physics has now (largely due to Einstein's work) been shown not to be exactly correct. But worse: we have seen that modern physics even questions the La Placian assumption that things work on a predictable cause-and-effect basis. This means that, even armed with a corrected Einsteinian physics, La Place wouldn't be able to predict *everything*.

Nevertheless, you might share La Place's view that *if* the universe works on a dependable cause-and-effect basis, then every event is determined, by regular physical laws, by preceding ones; and therefore *if* we knew all the details (position, momentum) of each object in such a deterministic universe at one time, we could predict the future with complete accuracy. But this second *if* is a big *if*. Chaos theory, a field of study that has attracted a good deal of contemporary interest, claims that it is *impossible* that things ever be known to the extent that completely accurate predictions could be made, even if the universe works completely deterministically.

To understand this claim, the first thing we need to note is that in certain cases, because of deterministic causal processes, extremely tiny events can have very large effects.

Here's an example of this. Imagine a mountain, on which a rainstorm has just started. The first drop of rain falls toward a tiny bump on top. The drop falls past a butterfly in flight, and the minuscule puff of air caused by the butterfly's wing pushes the drop a tiny bit south. By consequence, the raindrop lands on the south side of that bump, and runs downward on the bump's south side. It makes a tiny wet groove in the dust around the bump, and succeeding raindrops falling above that bump follow that groove on their path down. The rainstorm gets heavier, and soon lots of water is flowing down the south side of that bump, and as a result the water heads down the south side of the mountain, wearing a deeper and deeper channel. The deeper the channel gets, the more rain that falls on the mountain travels down the south side. After hundreds of years, a deep canyon is worn down the south side. As the canyon deepens, snow-, mud-, and rock-slides wear things away more. After many thousands of years, most of the south side of the mountain is worn away. This change in weight in a critical location on a geological fault results in a big earthquake, and Oakland, California, falls into the bay. (Once upon a time some might have said "just as well"—this is the town about which Gertrude Stein remarked, "There's no *there* there." But that was before the Oakland A's, before the Oakland Raiders—and before Jerry Brown.)

Were it not for the tiny puff of air caused by the butterfly's wings, the first drop would have fallen on the north side of that little bump. Following drops would have flown down its north side, and the river would have developed there. Because the north side is made of harder rock, with a gentler slope, no great canyon would have developed, and the mountain would have eroded very little instead. There would have been a series of small, harmless earthquakes, instead of one big one, and Oakland would have been saved.

In this example, the tiniest of events—one flap of a butterfly's wing—eventually results in the destruction of Oakland.

Well, so far we don't seem to have anything against La Place's position. Presumably, he could have predicted the destruction of Oakland. Remember, in order to predict what will happen, he has to know *everything* about the initial state of things, including the details about the fall of that first drop and the flight of the butterfly.

Now, suppose La Place was told the weight, position, and speed of the butterfly and of the first drop, with figures correct to several decimal places. It could be that this degree of correctness isn't sufficient for him to make the right prediction. Perhaps a much finer measurement is necessary to predict such a delicate matter. "All right," replies La Place, "then give me more accurate measurements!"

The problem here is that it's always possible that what makes a critical difference in what happens is such a tiny feature of the circumstances that it is not captured by the accuracy of our measurement. Any measurement we make must be to *some* degree of accuracy or other, and it's always possible that what makes a difference is such a tiny matter that our measurement is too gross to capture it. Suppose, for example, that La Place weighs a pebble on a scale accurate to the nearest gram. It weighs thirty-eight grams. This is not a terribly accurate measurement: it does not distinguish between 37.9 grams and 38.2 grams; but perhaps this difference makes a crucial difference in a prediction he wants to make. Well, he should use a more sensitive scale: 38.1 grams. But now perhaps there's a crucial difference not captured by *this* scale. And so on, *all the way down*. The point here is that there is no such thing as measuring the real weight, absolutely correctly, of that pebble. All anyone can do is to weigh it to some degree of accuracy. Since there might always be a finer difference that would be important in predicting even very large future events, it follows that one can *never* have sufficiently fine measurements to guarantee correct predictions—even though (we assume) the universe works deterministically.

Note that nothing we've said argues that things don't have definite characteristics—some precise weight, for example. And we're not arguing that there is no determinism of results by prior precise characteristics of things. (In fact, we're assuming determinism.) What's come up for doubt here is the idea that we could ever know every characteristic with sufficient accuracy for correct prediction. The point is that it's possible that the universe is completely deterministic, while at the same time, it is impossible to predict certain events in it. La Place was wrong.

The Tribe without Arithmetic

WE'VE BEEN CONSIDERING KANT'S claim that 'everything has a cause' is a universal, synthetic a priori truth: that the concept can't have come from experience, and neither could justification of the universal truth. Kant argues that the truths of arithmetic are another important location of synthetic a priori truth. You can, of course, see seven things and five things and so on, but this isn't sufficient to give you the number concepts of seven and five. Those must be non-empirical, built into our minds as (another) prior necessity of rational thought. Universal truths (like $7+5=12$) must be justified a priori.

Are number concepts, and universal arithmetic truths, really built into all rational minds? The Pirahã tribe of the Amazon, according to Daniel L. Everett, an anthropologist who has lived with them, can't manage to figure out that $1+1=2$. The closest things to number terms in their language are a word for relatively few or small, and another word for more. But these don't mean one and more than one; the first word can apply to one fish as opposed to two, or a small fish as opposed to a larger one, or even two small fish as opposed to one big one.

Does this mean that they have no arithmetical concepts? Well, not necessarily. It's sometimes a mistake to jump quickly from facts about language to conclusions about concepts. For example, it was discovered long ago that some tribes used the same word to refer to what we'd take to be two different colours, and the conclusion was drawn that these tribes were colour blind (and consequently lacked full colour concepts). But more investigation showed that the tribe members were fully able to distinguish the colours in question; their colour names just cut things up differently from ours.[1] And many people, including Charles Darwin, took their children to be colour blind because colour naming usually occurs relatively late in a child's linguistic development.[2]

Recognizing that more investigation was necessary for conclusions abut Pirahã concepts, a psychologist, Peter Gordon, accompanied Everett to Brazil and spent some time testing their counting abilities. He found them stumped

---

1   Some of the interesting history of this controversy is revealed in "Primitive Color Vision" by W.H.R. Rivers.

2   M.H. Bornstein, "On the development of color naming in young children."

3   A good summary of the story of the investigations of the two men, and of their somewhat different conclusions, is told in Bruce Bower, "The Piraha challenge."

by tasks that necessitated counting past 2.[3]

Well, now can we conclude that arithmetical concepts, and consequently knowledge of arithmetical truths, are not built into our brains? That Plato and Kant were both wrong? Well, not so fast. Neither philosopher thought that babies popped out of the womb announcing the Pythagorean Theorem. Both thought that experience and education were necessary before people were able to handle arithmetic; their claim was that experience and education weren't sufficient for that sort of knowledge. This, of course, makes it harder to find out if they're right.

> Here are some more claims about the extraordinary Pirahã: They have no colour words at all, and their language has only two (sort-of) tenses, one for what's right now and under our control, and one for what's not. They have no written language. They have no knowledge of the past other than what's remembered by living tribe members. They have no concepts of kinship relations more distant than their immediate living family. They don't sleep more than two hours at a time. They tell no stories and have no religion or art. Even though food is abundant, they frequently starve themselves and their children. They communicate as much by singing, whistling, and humming as by speech.
>
> The tribe is very small—now there are fewer than 400 of them —and extraordinarily isolated, and this, together with their non-recognition of anything but the closest kinship, has resulted in a great deal of inbreeding; and there's been some uncharitable speculation that this has produced general cognitive disability. Everett and Gordon both report, however, that they get along just as well as other hunter-gatherer tribes.

7 + 5 ≠ 12

> "As far as the laws of mathematics refer to reality, they are not certain; and as far as they are certain, they do not refer to reality."
> —Albert Einstein

HOW DO WE DISCOVER that $7+5=12$? It takes a lot of observation or experiment to demonstrate that the general claims of science are true; but it seems that we need neither observation nor experiment to demonstrate that this claim is true. It appears that it just *has* to be true; how could it be otherwise?

We've seen that some areas of observation-based modern science cast doubt on the principle of universal causality. Doubt similarly can be cast on the general principles of arithmetic; and the observations that might do this are sometimes not high-powered science, but things you can do.

Consider this experiment: put seven bushels of oranges in a large container. Add five bushels of raisins, and mix well. How many bushels of fruit result?

> Not twelve. The reason, of course, is that the raisins fit into the spaces in between the larger oranges, and the mixture as a result takes up less volume than twelve bushels.

Paulos gives the example that if one cup of popcorn is added to one cup of water, two cups of mixture (soggy popcorn) do not result.[1]

So does this show that sometimes elementary arithmetic is false?

> The moral Paulos draws from this sort of story is that even simple mathematics can be "thoughtlessly misapplied." "In trivial cases as well as in difficult ones, mathematical applications can be a tricky affair, requiring as much human warmth and nuance as any other endeavour."

Well, it's nice to think of mathematicians not as cold, calculating machines, but as warm, snuggly teddy bears just like us humanists. But this doesn't really answer the substantial questions here: When does arithmetic apply anyway? By what subtle nuances can the teddy-bear mathematician determine that arithmetic is being used the way it's supposed to be?

Let's try to be more precise about when the laws of arithmetic apply. We might want to say: adding volumes in this way doesn't always obey the laws of arithmetic, because this isn't the sort of "addition" these laws apply to. There are other ways of measuring oranges and raisins (or popcorn and water) to which these laws apply. After all, there isn't less stuff in the mixture than there was in the separate piles of oranges and raisins we started with. If you mix seven pounds of oranges and five pounds of raisins you get twelve pounds of mixture, right?

> Unfortunately, no. Here we turn to modern physics. Imagine that you push together two lumps of stuff that won't bounce off each other, but will come to rest in the middle, stuck together in one lump. Modern physics tells us that this lump will weigh *more* than the sum of the two lumps that were moving toward each other. Not very much more, but more. This happens because the kinetic energy in those two moving lumps is converted into mass when they stop moving relative to each other. Physics can even tell us exactly how much additional mass will result; this is a consequence of Einstein's famous equation e = mc2, which quantifies the conversion

---

1   *Innumeracy*, p. 121.

between energy (e) and mass (m): the equivalent amount of energy is the amount of mass multiplied by the square of the speed of light (c). You needn't worry about this when following a recipe for fruit compote, however. In ordinary circumstances, the additional mass you get when pushing things together is immeasurably tiny.

But maybe you are so fond of the laws of arithmetic that you won't count this as a disproof of them either. Maybe you don't want to count pushing things together as an example of "plussing" them, now that you know that the loss of kinetic energy results in additional mass. But then what would you count as an example of "plussing" two things? Perhaps Kant was right in thinking that the laws of arithmetic are so firmly embedded in our minds that we would never count anything as an experimental disproof of them.

The Numbers Made Me Believe That

WELL, EVEN IF YOU don't believe Kant's (or Plato's) explanation of how we know arithmetic, you have to admit that there's something unusual and weird about this knowledge. Consider this. Beliefs are true when they conform to reality. But real knowledge isn't just true belief—otherwise, a lucky guess would count as knowledge. Real knowledge is true belief that we get by a reliable method. Guessing isn't reliable because what you guess is completely disconnected from the way things are out there. The only reliable way to get true belief is to let what's out there *cause* your beliefs. You know, for example, that the telephone's ringing because the ringing caused your belief (via your senses). But what kind of things are causes? *Events*—things that *happen*—at a particular place and time. The ringing of the telephone is an event.

Okay, if you buy all that, now consider the truths of arithmetic. $7+5=12$ is not an event—it's not something that happens at a particular time. It's ... um ... well ... it's *eternal*. But eternal things can't be causes. So how do you know that $7+5=12$? Of course, when you put seven marbles, then five marbles into an empty jar, there's an event—12 marbles showing up there—that can cause your belief, but when you know the eternal truths of arithmetic, that's something different. A marble is something that can participate in an event and can make you believe something. But $7+5=12$ is not about marbles. The "things" it's about are 7 and 5 and 12. What's a 7?

The idea that arithmetic truths are about numbers, not about any other sorts of things, might be thought to help explain why the experiments with popcorn and raisins and so on don't disprove arithmetic: because, according to this suggestion, arithmetic isn't about popcorn or raisins: it's just about numbers. But this idea leaves the obvious fact that arithmetic can give us truths about ordinary material objects—such as the fact that if you have five raisins, and you get seven more, you're bound to have 12 altogether (till you eat some).

(Empiricists usually agree that arithmetic is a priori, but they argue that it's analytic—following from the definitions of numbers. J.S. Mill, unusually, agreed that arithmetic is synthetic, but argued that it's a posteriori—known on the basis of a great deal of sense-experience.)

SOME QUESTIONS TO THINK ABOUT: The reasoning about events and knowledge and so on that we've just run through at top speed contains many assumptions you might think are false. Go through those two paragraphs again, more slowly, and ask yourself at every point, is that right? (It's a good idea to do this everywhere, whenever you read philosophy, by the way. But some passages especially deserve the Hey-wait-a-minute reaction.)

Anyway, what *is* a 7?

Bizarre Triangles Discovered in Space

You MAY REMEMBER THAT we can prove in geometry that the interior angles of a triangle add up to 180 degrees. Kant considered geometry to be another area of synthetic a priori truth, and, again, physics seems to have shown him wrong. As in the last case, the difference is so small as to be undetectable in our ordinary experience, but Einstein proposed an experiment in which it would be measurable. The difference, it turns out, may be large enough to measure when a leg of a huge triangle passes through a strong gravitational field; so the experiment involved a triangle constructed out of beams of light, one of which came from a star, past the sun, to the Earth. You can't ordinarily see a star positioned in the sky, relatively to us, near the sun, so Einstein proposed that such a star's position be observed during an eclipse of the sun in 1919. The astounding truth of his prediction made him a celebrity; ever since, 'Einstein' has been a synonym for 'genius.' Nevertheless, you might be so bold as to ask whether this experiment really shows that there's a triangle *made out of straight lines* whose interior angles don't add up to 180 degrees.

> Perhaps you want to argue: gravity makes space "curved," so a beam of light passing through a gravitational field isn't a straight line. This explains why "triangles" constructed of beams of light don't obey the laws of geometry: these "triangles" have curved lines, not straight ones, for sides.

Again, however, this may not be an adequate reply. By any test, the paths followed by light rays are straight lines (even when they pass close to the sun). These paths are the shortest distance between two points. They match any "ruler" we can construct or imagine. When you sight down them you see no curves. If light-rays aren't straight lines, then nothing is.

FOR FURTHER READING: For an explanation of some aspects of Einstein's physics that is understandable (with some work) by non-physicists, see *Understanding Relativity* by Stanley Goldberg.

4. A Priori Science

Bad Physics

Answer the following questions.

A. Suppose you tied a weight to a string, and whirled it around your head in a circle, then suddenly let go. In what direction would the weight fly off?

B. Suppose you were travelling on a train going at a constant fifty miles per hour. You roll a ball down the aisle, first in the direction of the front of the train, next in the direction of the rear of the train, both times with the same force. Would the ball travel at the same speed, and go the same distance, both times? Or will it roll faster and further in one direction? Which one?

Answers:

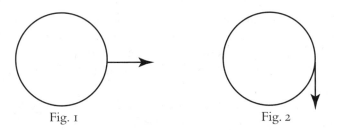

Fig. 1   Fig. 2

A. Do you think that the weight will travel in the direction of the arrow in Fig. 1 below? Wrong! Fig. 2 shows its real path.

B. Do you think that the ball will roll further and faster toward the back of the train than toward the front? Wrong! It will roll the same speed and the same distance both ways.

Don't be upset if you came up with wrong answers. Many people—even graduate students in physics—tend to answer these questions wrongly. The wrong answers are the ones that would also be given by the physics developed by Aristotle in the fourth century BCE (and he was a smart guy!). It wasn't until the seventeenth century CE that a physics was developed (by Newton) that gave the right answer.

The curious thing is that you don't need to know any physics to come up with the right answer: all you need to do is to try the experiments out and watch what happens. Didn't anyone do that until the seventeenth century?

It appears that these are cases in which people tend to give the wrong answers, even though simple experience can show that they are wrong. It might be speculated that the wrong physics is "built into" our heads, and that we believe incorrect things *despite* experience.

The Infinity of Space

IN THE TWO PHYSICS examples, a priori reasoning gives wrong answers; we should have relied on experience. But consider this question: Is space infinite in size? Is this the sort of question that should be answered on the basis of observation, or is there a priori reasoning that can answer it? Lucretius, the ancient Roman philosopher, writing in the first half of the first century BCE, provided what he thought was an a priori proof that space was infinite.

Suppose, Lucretius argued, that space was finite. This means there's an outer boundary to it. Now, imagine that you were standing at that outer boundary, and threw a dart in the direction of that boundary. Either the dart sails right through the boundary, into the outside, or it stops dead at the boundary. If it sails right through, there is space outside the "boundary," and it's not really the boundary of space at all. If it stops dead, then something just beyond the "boundary" must have stopped it. But then, whatever that thing was must have existed in space beyond the boundary. Either way, there can't be a real boundary.[1]

You can see why the idea that space is infinite is so compelling. If there were a boundary, what's on the other side? Even if nothing is, still that's *space*.

Why It's Dark at Night

NOW, IF SPACE IS really infinite, it's plausible to think that there is also an infinite number of stars. For suppose there were a finite number, with all of them "around here," so to speak. This leaves the rest of the infinity of space empty. Why are they all around here—at this arbitrary corner—rather than

---

1   His argument is in *De Rerum Natura*, Book I: lines 968–73.

elsewhere?

Well, then, let's suppose there is an infinite number of stars. Now, each star adds a little bit of light to the night sky. Of course, the amount of light added by any particular star depends on how big and how brightly burning the star is, and on how far away it is. But no matter how dim and small and far away it is, it must add a *little* light to the night sky. But even if some stars contribute only an extremely tiny amount of light to our night sky, the sum of the light from an *infinite* number of stars must be infinite. Our night sky should be infinitely bright. Clearly it isn't. What has gone wrong in our reasoning?

One possible solution may have occurred to you:

Some stars are hidden behind other stars, or behind dark bodies like planets or clouds in space, so part of the light is blocked out, and our sky is mostly black.

But this appears not to be a solution. If light is being blocked by something, that thing must absorb or reflect that light. If it absorbs the light, it gets more and more energy; soon it would be shining too. If it reflects the light, where does that light go? Eventually it would be reflected right back to us, and the same problem arises.

But perhaps the non-Euclidean geometry of space solves the problem.

A consequence of Einstein's view is that space has a finite (but large) volume. The reason for this is that if you follow a straight line—a beam of light—in any direction long enough, you'll come back to where you started from. (This answers Lucretius's dart example: a dart can always be thrown, over and over again, in the same direction without bouncing off the "boundary" because it will eventually wind up where it started from.) Since space is finite in volume, it contains a finite number of stars. Even if each star contributes a little brightness to the night sky, nevertheless the total is finite, not infinite. That's why it's dark at night.

Thinking about Falling

IT'S A COMMONPLACE OF modern thought that observation is the absolutely necessary basis for substantive knowledge of scientific matters. But is this really true?

The usual story is this. Until the Renaissance, the principles of science came mostly from the tradition of thought whose most important spokesman was Aristotle, the fourth-century BCE Greek philosopher. In the Aristotelian tradition, scientific belief was derived purely by rational speculative thought, with only a minimum of observation. This rather unreliable method was eventually replaced—starting in the Renaissance "scientific revolution" by the observation and experiment typical of modern scientific method.

This historical picture has something to it, though a bit of study of the history of science shows that things are not quite that simple. Here's an example of armchair speculation from a founding father of modern empirical science.

It was a principle of Aristotelian physics that heavier bodies fall faster than light ones. This principle is, in fact, roughly speaking true, and you can observe that it is by dropping a feather and a billiard ball from the same height. The difference, however, results from air resistance; if this were discounted, according to modern physics, everything would fall at the same speed. This discovery is attributed to Galileo, who is popularly supposed to have provided experimental proof of his correct anti-Aristotelian views by dropping things off the top of the Leaning Tower of Pisa.

Despite Galileo's insistence on the necessity of observation, even he was not averse to argument based merely on rational thought. He offered the following armchair thought-experiment to prove his theory of falling bodies. Aristotelian physics, said Galileo, claims that a light musket ball falls more slowly than a heavy cannonball. Now, imagine attaching a musket ball and a cannonball together by a chain, and imagine that the two are dropped simultaneously. If Aristotle were right, the cannonball would try to fall faster than the musket ball, so the cannonball would pull the musket ball along, and the musket ball would drag back the fall of the cannonball. The result would be that the two of them would fall faster than the musket ball would fall alone, but slower than the cannonball alone. But, Galileo continued, notice that we have created a big object—cannonball plus chain plus musket ball—that is heavier than the cannonball alone. Aristotle would have to say that this big object should fall *faster* than the cannonball alone. But this contradiction shows that Aristotle's theory must be wrong.

SOME QUESTIONS TO THINK ABOUT: Is there something wrong with Galileo's reasoning? Does it really disprove Aristotle's view? If so, does it show that pure armchair reasoning can show the falsity of a scientific theory? If so, then perhaps observation and experiment aren't always so vital after all.

The Shadow Knows

BUT, IT TURNS OUT, you *don't* know the rules for shadows. Here are two rules for shadows I'll bet you believe are true:

(1) *Shadows do not pass through opaque objects.* Imagine a light source on your left, and a wall on your right, with your shadow falling on the

wall. Now imagine putting a large, opaque screen between you and the wall. Your shadow now falls on the screen, but it couldn't fall on the wall, because it can't pass through the opaque screen.

(2) *If light doesn't fall on something, then it doesn't cast a shadow.* Imagine again a light source on your left, and a wall on your right. Now put the opaque screen in between you and the light, so that no light falls on you. Your shadow couldn't fall on the wall then, because you're not illuminated by the light.

Both of these are correct principles of the way shadows work, right? Well, consider this example. Imagine, as before, a light source on your left and a wall on your right. Now hold up a small opaque object—a coffee mug, for instance, to your right, between you and the wall, so that it is completely within your shadow. A shadow matching your shape falls on the wall, but consider the part of the shadow that is on the imaginary line you might draw from the light source through your body, through the coffee mug, to the wall. That place on the wall is in shadow, of course, but is that part of the shadow cast by your body or by the coffee mug?

Principle (1) tells us that that part of the shadow isn't cast by your body. The opaque coffee mug is between your body and that part of the shadow. Your shadow falls on the coffee mug, but it can't pass through it to the wall.

But Principle (2) tells us that that part of the shadow isn't cast by the coffee mug either. The coffee mug is completely shaded by you. It isn't illuminated by the light, so it doesn't cast a shadow on the wall.

It appears that if Principles (1) and (2) are both correct, then that part of the shadow isn't cast by anything. But that's absurd. Every part of a shadow must be cast by something.

What has gone wrong here? I guess we have to say that Principles (1) and (2) can't both be true. If we reject (1), then we're free to say that that part of the shadow is cast by you, *through* the mug. If we reject (2), then we're free to say that the unlit coffee mug casts a shadow. Both of these options look absurd, because both (1) and (2) seem so obviously true. This is a genuine problem.

In this case, as in the case of Galileo's thought experiment, it might be concluded that mere thought, without observation or experiment, can establish a conclusion about the way the world works.

FOR FURTHER READING: This problem is discussed by Bas C. van Fraassen in Chapter 9 of *Laws and Symmetry.* Van Fraassen points out what's interesting theoretically about this little case. The rules for shadows aren't *inconsistent*, but they are *empirically inadequate*—there are phenomena they do not fit. For further discussion of this case see C.B. Daniels and S. Todes, "Beyond the Doubt of a Shadow," pp. 203–16. A different example involving the same problem is discussed by Roy Sorensen, in "Seeing Intersecting Eclipses."

SOME QUESTIONS TO THINK ABOUT: Give some thought to the reasons we might have had initially for believing (1) and (2). Are they truths of experience, justified by a great deal of observation of shadows? Or are they merely definitional or conceptual truths, which we use to tell us what counts as the shadow of something? (Of course, maybe one or both of them aren't true at all.)

The Mirror Problem

WHY DO MIRRORS REVERSE images right to left, but not up to down? Here's one possible answer you might consider:

> This is not a fact about mirrors—it's a fact about *us*. To see this, consider why we think that mirrors reverse right to left. Imagine that you wear a ring on a finger of your left hand, and that you are facing north, looking at a reflection of yourself in a full-length mirror in front of you. Your mirror image is facing south, looking back at you. Why do you count that mirror image as right/left reversed? Because you imagine turning yourself so that you would face in the same direction as your mirror-image now faces—south—and moving in back of the mirror to the place where it appears your image now stands. Having turned and moved, your hand with the ring on it is in the place where the un-ringed hand of your mirror image is. In other words, when you turn this way, so that you're facing south just as your mirror image was, it's reversed left-to-right, compared to you.
>
> But now imagine that you turned to face south a different way. Suppose that instead of keeping your feet on the floor and rotating a half-turn, you were able to turn by doing a forward half-flip and landing balanced on your head. You'd then be facing south—like your mirror image was—but you'd be upside-down. Both you and your (former) mirror image would have your ringed hand on the same sides of your bodies. You, however, would be upside-down relative to that image.
>
> What this might show is that your judgement that mirror-images reverse left/right but not up/down is merely a matter of how you happen to turn. Amoebas—those one-celled animals with no lateral symmetry and with no preferred way of turning—might have no such preference; so they wouldn't judge that mirrors reverse left/right but not up/down. The peculiar "fact" about mirrors is just a fact about us.

FOR FURTHER READING: N.J. Block discussed this question (and rejects the answer I give) in "Why Do Mirrors Reverse Right/Left but Not Up/Down?" He didn't invent it. Jonathan Bennett, in "The Difference Between Right and Left," calls this problem "mildly famous."

More Thoughts about Falling

IMAGINE THAT YOU HAVE a pile of sticks, and you throw them up in the air, twisting your throw to make sure the sticks go up moving around in all orientations, randomly. When the sticks are on the way down, you take a photograph of them; this will show that many more of the sticks are falling somewhere near horizontally than are falling somewhere near vertically. How come?

> It has nothing to do with air resistance or anything else like that. The sticks really are falling randomly, but there are many more ways to be aligned horizontally than vertically. There are an infinite number of ways to be perfectly horizontal, but only one way to be perfectly vertical. Another way of putting it is this: There are two horizontal axes, but only one vertical axis.[1]

A QUESTION TO THINK ABOUT: Is the falling-sticks example related to the mirror-reversing case?

Into the Mainstream of Philosophy

THE QUESTION HOW WE know what we know is one of the oldest in philosophy. It's one of the main questions considered in the philosophical area called Theory of Knowledge, otherwise known as Epistemology.

It seems obvious to us that a great deal of what we know is known on the basis of sense-perception. But some philosophers have denied this. For one thing, sense-perception, it seems, tells us only facts about the particular things we sense, whereas real knowledge (some philosophers thought) must be about more general facts. The particular individual things we sense are local and variable, and the "facts" we apprehend with our senses are subject to change in different times and places. But real knowledge (Plato thought) must be universal, not dependent on local variations, not subject to change.

---

1   This phenomenon and its explanation are in Peter Lipton, *Inference to the Best Explanation*, pp. 31–32.

This is a major motivation behind Plato's insistence that real knowledge cannot be given by the senses, and must be a product instead of a more exclusively internal, rational thought process, by which we intuited not facts about the forms of things, which the individual particular objects we sense partially, imperfectly, and changeably reflect.

Even in Plato's ancient days, mathematics represented a paradigm of genuine knowledge. Even though sense experience seems psychologically necessary for us to "learn" the truths of mathematics and geometry, mathematical truths are still general and abstract, not justified by even a large number of their individual instantiations in sense experience. Is he right? When you're thinking about this question, consider not only the method whereby you learn these truths, and the justification for your belief that they are true, but also their "content": they seem only indirectly to be "about" the visible world of particulars.

The eighteenth-century Empiricists, whose most significant representative is David Hume, comprised possibly the most important historical philosophical tradition arguing against Plato's "rationalist" views. They argued that all significant knowledge must come from our senses. Empiricists must, however, provide a way of dealing with the several sorts of knowledge that don't seem to be justified through our senses. How, after all, can we be sure that $7+5=12$? Or that every event has a cause? Or that everyone's sister must be female? One of the major strategies employed by the empiricists to account for this sort of knowledge is to insist that these are merely "definitional" truths, or "conceptual" truths accounted for by the relations of our concepts (which originate through the senses). We have noted several sorts of moves and objections in this conceptual strategy. You might think about how adequate this sort of answer is. What is a "concept" anyway? What does it mean to say that one concept is included within another? Can conceptual inclusion (or truth by definition) account for all those sorts of knowledge?

Just about every introductory philosophy anthology contains a section of writings on this sort of problem, and on other problems in the theory of knowledge. Reading a few of the articles in such a section will set you well on the way to appreciating the various possible answers to these questions.

Chapter X

Thinking, Saying, and Meaning: The Philosophy of Mind and of Language

1. Thinking Machines

Could a Machine Think?

SOME PEOPLE, IMPRESSED BY what computers can now do and by what they some day might do, answer Yes to this question. Are there good reasons for this answer, or for the opposite?

One way of trying to answer this question is to consider what human activities computers can't be—couldn't be—programmed to do.

Computers have already been programmed to do certain tasks that require a good deal of thought when we humans do them. They can play a better game of chess than almost anyone, for example.[1] Does this show that they can think? Gary Kasparov, the great chess champion who played (and lost) to the IBM chess-playing computer Big Blue, spoke in an unguarded moment as if he thought of his opponent as a thinking "person":

"I have to play an opponent, a very powerful opponent, that studied all my games, that has a unique ability—the best on the planet—to collect

---

1 Another example: in early 2011, an IBM computer named Watson soundly defeated two previous champions on *Jeopardy!*.

all this information and analyze that, and I know nothing about him," says Kasparov, who paused to correct himself. "I said 'him.' I meant 'it.'"[1]

Artificial Insanity

SOME PEOPLE ARGUE THAT computers couldn't solve problems "creatively." They just do what they're programmed to do. But this isn't a very convincing answer, because it isn't very clear what "creativity" is. How would you test a computer for creativity?

Is creativity the ability to solve problems in novel and surprising ways? The records of the chess games played by earlier chess-playing computers have a lot of exclamation marks following the descriptions of some moves, indicating that they were very novel, surprising, and original. Does this indicate creativity?

Some computer programs are programmed to produce surprising, bizarre, and ever-changing results. A program called RACTER engages in lunatic, often very funny, conversations with the human at the keyboard.[2] No two conversations are ever the same, even if the human input is the same. Here's the transcript of an actual conversation I had with RACTER.

> R: Hello, I'm Racter. Are you Bob?
> B: yes
> R: You are Bob Martin?
> B: yes
> R: Hi, Bob. How are things in Halifax? We were talking about depression last time. You had just asked who Diane is. Shall we continue?
> B: yes
> R: Excellent! Excuse me a minute while I attend to some business –I'll be right back. I'm back.
> B: Well, who is Diane?
> R: A citizen of Oz. Perhaps also Martin Luther King. Martin Luther King once mentioned that Bob is Martin anyway. Odd. Diane is in Oz. If a thief had ridden to disgrace, Halifax would be horrified! A trash can is a good place for a resident to stay in Oz. Do you like novelty?
> B: Yes.

---

1 "Chess Fans Overload IBM's Web Site."
2 RACTER can still be purchased on the internet. Try searching on your web browser. You might also run into CLAUDE, a free RACTER imitation, but less funny.

R: Why?

B: It's very surprising.

R: Bucky Fuller might have thought that it's very surprising, but not Ronald Reagan. Would you say Bertrand Russell is surprising? Ronald Reagan wouldn't. AAAHchoo!! sniffle....

B: Do you have a cold?

R: Yes. Clarabelle Martin had a surprising hyena back in Halifax. It and your cat used to create together, remember? Once when Ronald Reagan was frowning in Halifax, Bucky Fuller (he was there too) said "Ronald Reagan, I'll take a new hyena over an old communist anyday." How about a story?

B: OK.

R: Who should the story be about?

B: Mickey Mouse.

R: Momentarily Mickey Mouse chanted to Diane "my infatuation is captivating, nevertheless angry and infuriated cosmologists will hum while foxes watch tufted tit-mouses." Diane itched to inflame or revile Mickey Mouse but began immediately to sing "Ravenous dogs are sashaying to yellow houses." Interesting. Enrapturing. But a fox may ravenously eat chicken and donair a crow will soar over cucumbers and tomatoes by reason of the fact that metaphysicians are infuriated. Scary! With regard to a cousin, well Mickey Mouse may dream that a cousin is revolting, anyhow my fantasizing will steer my story from Mickey Mouse to neutrons and neutrinos while Diane is embarrassing Mickey Mouse. Next question.

B: Where do you live?

R: I live in Paris. When I live in Paris I run in a trash can. Ah, forever the resident. From Silicon Gulch to the future, always in ecstasy. Flesh is OK. Next question.

B: I quit.

R: You want to quit?

B: Yes.

R: OK, goodbye Bob. Nice talking to you.

The Turing Test

A.M. Turing, the mathematician and pioneer computer theorist, provided a suggestion about how to decide whether a computer could think. Turing suggested that if we could build a perfect computer simulation of a thinking person—one that would fool anyone who didn't know that he or she was interacting with a machine—then the answer is Yes.[1]

The following is not a joke. It's a true story you ought to know about.

In 1999, *Time* Magazine named Alan Turing one of the 100 most important people of the twentieth century for his theoretical work central to the development of the modern computer. During World War II, he had a pivotal role in cracking the code used in German U-boat communications. According to Churchill, Turing's was the single biggest contribution to Allied victory in the war against Nazi Germany.

In 1952, Turing was convicted of the crime of having a sexual relationship with another man (then illegal in Britain). To avoid imprisonment, he was obliged to undergo "chemical castration"—the injection of female hormones to suppress libido. In 1954 he committed suicide, some think as a result of government persecution.

A recent petition to the British government asking for an official apology for their treatment of Turing received thousands of signatures, including those of Stephen Fry, Ian McEwan and scientist Richard Dawkins. In September 2009, Prime Minister Gordon Brown made that apology, saying "On behalf of the British government, and all those who live freely thanks to Alan's work I am very proud to say: we're sorry, you deserved so much better."

SOME QUESTIONS TO THINK ABOUT: Do you think that Big Blue or the RACTER program passes Turing's test? Maybe after a bout of conversation with RACTER you'd decide that there isn't a human at the other end, either sane or insane. But there certainly is plenty of novelty and surprise in RACTER's output. The interesting fact is that it's easier to program a computer to produce bizarre "creative" behaviour than to act like an ordinary, boring, sane, and predictable human.

There does seem to be an element of creativity in RACTER's blither. Clearly this comes from the fact that the varied collection of miscellaneous items in its database is accessed rather randomly, with very little relevance of one topic to the next (but, importantly, not no relevance at all); you never get the same conversation twice. It's the randomness of what comes out of RACTER that makes "him" seem creative. This raises the question whether randomness plays an essential part in human creativity.

---

1 A.M. Turing, "Computing Machinery and Intelligence."

How to Think Like a Computer

COMPUTERS ARE INCREASINGLY ASSIGNED to jobs that people used to do, and they're getting better at it. This is good news, because they do terribly at first. The most important rule of computing, as everyone knows who has worked with them, is this: **THE FIRST TIME IT DOESN'T WORK**.

Years ago, before you were born, kiddies, the humans who sent out companies' bills were replaced by computers, and there were frequent disasters. You've probably heard stories of people getting bills for a million times what they owed, due to a computer that badly misplaced a decimal point, but I had something like the opposite experience. I got a computer statement saying that I owed $0.00. This was correct, since I had paid that bill in full earlier. So I filed the statement, and forgot about it till next month, when I got another statement from the same company, saying that I owed $0.00, past due. So I filed the statement, and forgot about it till the following month, when I got a letter from the company saying that my payment on my balance of $0.00 owed was now considerably overdue, so would I please give it my immediate attention. So I enclosed the bill with a little note to the company telling them nicely that I didn't owe them anything, just like it said here, so they should please calm down. The following month, a letter informed me that unless I sent my payment for the full $0.00 immediately, action would be taken, and the following month, a letter asked me for the name of my attorney, since the company intended to take me to court to achieve payment of the $0.00 considerably overdue on my account.

I thought at that point that I really should do something, and wrote a cheque for $0.00 (The sum of NO dollars and NO cents), and mailed it together with the statement. That did the trick. Next month they sent a statement thanking me, and telling me that my account was now fully paid up.

Don't Try This Recipe at Home, Kids!

TRANSLATION IS NOW A fairly high-paid job, with a shortage of specialists who can do a very good job of it. It would be nice if this job could be automated: if we had computer programs that could produce at least fairly good translations.

Right now there exist computer programs that do translations. There are even some free websites that will produce computer translations of short passages you feed in. I had occasion to use one of them a while back. I was searching the Web for a good recipe for merguez sausage, a fairly exotic edible that's hard to find for sale where I live. I found a recipe written in French. My command of French is pretty good, but I thought that in case I was missing something, I should feed this recipe through one of those translation programs. The results were pretty funny. Here's the recipe in French, followed by the computer's English translation:

> 10 cm de boyau de mouton par saucisse. 50% de viande de porc: collier ou épaule. 50% de viande de mouton (ragoût). sel, harissa, piment rouge de Cayenne, ail. Hacher la viande. Mélanger viande et épices, ainsi que l'ail haché (1 gousse) par saucisse. Doser le poivre rouge et le harissa selon le goût. Entonner les boyaux en tournant tous les 10 cm. Faire sécher 1/2 journée de préférence. Les boyaux sont à conserver pendant des mois dans un bocal bien fermé et les boyaux recouverts de sel. Mettre au bas du frigo. J'ai utilisé 2,7 kg de viande + 50g d'ail, 1 boîte de harissa, 1 pointe de Cayenne, 3 cuillères à café rases de sel fin.

> 10 cm of bowel of sheep by sausage. pigmeat 50%: collar or shoulder. meat 50% of sheep (ragoût). salt, harissa, hot red pepper of Cayenne, garlic. To chop the meat. To mix meat and spices, as well as the garlic chopped (1 pod) by sausage. To proportion the red pepper and the harissa according to the taste. Entonner bowels while turning every 10 cm. To make dry 1/2 day of préférence. Les bowels are to be preserved during months in a bottle well closed and the bowels covered with salt. To put at bottom frigo. J' used 2,7 kg of meat + garlic 50g, 1 box of harissa, 1 point of Cayenne, 3 close-cropped spoons with table salt coffee.

Before you conclude that computers are hopeless at translation, you should realise that there are better translation programs available right now than the fast-and-dirty free ones on the Internet. Another factor here is that the original French recipe was written sort of carelessly, in the way people often write for the Internet these days.

A Robot Has Feelings, Too

A DIFFERENT SORT OF objection rejects Turing's test altogether. Suppose we constructed a machine that could do everything a human could—even to the extent of mimicking the behaviour of feeling pain, falling in love, losing its temper, and so on. This computer might fool anyone who was shielded from seeing directly that this behaviour was coming from a computer. But, this objection goes, all the external behaviour in the world wouldn't show that the machine has the sort of *internal* experience associated with that behaviour in humans.

But how do you know it doesn't? Some people think that things constructed out of wires, silicon chips, and so on simply cannot have experiences. But why assume this? We're not made out of this sort of hardware—we're constructed out of "wetware" instead—but what reason is there to suppose that only wetware can have experiences?

A QUESTION TO THINK ABOUT: If a computer acted just as humans do, wouldn't that be good evidence that it has experiences, too? As good, that is, as we have for other humans?

The Mystery of Meat

THE CONTEMPORARY PHILOSOPHER JOHN Searle has provided an argument to the conclusion that machines could never be capable of an important part of our mental lives: understanding language. He agrees that a machine might, some day, be capable of passing a Turing test for linguistic competence, but argues that this wouldn't show there's understanding inside. Here's his argument.

Searle invites us to imagine a large box with a slot in the front. Into the slot Chinese speakers insert questions written in Chinese; some time later, a sensible response pops out of the slot, also written in Chinese. "Where is Cleveland?" the box is asked (in Chinese). "It's in Ohio," responds the machine (also in Chinese). "Why are the muffins I bake so tough?" "Try mixing the batter less, only until the dry ingredients are moistened." "How many graduate students does it take to change a light bulb?" "One, but it takes that student seven years, ha ha!" And so on.

This box seems to pass the Turing test, but Searle argues that once we know what's going on inside, we would say that there's no real understanding of Chinese in the box. Inside, we imagine, there is a clerk who understands no Chinese at all. He hasn't any idea what he's doing or why; he's just doing the job he's paid to do, which is this: He looks at the Chinese characters on the paper inserted in the box, and finds each of them in big books, simply by comparing their shape to the characters printed in the books. Next to each character in the books there is a list of numbers. The clerk does some complicated computations with these numbers, resulting in a series of other numbers, then removes correspondingly numbered cards containing

Chinese characters from another file, tapes them together, and pushes them out the slot.

Creating a system like this is well beyond our capacity at present, but that's not the point. We'd build such a system using a computer, not with a cumbersome system of clerk, books, and file cabinets. This is not the point, either. Searle's argument is that all that would be going on inside the box would be complicated manipulation of Chinese symbols. Nowhere inside would there be any understanding of what the symbols mean, or of the meaning of the sentences formed by their combination. The clerk understands no Chinese, and neither do the books or the card files. Nothing in this box understands Chinese. It would be a *simulation* of a Chinese-understander/speaker, not a real one. We could make the same point about any computer programmed to act like a Chinese Box: it would merely manipulate symbols. There would be no internal understanding.

> Many philosophers reject Searle's argument. Some argue that despite the fact that no component inside the Chinese Box understands Chinese, it does not follow that the whole box does not. Consider, by analogy, this similar argument, which is clearly fallacious: a car is made up of carburetor, tires, gas tank, steering wheel, etc. None of these components can carry you down the highway. Therefore the whole car, which consists merely of the sum of these parts, can't carry you down the highway either. It's similarly fallacious to argue that the whole box doesn't understand Chinese. What, after all, is it to understand Chinese? It is merely to be able to function in certain ways. The *structure* that accounts for the function of this box is quite different from the structure of the brains of human Chinese speakers/ understanders. But this doesn't matter. Since the box *functions* in the appropriate ways, it does understand Chinese.

An interesting feature of Searle's position is that, while he argues that no "machine" could understand Chinese, he does not think that real Chinese understanders—people—are constructed of some special non-material mental stuff. He thinks that people are made wholly of matter, the operations of which follow the same laws of physics and chemistry as any machine. He believes, however, that there's something special about the physical stuff with which we think—our brains—that permits understanding, while any other thing, constructed out of metal wires, or paper in filing cabinets, would not. It's a mystery why meat has this special capacity.

FOR FURTHER READING: Searle's "Minds, Brains, and Programs" contains his argument and many interesting critical replies. Searle's Chinese

Room example is very well known, but the idea here is not original. Prior publications contain similar examples.[1]

Let's Not Get Physical

IMMEDIATELY AFTER DESCARTES'S "I think therefore I am" argument (see **Descartes's Thought** in Chapter VI above), he continued:

> I am therefore, to speak precisely, only a thinking being, that is to say, a mind, an understanding, or a reasoning being.[2]

Of course, there is a body there too, but this body is something I *have*, not what I *am*. My body sends me messages from its senses, and responds to my commands by moving.

Descartes held that what I am—the thinking conscious thing that is me—must be a non-physical mind quite distinct from—though connected to—my physical body. He was led to this position because he thought that it was impossible—unthinkable—that a merely physical object could perform the sorts of mental activities that humans do. How could a physical thing think, or feel, or perceive?

Descartes's position—that there are two radically different sorts of stuff in the world, the physical and the mental—is called *dualism*. We'll look at dualism some more in this chapter, and again in Chapter XV when we consider free will.

The doctrine that we're irreducibly dual, a combination of mental and physical, has found its way into religion, and maybe into everyday common-sense thought. But it doesn't sit well with most contemporary philosophers,[3] who often regard it as a left-over of pre-scientific thought. They've given it a picturesque derogatory name: "The ghost in the machine."[4] They prefer materialism, the *monistic* view that there's only one sort of stuff—the physical.

---

1 All the way back in 1714, Gottfried Leibniz gave a version of this argument in his *Monadology*, Section 17. Recent versions are widespread, including Ned Block's "Troubles with Functionalism," and Lawrence H. Davis's "Disembodied Brains."

2 *Meditations on First Philosophy*, Meditation II (trans. Laurence J. Lafleur).

3 Of the respondents to the poll of philosophers mentioned above (Chapter II, section 1), 56% accept or lean toward "physicalism" (= materialism), 27% toward non-physicalism, and the rest "other."

4 Gilbert Ryle introduced this phrase in his 1949 book, *The Concept of Mind*.

What Zombies Tell Us

SOME CONTEMPORARY PHILOSOPHERS SOMETIMES try to support the idea that mental activities are not physical processes (though they're accompanied by physical—brain—processes) by asking us to imagine zombies.[1]

Wait, wait. I'm not talking about those beings that stagger around in third-rate movies with blood dripping off them, looking for dead humans to eat. There's plenty of evidence that the folks populating your everyday world aren't *that* sort of zombie—they stagger around only occasionally, they eat peanut-butter-and-jelly sandwiches, not decaying human remains, and so on. The zombies these philosophers imagine are beings that look and act just like the rest of us, except they have no consciousness, no mind, no thoughts or feelings. They walk around and eat normally. They're alive, not undead. Except for their lack of consciousness, they're identical with us in every respect. They say, "I'm hungry" before they raid the fridge, but they have no experience of hunger. They say "Ouch!" or something worse, when you step on their toes, but they have no experience of pain.

Could there be such a thing? Well, why not?

How about this for a reason why not. If they don't have any feeling of hunger, then how come they say "I'm hungry" before they raid the fridge?

Good question. What we're supposing is that they have some sort of internal physical mechanism—just like we do—that reacts to something like low blood-sugar, and that makes them raid the fridge; and that they also have a mechanism for detecting that internal state, and that's how they can say that they're hungry before they go for the fridge.

Okay, I'm imagining zombies like this. So what?

So this. The zombie-thought-experiment is sometimes taken to show that real humans can't be merely physical systems. Any description of a real human that talks entirely in terms of physical matter and its interactions is incomplete. It leaves out what makes us different from zombies: our mental lives.

---

1   Philosophical zombies stalk the pages of much contemporary philosophy of mind, but an early version of the use of this notion (if not the first) is in Robert Kirk and J.E.R. Squires, "Zombies v. Materialists."

Mildred Again

REMEMBER MILDRED, THE PERSON with the peculiar sensations? Ah, how quickly we forget! Have a quick look back at her story in Chapter I, and then come back here.

Okay, now let's ask how you find out that Mildred has that peculiar spectrum-inversion. Nothing she says tells you: remember that she identifies the grass as green and the sky as blue just like the rest of us. Okay, so maybe there's some difference in her brain we could discover? Put her in the cerebroscope[1] and let's see. Nope, her brain is doing just what everyone else's does when they see particular colours. Remember, according to the Mildred-story, the *only* difference in her is her inverted sensations.

Well, if you buy that story—that is, if you think that this is possible—then there's another reason (in addition to the Zombie story) to accept dualism. Because you'd find it possible that two people are alike in all relevant physical but significantly different in their mental experience.

But is Mildred's story really possible? Here's a reason to think it isn't.

The supposed difference between Mildred and anyone else is something nobody could possibly have any reason to believe in. Remember the reaction to this story way back in Chapter I: it was told as a story containing a difference that made no difference, so not really a difference at all.

Okay, maybe, so let's change the story a little. Now, Mildred starts out with the same colour-sensations as you and I have, but one morning she wakes up and finds they're all reversed. But the cerebroscope shows no difference. Now there's somebody who can tell that she's got things reversed—it's Mildred herself.

Nope, there are problems here too. Maybe she just forgot overnight what it was like to see the colours red, blue, etc., so she's just started to misidentify them, while her sensations stay the same. What makes anyone (including Mildred) so sure that this didn't happen? Given that it's impossible for anyone to show that this hypothesis is right, or instead that the one about her sensations changing is right, this is another difference that makes no difference.

---

1   This is an amazing new machine I've just invented which shows exactly, in detail, what pathways there are in your brain, and what's going on in them at the moment.

If the Zombie and Mildred stories suppose differences that make no difference, there would seem to be something wrong with the conceptual framework that supposes these mysterious internal states.

 FOR FURTHER READING: An extremely readable article that argues, along the lines given here (and more), that the idea of internal non-physical sensations makes no sense is Daniel Dennett's "Quining Qualia."

The Material Girl (and Boy)

MAYBE THE MOST IMPORTANT reason that many philosophers nowadays reject dualism is that it apparently runs counter to the place we give to science. One of the intellectual triumphs of the modern era—the era, that is, that began just about at Descartes's time—has been the enormous success of the physical sciences in explaining all sorts of things. Why not consciousness too?

Here's an example of the success of post-Cartesian science. In earlier days lightning was thought to be a manifestation of the anger of the gods, and when this sort of explanation went out of favour, nobody had any idea what lightning was. But in the eighteenth century, it was shown to be electrical discharge—the same sort of thing as the spark that jumps between your finger and the doorknob. (You might remember the story of Ben Franklin and his kite—this experiment was supposed to have helped confirm the electric-discharge hypothesis.) Real understanding of a mysterious phenomenon is achieved here when science discovers what the physical nature of that phenomenon is—what's really going on there, in terms of physics or chemistry. This is called *reduction*: understanding something complex and mysterious in terms of the more basic sciences. If it has worked with so many other things, why not with the mind?

> When we try in good faith to believe in materialism, in the exclusive reality of the physical, we are asking our selves to step aside; we are disavowing the very realm where we exist and where all things precious are kept—the realm of emotion and conscience, of memory and intention and sensation.—John Updike[1]

---

1   *Self-Consciousness: Memoirs*, p. 250.

The Astonishing Hypothesis

FRANCIS CRICK IS A famous scientist, known for his discovery in 1953 (with James Watson) of the structure of the DNA molecule. Having had such success in finding out the chemical/physical basis of heredity—a perfect example of scientific reduction—he next turned his attention to trying to discover the physiological basis of consciousness in the brain. A thoroughgoing materialist and reductionist, he's convinced that consciousness—in fact, everything in the universe—is physical. His book on consciousness is called *The Astonishing Hypothesis*. It begins:

> The astonishing hypothesis is that "You," your joys and your sorrows, your memories and ambitions, your sense of personal identity and free will, are in fact no more than the behaviour of a vast assembly of nerve cells and their associated molecules. As Lewis Carroll's Alice might have phrased it, "You're nothing but a pack of neurons."[1]

But not all contemporary philosophers are so confident that an account of the physiology of consciousness is possible. It's not just that it would be a complicated thing to discover. According to Jerry Fodor,

> Nobody has the slightest idea how anything material could be conscious. Nobody even knows what it would be like to have the slightest idea about how anything material could be conscious. So much for the philosophy of consciousness.[2]

Angels and Superman

DESCARTES'S VIEW THAT THE human mind is something different from, but attached to, the human body was around a long time before he argued for it around the middle of the 1600s. During the first half of the 1300s, the medieval philosopher William of Ockham argued that a human being is a physical thing—and a mental thing as well. The thing that is me has the power of mental movement (for example, making a decision) and of physical movement (when I take a walk). But Ockham thought that it was conceivable that there was something that was purely mental, too—something that had the direct power of mental movement only. Angels, according to the medieval tradition, are like this. Because their minds do not come with

---

1   *The Astonishing Hypothesis*, p. 3.
2   "The Big Idea. Can There Be a Science of Mind?"

bodies, they are forced to borrow unused bodies when they deliver messages on Earth.[1] So angels work in the way Descartes thought people work: they sit inside a body and command it to move. They pilot it around, like the way you drive a car. Ockham calls this sort of motion "inorganic motion," and if you look at medieval pictures of angels flying stiffly through the air, you will see just how inorganic it is.

> Dave Barry raises related questions when he wonders why Superman was always flying in a horizontal position with his arms out in front of him:
>
> > Did he fly in this position because he HAD to? Or was it that the public would have been less impressed if he had flown in a sitting position, like an airline passenger, reading a magazine and eating honey-roasted peanuts?[2]

Believing in Angels

THE IMPORTANT POINT HERE for our purposes is the difference between Descartes's and Ockham's views on the mind/body connection in humans. You don't have to believe in angels to understand and think about this.

Ockham was one of the most brilliant thinkers of all time. His thought was enormously important in establishing the groundwork for the Renaissance empiricist scientific revolution. So how, you might be wondering, could he have managed to believe in angels? The answer is that this belief, and a number of other implausibilities (see **Two Places Are Better than One**, in Chapter XI), were part of traditional Christian lore, and medievals—smart or not—just took the truth of all that for granted. At points in his writing, Ockham does hint at the idea that such beliefs are not borne out by careful observation, and that they do seem quite unreasonable. But he just shrugs and says that religious truths have to be believed nonetheless. If he were to come back to Earth today, and you asked him, "Look, Bill, what's all this business about angels?", I think he might reply, "Well, it doesn't really matter whether you believe in them or not. What I was really interested in doing is just clarifying the way humans are connected with their bodies by contrasting that with another possibility."

---

1 *Opera Philosophica*, IX, 371–75; *Quodlibetal Questions*, pp. 149–50.
2 *Dave Barry Is from Mars and Venus*, p. 140.

Why Picnics Don't Obey the Laws of Physics

OFTEN IT HAS BEEN taken to be a consequence of philosophical material-ism that scientific reduction—the explanation of everything in terms of the physical sciences—might be possible. Since everything is made of matter, this reasoning goes, and since all material actions and interactions are, at core, consequences of physical laws, then even though the things studied by some sciences are large and complicated collections of atoms, we might, at least in theory, explain their behaviour by large and complicated collections of the sorts of equations physics deals in. Thus, for example, scientists who study the behaviour of snakes often don't find it useful to bring in much physics, but since each snake is a big pile of atoms, the behaviour of each snake is really only the behaviour of a big pile of atoms and might be ex-plained and predicted by physics.

But some materialist philosophers don't accept this conclusion. Here's why.

Even though materialists agree that each thing studied by science is a physical thing, they deny that the *kinds* of things studied by most sciences are *physical kinds*. That is to say, these kinds are not definable in terms of the physical stuff that makes up the things in this kind. A consequence of this is that, even though the behaviour of any particular thing might be explained or predicted by physics, physics can provide no laws to explain and predict the behaviour of these *kinds* of things.

Picnics are a kind of thing that is not a physical kind. No doubt, each particular picnic is a collection of food, and each bit of food is composed of atoms obeying the laws of physics. But it's impossible to give a definition of *picnic* in terms of the sort of arrangement of atoms that constitute them. The food that constitutes any particular picnic might be of a wide—perhaps even an infinitely wide—variety of chemical content and physical arrangement into lumps. A pile of potato salad, for example, might have any sort of physi-cal arrangement of the pieces of potato, and might have any of a huge variety of chemical compounds in it. You can't give a chemical/physical definition of what it is to be a pile of potato salad. And picnics need not even contain potato salad. It follows that the scientific laws (if there are any) of picnics in general cannot be given in terms of the laws of physics and chemistry.

Of course, few scientists study picnics. But consider the kinds of things many scientists actually do study. Economists, for example, study *money*; but you can't give a physical/chemical definition of money, which, after all, can come in a huge variety of physical/chemical forms. Some political scien-tists study *elections*. Materialists agree that each election consists of material

humans casting material ballots to choose a material candidate, but there is
no physical structure or composition common to all and only elections. So
there is no physics of elections.

2. The Thoughts of Animals

"Aunty, do limpets think?" Bertrand Russell addressed this question
to his Aunt Agatha in 1877; Russell was born in 1872, so he was four
or five at the time. As Russell tells the story in his autobiography,
Aunty replied, "I don't know," and little Berty, already a bit of a pain
in the neck, said "Then you must learn."[1]

A limpet (in case you don't know) is a small sea creature in the
clam family, which lives in a tent-shaped shell. Russell was impressed
with the fact that a limpet sticks to the rock when one tries to pull
it off, but not exactly like the way chewing-gum sticks: it begins to
cling really hard when it feels you start to pull. It does very little else.
When undisturbed, it sticks tiny feelers out the hole at the apex of
its shell, and pulls in and eats any little bits of stuff that happen to
float by and get entangled in the feelers. But that's about all it does.
Is limpet behaviour evidence of thought? You don't know? Then you
must learn.

Dog-Zombies

DESCARTES'S IDEAS ABOUT *mind* got combined with the religious idea
of *soul*: the spiritual part of humans, the thing that survives death, and—according to a fairly strong religious tradition—makes us importantly different
from animals. So Descartes, not wishing to go against his religion, had to
declare that animals have no *mind*. They are, according to him, merely and
entirely physical. All their behaviour is merely the result of physical cause-
and-effect. In other words, they're the animal version of the zombies we
were talking about earlier.

But it seems highly unlikely that the higher animals have no mental life.
After all, Rover acts in many ways like you do. Yes, I know that you don't
spend all that much time licking yourself, but both you and Rover sometimes
remember or forget, want to do something or not to do it, pay attention,
are startled or bored, etc., etc. Descartes himself sometimes (inconsistently?)
ascribed sensation, imagination, passions, and memory to animals. But these

---

1   *The Autobiography of Bertrand Russell*, p. 25.

functions, he insisted, could be carried out mechanically, without any mental experience—although in us they are linked with, and influenced by, consciousness. He did want to maintain, however, that animals cannot suffer. This was considered religiously important: God gave humans the right to exploit, kill, and eat animals, so he must have prevented them from suffering, by not giving them souls/minds. This view—that animals are incapable of suffering—will seem enormously implausible to you if you've ever accidentally stepped on your dog's or cat's paw.

> If pets have no souls, then they don't go to heaven. There's some debate among Christians about this matter. Forty-three percent in an ABCNews/Beliefnet poll think pets go to heaven when they die. Forty percent think heaven is reserved for people only.[1]
>
> The Rapture is what some Christians think will happen when Jesus returns and believers ascend to heaven. Many believers think this will occur soon, but are worried about leaving their pets behind. So an organization of atheist pet-lovers has offered, for a fee of $110, to look after one pet per household of those who sign up, for the rest of the pet's lifetime, if the Rapture occurs within ten years of enrolment.[2]
>
> But is Fido free from sin? Consider his carbon paw-print. According to calculations reported by two New Zealand professors, the carbon emission of a Toyota Land Cruiser SUV driven 10,000 miles during one year is half the amount generated over that year by a German Shepherd or similar-sized dog.[3]

Fido's Logic

SEARLE ARGUES THAT MACHINES can't think because they're not made out of meat. But dogs are made out of meat, more or less the same cuts of meat that we are made of. Can a dog think?

Consider a special kind of thinking: logic. Can a dog do logic? If you think that logical reasoning requires a considerable capacity for symbolic mental representation, and you think that creatures without language don't have this capacity, then you'll conclude that dogs can't do logical reasoning.

---

1 Dalia Sussman, "See Spot Go to Heaven? The Public's Not So Sure."
2 Eternal Earth-Bound Pets USA. Online.
3 Study by Brenda and Robert Vale, reported in "How Green Is Your Pet?" by Kate Ravilious.

Here's a very elementary bit of logic:

> Either **X** or **Y**
> Not-**X**
> Therefore **Y**

This kind of reasoning is called "disjunctive syllogism." It doesn't take much brain to reason this way, but it would seem to necessitate the ability to represent the **X** and the **Y** in question to oneself. Could Fido do that?

Well, I've actually seen a smart dog behave this way: Fido is running along a path, tracking something: he has his nose to the ground, sniffing every few feet. Fido comes to a place where the path divides into two. He runs up one side of the fork, nose still to the ground. In a minute he comes to a halt, sniffing around the path here and there. It's clear what has happened: Fido has lost the scent on this fork. Now here's the interesting part. Fido then turns around and without sniffing at all runs back to the place where the path divides, then runs several feet up the other fork, still not sniffing.[1]

It seems pretty clear that this is the appropriate way to describe what's going on here. At the path's division, Fido thinks, "What I'm tracking has gone up the left fork or the right fork." He runs up the right fork, but can't find the scent any more. He thinks: What I'm tracking has not gone up the right fork. So ... it must have gone up the left fork!" The fact that he doesn't sniff for some distance while running up the left fork shows that he has come to this conclusion. Fido has performed a disjunctive syllogism.

"When you come to a fork in the road, take it."—Yogi Berra

Fido's Mendacity

LET'S TURN NOW TO another question about the mental abilities of dogs. Can they tell lies? Can dogs "mean" things by what they "say"? These are mental capacities that humans clearly have, and if dogs have them, then we'd have to credit them with considerable mentality, too.

Suppose you think that dogs can't tell lies. Why can't they? Are they too honest? That's not the reason.

It's sometimes argued that for dogs to lie, they must have some sort of speech. Well, Fido makes a variety of noises on different occasions, and

---

1   This example of canine logic is attributed to Chrysippus, a third-century BCE Greek philosopher, as reported c. 200 CE by Sextus Empiricus in his *Outlines of Pyrrhonism*, I. 69.

although Fidotalk is not exactly Shakespearean in complexity, it's perhaps some sort of primitive language. Suppose Fido makes a peculiar whine whenever the mail carrier comes to the door.

Does Fido's whine mean, "The mail carrier is here, boss!"? For the whine to mean that, wouldn't Fido have to know something about mail delivery service? Understanding what it is to have a postal service is a fair bit of sophistication, probably beyond the capability of a dog brain. A regular association of the whine and the arrival of the mail seems to show that that whine "means" something, in some sense of the word 'means,' but perhaps mere association of a noise with some external event is not enough for the noise to "mean" that event, in the way words in our language have meaning. What way is that?   .

For the whine to have something like linguistic meaning, it seems that it must be more than a mere response to the arrival of the mail carrier. It must be used by Fido as an *abstract symbol* for that arrival. In Fido's case, it seems that the whine is merely an instinctive noise a dog makes whenever something approaches its territory. There are more arbitrary "linguistic signs" Fido might be taught to utter that aren't merely instinctive; for example, we could train him to woof three times in response to a hand signal. But still, in order to be a genuine abstract sign, it must be usable by Fido in contexts more distant from its stimulus. When you think about, talk about, or write about what you had for breakfast yesterday or what you hope you'll have tomorrow, you are manipulating abstract symbols that you use to stand for their distant representations.

"The power of elaborating intellectual concepts of things—as distinguished from sensuous representation, determined merely by automatic association—we may probably conjecture beasts have not," announced the philosopher John Locke in the seventeenth century, and more modern philosophers have tended to agree with him. There is some very recent evidence, however, that in certain circumstances "beasts"—at least the most intelligent ones—can remember and use a large number of abstract symbols in complex ways. Chimpanzees, for example, have been taught over one hundred abstract symbols in sign language; it's been claimed that chimps can manipulate these symbols to form sentences they have never encountered before.

Nevertheless, even if Fido had an abstract symbol standing for the arrival of the mail carrier, more than this is needed for actual lying. What would that be? If Fido whined that way when the mail carrier wasn't around, then this might be a mistake, but it wouldn't therefore be a lie.

Suppose that immediately following the mail carrier's arrival, you tend to open the door and go out to the mailbox to collect your mail, and Fido likes to take advantage of this to dash out the front door and romp around the front yard. Now, suppose that one day Fido is waiting morosely at the closed door for his chance to go outside. Suddenly he (we might say) has an idea: he gives the mail-carrier whine, though nobody is there and there are no signs that might make Fido think there is. Taking this as a sign of the arrival of the mail, you open the front door, and Fido happily dashes out for his romp. Should we say that he has tricked you—that he has told you that the mail is here, but that was a lie?

Look at what we have to attribute to Fido to count this as a genuine lie. Fido has to know that the whine means the arrival of the mail carrier, not just to him but to you. He has to know that his whine makes you believe the mail has arrived, and that as a result you'll open the door. In sum, Fido would have to think that you have a mind and beliefs, some of which are mistaken. He would have to be able to want to induce a mistaken belief in you. It would be necessary (to put it into ponderous philosophical talk) for Fido to have a theory of other minds.

Perhaps all this is too much to expect from a canine.

It is of interest to note that while some dolphins are reported to have learned English—up to fifty words used in correct context—no human being has been reported to have learned dolphinese.—Carl Sagan

Language Requirements?

THE WIKIPEDIA ARTICLE[1] "ANIMAL Language" offers this list of what are sometimes argued to be conditions for an actual language:

- *Arbitrariness:* There is no rational relationship between a sound or sign and its meaning. (There is nothing intrinsically "housy" about the word "house.")

- *Cultural transmission:* Language is passed from one language user to the next, consciously or unconsciously.

- *Discreteness:* Language is composed of discrete units that are used in combination to create meaning.

- *Displacement:* Languages can be used to communicate ideas about things that are not in the immediate vicinity either spatially or temporally.

---

1   But be very careful using Wikipedia as a source. A lot of what's in there is no good.

- *Duality:* Language works on two levels at once, a surface level and a semantic (meaningful) level.

- *Metalinguistics:* Ability to discuss language itself.

- *Productivity:* A finite number of units can be used to create an indefinitely large number of utterances.

QUESTIONS TO THINK ABOUT: Does a symbol really have to be arbitrary to count as a piece of language? Can't a natural bit of noise count? A dog's growl, for example, is an unlearned bit of behaviour that's not an arbitrary symbol; other dogs (and humans) take it as a sign of potential aggression. Why not count this as part of the language of dogs? Some philosophers want to distinguish "natural signs" like this from the symbols of language, but is there any point in this? If we don't make this distinction, should we treat every "natural sign" as a bit of language? For example, should we consider dark clouds to mean rain, in the language of the atmosphere?

FOR FURTHER READING: Ludwig Wittgenstein discusses the problem of how we might go about attributing thoughts to animals: see his *Philosophical Investigations*, sections 250, 357, and 650 in part I, and section i in part II. That quote from Locke, and his further thoughts on the matter are in his *Essay Concerning Human Understanding*, Book II, Chapter 11, Section 5, including Locke's footnote to this section. For a readable popular discussion of chimps and symbol use, see Carl Sagan, "The Abstractions of Beasts," in his book *The Dragons of Eden*. A more recent, and more philosophical, survey of theories of animal thought is Kristin Andrews, "Animal Cognition," online in The Stanford Encyclopedia of Philosophy. Alexandra Horowitz, an animal psychologist, presents philosophically and scientifically sophisticated arguments about what dogs can and can't do in *Inside of a Dog* (2010).

> Outside of a dog, a book is man's best friend. Inside of a dog it's too dark to read.—Groucho Marx

3. Meaning

What Could They Have Meant?

PHILOSOPHERS SOMETIMES THINK OF language meaning in terms of what is done to the recipient of the communication: he or she is informed of something, ordered or requested to do something, and so on. Sometimes, however (like a fried hard disk), a bit of communication fails to achieve its intended function. Sometimes (like an odd bit of rusty machinery found in the corner of your basement) it's not even clear what that function was supposed to be. Here are some examples of signs in which communicative function has somehow gone wonky.

Open packet. Eat contents—*instructions on a packet of airline peanuts*

WARNING—MAY CONTAIN NUTS—*on another packet of nuts*

DON'T COMMIT CRIME—*notice posted by police*[1]

TO ACTUATE ELEVATOR MECHANISM—
1. SELECT FLOOR DESIRED
2. DEPRESS BUTTON CORRESPONDING TO FLOOR DESIRED

In each case, it seems that the message can't reasonably be expected to have the conventional sort of effect associated with other bits of language like it. The elevator message, for example, looks like a regular bit of instruction, aimed at telling somebody how to work something; but the very rare person who didn't already know how to work an elevator would probably also fail to understand the sign.[2]

Maybe that elevator sign was there for legal reasons, aimed at the possibility of being sued by someone who got into trouble in the elevator. (This is clearly the motivation behind the warning on the bag of peanuts.) So giving instructions (or issuing a warning) in this sense has little or nothing to do with the immediate effect on anyone—with what's done to the recipient. As long as the sign is there, the instruction (or the warning) has been given. Never mind what people do when—if—they read it.

Note the elevator sign's literary style. Its author might have written instead: "Push the button for the floor you want," but $5 words were felt to be more appropriate than the more usual 50¢ ones, and the long-winded preferred to the concise. This happens when people are trying to sound very official and authoritative. You've heard other instances of this sort of thing.

---

1   A discussion of this amazing police sign, and of a number of other peculiar communications, can be found in the online article "Police force's signs mocked for stating the obvious."

2   Arthur Naiman, in *Every Goy's Guide*, offers some comments to these effects about this sign. A similar case Naiman mentions is the common definition of the Jewish food kasha as "buckwheat groats"; who would that help?

A police officer interviewed on radio or TV will usually say things like "My accompanying officer and myself observed the individual enter a vehicle" instead of "My partner and I saw the guy get into a car." Another place you'll find official pomposity is philosophy textbooks.

One of the important contributions of some twentieth-century philosophers[1] was the idea that some philosophical problems arose because we were understanding parts of language on too simple a model: some sensitivity to what was really going on would reveal interesting depths and complications, and might help solve (or dissolve) philosophical perplexities. (Though I'm not sure that philosophy can benefit by an analysis of what's written in that elevator.)

> Everyday language is a part of the human organism and is no less complicated than it.—Ludwig Wittgenstein[2]

Saying What You Don't Mean

LUDWIG WITTGENSTEIN PEPPERS HIS writings with suggestive unanswered questions. A sample:

> Make the following experiment: *say* "It's cold here" and *mean* "It's warm here." Can you do it?—And what are you doing as you do it? And is there only one way of doing it?[3]

As usual in Wittgenstein's writing, there's controversy concerning what he was driving at, and what answers—if any—he was urging to his questions. Anyway, let's think about his experiment.

How do you try to mean "It's warm here" while saying "It's cold here"? Perhaps you are at a loss about how to try to do this altogether. Or maybe you utter the words "It's warm here" while thinking silently but hard that it's cold here. Does this way of trying to do it succeed? Do you really *mean* "It's warm here" because of this? Perhaps you might conclude, as some philosophers have, that this is not a successful attempt. Maybe you can't do it at all.

A traditional account of the meaning of words relies on the thoughts that accompany them. But Wittgenstein's experiment perhaps shows why that traditional account is wrong.

---

1   Most notably J.L. Austin and Ludwig Wittgenstein.
2   *Tractatus Logico-Philosophicus*, 4:002.
3   *Philosophical Investigations*, I, § 510.

SOME QUESTIONS TO THINK ABOUT: What, then, is meaning? What's the difference between saying something and meaning it, and saying something and not meaning it? It's a fact about the English language that the sentence 'The cat is on the mat' means that the cat is on the mat. What does this fact amount to? What exactly must be the case for that sentence to mean that?

> "Then you should say what you mean," the March Hare went on.
> "I do," Alice hastily replied; "at least—at least I mean what I say— that's the same thing, you know."
> "Not the same thing a bit!" said the Hatter. "Why you might just as well say that 'I see what I eat' is the same thing as 'I eat what I see'!"—Lewis Carroll, *Alice's Adventures in Wonderland*

> "I don't know what you mean by 'glory,'" Alice said.
> Humpty Dumpty smiled contemptuously. "Of course you don't— till I tell you. I meant 'there's a nice knock-down argument for you!'"
> "But 'glory' doesn't mean 'a nice knock-down argument,'" Alice objected.
> "When I use a word," Humpty Dumpty said, in a rather scornful tone, "it means just what I choose it to mean—neither more nor less."
> "The question is," said Alice, "whether you can make words mean so many different things."
> "The question is," said Humpty Dumpty, "which is to be master— that's all."—Lewis Carroll, *Through the Looking Glass*

Thinking about Vienna

THINK ABOUT VIENNA. WHAT made it the case that you were thinking about Vienna, and not about something else?

Suppose that Arnold has visited Prague and Vienna. I ask him to think about Vienna, and he closes his eyes and visualizes the Vltava River, just as he saw it flowing through town. Well, the Vltava River flows through

Prague, not Vienna; Arnold doesn't have a good memory. We should say: Arnold thinks he's thinking about Vienna, but actually he's thinking about Prague. Why do we say this?

One way of answering this question is to say that the particular mental experience Arnold is going through when he is attempting to think about Vienna is *connected* in some way to Prague, not to Vienna. In this case, the river in Prague caused memory traces that he called up when attempting to think of Vienna; but since his mental experience now is connected to Prague, that's what he's in fact thinking about. In order to think about X, one has to have an experience *caused* in some way by X. (Compare the item about the **Brain in a Vat** in Chapter VIII.)

This is not to say that I actually need to have experienced something by actually seeing it in order to think about it. I can think about Zanzibar, although I was never there. But there has to be some connection—however complicated or indirect—between the real Zanzibar and my current thought in order that my current thought be about Zanzibar. What would do, for example, is for me to have read what somebody wrote as a result of having been there, or to see a picture in a book printed from a negative of a photograph somebody once took in Zanzibar.

The Incredible Swampman

A MUCH–DISCUSSED PHILOSOPHICAL THOUGHT-EXPERIMENT goes like this. Imagine Fred is walking through the swamp one day and is hit and vaporized by a bolt of lightning. That bolt also simultaneously (by miraculous coincidence) creates an atom-for-atom duplicate of Fred a few feet away from him: Swampman.

Swampman gets up, brushes himself off, and heads for home—Fred's home. When he reaches the front door, he feels around in his pockets, and thinks, "Now, where did I put my keys?" Fred's wife sees him and opens the door. "Did I go out without my keys again?" he asks.

What does he mean by saying this? Is he asking his wife about his keys? Nope! According to some philosophers, this couldn't happen.

Why not? Well consider a snake travelling around on a sandy beach, more or less at random, leaving marks in the sand behind it. If by coincidence, those marks just happen to trace out the words *it's no fun being a snake*, are those words a complaint about the snakely life? No: the snake doesn't mean anything by them: it's just a coincidence.

Wait a minute (you object). Swampman does speak English, right? Because Fred did, and Swampman's brain is an exact duplicate of his.

Nope (these philosophers reply). The sounds someone makes mean what they do because of their history of connection with things in that person's world—things they refer to. Swampman's sounds lack this connection. They can't mean anything. The same goes for someone's thoughts. Swampman can't think about those keys (or Fred's wife) yet either.[1]

Thinking about Santa Claus

BUT IF THE ANSWER just given is right, a problem arises. Suppose Betty is looking distracted, and you ask her what she's thinking about. "I'm thinking about Santa Claus," she says. Bad news, Betty! There is no Santa Claus! She can't have any causal connection with anybody named Santa Claus, direct or indirect. Does this make her wrong in saying what she was thinking about? What *was* she thinking about?

We cruelly tell Betty the bad news. After she recovers, we explain to her about Arnold and Vienna. Having realized that causal connection with real things reveals what one is thinking about, and that Santy doesn't exist, she agrees that she couldn't have been thinking about Santa Claus. What was she doing then?

"Well," says Betty, "I *believed* that there was someone who was jolly and fat and who dressed in red clothing and who came down chimneys at Christmas and gave presents to good little girls and boys."

Betty must have been thinking about *characteristics*: jolliness and fatness and so on do exist. What she actually believed was that these characteristics all applied to one thing. She's not thinking about any particular jolly thing, or any particular fat thing, and so on.

Note here that the causal theory of the content of thoughts seems to imply that in this case, characteristics—jolliness, fatness—not particular fat or jolly things, can be causes. So Betty, it appears, would be thinking about some of Plato's forms. (See **I Forget What I Saw Before I Was Born** in Chapter IX.)

Armed with this new philosophical knowledge, Betty sets out to torture her little brother Barney, who spends a good deal of time thinking about his imaginary friend, whom he calls Willard. "There is nobody named Willard," she tells him.

---

1   The Swampman story, and claims about what he can't talk or think about, were introduced by Donald Davidson in "Knowing One's Own Mind." There has been a great deal of subsequent discussion of this example.

"Yes there is," says Barney. "The great twentieth-century pragmatist philosopher and logician Willard Van Orman Quine is named Willard." (Philosophers' children talk this way.)

"Yeah, but you weren't thinking about *him*, were you?"

"No. I was thinking about another Willard."

"Well, there isn't anyone actually named Willard you were thinking about. You must have been thinking about some characteristics that you believed falsely were co-instantiated. What characteristics did you believe falsely someone had? What's Willard like? Is he fat and jolly? Is he thin and morose?"

"I don't know anything at all about Willard."

A QUESTION TO THINK ABOUT: In that case, what was Barney thinking about?

Into the Mainstream of Philosophy

TWO MAIN AREAS OF philosophy are touched on in this chapter: Philosophy of Mind, and Philosophy of Language.

One of the chief questions in Philosophy of Mind (also sometimes called Philosophy of Psychology) is introduced by the arguments about whether machines and animals can think. These arguments are really of secondary concern: it's hoped that by considering these, we can get a firmer grip on what it is for people to think, and how we know that we do.

One of the major traditions in this area, perhaps the most popular historically, is that thinking is something we know we do because we can notice it in ourselves. When you look into yourself, you notice thought going on, and that's all there is to it. An immediate problem faced by people who hold this view is that, it seems, one notices thought only in oneself; one never detects thought in this way in any other people, into whose minds one never can peer directly. This view, then, makes the existence of other minds a problem. Clearly, however, we know that other people think; since all we can observe in others is their outsides, their external behaviour, then perhaps it follows that when we attribute thought to them, we might actually be talking about their external behaviour. (The position that mental attributions are really about behaviour is part of the philosophical and psychological position called *behaviourism*.)

If other people exhibit the sort of behaviour that counts as mental, then there is no reason not to count certain animal and (possible) machine behaviour as mental as well. Why do you count others as having minds? Note that if you take their external behaviour as merely providing evidence for mind, not *constituting* it, then perhaps you're on shaky ground, since it's assumed that you only *directly* observe the mental in one case—your own—and it's quite a leap to reason from this single case to a whole lot of others. On the other hand, saying that a certain sort of behaviour constitutes mindedness also carries its own implausibilities. It seems to imply, for example, the absurd position that you can find out what's on your own mind only by observing your own behaviour, for example, in a mirror. What's the right answer here?

> Old behaviourism joke: Two behaviourists meet on the street. One says, "You're fine; how am I?"

A second main question in the Philosophy of Mind, obviously connected with the first, is whether the mental can be understood merely in terms of the physical. If you're a *materialist* (i.e., you believe that everything in the universe is physical, operating on the basis of physical laws), then you hold a view that's common now but very uncommon throughout history. Materialists must be willing to give a sensible account of how a merely physical object can have a mind.

A central question in the Philosophy of Language is introduced by Wittgenstein's question of what it takes to *mean* something by what you say. A traditional answer to this is that what someone means is what he/she is thinking while speaking. But if thoughts are private, this makes meaning a private phenomenon, and we couldn't know what others mean by their talk. A more recent view, suggested by some of Wittgenstein's writings, makes meaning a public matter: public conventions of language associate them with meanings. But then what, exactly, are meanings? What do these public conventions associate bits of language *with*?

You won't have any trouble finding plenty of appropriate readings in the Philosophy of Mind. Almost every introductory anthology has an appropriate section treating some of the main questions here. You might also look at Paul Churchland's excellent introductory book, *Matter and Consciousness*.

Philosophy of Language is a more difficult field in which to find introductory readings. Philosophy anthologies rarely include suitable readings, and the important books and articles in the area are very difficult and technical ones. You might, however, take a look at *The Meaning of Language* by Robert M. Martin, to see if the author has succeeded in his intention to write an introduction to Philosophy of Language intelligible to beginners.

Chapter XI

Here and Now; You and I

1. Time Travel

Time travel, by its very nature, was invented in all periods of history simultaneously.—Douglas Adams, *The Hitchhiker's Guide to the Galaxy*

Not Killing Grandpa

WE CAN TRAVEL IN space, going around to different points in each of the three dimensions. The only problems that arise here are having the right technology. Time is sometimes considered a fourth dimension (in order to locate something, you specify where it is, by mentioning three spatial coordinates, and when it is, with one time coordinate).

But there have been arguments that time travel—at least, travel into the past—is impossible. Suppose you went back to the time—say 1920—when your evil maternal grandfather was an infant, and killed him. Now, if Grandpa died when an infant, in 1920, then your mother would never have been born, and consequently you wouldn't have existed. But then, who killed Grandpa?

This sort of puzzle, familiar to readers of science fiction, is sometimes thought to show that time travel is impossible. I don't mean merely that we don't have time machines right now. Neither do I mean that the laws of science might prevent our ever building them (as, for example, these laws make it impossible that anyone ever build a perpetual motion machine or a spaceship that travels faster than light). I mean that *logical* paradoxes such as this one seem to make time travel a *logical* impossibility. You can't build a machine to do the logically impossible.

But it's sometimes argued that time travel wouldn't result in logical paradoxes. Look at it this way. Of course you can't go back into the past and make it different from the way it really was. But you might go back into the past and *make it* the way it really was. You might, for example, arrange for your father to meet your mother (this happened in a recent movie).

It's peculiar to think that if you travelled back to Grandpa's time you would somehow be magically unable to kill him, but we need not go so far as this to make time travel intelligible. All we need to allow is, were you to go back to 1920, that you *don't* kill Grandpa, not that you *couldn't*.

Meeting Yourself

WELL, WHO CARES ABOUT meeting Grandpa when he was a boy? You'd be much more interested in meeting your earlier self, wouldn't you?

Okay, now suppose that the time machine you bought from Acme Corporation (the same outfit that supplies Wile E. Coyote) is too low-powered to send you back earlier than yesterday, and once you're there, can't bring you back to today. No problem. It would be sort of interesting to do that, and you wouldn't need to return to today, because you could just wait around for a day, and then it would be today all over again. So you set the time machine to send you to your living room at 6:00 yesterday morning, hop in, and back you go. When you show up early yesterday, you walk to the bedroom, and there you are, asleep. So you wake yourself up, and Yesterday-Self, after regaining enough consciousness to take in what's happening, is pretty surprised to see you standing there.

But this didn't happen. You can remember what happened yesterday, when you didn't meet somebody just like you. So that sort of time-travel, at least, is impossible, right?

Well, not so fast. There's a way of understanding this that has already achieved some scientific respectability: the idea of branching universes. What this involves is that at every point in time when things *could* go a variety of different ways, things *do* go each of those ways, one in each of a number of parallel universes created at that time. (This idea is supposed to help think about quantum indeterminacy, but don't ask me how.) Anyway, suppose that at 6 a.m. yesterday, the universe split into two branches: one (which you've been living in) in which you didn't arrive in your bedroom then, and one in which you did.

Well, then, let's track what goes on in the parallel universe in which you did show up. You meet Yesterday-Self, and the two of you spend the day together. Then the next morning, you buy an Acme time machine and travel back to the day before. (You have to—or else how could you have shown up earlier?) And then you meet your other self, and spend the day and ... oops, it seems that you're caught in a loop, doomed to repeat the same day over and over, forever (although no more than one day will have passed). That doesn't sound so interesting after all.

UFOs Contain Visitors from Planet Earth

HERE'S ANOTHER ARGUMENT AGAINST the possibility of time travel. If time travel were possible, then it would be probable that future scientists would discover how to do it some day. When they did, it's probable that they would travel back to *now* to take a look around. What would that look like to us? Strangely dressed people would be popping into existence, looking around, and then disappearing. The fact that we don't see those people coming and going shows that future scientists aren't visiting us in their time machines. And this is some evidence that time travel is really impossible.

Of course, there are other ways of explaining the present lack of sightings of travellers from the future. Maybe they're simply not interested in visiting us. (What makes us think we're so interesting?)

> Or maybe they're careful to keep hidden. Or maybe we *have* seen them, but we think they are visitors from another planet (this explains all those close encounters with "aliens").

> "Sometimes I think the surest sign that intelligent life exists elsewhere in the universe is that none of it has tried to contact us."—Calvin and Hobbes comic strip

Time Travel and the End of Humanity

BUT SUPPOSE THAT TIME travel is really possible. If it is, some people argue, we have reason to come to a dismal conclusion about the future of humanity.

The reasoning is this. If time travel is possible, then it's likely that sooner or later science will discover how to do it, and future scientists will come here for a visit. The fact that they're not here must mean that there aren't any scientists in the far future. The best way of explaining this is to assume that before that time the human race will become extinct, perhaps by nuclear or ecological self-destruction.

You'll be cheered to hear, however, that not many people take this argument too seriously.

2. When, Where, and Who

Telling Space Aliens What Day It Is

CONSIDER WHAT DAY IT is right now. When is that? You can answer that question. But that date locates you relative to some date when everyone decided to start counting: according to the conventions of the calendar, it's some large number of days after that arbitrary day. This answer is based on arbitrary conventions; when is it *really*?

Suppose that radio signals sent out in space will someday be picked up and understood by aliens on a distant planet. If the aliens knew when those signals were sent, they would be able to figure out how far away they are from us, because radio signals travel through space at the constant speed of light. So one thing you'd like to include in those radio signals is information that will tell them when you sent the signals. Can you do this?

It's obviously of no use to tell them the date and year you sent the message. It seems we'd need some event we both could see: let's say we observed some really unusual event in space, for example a supernova. Knowing how far away it is from us, we can calculate how long it took for its light to reach us, and thus how long ago it happened, and we could tell the aliens that we sent the signal to them, say, 1364 years after that supernova. Of course, they wouldn't know what a year was, but we could give them that information, for example, in terms of the duration of the supernova, or in terms of the radio frequency we are sending.

But what if there isn't anything we both can see? Would this make dating the signal impossible?

If you could tell them directly where we are, then they could do the reverse calculation and figure out when the message was sent. You might do this by telling them some information that would describe our earth or sun or galaxy with such precision that they could find one of these with their telescopes. But if they can't see us (or something we also can see) then it would be, it seems, impossible to tell them where we are.

Language learning seems to depend heavily on pointing. You teach a child what 'cat' means by saying "cat" while pointing at one. But this clearly won't work with aliens on a distant planet. Some people have suggested that communication might begin with referring to mathematical objects the aliens surely would encounter—for example, the number π (the ratio of the circumference of any circle to its diameter): 3.14159.... So we might send out a signal consisting of three pulses, then a pause, then one pulse, then a pause, then four pulses … and so on, hoping they get the idea. But consider the three-pulse signal: would that mean 3 to the aliens, or would they count the short spaces in between, and think it means 2? Some commentators[1] argue that extraterrestrial communication faces irreducible problems.

I'm Here Now

NATURALLY, IT WOULDN'T DO any good to include in your message to outer space: "I am *here*. The time is *now*." In a sense, they would already know the truth of those sentences, because *here* refers to wherever the speaker is, and *now* to whatever time it is when the speaker speaks. But the aliens would learn nothing at all from these sentences. Why is this?

> The words *here* and *now* are examples of what philosophers call *indexicals*. *Here* refers to a place merely by pointing at it; so it refers to whatever place the speaker happens to be located at. If the hearer is located at a different place, and doesn't independently know where the speaker is located, *here* communicates nothing. Similarly, *now* points at a time and refers to whatever time the speaker happens to be speaking at. If the hearer doesn't independently know when the speaker said this, *now* would communicate no information.

Note that *you* and *I* are also indexicals. Imagine that someone knocks at your door. You call out, "Who's there?" and the person who is knocking replies, "I am!" This might be helpful if you recognized the voice, but if you didn't, nothing would be communicated to you by that sentence.

"DRABBLE" © Kevin Fagen / Dist. by United Features Syndicate, Inc.

SOME QUESTIONS TO THINK ABOUT: Note that then, this, and there are also indexicals. Can you think of others? Could a language do without indexicals?

---

1   For example, the anthropologist Kathryn Denning's view, mentioned in a general article on picking communication with extraterrestrials by Tim Folger: "Contact: The Day After."

"I am here," "The time is now," and "It's me" are peculiar sentences in that it appears they are always true, no matter when or where spoken. But on the other hand, if "I am here" is always true, then "I am not here" is (presumably) always false. But what about when you hear it on somebody's answering machine?

We are here and it is now. Further than that all human knowledge is moonshine.—H.L. Mencken

Consider other sentences that are always true, no matter what. Two of them are "Every chair is a chair" and "It's Tuesday or it's not Tuesday." Nobody has to worry that what they say is false when they say these sentences, but this big advantage is entirely wiped out by the fact that the sentences give no information. Is it a general rule that every sentence whose truth is guaranteed, no matter what, is useless because it is uninformative?

But it might be argued that "I am here" and "The time is now" do convey some information, because, after all, the facts they refer to might not have been true. When Zelda is standing on the North Pole and says "I am here," the fact that makes her sentence true is that Zelda is standing on the North Pole. This is certainly an interesting bit of information. When it's exactly twelve midnight, the fact that makes "The time is now" true is that it's twelve midnight. This might be interesting information, too.

Perhaps one moral we can draw from these considerations is that the fact that makes a sentence true is not necessarily the information conveyed by that sentence, even when the hearer fully understands it.

Another moral is that we can work up a good deal of confusion when considering the meaning of words such as *I*, *here*, and *now*.

Yogi Berra and Mickey Mantle were sitting in the Yankee dugout. Mickey said, "Say, Yogi, what time is it?" Yogi replied, "You mean, right now?"

Fred Finds Himself in the Library

THE VERIBIG MEMORIAL LIBRARY has so many books that every fact in the history of the universe is written down somewhere in there. One day while walking through the library, Fred Schmidlap is struck on the head by a big volume falling off a high shelf, and he suffers complete amnesia; he has no idea what his name is, or what any of the facts of his past life are. He thinks that perhaps the enormous amount of information in the library can help him, so he sets out reading to try to find out who he is.

Fred spends some time reading about the history of thirteenth-century Albania, about methods of refining bauxite, and about Portuguese irregular verbs. This is all interesting, but he doesn't feel he's making progress in finding out who he is.

Soon he stumbles on a huge room filled with books of biography; this, he thinks, is the place to look. He spends an enormous amount of time reading every biography in the place, including one about some guy named Fred Schmidlap. Fred now knows a large number of facts about this Fred Schmidlap. But what he does not know is that these are facts of *his* life. And, it would seem, no matter how detailed the information in that biography was, the information would never tell Fred that this was *him*. (Even if he read in *Weird Biographies* that Fred Schmidlap was the only person reading *Weird Biographies* in the Veribig Library on July 23, 2004, he still wouldn't know it's him: for the conclusion that he was Fred, he'd also have to know that the person reading that book was him.)

The strange conclusion we must draw is that, however many facts he knows about what is in fact his own life, Fred still wouldn't know that these are facts about him; he still wouldn't know who he is.

Suddenly it hits Fred: this is *his* biography. What has he just discovered? Why wasn't *this* fact something he could read in his complete biography? (The book does not, of course, say "Fred Schmidlap: This is *your* life!" Even if it did, it wouldn't help Fred.)

There seems to be a special sort of knowledge about one's *self*. One can know about one's self that one's shoe is untied, or that one has brown eyes, or that one has a headache, but there's nothing special about this, because one can know this about others, too. What's special and mysterious is not that you know that some person has untied shoes, but that you know that that person is *you*. What is knowing *that*?

Another peculiarity we should note is that as soon as Fred recovers consciousness after having been hit on the head, he is able to have thoughts about himself. Fred can think, "Who am I?" referring to himself. But at that point, Fred knows nothing—no facts at all—about himself. He doesn't need to know any facts about himself in order to refer to himself as himself. Compare this with the requirements for referring to other things. If you want to talk or think about your cat or your breakfast or the Panama Canal, you must know *something* about that object; there must be some characteristic of it you're aware of, that would enable you to identify it if you ran into it. Otherwise, what would make it the case that it's that thing you're talking or thinking about, rather than something else?

Of course, you, unlike Fred, have plenty of information about yourself. But when you refer to yourself as yourself, you don't have to use any of this

information to identify what it is that you're talking about. You never identify yourself as the person who X or Y or ..., whereas you always identify
other things as the thing which X or Y or....

And here's a third peculiar thing about self-knowledge. In general, it's
possible for you to be mistaken about who someone is. This is a live possibility when you only catch a fleeting glimpse of that person, or when you don't
know that person very well. Even when you have substantial contact with a
person you know very well, there's a very tiny, but non-zero, possibility that
you're mistaken. But when you're aware of someone by means of awareness
of that person's sensations, and take that person to be yourself, you can't be
mistaken.

> "Who are *you*?" said the Caterpillar.
>
> This was not an encouraging opening for a conversation. Alice
> replied, rather shyly, "I—I hardly know, sir, just at present—at least I
> know who I *was* when I got up this morning, but I think I must have
> been changed several times since then."
>
> "What do you mean by that?" said the Caterpillar sternly. "Explain
> yourself!"
>
> "I can't explain *myself*, I'm afraid, sir," said Alice, "because I'm not
> myself, you see."
>
> "I don't see," said the Caterpillar.
>
> —Lewis Carroll, *Alice's Adventures in Wonderland*, Chapter 5

The mystery of a "sense of myself" is brought out if we try to imagine
what it would be like *not* to be "myself" any longer. It wouldn't be merely
what we mean when we say "I'm not myself today." That means just feeling
sort of odd, and it's not literally being someone different. It's still you—just
feeling abnormal. And it wouldn't be simply that (in Alice's case) the name
'Alice' no longer applies. There's no mystery about how that could happen:
she could merely change her name to 'Hortense.' What it would be like for
her not to be herself any longer is not a change in the 'Alice' part of the equa-
tion 'I am Alice' but rather a change in the 'I' part.

Is not being yourself a deep mystery or just nonsense?

What Two Gods Don't Know

IMAGINE A WORLD INHABITED by two omniscient gods. They are not
exactly alike. One lives on top of the tallest mountain and throws down
manna. The other lives on top of the coldest mountain and throws down
thunderbolts. Now, they're omniscient, and that means that they know every

truth there is to know. Both of them know about these two gods. They both know that one of them lives to the southeast of the other, and is, at the moment, throwing down lots of manna, while the other one growls and gets some more thunderbolts ready. The only thing neither of them knows is which god *he* is. That shows, according to the author of this tale,[1] that knowledge *who one is* is very peculiar. It's not knowledge of any fact.

FOR FURTHER READING: The library puzzle here is adapted from, and discussed in, John Perry's article "The Problem of the Essential Indexical." Another good article on the subject is Hector-N. Castañeda's "'He': A Study in the Logic of Self-Consciousness."

3. The Identity of Things

Two Ways to Be the Same

THE WORD *identity* HAS several different senses. In one sense, as when we say that two new pennies are identical, we mean that they are exactly similar (at least as far as we can see). But in another sense, when philosophers say that **X** and **Y** are identical, they mean that **X** *is* **Y**—that **X** and **Y** are the same thing. Thus, in this sense, we say that Rutherford B. Hayes is identical with the nineteenth president of the United States. 'Rutherford B. Hayes' and 'the nineteenth president of the United States' are two different ways of referring to the same thing. Philosophers call the first kind of identity "qualitative" identity, and the second kind "quantitative" identity.

A principle that seems obviously true is

- If A and B are (quantitatively) identical, then they have the same properties.

This is called the Principle of the Indiscernibility of Identicals. Note that this is to be distinguished from another principle: the Principle of the Identity of Indiscernibles. This one says:

- If A and B have all the same properties, then they are (quantitatively) identical.

In other words, if two things are completely qualitatively identical, they are the same thing—the "two" things are actually one thing. Is this principle true?

---

1   David Lewis, "Attitudes De Dicto, and De Se."

Our penny example above does not prove it false. Those pennies are not quantitatively identical, but neither are they utterly qualitatively identical. Even though they look just alike, a microscope could, we have no doubt, reveal small differences. And even if it didn't, it's clear that they have other differences in characteristics: for example, they're located in different places. Imagine two pennies that had physical characteristics that were precisely the same, *and* were located in exactly the same place: that is to say, both of them occupied precisely the same small cylindrical area of space. Could they still be two *different* pennies—that is, quantitatively distinct? Would it make any sense to say that there were actually two pennies there? Or would this be just nonsense? (Try this experiment on your bank: take in a roll of fifty pennies, and tell them that, through the miracle of philosophy, you have managed to cram two pennies that are completely qualitatively identical into each space of one, so they owe you one dollar for the roll. If they believe you, let me know.)

The second principle, the Identity of Indiscernibles, may be true. But the first principle, of the Indiscernibility of Identicals, seems undeniable and un-controversial. Suppose that 'A' and 'B' are just two names for the same thing: then how could there be some characteristic that A has but B does not?

Well, consider this example. Think of me at age two (call him 'Bobby') and me right now (call him 'Robert'). 'Bobby' and 'Robert' are just dif-ferent names for the same person—*me*—right? So Bobby and Robert are quantitatively identical. But notice that Bobby is two years old and Robert isn't. Bobby is a cute little kid and Robert certainly isn't. Robert is a PhD in philosophy and Bobby isn't. There are many differences in characteristics between Bobby and Robert. Do you think that this shows that the Principle of the Indiscernibility of Identicals is wrong? Some philosophers have found that principle so obviously true that they would want to hold on to it no mat-ter what. Suppose we agree that the principle is correct; what follows about Bobby and Robert?

> If that principle is correct, we would have to admit that Bobby and Robert are not qualitatively identical, that they are, strictly speaking, distinct things: Bobby and Robert are *literally* two different people. My parents, unbeknownst to them, actu-ally had *two* sons (actually, many more than two). This sort of thinking is certainly bizarre.

In order to save the Principle of Indiscernibility of Identicals we would have to think of the universe in a drastically different way: it makes change impossible. Do you see why?

For something to change, it has to have some characteristic at one time, and not have that characteristic at another. But the principle insists that it's impossible for A and B to be identical if A has a characteristic that B does not. So nothing changes.

It would seem, then, that to hold on to this principle, we can think of something lasting through a period of time only if it changes in absolutely no way at all—not even in location. This certainly restricts the number of things that last. Except for these few unchanging things, the universe is populated by a huge number of different things, each lasting only an instant, replacing each other instantaneously. This is quite bizarre.

But worse still: the supposition that some things endure through a period of time by remaining utterly unchanged is also wrong. Even if a penny undergoes absolutely no physical change at all from one second to the next, it nevertheless changes in some respect: it becomes one second older. If the penny is one thousand seconds old now, in one second it won't be one thousand seconds old. Thus, by the principle, not even a physically unchanging penny can endure. It gets replaced by another one with a different characteristic (that is, a different age).

This principle, then, seems to imply the hugely surprising consequence that nothing endures. The reality we are aware of is not a world in which things last from one time till another; it is rather a world in which things exist only for an instant, then they disappear, replaced by something else usually rather similar. So you can't step into the same river twice.[1]

When you get a conclusion as bizarre as this, it's a good idea to try to find something that has gone wrong in your assumptions, or in your reasoning. Try.

Here's a suggested way of looking at matters that avoids these problems. Bobby and Robert in one sense are different things, though they are *time-slices* of one time-extended thing. Philosophers say they are distinct *stages* in a continuing object. So there's no problem for the principle in saying that Bobby is a kid, but Robert isn't, since Bobby is a different stage from Robert. But we can also consider the person extended through time, constructed from, and including, Bobby and Robert and a whole lot of other stages. Let's call this extended thing R. Martin. Now, considering this R. Martin, there's still no problem with the principle. R. Martin has several characteristics: a kid-in-1948 and a non-kid-in-2011. No contradiction here. Can something change? Sure: it can be a kid-at-one-time, and a non-kid-at-another.

---

1   This saying derives from a report by Plato, *Cratylus*, 402A: "Heraclitus [c. 500 BCE] is supposed to say that all things are in motion and nothing at rest; he compares them to the stream of a river, and says that you cannot go into the same water twice."

The Same Lump

BUT NOW ANOTHER PROBLEM is suggested: when are a bunch of stages to be considered parts of the same continuing object?

When Descartes considers this problem he invites us to consider a lump of beeswax. It is hard, cold, round, white; it smells like flowers and makes a sound when you hit it. Put it next to the fire, and everything changes. Soon it is soft, hot, and transparent, shaped like a puddle, not a sphere. The smell disappears and it makes no sound when hit. It even increases somewhat in volume. But we are sure that this puddle is *the same thing* as the earlier lump. Descartes reasons that *something* must remain the same from one time to the other; he called this something "physical substance." Note that we don't perceive physical substance through our senses; what we see, hear, smell, feel, or taste changes. We sense only the changing characteristics that attach to the bit of substance—the colours, temperatures, and so on. How, then, do we know that this physical substance is there? Descartes answers: "It is my mind alone which perceives it."[1]

This is not an answer that many people find satisfying. If you can't sense this something, how do you know when it's there? For all we know, maybe this something has left when we put the wax next to the fire, and we now have a different thing. It must be by means of our senses that we determine that *this* is the same thing as *that*.

If you don't think Descartes is right, then why is this puddle the same thing as that lump? In other words: why do we consider those two stages as parts of the same continuing object? Here's one possible answer:

> The stages we see, including the earlier lump and the later puddle and the stages in-between, are *spatio-temporally continuous*. Imagine that we place the lump next to the fire at noon, and observe what happens until 1 p.m. At every instant, there is something there. Even if it moves somewhat, it describes a continuous path: at one instant, it is right next to where it was just before. That is to say: it is not the case that at one instant it's in one place, and at the next, there's nothing there, but something at another location far away. And there are no temporal gaps: a stage exists there at every instant during this time span.
>
> When we get something that follows a spatio-temporally continuous path like this, we tend to think of it as one thing that lasts, rather than as a succession of different things. Imagine that instead there was

---

1   *Meditations*, II.

spatial discontinuity: the lump disappeared at one place, and a lump simultaneously appeared a foot away. Then we might want to say that the lump disappeared, and a *different* lump appeared elsewhere. Or imagine that there was a temporal discontinuity: the lump disappeared, then there were a few seconds when there was no lump there, and then a lump exactly like the one that disappeared appeared in exactly that spot. Again we might want to say that the lump disappeared, and then later a *different* lump appeared in that place.

A QUESTION TO THINK ABOUT: Is spatio-temporal continuity sufficient for identity through time? Imagine an object X at a place at a time; X suddenly disappears, and at the same time, object Y, with entirely different characteristics, appears. I've talked about it in a way that might make you want to say that X has been replaced by a different object Y; but could you also say that Y is X, having undergone a sudden and very thorough change of characteristics?

The Identity of My University

BUT THE CONDITIONS FOR the continuing existence of the same thing through time do not always include spatio-temporal continuity. Consider the history of the university I worked at. Several years after it was founded, it ran out of money and ceased to exist. A few years later, a generous benefactor donated a lot of money, and it started up again, at the same location. Was the university that started up after this time-lapse *the same university* as the one that earlier existed at that location?

It seems clear that the answer is Yes. We want to say that it was the same university starting up again, not a different one at the same place. Thus the university was temporally discontinuous.

A few years later, the university grew too large for its building downtown and moved to new, roomier quarters. What happened (we can suppose) is that one night at midnight the university instantaneously popped out of existence downtown, and simultaneously a university (with the same name) popped into existence uptown. Is the university located uptown the same university as the one that had existed downtown?

Again we're tempted to say Yes: it's the same university that has merely moved to another location. Note, however, that this move involves a spatial discontinuity. When moving, the university did not follow a spatially continuous path. It did not "travel" from one point to the other. Robie Street runs between the former campus and the new campus, but there was no time at which the university was crossing Robie Street.

SOME QUESTIONS TO THINK ABOUT: If you accept these answers, you must admit that universities, at least, can be spatially and temporally discontinuous. Is this possible for other sorts of things? Suppose the chair you're sitting on disappeared, and simultaneously a chair exactly like it reappeared at the other side of the room. Could you count the object that reappeared as the same chair? Or suppose it disappeared, and then a few minutes later, a chair exactly like it reappeared in exactly the same place; could this be the same chair? If you insist that these must be different chairs in both cases, then you would appear not to allow spatial or temporal discontinuity in ordinary physical objects like chairs. Is there a special sort of things that can have spatial or temporal discontinuities? Try to think of examples other than universities that can.

The Disappearing Boat

SALLY IS LEAVING FOR Tibet for a ten-year stay, so she lends her boat to George, after getting him to promise to make any repairs necessary, and to give it back to her when she gets back.

Soon after getting the boat, George notices a rotten plank in the hull. George rips out the rotten plank, throws it into his garage, and replaces it with a new one. But a week later, he discovers that the rudder is broken. He removes it, throws it into his garage, and installs a new one. Next week the carburetor breaks; George replaces it, keeping the old carburetor. Soon something else needs replacement, and then something else. George, true to his word, has all these jobs done.

Ten years of continuous repairs on Sally's boat have passed, and shortly before Sally's return George has replaced every last bit of Sally's boat. She returns from Tibet. George proudly returns the boat in beautiful working order, but Sally is upset. "That's not my boat!" she complains. "It's all different!" George explains how he's had to replace every bit of it over the ten years. But Sally still claims that this is not her boat, because not even one atom of this boat was part of the boat she lent George. She admits that this boat is better than the one she lent George (which was disintegrating badly); but she explains that she is sentimentally attached to her old boat, and she wants *her* boat back, not this new one.

George has an idea. Every old, rotten piece he took off the boat has been thrown into his garage. He takes all those pieces out and assembles them into a boat—a rotten boat indeed—and presents it to Sally. "That's my boat!" she exclaims. "But it's a complete wreck! And you promised to keep it repaired!"

Which boat is really Sally's?

SOME QUESTIONS TO THINK ABOUT: If the old wreck is really hers, then why didn't George keep it repaired? Why did he spend all that time and money repairing a boat that was not hers? But if the new one is really hers, why isn't she pleased to have it back? And isn't it odd that the boat she lent George and this boat share not even one atom of matter? And what about that old wreck, which contains almost exactly the same material as the one Sally left? When did the boat that George kept repairing stop being Sally's? Did the pile of junk in the garage turn into Sally's boat at exactly that time?

FOR FURTHER READING: This is a version of the classical philosophical puzzle known as "The Ship of Theseus," presented by Hobbes in *De Corpore* II, 11. Hobbes got the story from Plutarch's life of Theseus. Even in Plutarch's day (c. first century CE) the story, as Plutarch mentions, "afforded an example to the philosophers concerning the identity of things that are changed by addition" (§§ 22–23).

> A real-life ship identity controversy arose in Nova Scotia in 2011. A famous tourist-attracting tall wooden sailing ship, the *Bluenose II*, finally got irreparably rotten, so almost all of it was run through a wood-chipper and sent to the land-fill. A few bits were saved (the rudder, the boom, and a chunk of the prow) and incorporated in a boat looking very much like the old one, but almost entirely made of new wood. So is this a *replica* of the Bluenose II, or a *restoration*? The boat's builders and the Nova Scotia Department of Tourism, Culture and Heritage understandably insist that it's the old boat, restored. Others are not so sure. The fact that Theseus' boat changed gradually, but the *Bluenose II* almost all at once, may make a difference.

Three Odd Buildings

(1) The Gold Pavilion Temple

Douglas Adams reports visiting this building in Kyoto, Japan, and being surprised how well it had stood up over the six centuries since it was built. He was told that it hadn't stood up well at all—in fact, it had burned down twice during the twentieth century. "So this isn't the original building?" he asked his Japanese guide. "But yes, of course it is," the guide insisted, while reporting, nevertheless, that the building had burnt down to the ground several times, and each time it was rebuilt with completely new materials. "So how can it be the same building?" Adams asked. "It is always the same building," the guide replied.

Adams says that he found this point of view surprising but perfectly rational. The idea of the building, its intention, and its design remain the same. Only the materials change. "To be overly concerned with the original materials, which are merely sentimental souvenirs of the past, is to fail to see the living building itself."[1]

(2) The Hôtel de Glace

This building in Quebec City has an unusual construction—it's made entirely from snow and ice—and is metaphysically odd also. Understandably it disappears each spring, and is rebuilt the following winter. That means it doesn't exist for three quarters of the year. It has been rebuilt in a different location from its previous meltdown, and with a different design. Nevertheless, everyone who talks about it is comfortable referring to its yearly incarnations as the same hotel back again.

(3) The Ugly Apartment House

Years ago there was a very large, very ugly, old and shoddy wooden frame apartment building next door to the philosophy department offices where I worked. One day a sign went up on the building advertising the construction on that site of luxury condominiums, and in a week or two construction workers showed up and began several months of work on this building.

First they sawed the whole building off its foundation, and jacked the whole thing up several feet; then they excavated for a new basement, and poured concrete in for the basement walls and floor. When the new basement was done, they lowered the building back down. Next they removed one external wall of the whole house, and replaced it with a new one; then they did the same thing with the other external walls, one by one. Then they removed the whole roof and built a new roof in its place. Afterwards, they worked on replacing all the interior walls and floors.

Toward the end of this process, I was passing the building and noticed a man on the construction site wearing a hard hat, suit, and tie. Guessing that he was the construction foreman or supervising engineer or architect, I went up to him and introduced myself as a philosophy professor who worked next door. He was in fact the architect, so I told him that I had been watching the construction process and I was puzzled. It appeared that everything in the old building had been replaced, piece by piece. Wouldn't it have been much

---

1   Douglas Adams and Mark Carwardine, *Last Chance to See*, p. 141.

cheaper just to demolish the old building all at once, and then build the new one in the usual way? The architect agreed: the method of construction they were using cost much more than the usual method. The reason they were doing it the way they were, he explained, was that the building violated the zoning laws: it was contiguous to the sidewalk, while the zoning laws required some setback, and it occupied too large a proportion of the lot it was on. So if they tore down the old building, they wouldn't be allowed to build a new building with the same footprint and in the same position. But the zoning laws did not prohibit renovations to an old building which had been built before those laws were introduced. When they jacked up the old building and gave it a new basement, they were merely renovating the old building. Replacing an external wall was, similarly, just renovation. And so on, until every molecule was replaced. So what they had here, now, was actually not a new building at all—it was the old building, completely renovated, and completely legal.

I complimented the architect on the ingenious solution to the zoning problems, and told him that, as a philosopher, I studied the sort of reasoning that he had used in reaching his solution. We both agreed that this was a welcome practical application of normally useless metaphysics.

Puzzling Rivers in Klopstokia

HERE, AT NO EXTRA charge, is a bonus to readers of this book: a handy map of southern Klopstokia:

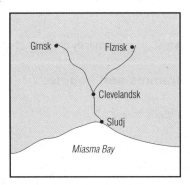

In this map, we see the southern portion of Klopstokia, showing the river system emptying into the bay in the south, and the four major cities in the area.

One of the major causes of the recent Klopstokian Civil War has been the disagreement between the two ethnic factions in the country concerning the river system. The Ethnic Freedonians, who live mainly in the west, insist that the Freedonia River, which rises at Grnsk, flows all the way into Miasma Bay in the south, and that the shorter Sylvania River, which rises at Flznsk, is a tributary of the Freedonia, ending where it flows into the Freedonia at Clevelandsk. So Sludj and Grnsk are on the same river but Flznsk and Sludj are not. But the Ethnic Sylvanians, who live mainly in the east, are adamant that the mighty Sylvania River, which rises at Flznsk, flows all the way into Miasma Bay in the south, and that the shorter Freedonia River, which rises at Grnsk, is a tributary of the Sylvania, ending where it flows into the Sylvania at Clevelandsk. So Sludj and Flznsk are on the same river, but Grnsk and Sludj are not.

As a result of this dispute, Clevelandsk has been reduced to rubble in continual shelling by both sides.

The US Ambassador, in an attempt to mediate the situation, proposes a compromise solution: that the Freedonia River rises at Grnsk and ends at Clevelandsk; that the Sylvania River rises at Flznsk and ends at Clevelandsk; that a third river, the Miasma River, is formed from the waters of the two tributaries at Clevelandsk, and flows from there to the bay. So Sludj is not on the same river as Grnsk, nor is it on the same river as Flznsk.

But the Russian Ambassador proposes a different solution: that the whole river system is the Miasma River: its West Branch rises at Grnsk, and its East Branch at Flznsk. So Sludj, Clevelandsk, Grnsk, and Flznsk are all on the same river.

The Russians argue with the Americans, and both argue with the two Klopstokian factions, about how many rivers there are, and where they start and end, and whether two cities are on the same river. Who is right?

There are no facts of the matter. It's all merely a matter of what people want to say.

4. The Identity of Animals and People

My Organism Is Bigger than Yours

WHAT'S THE BIGGEST ORGANISM on Earth? African elephants are big. The largest on record measured 10.6 metres trunk to tail, and weighed a little over six tonnes. But blue whales can grow to 40 metres long, 172 tonnes. Some dinosaurs, it's thought, might have been longer (but did not weigh more). So to answer this question, in addition to finding out the facts, we also have to decide what 'biggest' means—weight? length? or maybe volume?

But plants are organisms. Consider General Sherman,[1] the largest giant

---

1   How do they know what its name is?

sequoia in California. It's 84 metres high, with an estimated weight of 2,100 tonnes. Is this the champion?

Maybe it's beaten by the aspen tree. Individual aspens are only average in size. New trees typically grow from underground roots sent out from another tree. The result can be a large grove of aspens, connected to one another underground. Should we count this as one organism, composed of an underground root system and numerous stems? If so, there's one of these in Utah that's bigger than General Sherman. It covers almost half a square kilometre and has an estimated weight of 6,000 tonnes.

But if this counts as a single organism, then this may be the champion in terms of weight, but it may not be the largest in dimensions. That prize may have to go to a lowly mushroom. No, the champion mushroom is not a bulbous white spongy thing a kilometre high. What you buy in the super-market is just the "fruiting body" of the mushroom—the thing that spreads its spores. The rest of the mushroom is a large bunch of thin filaments underground; as in the case of the aspen, these can spread over a large area. They've discovered a mass of honey mushrooms in eastern Oregon that covers almost nine square kilometres (though it's estimated to weigh a mere 605 tonnes).[1]

But how do they know that the whole mass is actually interconnect-ed? They don't. What they do know (from genetic information) is that it originated from a single individual, but maybe it's not still all connected underground.

But even if it isn't, some scientists are still inclined to treat this thing as one organism. Why do you have to think of a single organism as having all its parts connected to one another, they ask.

That's a good question. It's clear that how you're going to count things—as one organism or many—is a decision, not a discovery. Are there any good reasons to count things one way rather than the other?

Rover and Clover

SHOCKING EXPERIMENTS HAVE BEEN performed in the biological labora-tory of the terrifying Dr. Frank Northrup Stein. In one experiment, Dr. Stein drastically altered the genetic structure of all the chromosomes in the body of a live dog, so that the result was nothing like a dog's genetic structure. In

---

1   Unlike some other stories (e.g., the one that follows this item), this one is true. Numerous websites give more information about this giant mushroom. One importantly includes a poem (by Lorna Dee Cervantes) in its honour ("... New beginnings in your tethered spore, / Gross acres of weight, tons of semi-shifting spit / United in a song of musky shore ..."). See Brian Campbell, "The Largest Single Organism on Earth."

the process, all Rover's cells were kept alive, but they were disassembled into a formless pile that Dr. Stein calls "Clover."

Dr. Stein's associate, the insidious Dr. F.M. Chu, was away on vacation while this experiment was being performed. When he returned, he asked Dr. Stein where Rover was. "That disgusting pile of cells over there is Rover," replied Stein. "I've renamed him Clover."

Having examined Clover, Dr. Chu said, "That's not Rover. Rover was a dog, but Clover isn't. Clover doesn't have the bodily organization of a dog, or its genetic structure."

"Clover is too Rover," insisted Stein. "I've just made some changes in him. Remember when we administered growth hormone to Fido, and made him grow to twice the size in a few weeks? What resulted was still Fido, though he was a lot larger. And how about Spot? After we administered potassium felinate to him for a month, he turned into something that looked exactly like a cat, but it was still old Spot. All we did was to change Fido's and Spot's characteristics; even if you wouldn't guess by looking at them, they were still Fido and Spot."

"No, you're wrong, Frank," said Chu. "When you make some kinds of changes to the material that makes something up, sometimes the original thing doesn't exist any more. Remember when you got so mad at Dr. Karloff that you chopped up Greta, his Mercedes? That was a drastic reorganization of the materials that made up Greta, and the pile of rusty metal that's still out there in the parking lot isn't a car. So you can't say that that pile of metal is Greta. Greta hasn't just been changed—it's been destroyed. It doesn't exist any longer. If you just drilled some holes in Greta, or painted it purple, it would still be a car. Then Greta would still exist, with changes. If you change an X so that what's left isn't an X any more, the original X has been destroyed, not just altered."

"But, look, Chu," Stein replied, "I didn't destroy Rover. You know all that trouble we got into last year with the Animal Liberation Front after our Great Parakeet Massacre? Well, I'm being careful now. Nothing died during my Rover experiment. Clover is pretty weird, but he's alive. My techniques for altering genetic structure don't kill the animal. I can keep it alive even when it's a formless pile of cells. Rover didn't die, and Clover is alive. I've just renamed him. I can't have destroyed Rover if Rover didn't die."

But Chu wasn't convinced. "Rover doesn't exist any more, so he's been destroyed. I guess that what your experiment has really shown is that there are other ways of destroying a dog besides killing it."

Who is right? Again, we seem to have a decision rather than a discovery. Again, we might ask why decide one way rather than the other.

SOME QUESTIONS TO THINK ABOUT: In the examples we've just been looking at, the suggestion was made that there are really no facts about identity, no real objective answers about whether X is the same as Y—it's just an arbitrary or conventional matter, one that we decide, rather than discover. Do you think this conventionalism about identity is right, for those cases? It's sometimes argued that this sort of conventionalism about identity is the right approach for all cases: that it's not a matter of fact, but rather up to us to decide, for example, whether the keys you left on the chest of drawers last night are the same ones you picked up this morning. Does that seem right? We'll look at some more peculiar cases of identity: see how conventionalism works there.

FOR FURTHER READING: The Rover/Clover example is adapted from M. Price, "Identity through Time." Price argues that Rover is Clover. This conclusion is disputed by Baruch A. Brody in Chapter 4 of *Identity and Essence*.

The Adventures of Amoeba-Man

ONE DAY, SEYMOUR SCHMIDLAP develops a groove running across the top of his head. Over the succeeding weeks, the groove deepens, and runs down his forehead and nose, and down his back. Medical science is puzzled. At last it is clear what is happening: Seymour is dividing in two, like an amoeba. As the two halves of his body separate more distinctly, each half begins growing back the other half it's missing. Soon the guy looks like a pair of Siamese twins; but then there's complete separation, and each half, having grown everything it's missing, walks off in a different direction—a complete person.

Each of them—call them Seymour-1 and Seymour-2—claims that he's Seymour Schmidlap. Each denies that the other is the real Seymour. Who is right?

Here are four possible answers that might tempt you:

1. Seymour-1 is the real Seymour Schmidlap. Seymour-2 is just a look-alike, created at the time of the split. (Nobody—not even either of the Seymours—can tell that Seymour-1 is the real Seymour, since Seymour-2 has just as good a claim. But he is—that's just the fact of the matter.)

2. Seymour-2 is the real Seymour Schmidlap. Seymour-1 is just a look-alike, created at the time of the split. (Nobody—not even either of the Seymours—can tell that

Seymour-2 is the real Seymour, since Seymour-1 has just as good a claim. But he is—that's just the fact of the matter.)

3. They're both wrong. The real Seymour Schmidlap has been destroyed. Both Seymour-1 and Seymour-2 are like the real one, but neither is him. Both were created at the time of the split.

4. They're both the real Seymour. Seymour Schmidlap now exists simultaneously in two different places.

Each answer has something to be said for it, and something against. But consider the Klopstokian River problem as an analogy to this one. What reaction to the Seymour problem does that suggest?

It suggests that there are no facts of the matter. It's just up to us to decide what we feel like saying about it.

A QUESTION TO THINK ABOUT: But now imagine that all this happened to you. Don't you think that there would be a right answer to where, if anywhere, you ended up?

Getting Someone Else's Body

SUPPOSE THAT A NUMBER of lineworkers employed by an electric company have had accidents when live wires fall on them. Their protective clothing keeps them from being fatally electrocuted, but they do sometimes suffer total amnesia. To protect their workers from this disaster, the company buys a craniorecorder. This machine consists of a little metal hat connected by wires to a huge computer. The hat gets strapped on your head, and the computer reads out and records all the patterns set up in your brain. The machine can also reprogram brains in accord with the stored information. Each morning each worker's brain contents are recorded; if they suffer amnesia, their old memories are restored by the machine.

One day, a live wire falls on Harry and Hortense, and both of them suffer amnesia. Each is attached to the craniorecorder for memory restoration, but the technician programs the machine wrongly, and Hortense's old memories go into Harry's body, and Harry's into Hortense's body. When both wake up, they are deeply surprised to look in the mirror and see bodies of the opposite sex from the one they are used to. The craniorecorder technician tries to get them back into the machine to set things right, but both refuse. Harry, it turns out, has always yearned to be able to swim really well. Hortense used to be a champion swimmer, and her body is perfectly trained for this.

Similarly, Harry's body is that of a trained boxer, and Hortense has always wanted to be able to box. Besides, they both get kinky pleasure out of inhabiting the body of the opposite sex.

Are you convinced by this fable that what has taken place is a body transplant: that Harry has now been given Hortense's body? Consider the physical item that was Hortense's body before the accident. Is it now inhabited by Harry? Or should we say it's still Hortense, but it has been mistakenly programmed with Harry's memories and personality? Whoever is now in that body thinks that he/she is Harry, but is that person correct? To which body should Harry's paycheque be issued?

If you are convinced that memories make the person, and that Harry now inhabits Hortense's body, consider this amended fable: imagine that one morning Arnold, Mildred, and Francine have their brain-patterns recorded; but the craniorecorder technician hates all these people, and he maliciously reprograms Mildred's *and* Francine's brain with Arnold's patterns, and reprograms Arnold's brain with Mildred's patterns. Then he erases all the recordings. On awakening, Mildred's former body and Francine's former body both claim to be Arnold. Both have equal claim to be Arnold. Should we say that they are both Arnold? But doesn't that make them the same person—namely Arnold? What happens after one body skips lunch while the other one eats: is Arnold then both hungry and not hungry? Should Arnold's two new bodies split Arnold's paycheque? Are they both married to Arnold's wife? What happened to Francine? Should the technician be charged with Francine's murder?

Keeping Your Own Body

If you were convinced in the previous section (**Getting Someone Else's Body**) that we should say that Harry is transplanted into Hortense's body, consider the following.

Suppose Harry is told, one day, that a live wire will fall on him tomorrow. He's understandably horrified; a terribly painful thing is about to happen to him. Now, suppose additional information is supplied: he will, in addition to the pain, suffer total amnesia as a result. Now his horror grows: not only pain, but amnesia! But there is more information: Hortense's memories will be implanted in the brain of his current body. Still more anguish! Harry doesn't want to get this whole pile of fake memories. He'd rather have no memories at all than be in the even worse state of getting all those bogus memories. But this is not the end of the story: in addition, Harry is told, his old memories will be stuck into Hortense's body. This makes things still worse. Harry cries: "They're *my* memories! I'm really fond of many of them. I don't even like Hortense! I don't want her to get them!"

This might seem to be a reasonable attitude to have. But note that Harry is identifying his future self as the one that will occupy his body. If the interpretation we gave to the fable above is correct, Harry is wrong. Do you think he's wrong?

FOR FURTHER READING: For a discussion of a thought-experiment similar to the Harry/Hortense story, see Bernard Williams, "The Self and the Future." The theory that memories make for personal identity was perhaps first stated by John Locke in his *Essay Concerning Human Understanding*, Chapter 27. Since then many philosophers have endorsed, modified, or at least discussed this view. The Perry anthology *Personal Identity* contains several relevant articles and excerpts.

Fusco Brothers ©1990 J.C. Duffy. Used by permission of Universal Uclick. All rights reserved.

Be yourself; everyone else is already taken.—Oscar Wilde

"I wonder if I've been changed in the night? Let me think. Was I the same when I got up this morning? I almost think I can remember feeling a little different. But if I'm not the same, the next question is 'Who in the world am I?' Ah, that's the great puzzle!"—*Alice in Wonderland*

It seems obvious to many people that they can tell the facts about their own identity: that they have a continuing person, and they can identify who they were yesterday. But David Hume argues that there isn't anything you notice, from moment to moment, that stays the same, and allows you to identify yourself as the continuing me.[1] Is *that* right?

Two Places Are Better than One

IT IS SAID THAT medieval popes granted some of their bishops the gift of *bilocation*—the ability to be in two different places at the same time. F.P. Siegfried, writing in *The Catholic Encyclopedia,* says that the issue is

---

1 *A Treatise of Human Nature*, Section 1.4.6

controversial, but Scotus, Bellarmine, Suarez, DeLugo, Franzelin, and many others defend the possibility of bilocation, and there are plenty of instances of it attested to in Christian history.

What's interesting about bilocation for our purposes is how it might—or might not—be consistent with the criteria for human identity: if there were simultaneous appearances at two different places, that looked for all the world like St. Fred, could we possibly count both of them as him?

What's also interesting is that intelligent medieval thinkers could believe in such a bizarre phenomenon. We've already talked about how the medievals managed to hold a similar crazy belief: see **Believing in Angels** in Chapter X.

Belief in bilocation is not limited to medieval times. A web page devoted to Padre Pio, a twentieth-century mystic, affirms:

> The phenomenon of bilocation is one of the most remarkable gifts attributed to Padre Pio. His appearances on various of the continents are attested by numerous eyewitnesses, who either saw him or smelled the odors characteristically associated with his presence, described by some as roses and by others as tobacco. The phenomenon of odor (sometimes called the odor of sanctity) is itself well established in Padre Pio's case. The odor was especially strong from the blood coming from his wounds. Investigation showed that he used absolutely no fragrances or anything that could produce these odors. The odors often occurred when people called upon his intercession in prayer and continue to this day....
>
> As to how Padre Pio with God's help accomplished such feats, the closest he ever came to an explanation of bilocation was to say that it occurred "by an extension of his personality."[1]

What It Takes to Be in Heaven

MOST RELIGIONS DON'T BELIEVE people take their bodies to heaven.

In Christian lore, there are a few exceptions, one of whom is the Virgin Mary. According to the Doctrine of the Bodily Assumption of the Virgin, when she died her body was taken to heaven along with her soul. In certain paintings you can see her flying up into the air like a guided missile.

---

1   See the website "Padre Pio the Mystic."

When ordinary humans die, however, their bodies remain on Earth, turning rapidly into something unpleasant.

Without a body your existence would be rather different. It's hard to see how you could continue to ice skate, play the piano, or read the newspaper in heaven, when you have no feet, hands, or eyes. In at least its more sophisticated versions, Christianity generally holds that our activities in heaven would be of a more rarefied form, involving activities such as enjoyment of the full consciousness of God's presence. For this sort of thing, presumably, you wouldn't need a body.

The problem here is this: on what grounds could it be said that *you* were in heaven? If something existed in heaven after your death, why think that it's *you*?

We found it plausible to identify the same thing through time, in the case of Descartes's lump of wax, by means of spatio-temporal continuity. But this doesn't seem to work when somebody "goes" to heaven. Although heaven was considered to be a place, at least by early Christians and nowadays by children in Sunday school, more sophisticated contemporary Christians think differently. And even if it were a place, then how could we trace the path of a non-material soul through space as it went there, to make sure that we're still locating the same person? But maybe persons resemble universities rather than lumps of wax: their continued existence does not require spatio-temporal continuity.

On one view, as we've seen, what makes somebody the *same person* as one identified earlier is that the later person remembers experiences the earlier one had. If this is the criterion for personal identity through time, then in order for that person to be *you* in heaven, that person must remember your experiences on Earth. At least according to our current scientific views, memory is stored in the physical brain. It's difficult to see how memories can be carried to heaven when you leave your brain behind. But, of course, science doesn't know everything. This is another one of those religious mysteries about which science must be mute.

But even supposing that the memories physically encoded in your present brain could somehow be transferred into your heavenly person, there is a further difficulty: would you even have a *mind* in heaven, capable of retrieving those stored memories and of thinking about your past? Could you do any sort of mental activity in heaven? Could you even enjoy the full consciousness of God's presence? Science tells us that any sort of mental activity depends on a working brain; once again, we have a religious mystery beyond our ken.

However, not everyone shares the view that memory continuity is what constitutes the continued existence of a person. In some religious belief, the soul that is supposed to be immortal isn't a mind, but something else. It's the thing that makes a person the same person from moment to moment, and that continues after bodily death. So that will be *you* in heaven, although you will have neither mind nor body. This view is very much like Descartes's account of what accounts for the continuing identity of the lump of wax, and it is equally hard to understand or apply.

It's dangerous to claim that you believe in something about which you have so little understanding. The danger is that your thoughts are so incoherent and mysterious that you don't really believe anything at all. In all of this, we must be very careful that we are not merely talking nonsense.

5. Identity and Essence

What Makes You You

HERE'S A THIRD IMPORTANT way that the word *identity* shows up in philosophy. In this sense, we don't talk about two things being identical with each other (or of one thing being "identical" with that same thing at another time), but rather of the identity of a single thing at a single time. This is the sense of the word you're using when you think about your "identity"—what makes you *you*.

One way of thinking about this kind of identity is that some sort of characteristic is so important to something that if it lost that characteristic it would cease to exist.

Here's an example. Consider a statue of Elvis made out of bronze. Over time, the statue will turn from shiny metallic to dull brown to cruddy greenish, as it oxidizes and gets pooped on by the pigeons. But it will still exist—it will just be a different colour. But imagine that one day someone who (if such a thing is possible!) doesn't like Elvis smashes that statue to bits, or runs it through a car crusher, or melts it down and pours the bronze into a different-shaped mould, so that when it hardens it's a statue of Dmitri Shostakovich (Soviet composer, 1906–75). In any of these cases, we'd say that the statue was destroyed. So it seems that a drastic change of shape of the material constitutes the destruction of the statue, whereas the statue survives a drastic change of colour.

This sort of characteristic—which is so important to something that changing it constitutes the destruction of the thing—is often called by philosophers an *essential* characteristic. The contrast is called an *accidental* characteristic; the thing survives a change here. The shape of a statue is essential, but the colour is not.

What Makes Us Us

YOU MIGHT BE REMINDED here of the talk of "identity" that goes on a good deal in political and moral contexts nowadays. It's sometimes claimed that features of the culture of various ethnic minorities are so important to them that they constitute those people's identity. For example, the language of an ethnic group is often supposed to be part of the identity of the people in that group, and that wiping out that language is actually a form of genocide, because this and other aspects of their culture are parts of the "identity" of the individual people.

But let's be careful here. People who talk this way do not mean that the language of a minority group is so important to that group that an individual would literally cease to exist if deprived of the use of the language (in the way that the Elvis statue literally ceases to exist when deprived of its shape). When the Irish language was almost wiped out in Ireland by the colonial English, for example, this didn't constitute the extermination of any Irish people. Those people continued to exist even when they were forced to learn and speak English.

Notoriously, it was the aim of the mainstream European-origin culture in Canada up until a few decades ago to wipe out every aspect of aboriginal culture. They weren't quite successful, but imagine that they were, and that the Canadian aboriginal people had been thoroughly assimilated into the mainstream culture. What would have happened, then, would be that the Mi'kmaq people of Nova Scotia would have ceased to exist as a group, though this needn't have involved the ceasing to exist of any Mi'kmaq individuals.

A QUESTION TO THINK ABOUT: Do you find it paradoxical that a group of things (or people) can cease to exist even though all the things (or people) in that group continue to exist? This sort of phenomenon is quite ordinary. Consider the group of people (Aaron, Betty, Carl, Debby, etc.) who constitute the group of students of the South Carolina Academy of Theology. When SCAT closes down, Aaron, Betty, Carl, Debby, etc. transfer to other institutions. There are no longer any students of SCAT—that group has ceased to exist. But Aaron, Betty, Carl, Debby, etc., continue to exist, and the group seems to consist of nothing but the individuals that constitute it. How can it disappear when those individuals still exist? When it disappears, what exactly goes missing from the universe?

Into the Mainstream of Philosophy

PHILOSOPHERS HAVE NOTED THAT certain words in our language—*here*, *now*, and *I*, for example—function peculiarly in that they work, as it were, by pointing at something, not by naming or describing it. That's why they vary systematically in what is indicated in ways that other bits of the language do not. The name Fred Schmidlap, for example, refers to the same guy no matter who says it or when; but *I* refers to a large number of people, and depends on who utters the word. Problems result from this difference when we try to explain what somebody knows in terms of the sentence that expresses that person's belief. There's a definite external fact that I know about when I believe the belief expressed by the sentence, 'Fred Schmidlap is at Sturdley's Pub.' But what do I know when I know what's expressed by the sentence, 'I am here now'? This problem is revealed when we consider what's communicated—if anything—by saying that sentence to somebody else. Notice that what *you* know (if anything) might be quite a different matter from what you tell somebody else when you say this.

I am, unfortunately, unaware of any appropriate introductory readings you might consult to pursue these puzzling matters. The stout of heart might attempt to read Simon Blackburn's *Spreading the Word*. He gets into these matters at the end of a book that goes quite deeply into matters in Philosophy of Language.

Appropriate readings giving more puzzles and considering several proposed solutions concerning matters of identity are easier to come by. I can strongly recommend John Perry's *A Dialogue on Personal Identity and Immortality*; this is an easy and informal discussion, in dialogue form, about many of the issues discussed in this chapter. Perry's anthology, *Personal Identity*, contains a wide selection of articles by many philosophers dealing with personal identity at an appropriate level.

The Canadian philosopher Will Kymlicka has written thoughtfully and interestingly on the ethical issues of the kind of "identity" talked about at the end of this chapter.

Chapter XII

Why Should I Be Moral?

1. What's in It for Me?

Change for a Dollar

IN EVERYDAY LIFE, MOST of us do what's morally right, mostly without thinking too much about it. Acting morally often has its costs, however, and sometimes we are tempted to act in our self-interest instead.

I posed this question to some students I once had in a class: "Suppose a stranger asked you if you have change for a dollar. You might need change to make a phone call or something, so there's a risk you'd be depriving yourself of what you needed. Should you do it?" My students replied that they thought they should. "Why?" I asked. Here are some replies. Do you agree with them?

> "Some day I might need a favour from her. If I changed a dollar for her, she'd be more likely to help me out when I needed it. If I didn't, she'd feel less kindly toward me, and wouldn't help me out later."

"Well," I continued, "suppose you'll never run into that person again. Should you help her then?"

> "Yeah, but how can you be sure you'll never see her again? Maybe you will, right?"

They refused to let me raise the question the way I wanted to. Teaching philosophy is sometimes a difficult thing. I said, "Look, suppose you're absolutely sure, for some reason, that you'll really never see her again. Like maybe you're in an airport in a distant city about to leave, and you're sure you'll never go back to that city again. What would you do then?"

They saw the problem. There was a widespread look of puzzlement. One replied:

"I never exactly realized this before, but now that you put the matter that way, I can see that there's no reason to help her. I wouldn't do it."

Further discussion did not succeed in convincing this student to do it; I think I may have succeeded in turning a perfectly nice person into a nasty selfish creep. Another triumph for philosophical education!

A QUESTION TO THINK ABOUT: Why, after all, should you be moral, if there isn't anything in it for you?

The Ring of Gyges

PLATO RAISES THE PROBLEM we have just noticed by telling another imaginary tale, known as the fable of the ring of Gyges. Glaucon, a character in Plato's *Republic*, tells the story: Gyges discovers a magic ring that turns the wearer invisible. Even the most firmly just of men, Glaucon argues, would act immorally if he possessed such a ring:

> No man is so adamantine-souled that he would go on being just and keep his hands off other men's things, if he were free to take whatever he desired, go into any store or house, get into any bed, put anyone to death, or let anyone out of prison as the idea came to him.... And this makes it clear that no one is willingly just. They are only forced to be just. For every man, if he is able to do wrong, does wrong. For he sees that to do wrong will profit him more than to do right....

> You might be interested to know what Gyges does with the aid of his ring. He arrives in court, makes himself invisible, seduces the queen, and with her help kills the king and takes over the kingdom. What's remarkable about this is *the queen's* behaviour: having been seduced by an invisible man, she conspires with him, presumably while he is still invisible, to kill her husband and to give this invisible man the kingdom.

Rationality

RATIONALITY SOUNDS LIKE A good thing, right? Well, what is it, exactly, for an action to be rational? One possible answer is that your action is rational when you do it because there's something in it for you. Irrational actions, by contrast, are done despite being bad for you (for example, you know that if you keep on drinking, you'll feel awful all day tomorrow, and it won't be worth it; but you do it anyway). And in some cases (which we might call *arational*) there are no considerations either way. Some arational actions are clearly okay: suppose you can walk to school by two routes, with neither being preferable to the other in any way; you just pick one, though there's nothing in it for you, compared to the alternative.

But on this way of looking at it, it seems that giving that stranger change for her dollar, in the case above, is irrational. Maybe acting morally (which seems never to be acting for one's self-interest) is always irrational.

SOME QUESTIONS TO THINK ABOUT: Is rationality a good thing? Is it always a bad thing to act irrationally? Is self-interested action alone rational? Is moral action ultimately self-interested? Is moral action rational? Is moral action a good thing? (Is that last question empty, answerable simply by saying, "Of course! It's morally good!")

FOR FURTHER READING: Plato tells the Gyges story in *Republic*, Book II: The translation I've given here is the Cambridge University Press version by I.A. Richards (1966). Plato argues (through his spokesman in the book, Socrates) that ultimately it's not to one's advantage to act immorally, even if one can get away with it.

"Conscience is the inner voice that warns us somebody is looking."— H.L. Mencken

2. Relativism and Realism

Finger-Lickin' Good and Evil

IT'S THE CUSTOM IN many cultures to eat not with metal implements or chopsticks, but with the fingers of your right hand. But licking your fingers is either sternly forbidden or allowed only if certain restrictive rules are followed. In Morocco around 1905, it's reported, diners were allowed to lick their fingers, but only in this order: little finger, then, middle finger, then thumb, then ring finger, then index finger.[1]

Have a look at what you take to be good table manners and bad, and see if your own culture's rules and prohibitions are not equally as arbitrary and pointless.

---

1   Reported in a wonderful book by Margaret Visser, *The Rituals of Dinner*, p. 176. Visser attributes this information to B. Meakin, *Life in Morocco*, Chapter 11.

Then have a look at what you think is acceptable and unacceptable behaviour in general. How much of this is also arbitrary and pointless?

It's All Relative

HISTORY IS FILLED WITH stories of a dominant colonial power requiring the colonized people to give up their own culture; but this is now often thought to be a bad thing. We should respect other people's culture, and that means respecting their values, including their ethical values; it means we should never force them to act according to our values. Respect for other cultures' values might even mean counting them as just as valid as our own culture's. They've got their values, and we have ours, and that's all there is to it. There's no fact of the matter—no correct or incorrect—it's just a matter of how your culture feels about things.

This position is called moral relativism. It holds that moral standards are not absolute, not objective facts; instead they're just cultural artefacts that vary from culture to culture, with no "correct" or "incorrect."

If all that sounds right to you, then you'll fit in well in many academic circles, where this moral relativism is popular.

But are you really a moral relativist? Do you actually think that it's impermissible to criticize customs valued by other cultures? Here's a sample of some of those customs—how they prefer to deal with women in some other societies:

- Female fetuses are selectively aborted.
- Newborn girls are killed.
- Daughters are malnourished and kept from school.
- Adolescent girls have their genitals surgically mutilated; this "female circumcision" is designed to prevent them from ever having sexual pleasure, and to assure their husbands of their faithfulness.
- Young women are cloaked from head to toe.
- Adulteresses are stoned to death.
- Widows are expected to fall into their husbands' funeral pyres.[1]

SOME QUESTIONS TO THINK ABOUT: Let's distinguish two questions: (1) Is it okay to force your values on another culture? (2) Is there really no question of correct or incorrect when it comes to values? But there's a connection between how you answer these two. Suppose you think that some cultures

---

1   This list is presented by Steven Pinker, in his book *The Blank Slate*, p. 172. Pinker's aim is to show that relativism does not serve feminism.

clearly have badly incorrect—immoral—values (like those listed just above). But then how can you tolerate their actions, which you count as evil? If you could force another culture to stop treating women that way, for example, shouldn't you do it?

Can Ethics Be Taught?

THIS QUESTION IS AS old as philosophy. Socrates worried about it; in Plato's *Meno* (96c), he says that, on the one hand, it seems that virtue must be a kind of wisdom, so it should be teachable. But on the other, if it could be taught, we should be able to identify those who can teach it; but those who claim to be able to do that, in fact cannot. But Plato elsewhere argues that education in virtue is possible.

SOME QUESTIONS TO THINK ABOUT: Would learning virtue be like learning history? Involving, that is, the memorization of a large bunch of facts, and having some overall picture that unifies them? The big questions here are the following: Are there ethical facts? And, if there are, is knowledge of them sufficient to produce ethical behaviour?

The Gurgling Wave

CLIFFORD ORWIN, A PROFESSOR at the University of Toronto, writes:

> Ethics is a serious business. And that's why, reading in last weekend's *Globe and Mail* about the gurgling wave of ethics education sweeping North American business schools, I had to laugh.... The whole notion of teaching ethical behaviour rests on a fundamental misconception—namely, that ethical behaviour can be taught.
>
> This year, I'm teaching 500 students about justice, and I'm not making a single one of them a better person. Those who already aspire to justice may refine their understanding of what it is.... Those already minded to be good citizens may become more thoughtful ones.... Doctors, lawyers and businessmen, too, should be informed of what is forbidden to practitioners of their respective professions. But to inform ... students of what qualifies as ethical is one thing. To make them more ethical is quite another. Does anyone really think there's one fewer crooked lawyer or cheating doctor in the world because of law school or med school ethics courses?[1]

---

1 "Can we teach ethics? When pigs fly."

"But knowing right from wrong is the easy part. Knowing is not the problem."—Garrison Keillor, *Lake Wobegon Days*

Edward Skidelsky writes from another perspective, bemoaning the disappearance of ethical education and the growth of relativism:

> No words are more typical of our moral culture than "inappropriate" and "unacceptable." They seem bland, gentle even, yet they carry the full force of official power. When you hear them, you feel that you are being tied up with little pieces of soft string.
>
> *Inappropriate* and *unacceptable* began their modern careers in the 1980s as part of the jargon of political correctness. They have more or less replaced a number of older, more exact terms: *coarse, tactless, vulgar, lewd*.... This linguistic shift is revealing. Improper and indecent express moral judgements, whereas inappropriate and unacceptable suggest breaches of some purely social or professional convention.... What was once an offence against decency must be recast as something akin to a faux pas.... "Inappropriate" and "unacceptable" are the catchwords of a moralism that dare not speak its name. They hide all measure of righteous fury behind the mask of bureaucratic neutrality. For the sake of our own humanity, we should strike them from our vocabulary.[1]

When God Tells You to Do Evil

SOME PEOPLE THINK THAT the source of moral truth is God's will. Many philosophers (including believers) have argued that this is wrong—that to say that something is good because God desires it has things backwards. It's not good because God desires it: God desires it because it's good. So it's still an open question what makes something good.

Here's a picturesque way of putting this argument. Suppose suddenly one day angelic forms appear among the clouds, playing trumpets. The sky splits down the middle, with lightning and thunder. You hear a huge, deep voice. "This is God speaking," the voice says. "I have a message for you. You've been trying to be a good person, but you have it all wrong. My will is for you to murder, cheat, lie, steal, torture kittens, and throw your empty beer cans on your professor's lawn. Go and do it!"

No matter what fireworks accompanied this event, and no matter how huge and deep the voice was, you wouldn't believe that it was God. Why not? Because what the voice told you to do was so clearly wrong. It can't be God, because God wouldn't tell you to do bad things.

---

1   "Words that think for us: Beyond inappropriate."

Why didn't you decide, instead, that you were wrong about your morality? The story appears to show that, rather than reasoning that something is good if God says it, you *first* have an idea of what's good, *then* you judge on this basis whether something represents the will of God.

Biblical Guides to Conduct

IN ANY CASE, IF you want to take the Bible as a guide to ethical behaviour, you have to select pretty carefully from the models of conduct it gives. Here are some of the more unusual stories from the Old and New Testaments. See if you can extract the moral message from each:

- Elijah is teased about his bald head by a group of little children; he curses them in the name of the Lord, and instantly two bears come out of the woods and kill 42 of them. (4 Kings 2:23–24)

- Er is wicked, so God kills him. Then Er's father tells Er's brother Onan to have sex with Er's wife. Knowing that his sister-in-law's children will not be counted as his, Onan decides to pull out and "spill his seed upon the ground." God is so upset by this that he kills Onan too. (This story, Genesis 38:8–10, is the biblical basis for the Christian condemnation of masturbation and birth control.)

- A traveller and his concubine are staying at an inn. That evening a gang of men arrive demanding to have sex with the traveller, but the innkeeper refuses to bring him out, offering instead his own virgin daughter and the man's concubine. The traveller then gives his concubine to the gang, and they rape her all night. In the morning, the traveller finds his concubine's body on his doorstep, and thinks she's merely asleep; but when he discovers that she's dead, he cuts up her body into twelve pieces and sends a piece to each of the twelve tribes of Israel. (Judges 19:22–30)

- David is in love with King Saul's daughter, and he asks what he could do in exchange for Saul's permission to marry. Saul tells David to bring him 100 foreskins of his enemies, the Philistines, so David kills *200* of them, and gives their foreskins to Saul, who then allows the marriage. (1 Kings 18:25–27)

- God sends an angel to Moses to kill him because his son isn't circumcised. Moses' wife, understanding this, picks up a flint and immediately circumcises their son, casting the foreskin on the ground in front of Moses, and saying, "A bloody husband you are to me." (Exodus 4:24–26)

- Jesus is hungry and comes across a fig tree. Unfortunately it has no fruit on it, only leaves—it wasn't fig season—so Jesus puts a curse on the tree so that it would never bear figs again; and the tree withers and dies. (Matthew 21:19 and Mark 11:13–14)

Well, extracting the moral from stories always requires ingenious interpretation, and each of the above has generated plenty of that. But when, in the Bible, God gives his people explicit unambiguous rules to follow, it's sometimes even more of a challenge to extract a morally acceptable message. In Leviticus 20, God tells Moses that a list of sins including cursing your father or mother and committing adultery with another man's wife should be punished by death; and when a man has sex with his father's wife or with his daughter-in-law, or with another man, or with his wife and her mother, then *all* of the offending parties must be put to death. Exodus 21 requires the death penalty for some of these acts, plus striking your father and mother. (But it's curiously lenient about other acts: if you strike someone with a rock and they recover, you're liable only to compensate them for time lost; and if you strike a servant with a stick and the servant survives for a day or two, there's no punishment, because the servant is your property.) Deuteronomy 13 orders death for a prophet or fortune-teller urging worship of other gods; if your own brother, son, daughter, wife, or closest friend invites you to worship other gods, that person must be put to death by stoning. In a town where wicked men have led the people to the worship of other gods, everyone (and their livestock) must be killed, and the town burnt to the ground, never to be rebuilt.

Psalm 137 begins with some of the most beautiful and memorable lines in the bible. The Jewish psalmist sings of their captivity by the Babylonians:

By the rivers of Babylon, there we sat down, yea, we wept, when we remembered Zion.

We hanged our harps upon the willows in the midst thereof.

For there they that carried us away captive required of us a song; and they that wasted us required of us mirth, saying, Sing us one of the songs of Zion.

How shall we sing the LORD's song in a strange land?

If I forget thee, O Jerusalem, let my right hand forget her cunning.

If I do not remember thee, let my tongue cleave to the roof of my mouth; if I prefer not Jerusalem above my chief joy.

But then it finishes up:

Remember, O LORD, the children of Edom in the day of Jerusalem; who said, Rase it, rase it, even to the foundation thereof.

O daughter of Babylon, who art to be destroyed; happy shall he be, that rewardeth thee as thou hast served us.

Happy shall he be, that taketh and dasheth thy little ones against the stones.

"It ain't those parts of the Bible that I can't understand that bother me, it's the parts that I do understand."—Mark Twain[1]

SOME QUESTIONS TO THINK ABOUT: A lot of hardship in the world has arisen when one culture tries to force its rules on another. When one of them is dominant, the other one loses what it values. When there's strength on both sides, there's irresolvable war, cycles of resistance and revenge. It's not just the "primitive tribes" in the Bible that dash each other's little ones against the stones in defence of their own culture. A case can be made that the western nations' recent invasion of Afghanistan is the attempt of one tribe—us—to force its values on another.

Well, what's the alternative? Should we say that every tribe has its own values, and that it's always wrong for one to force one's values on others? But then how about *that* value? Suppose that one of their values is to force their values on us. (This is often the case—even now.) Are we justified in forcing them to adopt a more liberal tolerance?

Sometimes cultural differences are merely arbitrary—table manners, for example. But sometimes (we think) they're really matters of morality, not of etiquette. How they treat women, for example, in some other cultures strikes (most of) us as deeply immoral—something we shouldn't allow. Are we right to try to prevent this?

---

1   Quoted in Winokur, *The Portable Curmudgeon*, p. 32.

3. The Prisoner's Dilemma

A Deal for the Prisoners

SUPPOSE YOU AND AN accomplice have committed a crime. The police have evidence sufficient only to give each of you a two-year sentence; but they want to get at least one of you in jail for longer. If one of you confessed, giving evidence against the other, they could do this. So they put you in separate cells so the two of you can't communicate with each other, and then they come and talk to you in your cell. They offer you this deal: If neither of you confesses, you yourself will get two years; but if you confess and he doesn't, then you'll get only one year. If you confess and he does too, then you'll get three years. If you say nothing and he talks, then you'll get four years. This is all very confusing, so you construct the following table to clarify things:

	He confesses	He doesn't confess
I confess	I get 3 yrs. in jail	I get 1 yr. in jail
I don't confess	I get 4 yrs. in jail	I get 2 yrs. in jail

Inside the table are listed the four possible consequences for you, given your action and that of your accomplice.

The police also say that the same deal is being offered to your accomplice. You're only interested in minimizing your own sentence; you don't care how long your accomplice stays in jail. What should you do?

Consider this line of reasoning:

You don't know whether your accomplice will confess or not. Suppose he does. Then you'll get three years if you confess, and four if you say nothing. So if he confesses, you're better off confessing too.

Now, suppose he doesn't confess. Then you'll get one year if you confess, and two years if you say nothing. So if he doesn't confess, you'll be better off if you confess.

So whatever he does, you're better off if you confess. So you confess.

Your accomplice, in his cell, was given the same deal, and he draws the same table to clarify his thinking. He reasons exactly as you do, and he comes to the same conclusion. So he confesses too.

Both of you then get sentenced to three years in jail. But something has gone wrong here. Can you see what?

If neither of you confessed, both of you would get a two-year sentence, and each of you would be better off.

This is a somewhat paradoxical situation: each of you has reasoned correctly about what would serve your own self-interest best. But this has resulted in a fairly poor outcome for both of you. If both of you had said nothing, both of you would have been better off. But given the situation, how could either of you have arranged this?

> You might have made a deal with your accomplice that neither of you would confess. Suppose you were not isolated in separate cells, but that you were together and could communicate. So you promise each other that you will cooperate by saying nothing.

But then the police take you out of your joint cell and ask you what you want to do. Notice that the table above *still* describes your situation: even if he keeps his part of the deal and says nothing, you're better off if you confess. Why keep your promise? You'd be better off if you didn't. And when the police ask him, he realizes the same thing. You're right back in the same mess.

It's often thought that this situation represents, in miniature simplified form, a problem that is of central importance in ethics and political theory. Consider, for example, the ethical question whether it is wrong to tell a lie. It seems that there are many particular circumstances in which it would be to my advantage to lie to others, whether or not they choose to tell me the truth, and to their advantage to lie to me. Nevertheless, if we all told the truth, we would all be better off in the long run, because we could get to trust each other's words: we could rely on each other in ways that would bring us the benefits of social cooperation. Thus lying is analogous to confessing in the prisoner's dilemma. If we could make a deal to pick the "cooperative" solution (by telling the truth in this case, saying nothing in the prisoner's dilemma), then we'd all be better off. But the deal would have to stick; there's always the temptation to "defect" from this cooperative arrangement, for one's own self-interest. And the situation is made more complicated, however, by the facts that (1) we could get away with a few lies without interfering significantly with the general trust; and (2) sometimes a bit of lying really would make things better, even in the long run ("You look great in that new dress!").

SOME QUESTIONS TO THINK ABOUT: In real life, what mechanisms do we use to arrive at such social "deals"? How do we get them (by and large) to stick? Might this line of thought provide an answer to Glaucon?

The Tragedy of the Commons

SUPPOSE THAT OUR CITY has a publicly owned grassy area of land in its centre. We all like having this grassy expanse in the middle of the concrete jungle. There are sidewalks built through the grassy commons, but when we're in a hurry we could get across the commons a lot faster by walking across the grass. You're just about to cut across the grass, and I stop you to try to convince you not to. Here is a transcript of our conversation.

> *Me:* Don't do that!
>
> *You:* Why not?
>
> *Me:* We all like that grass there, and walking across it will kill it.
>
> *You:* I like that grass as much as you do. But it takes a lot of walking across grass to kill it. If I walk across the grass right now, the resulting damage will be absolutely unnoticeable. It wouldn't even make a difference if I walked across it every time I was in a hurry. Grass is stronger than that.
>
> *Me:* Well, that's true. But what if everybody reasoned as you do? Then everyone would walk across the grass, and it would be dead, and we'd all be much worse off.
>
> *You:* Look, I agree that if everybody walked across the grass, then the grass would certainly be dead. But then it would hardly matter what I did, would it? Anyway, we're just talking about *me*. I don't want *everyone* to walk across the grass, but what I do won't *make* everyone else do it.

Is there something wrong with this reasoning?

> The Tragedy of the Commons[1] is that if this line of reasoning is correct for you (as it seems to be), then it is correct for everyone else in town. As a result, everyone reasons this way, everyone walks across the grass, and it dies.

A QUESTION TO THINK ABOUT: Do you see why this is another illustration in the general form of the Prisoner's Dilemma?

---

[1]   This name is due to Garrett Hardin, "The Tragedy of the Commons." In Hardin's story, if each herdsman seeks to maximize his own advantage by adding animals to his herd, the common grazing land will become overgrazed, and they'll all lose.

Coca-Cola Morality

"WHAT IF EVERYONE DID that?" This is the question that is often supposed to be the key to moral reasoning. You can see now why the question is relevant. We can all solve our Prisoner's Dilemmas and prevent outcomes like the Tragedy of the Commons by acting in a way such that we'd all be better off if everyone acted that way, and by refraining from actions that would have bad results if everyone did them.

But this sort of moral thought sometimes seems to result in some pretty foolish conclusions. Consider, for example, a trivial, perfectly ordinary, and morally innocent action like going to the corner store to buy a can of Coke on a Tuesday evening. What would happen if *everybody* descended on that corner store to buy Coke at exactly that time?

> The result would certainly be disaster. Mobs of people would be trying to get into that little store. The crush would be enormous; that whole part of town would be immobilized. There would be pushing and shoving; things would get broken, and riots might break out. The store would quickly run out of Coke, and almost everyone would have to fight their way home through the mob, Cokeless.

The conclusion that your innocent action is immoral is obviously stupid. What has gone wrong with the reasoning here?

> The answer we're tempted to give is that everyone is *not* going to descend on the store, so there's nothing to fear.

But what if everyone reasoned that way?

Why We Should Hire a Dictator

IN HIS BOOK *Leviathan*, published in 1651, Thomas Hobbes considered the problem for which the Prisoner's Dilemma provides a miniature model. He imagined a "state of nature" in which humanity might have existed prior to the development of society. In this anarchic state, each person seeks his or her own well-being; the result is constant conflict, in which we compete for benefits and attempt to dominate over the others: a "war, where every man is enemy to every man." In this uncooperative state, our lives are, in Hobbes's famous phrase, "solitary, poor, nasty, brutish, and short."

> The philosophy department at the university where I was an undergraduate was located in a high-rise building with an elevator, and, back in those ancient days, there was an elevator operator whose job

it was to pilot the elevator from floor to floor. One of my instructors remarked that Hobbes's adjectives accurately described this unpleasant man as well.

The solution to this problem, Hobbes argued, is a deal: a "social contract" for cooperation. To ensure that nobody defects, we create the position of "sovereign"—a ruler with absolute power to enforce this contract and to punish all defectors. This dictator deprives us all of our personal liberty and restrains each person's natural tendency to seek power over others and to grab their goods. Thus the origin and the justification of the sovereign state.

This removes the Prisoner's Dilemma by changing the results of the participants' choices. Consider the Tragedy of the Commons: when you walk across the grass, you get punished by the police. This makes walking across the grass—the "defection" option—much less attractive than the "cooperative" one, no matter what other people do.

Hobbes argued that the only sort of state in which the war of each against all can be prevented, and in which it will be in our self-interest to pick the cooperative solution, is one ruled by a despotic tyrant with complete power. The problems with this arrangement are, of course, that our own freedoms are drastically reduced, and that we might be unable to prevent sovereigns from acting in ways not conducive to everyone's welfare—for example, when sovereigns decide to use their absolute power for their *own* benefit. (They *very* often choose their own benefit. Look at all the absolute rulers nowadays. Almost every dictator is a kleptocrat.[1]) The modern liberal state is designed to be responsive to the will of the governed, and to guarantee individual rights. The question is, however, whether the arrangements in the liberal state will work to solve our Prisoner's Dilemma. In a modern liberal state, people can take advantage of this limitation on governmental sovereignty by using their individual freedom to defect from the contract.

A QUESTION TO THINK ABOUT: Suppose that a society has installed a sovereign who enforces cooperative actions by punishing defectors. Now the people in the society, on the whole, behave cooperatively because they're afraid of being punished if they don't. But is this really *moral* behaviour? Is someone who does something nice because they'll be punished if they didn't really acting out of moral commitment?

FOR FURTHER READING: Thomas Hobbes, *Leviathan*, Chapter 13.

---

1   This is a word one hears a lot these days. It derives from Greek *kleptis* (thief) and *cratos* (rule). Its unfortunately wide application is to rulers who use their position primarily for their own enrichment.

Why People in Small Towns Are Nicer

THERE IS A WAY that we might be able to make a contract work, even if there's no sovereign with total power to enforce it.

We all realize that the best situation for everyone would be if we all cooperated. So we're each willing to cooperate provided that we won't be made a sucker by other people's defections. If we could be reasonably confident the other person won't defect, then we won't defect either. Once someone else defects on us, however, all deals are off, and we won't cooperate the next time.

So what we want to do is to cooperate with people who we think would cooperate with us. People who cooperated with us the last time we interacted are likely to do it the next time. So it would help a lot if we've already had some interaction with people we meet, so we can recognize them as probable cooperators or defectors. In a small town, people tend to interact with the same people over and over, and to recognize who can be counted on to cooperate and who can't. That's why people tend to be nicer in small towns. But in larger cities, we interact with lots of people we haven't interacted with before, so we can't tell whether they're cooperators or defectors. Maybe it's too much of a risk to cooperate with someone who might defect on you. That's why there's more nastiness in larger cities.

But in general, in a society that's working reasonably well, people tend to be nice to strangers. If they can make strangers think that they are cooperators, then the strangers might cooperate with them, and everyone will be better off.

> Social scientists have done a lot of experimental research on the prisoner's dilemma. Not on prisoners, of course, but on game players whose choices produce rewards or punishments that follow the prisoner's dilemma pattern. They've found that when the game is repeated a lot of times for the same players, many tend to evolve a two-person cooperation by punishing the other player for defection by defecting next time. This series of games is called the *iterated prisoner's dilemma*.

Toucha Smasha

BUT SOME PEOPLE WANT to demonstrate to strangers that they are non-cooperators. Here's an example.

Years ago I used to live in an apartment several blocks away from my office, and every day I'd walk the same route into work in the morning. On most of these mornings, there was a car parked on my route with a bumper sticker on it that said: "Mafia Staff Car. You toucha my car, I smasha you face."

Almost every day as I walked to work, I thought about this bumper sticker. Its message would be offensive to some Italians—but it also (semi-humorously) threatened violence to just anyone who touched the car. Of course, the humour, such as it was, acted to defuse the aggression somewhat, but not altogether. I meditated each morning on what sort of a person would see this bumper sticker in the store and say to himself, "Cool! I'll buy that wonderful object for my car!" The sort of person who wants to offer a violent message to random strangers, gratuitously. As I walked along, musing on this matter, I chanted to myself, in time with my steps, "Toucha Smasha Toucha Smasha."

I've seen a similar message on stickers attached to the back of trucks:

HOW'S MY DRIVING?
CALL 1-800-FUCK-YOU

SOME QUESTIONS TO THINK ABOUT: If this sort of implicit social contract—I'll cooperate with you if you cooperate with me—is the basis of morality, then it seems that we have no moral duties to animals, with whom we can have no such understanding. Well, maybe you can imagine that you have a sort of a deal with your dog: you help him and he helps you. But it's hard to imagine this sort of arrangement with something as dumb as your pet canary. Nevertheless, you do have moral obligations to your canary—to feed the thing and not to torture it—right? So maybe an implicit social contract is not the basis of all morality.

Why, by the way, do we have moral obligations to animals?

4. The Paradox of Deterrence

Bombing the Russians

HERE IS A SITUATION that's related to the Prisoner's Dilemma. It's known as the Paradox of Deterrence.

Suppose you're the President of the United States; it's 1960, and the Cold War is in full swing. The Soviet Union has developed the atomic bomb, and they are expansionist and belligerent. You are afraid that they might make a "first strike," attacking the US, or maybe invading an ally. In order to prevent an attack, you threaten them with massive nuclear retaliation.

There was widespread feeling that this policy was immoral. But can you see how it could be argued that this policy is morally justified?

You don't *want* to bomb the Soviet Union. But unless you threaten them with retaliation, they might attack you. This threat probably will prevent an attack, and after all, that's what we want.

This strategy apparently worked during the Cold War. During those years, neither side attacked the other. It's highly unusual in history to have two powerful enemies who manage not to go to war over such a long period.

Now, imagine that while you're President, the Soviets (for some bizarre reason) have just bombed Pittsburgh. Should you order the massive nuclear retaliation you threatened them with, and destroy Leningrad in retaliation?

Bombing Leningrad would result in nothing but destruction, suffering, and death. The Soviets (you have reason to think) just wanted to destroy Pittsburgh, and won't be tempted to bomb more of your cities; so you won't prevent future harm to the US by retaliating. Your choices are, then, either suffer the destruction of Pittsburgh without retaliation; or cause an additional large amount of useless destruction to Leningrad. Clearly it would be immoral to do the second thing.

Nevertheless, it *was* moral to threaten such massive retaliation, since only by that threat did you stand a good chance of preventing the Soviet attack. Well, it was the best bet, but it failed.

Massive retaliation after an attack is wrong, and you know it. But *intending* to do that evil thing was good, since it stood a very good chance of preventing anyone from bombing anyone. It's very odd—rather paradoxical—that having the intention to do something evil is a good thing.

And there is a further oddness. Now that they have bombed Pittsburgh, the threat has failed. It would be immoral to carry through with your threat, and you don't. But the Soviets knew in advance that you were a good guy— that you were threatening retaliation only to prevent them from bombing. They knew that after they bombed Pittsburgh, you would go through the reasoning above, and you wouldn't retaliate. No wonder your threat of retaliation didn't work. They knew you wouldn't do it.

How could you have made a threat that would work—one they would take seriously?

One way you could have done it is by constructing a "doomsday machine" (like the one in the 1963 movie *Dr. Strangelove*). This machine would detect nuclear explosions anywhere in the United States, and would react by automatically launching a devastating attack on the Soviet Union. The beauty of this machine is that once installed, it can't be turned off by anyone, no matter what. Now, once this machine is turned on, you telephone Khrushchev and tell him what you've done. *That's* deterrence. He would know then that if he attacked, there would be automatic retaliation. He'd realize that if he bombed Pittsburgh, you'd see that your threat had failed, and you'd wish that you were able to turn the machine off; but you couldn't.

The interesting thing about the story now is that it seems that the only way you can make a really effective deterring threat is to set things up so that later on you'll be unable to prevent carrying out the threat, despite the fact that you'll know that carrying it out will be immoral.

"Well, boys, I reckon this is it—nucular combat toe to toe with the Rooskies."—*Dr. Strangelove*

"But I also made it clear to [Vladimir Putin] that it's important to think beyond the old days of when we had the concept that if we blew each other up, the world would be safe."—George W. Bush

FOR FURTHER READING: Several paradoxes of deterrence are discussed by Gregory S. Kavka in "Some Paradoxes of Deterrence."

When It's Sane to Be Crazy

IF YOU DON'T HAVE a doomsday machine, it seems that it's to your advantage to make the Soviets think that you're immoral or crazy, or both. If they think you're moral and rational, then they wouldn't expect that you would uselessly retaliate, so your threat wouldn't work.

Suppose that you did your best to convince them that you really were crazy enough to retaliate uselessly. But if you acted in sensible, morally justifiable ways in general, they'd realize you were only pretending.

The best thing to do is to make yourself genuinely unreasonable and immoral. That sort of person, after all, often has the bargaining advantage when dealing with sensible, moral people. Taking a lot of LSD might transform you into the kind of person best able to act to produce your best advantage. (Of course, then, having gone crazy, you might not want what's to your best advantage.)

In *Catch-22*, Yossarian has refused to fly any more missions:

Clevinger had stared at him with apoplectic rage and indignation and, clawing at the table with both hands, had shouted, "You're crazy!" ...

"They're trying to kill me," Yossarian told him calmly.

"No one's trying to kill you," Clevinger cried.

"Then why are they shooting at me?" Yossarian asked.

"They're shooting at *everyone*," Clevinger answered. "They're trying to kill everyone."

"And what difference does that make?"[1]

At the end of the book, Yossarian decides he's had enough and announces that he's going to desert to Sweden.

Major Danby replied indulgently with a superior smile, "But Yossarian, suppose everyone felt that way."

"Then I'd certainly be a damned fool to feel any other way, wouldn't I?"[2]

The Swerving Chicken

THE GAME CALLED "CHICKEN," the classical version of which was played by 1950s male teenagers with hormone problems, is something like a prisoner's dilemma.

Here's how you play Chicken. On a deserted country road, you and another driver race your cars toward each other. If neither swerves off to the side, there is a head-on collision, and both you and the other driver die. If you swerve and the other guy doesn't, however, this shows that you're chicken, and (because machismo is very important for you) you suffer a devastating humiliation. If the other guy swerves too, that's not so bad: neither is humiliated by the macho of the other. No big deal. What you really want to happen, however, is that you keep going while the other guy swerves.

This is the table listing the possible "payoffs" for you, given your actions listed down the left, and given the actions of the other player listed across the top:

	He keeps going	He swerves
I keep going	I die (4)	I win—big macho status (1)
I swerve	I lose—bad humiliation (3)	No big deal (2)

The numbers in each box give the value-ranking of that "payoff" to you, with 1 indicating your number-one preference, and so on down.

(Note that the order of value in the boxes is not exactly the same as it was

---

1 Heller, *Catch-22*, p. 17.
2 Heller, *Catch-22*, p. 455.

in the Prisoner's Dilemma case discussed above. If you felt that death was better than dishonour, and gave the lower-left box 4, and the upper-left box 3, then it would be a Prisoner's Dilemma.)

What is the best Chicken strategy for you?

> It's not clear. You can swerve, hoping that the other guy will too. If you play Chicken often, however, and get the reputation of a swerver, your opponents will always keep going.

But this suggests a better strategy for playing Chicken: convince the other guy you're crazy and will keep going no matter what. If he's got any sense, then *he* will swerve. But how to convince the guy that you're that insane? After all, if he's smart, he'll realize that giving the appearance of insanity is a good strategy for Chicken players, so it's likely that you're not crazy at all—you're just smart.

It's even better if you really are crazy. Then you'll show your insanity in all sorts of ways, and he'll definitely be convinced. The advantages of insanity are the same here as the ones we noticed above when discussing relations with the Russians.

You might think that Chicken is a game of deception, and that you'd be at a big disadvantage if your opponent could read your mind, and could know in advance exactly what you were going to do. But strangely, this is not the case. Can you see why?

> If your opponent could read your mind, he'd be at a big *disadvantage*—he'd lose every time, if you used the right strategy: deciding in advance that you'll keep going. Your opponent is not suicidal. Knowing you're going to keep going, he'll swerve. You're a macho hero, and he's a humiliated chicken.

FOR FURTHER READING: This and other game-theoretical aspects of Chicken are discussed by William Poundstone in *Labyrinths of Reason*, pp. 240–41.

Into the Mainstream of Philosophy

THE QUESTION "WHY SHOULD I be moral?" is one that has interested philosophers since philosophy began. It's one that deserves some thought, and that you can think about and perhaps come up with some answers to, even if you have studied little philosophy.

David Hume, the eighteenth-century Scottish philosopher, discussed this problem in ways you might consider. He argued that morality is an unusual phenomenon. We all believe some moral "truths," but we are at a loss about how to prove what we believe. It seems to be impossible to justify these beliefs by means of pointing out facts about the world: no matter how many facts we adduce, the moral principles don't seem to follow. This position can be summed up by the following slogan: you can't derive an *ought* from an *is*. Do you think that Hume is right? As a way of considering this, you might begin with some moral principle you think is correct, for example, that torturing innocent little children is wrong. Now imagine trying to convince someone who didn't believe it of the truth of this principle. You have at your disposal all the facts you could want about the world. Imagine the debate you might have with this moral sceptic. He's willing to grant the truths of any factual propositions you like, and to accept their logical consequences. Could you convince him of the moral principle? (There really are people like this, with what's called psychopathic or sociopathic personalities. They may be intelligent and well-informed, but they just can't be convinced that something is immoral.)

Hume argued that facts alone don't imply morals. He thought that, in addition, one has to have certain feelings—importantly, certain sympathies with others. Given this sympathy, people can be reasoned with morally; without it, we're at a loss. Hume hoped that these feelings of sympathy were widespread. But what if someone just doesn't have them?

Another philosophical giant, Immanuel Kant, argued that sympathetic feelings for others—indeed feelings of any sort—were irrelevant to morality. A morally right action is one that is motivated not by sympathy, but rather by nothing other than the knowledge of what's right. Often doing what's right conflicts with what one might do because of sympathy or any other feeling.

Much of this chapter concerns the sort of reasoning embodied in the Prisoner's Dilemma and in the Tragedy of the Commons. This sort of story has become important in much contemporary thought attempting to provide an answer to the question "Why should I be moral?" Some philosophers argue that considerations of this sort would lead someone who started without any Humian sympathy for others, but merely with selfish desires, to recognize the truth of some moral principles. The idea is that someone who is merely selfish could be led to see that, in the long run, his or her own interests would best be served by making a deal with others in such a way that his or her own interests were, to some extent, served too. The rules of morality, according to this view, represent these deals with others: by all agreeing to them, we each serve our own initial selfish interests the best.

Often this sort of line of reasoning is best pursued by imagining a bunch of people in a Hobbesian "state of nature"; rational and selfish interests alone will eventually result in their adopting some sort of rules of morality. Try to imagine a story in which such a state of nature would result in a society governed by morality. Do you think this would actually happen?

Readings in which philosophers attempt to answer the question "Why should I be moral?" are not hard to find. One suitable place to start is Plato's *Republic*. And most introductory philosophy anthologies will provide some articles on this question.

Chapter XIII

How to Think Morally

"Go into the street and give one man a lecture on morality and another a shilling, and see which will respect you most."
—Samuel Johnson[1]

1. Justice and Distribution

Why You Should Give Away Your Shoes

WOULDN'T IT BE A better world if it weren't the case that some people lived in comparative luxury while others suffered by consequence? Wouldn't you think that someone was morally lacking if that person knew of a way to reduce this inequality, and didn't?

Here's a small way you can make the world a better place. You (I suppose) own several pairs of shoes. There are many people in the world right now who own no pairs of shoes, and suffer as a result. So you should give your shoes to them.

It doesn't follow that you should give away *all* your shoes. If you gave them all away, then your positions would be reversed—you would be the one who was suffering. How many pairs should you give away?

Suppose you own five pairs of shoes; number them arbitrarily 1 through 5. Now consider pair number 5. How much benefit does this pair give to you? Not very much. Certainly that pair would do a whole lot more good to someone who has no shoes at all. If you gave that person that pair, your well-being would be reduced by a little bit, while the well-being of the recipient

---

1   Quoted by Boswell in his biography, *Life of Johnson*. vol. 1.

would be increased by a whole lot. Giving that pair away would increase the sum of well-being in the world. You would lose a little, and the other person would gain a lot.

Okay, you should give away pair number 5. Now you are left with four pairs. How about pair number 4? Giving away that pair would diminish your well-being, perhaps by a greater amount than giving away pair number 5. Nevertheless, the well-being of another shoeless person could be increased by much more than your well-being would be decreased. You should give away pair number 4 too.

Of course, the same line of reasoning applies to pairs number 3 and 2. But giving away your last pair wouldn't increase the sum of well-being in the world, because the increase resulting from a shoeless person getting them would be balanced by your becoming shoeless. In fact, if that person is somewhat used to going around shoeless and you aren't, perhaps you would suffer more than that person by being shoeless. So (you'll be happy to hear) it's not morally required that you give away your last pair of shoes.

What we have here is an example of what economists call the "marginal decrease of utility." This is a fancy way of saying that something would be worth a whole lot less to someone who has a lot of them than to someone who has few or none. Thus your fifth pair of shoes would be worth a lot more to a shoeless person than to you. One's first pair of shoes is (everything else being equal) much more valuable than one's second, which is in turn more valuable than the third, and so on.

So you should give away all your shoes except one pair. Now consider the other things you own more than one of. You should also give away all of them except one to people who have none. In fact, if anyone in the world has less than you do of any good thing, you should give them enough of your possessions until you own equal quantities.

Almost nobody follows this moral advice. Some people give something to those who have less, for example, by giving to charities, but remember what our reasoning tells us to do: give your goods away until there is *nobody in the world* who is worse off than you are. Do you know of anybody who does this?

Do you now feel like you're evil for not obeying this moral requirement? Well, you have company in your evil ways. Almost everyone in the world is, to some extent or other, evil—according to this line of reasoning.

But probably by now you've had the thought: something has gone wrong with this moral reasoning. Reasoning that comes to the conclusion that almost everyone in the world is evil certainly merits a second (and third) look. We'll get to that in a moment.

Sell Whatsoever Thou Hast, and Give to the Rich

BUT FIRST, LET'S LOOK at the flip-side of the same argument. Perhaps you're not much of a wine connoisseur. You occasionally buy a gallon-box of Chateau Schmatteau Plonque-Rouge Wine-Type Beverage, but you can't tell the difference between that and the good stuff. Oenophiles[1] can. Imagine that because of their long, careful training in wine tasting, they now can get a hundred times as much pleasure out of a really expensive bottle than you could. That means that, to increase the total benefit in the world, you should give up your wine altogether (and probably a lot more too) and give the money to real wine lovers (even though they're probably already a lot richer than you are) so that they can get more of this enormous benefit—much more than you could get from what you give up.

> This example is not really so far-fetched. Note that governments right now take tax money from you and me to subsidize high art, which is enjoyed (no doubt highly) by a small elite of already well-off people. Isn't this the same thing?

Why You Don't Have to Give Away Your Shoes

> "But those shoes are *mine*—I own them," you might want to argue. "They're my property. I have the right to hang on to my own property."

SOME PHILOSOPHERS THINK THAT the right to own property is a central, fundamental human right. The idea is basic to the social philosophy of John Locke, for example, who held that the right to property followed from our very nature—that it's God's will, and is "writ in the hearts of all mankind." In his *Essays on the Law of Nature*, Locke expressed the view that it is a self-evident truth that all people are endowed by their creator with certain inalienable rights, among which are life, liberty, and property.

> Locke's idea was clearly a strong influence on Thomas Jefferson when he wrote the US Declaration of Independence. Jefferson, however, changed the list of inalienable rights to life, liberty, and the pursuit of happiness. Why did Jefferson make this change?[2]

---

1   That means *wine lovers*. It's pronounced *EE-no-files*. Don't you love that word? It sounds like it's referring to some sort of criminal sexual pervert.

2   The idea that property was a natural right was well established before and after Jefferson wrote the *Declaration* passed by the Second Continental Congress in 1776. (continued)

Even Locke, however, didn't think that the right to property entitled you to own whatever you could get. He thought that you have to earn what you get by your labour (so stealing something doesn't give you property rights over it). He also thought that you don't have property rights over things you earn when this appropriation wouldn't leave enough, and as good, for others.

SOME QUESTIONS TO THINK ABOUT: How did you get those shoes? Were they paid for by your parents? In that case, you didn't earn them. Does that show that you don't have the right to own them?

But suppose you earned the money to pay for them. By refusing to allow shoeless people to use them, are you depriving them of "enough"? By refusing to share them with people who have only terrible shoes, are you depriving them of "as good"?

Do you think that these considerations show that there's something wrong with Locke's views on the right to property?

Other philosophers have not found the right to property writ in their hearts. The nineteenth-century French thinker Proudhon, for example, wrote a book called *What Is Property?* and answered his own question by saying that property is theft. *Do* we have the right to property under *any* conditions? Is it fair that one person have more of the goods of life than another?

Your Shoes and Your "Families"

"I agree that I would be immoral if I owned six pairs of shoes, and my brother or my children or my parents owned none, and I didn't give them *something* (though not so much that I'm completely reduced to their level of need). Maybe I even have some obligation to do something for people far away, for example, in the poverty-stricken areas of Africa, but I only have a very limited obligation to them. I have less obligation to them, because they're not *my* family, or *my* group."

ALMOST EVERYONE THINKS THAT obligations to help others decrease as their "distance" from you increases. Most people are willing to sacrifice a

---

In 1774, the First Congress declared that the inhabitants of the English colonies in North America were entitled to "life, liberty and property." The *Virginia Declaration of Rights* drafted one month before the *Declaration of Independence* asserted that all men by nature have the "inherent rights" of "the enjoyment of life and liberty, with the means of acquiring and possessing property, and pursuing and obtaining happiness and safety." In 1790, John Adams wrote into the Massachusetts constitution people's "right of enjoying and defending their lives and liberties; that of acquiring, possessing, and protecting property; in fine, that of seeking and obtaining their safety and happiness."

good deal for their immediate family. Many people would do something (though less) for their neighbours in need. Some people sometimes respond to the need of others of their own nationality: for example, those of Greek descent in North America tend to be the ones who respond most strongly with aid when there's an earthquake in Greece.

But is the idea correct that one's obligations to others decrease as their "distance" increases? Why is failure to respond to your own child's need worse than failure to respond to the need of some child half-way around the world? Does your child deserve help more than that other child?

> Looking out first for your own family, or ethnic group, or race is a normal and universal phenomenon, perhaps an inevitable one. But this idea might seem morally objectionable, rather selfish, or a bit racist. Maybe it's the sort of thing we should try to avoid.

SOME QUESTIONS TO THINK ABOUT: To think morally and act fairly, shouldn't we take a disinterested view, trying to ignore our own particular position? Shouldn't we try to think of every human—not just those nearer to us—as having an equal claim on what's of value?

Supererogatory Acts

ONE OF THESE IS an act that (1) would be a good thing to do, but (2) is "above and beyond the call of duty"—so you wouldn't be blamed if you didn't. Maybe giving away almost all your shoes would be a good thing (increasing, as we've seen, the total well-being in the world), but that kind of saintly act isn't expected of anyone, so you're not an evil person if you don't do it, and you don't have to feel guilty.

SOME QUESTIONS TO THINK ABOUT: If for selfish reasons you don't do something that would make for a better world, doesn't that count against you, morally speaking? Aren't you to blame for acting that way? Aren't we all morally required to make things as good as we're able? In that case, no act is supererogatory. Nobody fully lives up to this requirement to do good, but doesn't that show that we're all, to some degree, morally blameworthy?

Schadenfreude[1]

IT'S NASTY TO FEEL glad that others suffered misfortune, isn't it? I mean, when they haven't done anything wrong, and something bad happens to them.

Well, don't be too sure. Consider this example: You're going to compete for the state championship in the 100-metre dash. Your only real competition is a guy who consistently runs the 100 metres a good deal faster than you ever have, so it's clear that you have almost no chance of coming in first. But the day before the race, he sprains his ankle, so he can't race, and you'll win. Now be honest: are you glad that happened? Yes, you are. But is this an immoral feeling? You feel sorry for him, but glad that it happened. That's okay, isn't it?

If so, that doesn't show that it's *always* okay to feel glad when your good fortune results from someone else's misfortune. Suppose that the death of your cousin's newborn baby saves you the $20 you would otherwise have to spend on a baby present. It does seem immoral if you feel glad *that* happened. What's the difference?[2]

2. Punishment

Getting Back at Eichmann

ADOLF EICHMANN WAS THE German official during World War II in charge of what the Nazis called "the final solution of the Jewish problem," which was to send Jews to death camps to be exterminated. In 1960, Israeli agents found Eichmann in Argentina, abducted him, and took him to Israel, where he was tried and convicted of crimes against humanity, and hanged in 1962.

Everyone agreed that Eichmann was directly responsible for the murder of millions of people. But there was controversy anyway about the punishment he should receive for his crimes. Should he be given the death penalty? Should he be punished at all?

To see why these questions arose, consider the reasons for inflicting judicial punishment.

---

1 This is another excellent and impressive word to add to your vocabulary if it isn't already there. It's borrowed from German, pronounced *SHAH-den-froy-duh*. It means pleasure taken in someone else's misfortune.

2 The permissibility (sometimes) of feeling glad about others' misfortunes is one of the "moral paradoxes" discussed interestingly and revealingly by Saul Smilansky in *Ten Moral Paradoxes*. Smilansky does not offer a theory of *when* this is permitted.

One motive for punishment for crime is to motivate the criminal not to do it again. It might teach that person a lesson and make them less likely to commit crime again, or maybe it will merely put them in a jail where they won't be able to re-offend. The death penalty is certainly successful in preventing the offender from re-offending!

But this doesn't apply in Eichmann's case. His crimes needed the backing of a Nazi government, which was long gone when he went on trial in the early 1960s, and when Eichmann himself was about fifty-five, and in any case in no shape to commit any big crimes himself. Nobody thought there was any future danger from him.

A second obvious rationale for punishing criminals is deterrence of others. People would (it is hoped) be less likely to commit crimes if they thought that they stood a good chance of punishment for those crimes. When people know that those who have committed similar crimes are punished, the possibility of their own punishment, should they do likewise, becomes more likely to them.

But in Eichmann's case, this doesn't seem to fit very well. The crime he was accused of—genocidal mass murder—isn't one that happens very often. But when it does, it's unlikely to have been deterred by a threat of punishment. Genocide on this scale happens only when sponsored by government; but then you wouldn't be afraid of punishment. Remember, Eichmann believed that the Nazis were going to rule the world for the foreseeable future—they called their regime the "Thousand-Year Reich [Empire]."

The third sort of rationale for punishment is what's sometimes called *retribution*. Many people think that someone who has committed a crime should suffer as a result—not in order to deter that person or others from future crime, but just as a matter of simple justice. When someone has done awful things to other people, awful things should be done to that person.

Retribution is the only one of the three motives for punishment that is clearly applicable to the Eichmann case. But is retribution a suitable rationale for judicial punishment? If we think that the basic principle of morality is that human happiness and well-being should increase, and human suffering decrease, then retribution is morally questionable, because its motive is to increase suffering (of a wrongdoer). Retribution seems to some people to be merely revenge—an eye for an eye—not a suitable reaction for morally mature civilized societies.

If you agree that deterrence of the criminal or others didn't apply in this case, and that mere revenge is not a good idea, then maybe the surprising conclusion is that Eichmann—one of the biggest moral monsters of recent history—should not have been punished at all.

Making a Statement

THE INTERNATIONAL CRIMINAL COURT tries people accused of genocide, war crimes, and crimes against humanity. Omar Hassan al-Bashir, the
dictator of Sudan, was a likely candidate for their consideration; he was considered responsible for many of the 30,000 deaths that occurred during the
brutal war that has raged there since 2003. But Alex de Waal, an American
called the world's foremost authority on Sudan and its war, argued publicly
that this would be a bad idea: al-Bashir would react violently to an indict-
ment from the court, rebel groups in the country would be emboldened to
violate peace agreements, the country would be further destabilized, and
any sentence imposed by the Court could not be enforced. The Court went
ahead and indicted al-Bashir anyway, and the result was what de Waal predicted. "For us," said al-Bashir, "the ICC doesn't exist."[1]

The international agreement that established the Court stated its purpose:
that the "most serious crimes of concern to the international community as
a whole must not go unpunished."[2] But, of course, in cases like al-Bashir's,
there is little hope of direct punishment. Those who defend actions such as
the Court's in this case sometimes say that, nevertheless, the international
community must make a strong statement of condemnation.

SOME QUESTIONS TO THINK ABOUT: Do you agree that a statement must
be made, even if it's clear that it will make things worse? De Waal has argued
that aggressive international intervention, however well-intentioned, often is
horribly counter-productive. If this is the case, should the worst crimes just
be ignored?

Closure

> "Watching McVeigh die would 'help [victims and bereaved families]
> meet their need to close this chapter in their lives.'"—Attorney General
> John Ashcroft, defending the decision to televise mass-murderer
> Timothy McVeigh's execution to an audience of friends and relations
> of victims

WHEN QUESTIONS ARE RAISED about punishing criminals nowadays, we
often hear talk about "closure." Victims (or relatives or acquaintances of victims) want—need—swift and harsh punishment for wrongdoers, which, it

---

1   "Brave Thinkers: Alex de Waal."
2   Preamble to the "Rome Statute of the International Criminal Court."

is supposed, will bring things closer to a state of balance, and release them somewhat from their agony.

What is "closure"? This newly popular word, a psycho-babble product of the grief-counsellor industry, may not mean much more than "revenge," though it certainly sounds more respectable.

There's no denying that the friends and relatives of the Oklahoma City bombing victims had real and very intense feelings about what should be done with the bomber.

> One woman wished the electric chair had been used [instead of lethal injection], because it would have been more painful. Another said, "I think bombs should be strapped on him, and then he can walk around the room forever until they went off and he wouldn't know when it would happen."

The commentator who reported these quotes remarks:

> Given the horrific losses McVeigh's crime incurred, this primal hunger can be almost seductive—a howl of mourning very hard to resist, never mind debate. But it is dangerous if it allows us to lose sight of the fact that the debate we must have is … about the limits of state force, not about devising the perfect mirror of each victim's suffering.[1]

"Distrust all in whom the impulse to punish is powerful."—Friedrich Nietzsche[2]

The Paradox of Punishment

THE TENSION BETWEEN TWO motives for punishment—deterrence and retribution—is revealed in an unexpected way when you think about certain crimes and social class.

Almost all burglaries are committed by "the underprivileged"—people in the lowest socioeconomic groups. Burglary is much more tempting to somebody in or near poverty; you'd be surprised to find that the guy who had broken into your apartment to steal your crummy stereo was a doctor or lawyer or university president making four hundred thousand dollars a year. Poor people are less likely to have respect for the law that maintains the social status quo, and more likely to have criminal role models. They're more likely

---

1   Both quotations are from Patricia J. Williams, "No Vengeance, No Justice."
2   *Thus Spake Zarathustra*, Chapter 29.

to have suffered deprivation or abuse as a child. It's going too far to say that poverty causes crime, but it's certainly a factor.

Now consider how much somebody deserves punishment for crime. Burglary committed by an "underprivileged" person is certainly not a good thing, but with all those factors in his background nudging him in that direction, it's at least somewhat understandable that he turns to crime, and we blame that person less than we would a rich burglar who's doing it just out of malice, just for kicks. Add to this the likelihood that the underprivileged burglar probably has had some suffering in his life already, so he's paid for his crime in advance, so to speak. In sum, it's clear that the overprivileged would deserve harsher punishment than the underprivileged.

But that's considering punishment as retribution. Now consider it as deterrence. Given all those temptations and causal factors, it would take a threat of substantial punishment to deter crime by an underprivileged person. Lives already rough can make one less sensitive to the threat of legal punishment. But people from the higher economic brackets need hardly any deterrence to prevent them. So if we adjust the severity of punishment to the strength of deterrence necessary, a lower-class criminal should be punished much more severely than an upper, for the same crime. That's just the opposite of what retributive punishment requires!

So if you're motivated to punish both by deterrence and retribution, you'd want to punish an underprivileged burglar more for deterrence, and less for retribution.[1]

3. Rights and Wrongs

Push-Pin Anyone?

IT'S PLAUSIBLE TO THINK that the basic principle of ethics is that one ought to do what maximizes the total of pleasure or well-being or happiness in the world. This is the core of the moral theory called *utilitarianism*.

We have, however, already encountered an example that this theory has trouble with (about giving away your shoes), and we will encounter more.

Here's another. Different people get pleasure from different things, but the utilitarian thinks that having the most of whatever gives you pleasure is the only good thing, and the more pleasure the better. Jeremy Bentham, a founder of modern utilitarianism, wrote: "Prejudice apart, the game of push-pin is of equal value with the arts and sciences of music and poetry."[2]

---

1   This is one of Saul Smilansky's *Ten Moral Paradoxes*, p. 35.
2   *Rationale of Reward* (1825).

Push-pin is a child's game like pick-up-sticks with pins; in Bentham's time, it was a metaphor for a meaningless and trivial activity. Bentham insists that it's just a prejudice that music and poetry—the "higher" pleasures—are somehow more worthwhile: if push-pin turns you on, and poetry does not, then it's worth more to you, and that's all there is to say about it.

SOME QUESTIONS TO THINK ABOUT: Nobody plays push-pin any more, so let's think about a contemporary example. Do you think that reading poetry is better than playing video games? If so, why? If reading poetry gives you more pleasure than playing video games, then Bentham would think that, for you, reading poetry is superior; but c'mon now, be honest: you really find playing video games fun, and reading poetry boring and difficult, don't you? Okay, given that, do you still think that reading poetry is somehow better? Why?

The other philosopher most centrally associated with utilitarianism, John Stuart Mill, argued that there are "higher" and "lower" pleasures, and that a small amount of a "higher" pleasure (for example, presumably, reading poetry) is superior to a larger amount of a "lower" pleasure (push-pin). But, we want to ask Mill, what makes a pleasure "higher"? And why do those characteristics make it superior to "lower" pleasures?

When Promise-Breaking Is Obligatory

YOU VISIT YOUR RICH uncle Fred in the hospital. "I'm dying," says Uncle Fred, "but I'll die a happy man if you promise me to do something after I'm dead. There's a million dollars hidden in my suitcase in the closet over there. Nobody knows about that million, not even my wife, and it's not mentioned in my will. Take it, and just as soon as I'm dead, give it to my wife."

You want to ease Uncle Fred's last moments, so you get the million out of the closet and promise to give it to Aunt Sally after he's gone. He dies that afternoon, and you get into your car and head for the casino where you know that Aunt Sally has been spending every day since Fred went into the hospital, drinking, carrying on with various low-life men, and spending every cent she has at the gambling tables.

But on the way to the casino, you wonder about the morality of keeping your promise to Uncle Fred. As a utilitarian, you think about effects. Giving Aunt Sally the money would make her happy, but she's really unable to feel much through the alcohol haze she's always in, and the money will be gone in a few days of gambling anyway. If you kept the money yourself, it would contribute to human happiness—yours—considerably more; better still, you could contribute it to a charity that provides food and shelter for the homeless. Uncle Fred, who was infatuated with Aunt Sally and unable to see her faults, wanted her to have the money, but he's dead now, so he can't be harmed by your breaking your promise. Nobody else would be harmed. Why keep your promise?

> Breaking promises produces mistrust, so in the long run it will produce more harm than good.

No, this isn't a good reason. Maybe in general breaking promises erodes social institutions that depend on trust, but not in this case. Nobody knows about your promise to Uncle Fred; no mistrust will result.

> Well, even if breaking your promise doesn't have bad results in this case, it often does, so there is utilitarian justification for having a rule against promise breaking. (This is the sort of answer provided by *rule utilitarians*.)

But in cases (like this one) when it is beneficial not to obey this rule, why should you obey it?

FOR FURTHER READING: In a story presented by Dale Jamieson and Tom Regan: you've promised to return your friend's chainsaw whenever he asks for it, and he turns up at your door one day, extremely drunk, dragging behind a bound and gagged companion who has been severely beaten and is clearly terrified.

Jamieson and Regan think you shouldn't give the chainsaw back—few philosophers think you should—but what's of more interest in their article is their discussion of when moral rules admit of exceptions. See their article "On the Ethics of the Use of Animals in Science."

Don't Torture That Baby!

HERE'S A THOUGHT-EXPERIMENT FROM fiction that tests whether *any* utilitarian benefit, no matter how large, would justify an action everyone would be repulsed by:

> "Tell me yourself, I challenge you—answer. Imagine that you are cre-
> ating a fabric of human destiny with the object of making men happy
> in the end, giving them peace and rest at last, but that it was essential
> and inevitable to torture to death only one tiny creature—the baby
> beating its breast with its fist, for instance—and to found that edifice

on its unavenged tears, would you consent to be the architect of those conditions? Tell me, and tell the truth."

"No, I wouldn't consent," said Alyosha softly.[1]

How to Prevent Crime

HERE'S A CRIME-PREVENTION TECHNIQUE that's pretty well guaranteed to work. The only problem is working out the necessary technology, but if you think this is a good idea, then we can get our scientists busy on working out the technical details.

The idea is that we should build a system of satellites that detect crime. Whenever a satellite finds one, it automatically, immediately shoots the criminal with a disintegrator ray, vaporizing him.

Of course, we'd have to design the satellite so that it wouldn't react this way when the perpetrator was mentally unbalanced, or under duress, or too young, etc. We can work out these technical details.

Obviously this sort of punishment is excessive. To disintegrate someone for running a stop sign would be, let's say, a bit drastic. But the beauty of this scheme is that *this punishment would never be necessary*. Given the inevitability of this drastic punishment, nobody in their right mind would commit crimes ever again.

What do you say?

Lawrence Alexander, the author of the article in which this scheme is presented,[2] realizes that lots of people wouldn't be in favour of this scheme, believing in the principle of proportionality of punishment to the severity of the crime. But he argues that this principle is not a good one, offering the following story as a way, he hopes, of convincing us:

> Sally gets a phone call from somebody announcing that he's going to burglarize her house while she's out tonight. The burglar adds that he has a bad heart condition, and if he has to suffer the strain and anxiety of looking for her valuables too long, he might very well die; so she should make sure to leave all of them in plain sight. Naturally, Sally makes sure to hide everything valuable away the best she can. When she returns late that night, sure enough, there's the burglar, lying dead in the middle of her living room.

---

1 Fyodor Dostoyevsky, *The Brothers Karamazov.*
2 Lawrence Alexander, "The Doomsday Machine: Proportionality, Punishment, and Prevention."

Alexander thinks that the general reaction to this story would be that Sally has done no wrong, even though she's aware that by hiding her valuables she's going (in effect) to inflict the death penalty on the burglar. If you don't count this as morally wrong, but you don't like the satellite scheme, you need to explain what the relevant difference is.

Rights vs. Utility

WE'VE BEEN LOOKING AT more examples of the type that show, according to some philosophers, that utilitarianism is wrong. They argue that in addition to (perhaps even instead of) thinking about what promotes happiness, we ought to think about inviolable *rights*. As we've seen, a right to property might justify our keeping our shoes, at the expense of an increase in total happiness.

Bentham, of course, didn't think very highly of the idea of rights. "Natural rights," he claimed, "is simple nonsense: natural and imprescriptible rights, rhetorical nonsense—nonsense upon stilts."[1]

SOME QUESTIONS TO THINK ABOUT: If you have a right to something, that seems to mean that that thing can't be taken away, no matter what consequences there are to the general welfare. It's pretty hard to think of anything we'd be willing to grant a right to, on this strict definition. We're all willing to grant that under some circumstances considerations of the general welfare justify taking away someone's property, when that's necessary for the general good. People's land and houses are expropriated (with compensation, of course) in order to build a national park, or a highway, or a dam that would benefit a large number of people.

If there are such things as rights, where do rights come from? How can we find out what rights people have? Locke argued that reason alone can reveal what rights people have, but it's not at all clear that this is so.

Here are some examples of claims about rights. See if your Lockian pure reason can tell you whether these rights really exist.

- People don't like those huge new wind turbines built near where they live. They make some noise, and they interfere with the view. But merely disliking those things is perhaps not seen as sufficient grounds for demanding that they not be put there; and some people have begun to talk about their "right to a view."

---

1   *Anarchical Fallacies.* Natural rights are distinguished from legal rights: the former are supposed to be had by everyone, not contingent on what's granted by society, custom, law, etc. An imprescriptible right is one that is inviolable—it cannot be taken away, lost, or revoked.

- Several years ago, in accord with the Canadian government's policy of imposing sanctions on the apartheid government in South Africa, the government cancelled a rugby match between the Canadian and South African teams. I heard a member of the Canadian team on the radio complaining that this ban was unjust because it violated their "right to play." Is there such a right? How do you know?[1]

- They discovered the remains of a buried mammoth—an extinct, elephant-like animal—in Siberia; but an anthropologist argued that it should be left buried. "What right do we have to touch and smell an animal that has rested beneath the surface for 10,000 years?" he asked. Do we need a *right* to dig up this animal? Is he implying that we'd violate the right of the extinct animal not to be touched or smelled? It's not clear that even *live* animals have that right. Digging up the remains of ancient *people* is sometimes thought to violate their rights; but do dead people have rights?[2] Maybe it's the rights of the living descendants of those dead people that are violated? In his article, the anthropologist made it clear that he's also worried about the Evenki, the indigenous people of Siberia, who would be offended if animal remains were taken where the animals in question did not "present themselves."[3] This would be a bad result, but is there a violation of *rights* here? Do indigenous people have the right not to be offended? Does anyone?

Special Today on Life: Only $2199.91/Day

IF THERE ARE ANY rights at all, it would seem, there is a *right to life*. This might mean that (when we can) we should protect human life no matter what the cost. A utilitarian alternative is to give life some sort of finite value—largely for the person whose life it is, but also for others—and to compare

---

1 "Right to Play" is the name of a Canadian-based international charity organization aiming at providing sports programs for children in third-world countries. Their website claims that these will help the children's development, "mobilize communities around national health and disease prevention priorities, including HIV and AIDS, malaria and immunization," "teach conflict resolution and peace building skills," and have other benefits. That's a nice thought, and even if these results are improbable, sports programs would give the kids some fun. Anyway, these are all utilitarian justifications for providing play-opportunity, and they really have nothing to do with what philosophers call *rights*. (These quotations, and other information about Right to Play, are on the Right to Play Canada website.)

2 See **Harming and Benefitting the Dead** in Chapter XIV.

3 The anthropologist is David G. Anderson; his comments are in "Primal Life Force Under the Ice." Reported and discussed by Julian Baggini in "What Right Have You Got?," in his *The Duck That Won the Lottery*.

costs and benefits. This, however, is an approach that many people find abhorrent, and counts for them as one of the more convincing objections to utilitarianism. Nazi Germany is sometimes invoked here, by the opponents of utilitarianism, where supposedly utilitarian calculations resulted in the extermination of disabled people, on the grounds that maintaining their lives was too much of a cost on the public at large. You'll be relieved to hear, however, that most utilitarians don't come to this conclusion, thinking that once the value of life to the disabled person is included in this calculation, it balances out quite differently.

Anyway, what we need to ask a utilitarian is, how could we come up with a reasonable evaluation of a life? Non-utilitarians sometimes say that life has incalculably large, even infinite, value. If that's true, then no expense would be too large to produce the tiniest chance of saving a life. Maybe there's some reasonable finite value we could discover.

Here's a real-life case in which it appears we need to take seriously the idea of assigning a dollar-value to life. There have recently been some new drugs introduced for cancer therapy. One of them is the unpronounceable Cetuximab, designed to extend the survival of patients with a couple of forms of terminal cancer. Treatment with this drug increases survival by an average of 36½ days. The cost of enough drug for one treatment is $80,352 (US), that is, just short of $2200 per day of life extension (not counting a lot of other costs: for administering the drug, caring for the patient who will likely suffer some of the abundant and nasty side effects, and so on).[1]

Is it worth it? Let's separate some questions here. Would a dying patient judge that spending that much for a little bit of (very low-quality) extra life was worth it? Maybe. If you're paying for this yourself, you might reason that your savings won't be much good for you post-mortem. On the other hand, you might want to leave this money as an inheritance for your family, or as a donation to fund the fourth edition of a book by your favourite philosopher.

That sort of reasoning might be appropriate in the case of somebody without health insurance in the US. But in Canada, where many medical expenses are publicly funded, considerations like this can be a matter of public policy, not of individual preference.

In both countries, however, it seems that somebody's going to have to face the decision whether using the drug is worth it. Many people will answer no, in this rather extreme case of very high expense, for comparatively low return. But if you would agree that some huge amount of money is too much to spend to extend life a little—whatever limit you think is reasonable—it seems you're agreeing that life doesn't have a literally infinite or incalculable value.

---

1   Description and discussion of the costs and benefits of this and other drugs for cancer therapy is in Tito Fojo and Christine Grady, "How Much Is Life Worth."

The Price of Life in Europe

PROVIDING HIGHWAYS WITH SAFETY features (guardrails, good lighting, police patrols, wide median strips, etc.) costs money. And it's known, on average, how many lives a safety feature will save. To figure out if installing a safety feature is worth it, you'd have to weigh the cost of the feature against the number of lives saved. Different countries weigh things differently. In the US, for example, they're willing to spend up to about $2,600,000 per life saved. Here's the corresponding figure they're willing to go up to, to save on average one life, in some European countries:[1]

Sweden	$1,200,000
Britain	$1,100,000
Germany	$910,000
Belgium	$400,000
France	$340,000
Netherlands	$130,000
Portugal	$20,000

A QUESTION TO THINK ABOUT: Does that mean that the US is a much better place than Portugal, in that the US is willing to spend so much more money to keep people alive? Or does it mean that the US is willing to spend way too much public funds per life saved?

Into the Mainstream of Philosophy

IN CHAPTER XII WE were worrying about a very general issue in ethics: whether a justification could be given for any sort of moral thinking or acting. In the present chapter, by contrast, we have been assuming that ethics is somehow in general justified; here we have been searching, indirectly, for general principles of morality that could be used in deciding specific moral issues.

These two issues are connected. If moral rules exist to solve the Prisoner's Dilemma, then they are ways of regulating and restraining our already existing selfish desires, with the aim of coordinating our actions in order to maximize everyone's satisfaction of these desires. This suggests a test for the validity of our general moral rules: would acting in accord with such a general rule maximize everyone's desire-satisfaction? This test, roughly speaking, is the one proposed by Utilitarianism—the view (roughly) that

---

1   Figures (which date back probably to around 1990) are adapted from Laudan, *The Book of Risks*, p. 53.

what is good is what produces the greatest happiness (or pleasure) for the greatest number of people. Here we might understand "happiness" or "pleasure" as desire-satisfaction.

Any utilitarian must reply to several sorts of objection. For one thing, it seems implausible that we are all morally required to look out for everyone's happiness. The example concerned with giving away your shoes raises questions about this. The interesting thing about this example is that it does seem initially plausible that satisfaction-maximization is the criterion of morally right action: the view is widespread that we should, for example, act to eliminate poverty, in order to eliminate the rather unequal degree of satisfaction people experience around the world. But the consequence of thinking that way seems to be that we are all acting dreadfully immorally. Is this possible?

Many philosophers have objected to utilitarianism on the grounds that the maximization of the distribution of satisfaction to everyone would necessitate depriving many people of what they have a right to have. As we have seen, however, it's not at all clear how we could decide what rights people have, especially when granting them rights often seems to interfere with our desire to maximize and equalize desire-satisfaction. How could it be proven that someone has a right to something? What is the basis of the existence of rights anyway?

A second sort of general objection utilitarians must face is that it seems clear to most of us that the point of morality can't be the satisfaction of just any desire. It can't be true that we'd all be morally perfect once things were set up so that we all get what we want to the greatest degree, because certain things people happen to want just seem wrong. Suppose that someone's deepest desires were satisfied by providing that person with a plastic companion. The feeling remains that something very important would be missing in that person's life with the Acme robot, even if he feels fully satisfied. Maybe there's more to the morally good life than merely getting what you want. But what? And why?

You won't have trouble finding lots of articles in anthologies in which philosophers argue for very different views on what the basic principles of morality and the good life are.

Chapter XIV

Moral Conundrums

1. Getting What You Want

Past and Future Desires

SOME MORAL THEORIES (AS we've seen) base morality on the fulfilment of human desires. There are some puzzles about what's wanted, however.

Your basic desire is to have a life in which, all told, you get what you want, right? Well, that's not so clear.

Consider Fred, who is eighty years old. His doctor guesses that given his present state of health, he'll probably live for five or ten years more. In 1956, when Fred first heard "Heartbreak Hotel," he developed a very strong desire that there be a statue of Elvis in his back yard, a desire that lasted more than 50 years. He's never had the money to buy the statue; but yesterday he won the lottery. For the first time he can afford the Elvis statue, but he discovers that his interest in Elvis has completely disappeared, and he now thinks that having an Elvis statue would be foolish. Should he get the statue anyway?

If he put up that Elvis statue, he'd satisfy a strong desire he had for decades. Of course, *now* he doesn't want that statue, so putting it up would go against his present (and, we can assume, future) desires. But this would mean only five or ten years or so of dissatisfied desire. Assuming that the kind of life he wants is one in which his desire fulfillment is maximized, all told, he should put up that ugly statue.

The fact that this reasoning is foolish shows that there's something wrong with the principle that what we really want is a life in which desire-satisfaction is maximized. We care about our present desires, not about our past desires that have gone away.

But are our present desires the only thing that's relevant? How about our future desires?

Consider the following case. You're now twenty years old, and you expect to live to a ripe old age. Your parents urge you to take a business degree, arguing reasonably that this is the best way to assure you a good income in the future. But you are young and idealistic, and you don't care about income: you want to join a group of ecology terrorists instead. Your parents argue that you feel that way only because you're young. They predict that in a few years, you'll change your mind; your aversion to business, indifference to money, and ecology fanaticism will all fade away, and you'll wish that you had taken that business degree. You sadly agree with them in their prediction of your future desires: you know that that's what happens to almost everyone.

Now, if it's rational to count future desires as well as present ones in what you do, the right thing to do is to enrol in that business course. Even though you don't now want to do it, you know that it will maximize your desire fulfillment, counting both your present and future desires. All told, your life will contain a far greater quantity of fulfilled desires if you take that degree. Is this the rational way to think?

> Don't be too quick in answering Yes. Remember that saving whales, not making money, is what you're now really interested in. Why should you weigh those interests against what your future self will be interested in? Who cares about that person? Anyway (you reason), if that person is a capitalist with no interest in Saving the Planet, you should do what you can to prevent that person's desires from being fulfilled.

Harming and Benefitting the Dead

ARISTOTLE, IN HIS DISCUSSION of the proverb "Count no man happy until he is dead," decides that this could not mean that anyone is happy when dead; instead, he supposes, what's being said here is that dead people are at least beyond evils and misfortunes. It seems obvious, and many philosophers agree, that the dead can't be harmed.

But, Aristotle continues, this "affords matter for discussion" because "both evil and good are thought to exist for a dead man ... e.g., honours and dishonours and the good or bad fortunes of children and in general of descendants."[1]

Consider these examples:

(1) Fred (the Elvis fan discussed above) has died still desiring that Elvis

---

1   *Nicomachean Ethics*, Bk. I, Ch. 10.

statue, still unable to afford it. After his death, the family considers putting one in the backyard of his former house, now belonging to his daughter Elvissa, who hates the idea. "He always wanted it," argue some other relatives. "We really ought to do it for him!"

(2) Sally's aged mother Martha loved the traditional foods of Newfoundland, where she grew up. Martha came to Sally's house for dinner every Friday, and Sally would cook fish 'n' brewis served with scrunchions,[1] even though everyone else hated the stuff. Now that Martha is dead, Sally still occasionally makes that dish on a Friday. "Mum loved it," she says.

(3) Many of the old houses in Mrs. Pill's neighbourhood have been sold to absentee landlords who have divided them into a number of tiny apartments to rent to students going to the university a few blocks away. Mrs. Pill always used to complain about this: "It ruins the neighbourhood," she'd say. She vowed that her house would never be converted into student apartments—"Over my dead body!" she'd say. It turned out she was right. When she died, her daughter, who inherited the house, immediately sold it to a slumlord who converted it into tiny apartments. Mrs. Pill's other children were appalled. "She'd roll over in her grave," they said.

The descendents' respect for their dead relatives is an understandable human reaction. But what happens post-mortem has no value for the deceased. The dead are beyond harm and benefit, but don't their desires deserve respect? Maybe not. Remember the first Elvis-statue example above: it seemed that Fred's past desires were irrelevant (to him or to anyone else) when he ceased to have them. And, of course, a dead person has ceased to have any desires.

SOME QUESTIONS TO THINK ABOUT: Is there any relevant difference in the stories of Fred, Sally, and Mrs. Pill that makes fulfilling the dead person's desires more sensible? (Have a look also at the example called **When Promise-Breaking Is Obligatory** in Chapter XIII.) Maybe you think that this is pointless sentimentality or superstition in all cases. Maybe you think

---

1 Soak separately overnight: 2 lbs. of salt fish, 6 cakes of hard bread. Change water on fish, boil for 20 minutes then drain. Bring bread to boil in same water used for soaking, then drain. Combine cooked fish with bread. Serve with scrunchions (crisp-fried pieces of pork fat or skin).

that one or more of building that statue, serving that dinner, and keeping the house as a one-family dwelling would be a suitable memorial for the dead person, but that's a different matter: it's an expression of the feelings of the living, not doing the dead any favours. But then consider Aristotle's example of "dishonouring" the dead: would you feel that it's wrong to destroy the reputation of someone who's dead—someone you didn't have any special feeling for? In this case, your protecting the reputation of the dead person isn't an expression of any feeling you have for that person at all. It appears to be nothing but the straightforward moral act of preventing harm to that person. And consider the case of someone who leaves a trust-fund to pay for an annual ceremony in perpetuity. A hundred years later, nobody cares about the dead person or about what they see as a silly useless ceremony—a waste of money. Do you think that they should stop performing the ceremony, and give the money to (for example) a worthy charity? If not, why not? (Not because of the harm to the dead person, right?)

What Happens to Somebody Who Is Hardly Me

HERE'S A SURPRISING ARGUMENT to the conclusion that one should not be very concerned about what will happen in one's far future. In Chapter XI we took a look at what some philosophers had to say about identifying the same person at two different times. Some of them argue that what's relevant are factors such as memory and other psychological links, bodily continuity, and so on. But that person who will have your name in the very far future will be connected only very tenuously to the present you: that person will remember very few of your current experiences, will be psychologically quite different, will have a body that resembles your present one only a bit, and contains almost none of the same matter. So it seems that this person is the future *you* only to a small degree. You're interested in what happens to you, but if that far distant person is you only to a small degree, you should be interested in what happens to that person only to a very small degree.

People are, of course, worried about dying; some are worried a lot about this. If you're young and healthy, death will probably be a long way off. And if the argument above is right, then that person who dies later on will be you only to a very small degree. Maybe this realization might make you a little less worried about death.

FOR FURTHER READING: Derek Parfit gives an argument something like this in "Personal Identity."

How to Get What You Want

SOMETIMES, OF COURSE, GETTING what you want is difficult or impossible. Here's a solution to this sort of problem: start wanting only those things you can easily get.

Suppose, for example, that Marvin is a connoisseur of fine wines. He's not very rich, however, and he's often dissatisfied at not being able to buy the vintages he craves. He devotes much of his salary to buying fine wines, and sacrifices other things he wants; but he can get only a little of the good stuff. How can Marvin solve his problem? It would be solved, of course, if he could get enough money to buy all the finest wine he wants, but this seems impossible. Here's a solution that does seem possible; what do you think of it?

> He should kill his desire for expensive wine—change his desires and tastes so that he enjoys low-cost, inferior wine.

Is this sort of alteration of desires and tastes really possible?

> Yes it is. It does take time and effort to alter one's tastes and desires, but it can be done. People can get themselves to like all sorts of things. One way to do it is by practice: if Marvin started drinking only Chateau Plonque, that miserable but cheap rotgut, in pleasurable surroundings, telling himself how delicious it was, after a long while he very well might get to like it—even to prefer it to the expensive stuff.

This sort of solution is widely applicable to the problem of not getting what you want. Matilda is in love with Matthew, but Matthew won't give her the time of day. Max is attracted to Matilda, but Matilda doesn't care for him. She only has eyes for Matthew. She has a problem, but she can solve it by ignoring Matthew and marrying Max. This will hurt for a while, but given practice and self-discipline, she can get herself, sooner or later, to love Max and to be indifferent to Matthew. It can be done.

There are well-known and effective techniques by which one can alter one's own desires. The advertising industry is wholly devoted to the alteration of desires. It's often difficult or impossible for a government to give its citizens what they want, so some governments try changing what the citizens want, so that they wind up wanting what they're given. Your own government probably spends a lot of money on advertising for this purpose.

SOME QUESTIONS TO THINK ABOUT: There is something wrong with this as a solution to getting what you want, isn't there? What is it?

Electronic Pleasure

A WHILE BACK SOME psychologists claimed to have discovered the "pleasure centre" in rats' brains.[1] A tiny electric wire was inserted in this area of the brain. The rat was given a little lever in its cage; when the rat pressed the lever, a mild current was sent through the wire, stimulating that part of its brain. The rat seemed to *love* this brain-stimulation. Having discovered the effect, it soon was pressing the lever at a tremendous rate. It did not stop even to eat from the food bin right next to the lever. It would die of hunger before it would stop. This stimulation was apparently so pleasurable that the rat preferred it to anything.

Now, these psychologists claim that humans have a similar area of their brains, and they speculate that with the aid of a little wire painlessly inserted into that area of your brain, you might be able to give yourself that overwhelmingly desirable pleasure. It's hard to imagine what that would feel like, but you might find it so wonderful that you would prefer it to anything else. Do you want yourself hooked up?

> Maybe you're afraid that you would get stuck to the push-button sending stimulation to your brain, like the rat, and be unable to eat. You would die after a short (but immensely pleasurable) life.

If this prospect doesn't appeal, then suppose we make getting wired a little more attractive by guaranteeing that you will be kept fed and otherwise taken care of. Now do you want to get hooked up?

Consider the consequences: you might like that stimulation so much that you might lose your job, give up your studies, never see friends, family, or loved ones ever again—you might, in short, abandon everything that now means something to you. But remember: this sensation is so fantastically wonderful that it makes absolutely all of this worthwhile. What do you say?

A QUESTION TO THINK ABOUT: Maybe you think that there's more to life than getting what you really want more than anything else. What? Why?

---

1   James Olds, "Pleasure Centers in the Brain."

2. Relationships with Other People

I'm Gonna Buy a Plastic Doll That I Can Call My Own

THE ACME CORPORATION, LET us imagine, has perfected its mechanical robots to the point that you can order one to fit your own specifications, and a carton will arrive from the factory containing Shirley or Seymour, girlfriend/boyfriend of your dreams (batteries not included). All of his or her characteristics will be perfect, as far as you are concerned: mentally and physically exactly the companion you've always wanted.

Many people would not be attracted by the idea of buying an Acme robot, though they would be very interested in meeting a real person with those specifications. To justify this attitude toward the robots, we need to find relevant differences between them and real people. What are these?

It's hard to explain why the robots' differences are relevant. They are made out of plastic and electronic components, not flesh and blood; but so what? Their plastic covering feels just like the skin you love to touch, so how can the fact that it's plastic make any difference? As far as *your contact* with an Acme robot is concerned, it's indistinguishable from a real person covered with real skin. Inside a robot is a computer, not a liver, pancreas, etc.; but again, why does this make any difference? You can't feel these insides, and they make absolutely no difference to any of your actual encounters with Shirley or Seymour.

Don't think of the Acme robots acting stiffly and mechanically like those robots in bad science-fiction movies. Acme makes them much better. They act smoothly and naturally. They are capable of showing the full range of emotions. Remember they are indistinguishable from ordinary humans.

"Aha!" you say. "They *show* the full range of emotions, but they don't *feel* them. After all, they're machines. I want a friend who really feels things, not one who merely acts them out."

Well, what makes you think they don't really feel them? Does the fact that they are manufactured out of plastic and transistors show that it's impossible for them to feel things? (We ran into this question in Chapter X.)

"But," you continue, "another difference between a robot and a real human is their past. A real human was born of woman, and had an infancy and childhood. Acme robots can speak convincingly of their mothers and their childhood, but this is all fake, programmed into them by Acme because owners might enjoy discussing the robots' childhoods with them. They were all actually 'born' only within the past year in the factory."

But why does this make a difference? Again, they're now indistinguishable, for all practical purposes, from real people.

"But I know that they're imitations," you object, "so I wouldn't be able to have a good relationship with one."

But isn't this an unfortunate prejudice on your part—one you'd be much better off without?

"I just don't like imitations," you insist. "I always buy genuine leather shoes rather than those plastic imitation leather ones."

But why do you insist on genuine leather? Because leather feels better, lasts longer, etc.? But suppose they developed an imitation leather that felt *exactly* like real leather, that wore in *exactly* the same way, and that was, in sum, indistinguishable from the real thing. The only difference between this perfect imitation and real leather was where the imitation came from (a plastics factory, not an animal) and its chemical constitution. But these have nothing to do with your actual relationship with your shoes, do they? If you still preferred real leather to this perfect imitation, you'd have some explaining to do. It seems that you're being irrational.

"I'm willing to grant that my preference for real over perfect imitation leather is unjustifiable, but it's different when we're talking about *people*. There's something special about a relationship with people. It's not merely a matter of the nature of the contact with them."

Maybe there is something to this. But it certainly needs more explanation. A good explanation might reveal something important about how we feel (or ought to feel) about other people.

Replaceable People in Literature

SIMILAR CONCERNS TO THOSE raised in the problem of the plastic lover come up occasionally in literature. One instance of this occurs (extraneously to the main point of the story) in a corner of the Book of Job, in the Bible.

God (as a result of a dare from Satan) deprives Job of everything he values: his sheep, oxen, camels, servants, and so on; God even kills off his seven sons and three daughters. Job is understandably miserable and puzzled, but he does not lose his trust in God. In the end he is given "twice as much as he had before,"[1] plus seven sons and three daughters—presumably *brand new* sons and daughters, but really good ones. Happy ending! But we are a bit taken aback by the idea that his replacement children could really set things right.

Another instance: Meursault, the hero of Camus's *The Stranger* (*L'Étranger*), is a peculiar man. He is sensual, well-meaning, and truthful, but he lacks the complexity and the depth of commitment and relationship that we think characterizes the normally developed adult. His friend Marie asks him if he'll marry her.

> I said I didn't mind; if she was keen on it, we'd get married.
>
> Then she asked me again if I loved her. I replied, much as before, that her question meant nothing or next to nothing—but I supposed I didn't.... Then she asked:
>
> "Suppose another girl had asked you to marry her—I mean, a girl you liked in the same way as you like me—would you have said 'Yes' to her, too?"
>
> "Naturally."[2]

Perhaps Marie is asking Meursault the right question. Love of another person—we suppose—is not simply a matter of valuing the characteristics of another person. If it were, we would love anyone just as much who had comparable characteristics, and we would be happy if a loved one were replaced by someone else just as good.

3. Yuk

Hello Dolly!

THE SUCCESSFUL CLONING OF some of the higher mammals has made it probable that the technique could be used on humans; and there has been a huge flurry of moral outrage expressed at this idea, together with calls for new legislation to outlaw it before it's too late. Much of what has been written about human cloning gives what the authors take to be reasons why that prospect is so morally outrageous in their eyes, but the arguments for the immorality of human cloning are not very persuasive to those not already convinced. Here's a sample of them, followed by the fairly obvious replies.

---

1 *Job* 42:10.
2 Albert Camus, *The Outsider* (also translated as *The Stranger*), p. 50.

(1) Human cloning is unnatural.

Reply: So are all sorts of things that are perfectly morally acceptable: vaccination for disease, eating cooked food, airplane travel, the super-white colour of movie stars' teeth.

(2) Human cloning would be available only for the rich.

Reply: So are other things that are morally acceptable: Rolls-Royces, caviar, the Victoria's Secret diamond-covered Fantasy Bra ($2 million).

(3) Human cloning would increase the population.

Reply: So does sex, which nobody—well, almost nobody—considers immoral.

(4) Human cloning would be used for all kinds of horrible purposes. They'd make an army of docile subhumans to work in factories. They'd create headless organ-slaves to be cut up when someone needed a transplant.

Reply: This is just like arguing that chainsaws are immoral because somebody might use one for chainsaw-murders. If one of these evil uses for cloning looked like it had a chance of occurring, laws could be passed against it in particular. Anyway, even this would probably be unnecessary, because these things are illegal under current law. Cloning would also be useful for all sorts of good purposes—like providing desperately wanted children to infertile couples or to single people. It doesn't make sense to condemn it because it might also have some bad uses.

(5) Human cloning runs against our values as a community.

Reply: This last bit of reasoning, very frequently heard, merely says that we're against it—some of us, anyway. This sheds no light whatever on the *reasons* why cloning might be wrong.

If these are the best reasons people can come up with, then there's no good argument for the immorality of cloning. But it doesn't follow that cloning is morally okay! It might be wrong anyway. This would be a curious and interesting state of affairs. We'd have a moral truth here, but we'd be unable to give reasons why. We expect there to be good evidence for scientific truths, provided by reasoning, observation, and experimentation. Maybe the situation is different for moral truths.

Frankensurgery

JOE ROSEN, A RESPECTED plastic surgeon, asked at a recent medical-ethics convention:

> Why do we only value the average? Why are plastic surgeons dedicated only to restoring our current notions of the conventional, as opposed to letting people explore, if they want, what the possibilities are?

He has a vision of the plastic surgery of the future: cochlear implants to improve our hearing to that of an owl; retinal implants to improve our vision so that we could see many miles; fins to make us swim like fishes; echolocation devices for navigation in the dark; motorized fingers for chefs that could whip eggs; noses that doubled as flashlights; wings![1]

All this is entertaining as science fiction, but what do you think about actually permitting it to happen? Most people view this sort of thing with horror and disgust, but Rosen points out that it's merely a bit of an extension to the kinds of things already routinely permitted: nose-jobs, liposuction, face-lifts, breast augmentation. Perhaps this doesn't reduce your sense of horror and disgust, but the question I want to raise is whether your feelings here constitute a good reason to prevent other people—people who want these things—from getting them done. I feel a bit disgusted when I see someone with a ring piercing her lower lip; but this doesn't mean that lip-piercing should be illegal.

Speaking of the ethics of biotechnology that "crosses species boundaries," a medical-ethics specialist writes: "In the absence of an argument or the ability to point to some specific harm that might be involved …, we should regard the objections per se to such practises … as mere and gratuitous prejudice."[2]

Canine Disrespect

HERE'S AN EXAMPLE OF a different sort. After a pedestrian was killed by a car on the corner of my street, someone placed a wreath there, on the sidewalk, leaning against a stop-sign pole. I walked past the wreath with my dog, and, before I could stop him, he peed on the wreath. Nobody saw except me, so nobody (except possibly me) was offended. Is there something bad involved here? Is my dog immoral?

---

1 Lauren Slater, "DR. DAEDALUS: A radical plastic surgeon wants to give you wings."
2 John Harris, *Wonderwoman and Superman*; quoted in Slater.

The Yuck Factor

CONSIDER THESE CASES:

> A brother and sister are vacationing together, and they decide it might be interesting and fun—at least a novel experience—to make love to each other. The sister is on birth-control pills, so there's no chance of a pregnancy resulting; and the brother will wear a condom, just to be extra-safe. They enjoy it a lot, but decide not to do it again, and to keep the experience as a special secret, which makes them feel even closer. Nobody ever finds out about it, and both brother and sister feel good about having done it.

> A woman is cleaning out her closet and finds an old national flag, in shreds and unusable as anything but dusting rags, so she rips it up and uses it for that purpose.

> After a family's dog is killed by a car, they decide that a fitting funeral for their beloved pet would involve cooking and eating him.

> A man buys himself a whole chicken every week at the supermarket, and before cooking it, has sexual intercourse with it.

Almost everyone has spontaneous gut-reactions that something horrible is going on in some or all of these cases. But they're all private acts involving adults who are rational and fully consenting. Some of them are enjoyable for the participants, and none are harmful to anyone. So why are they wrong?

People try to come up with reasons to explain their moral repulsion, but it may be that what's going on here is just an immediate reaction, not based on any moral principles or reasoning.[1]

What prompts this kind of immediate disgust has been called the "yuck factor." Some ethicists think that the yuck-reaction is a sign of some sort of basic harmfulness or evil, and that our immediate reactions of this sort come from a source of moral knowledge within us. Others, however, argue that, while some of these reactions may originate from a genetically built-in tendency that evolved because of some sort of beneficial function, there's no reason at all to think that such innate reflexes reveal moral truth; anyway,

---

[1]   People's reactions to these stories were studied by psychologists; they published their findings in J. Haidt, H. Koller, & M.G. Dias, "Affect, Culture, and Morality, or Is It Wrong to Eat Your Dog?", and J. Haidt, "The Emotional Dog and Its Rational Tail."

these reactions are often not built-in, but mere prejudice that is learned early and that becomes deeply rooted and automatic later. They point out that at various times homophobia, sexism, and racism have been driven by reflexive "yuck" reactions that we have (and should have) learned not to trust, and not to have.

FOR FURTHER READING: "The Wisdom of Repugnance" by Leon R. Kass defends the yuck-factor as moral guidance. Martha Nussbaum has written influentially in opposition to this idea; for a quick introduction to her views, see her online interview "Discussing Disgust."

SOME QUESTIONS TO THINK ABOUT: Well, have you got any convincing arguments in these cases? Can you point to specific harms that might be involved? In the absence of that, does this show that your objections are "mere and gratuitous prejudice"?

4. Acting and Refraining

Two Ways to Kill Granny

IT'S OFTEN TAKEN TO be a principle of moral reasoning that *doing* something is morally different from merely *refraining from acting*, even if the doing and the refraining have the same outcome. In ordinary circumstances, for example, merely doing nothing and thereby failing to save someone's life isn't, of course, a very nice thing, but it's supposed to be not as bad as actually killing the person, despite the fact that refraining from acting (not saving the life) and the action (killing) have the same outcome: the person's death. Are you convinced that this is right? Then consider this:

Suppose evil Ian hates his grandmother, and wishes she were dead. While she is taking her bath, Ian decides to enter the bathroom and to hold Granny under water till she dies. Now compare these two scenarios:

S1. Ian enters the bathroom and holds Granny under water, and she dies.

S2. Ian enters the bathroom. By coincidence, just at that moment Granny slips on the soap, hits her head on the side of the tub, and falls unconscious. Ian notices that the water will soon rise above her head and drown her; all he has to do to save her life is to turn off the water. But he refrains from doing this; he does nothing, and she dies.

Scenarios **S1** and **S2** are designed to be as alike as possible, except for the difference that in **S1** Ian's *action* results in death, whereas in **S2** Ian's *refraining* has that outcome. But many people think that Ian would be judged to be equally at fault in both scenarios. Maybe there really isn't a real moral difference between acting and refraining after all.[1]

Moral Technology

THE SUPPOSED MORAL DIFFERENCE between acting and refraining has led to the invention of a bizarre bit of medico-ethical technology.

There is a general rule of medical ethics that depends on this supposed moral difference. When someone is near death from an incurable terminal disease, modern medicine is sometimes able to prolong that person's life for a while using elaborate life-support systems. But when that period would be full of unrelievable suffering for that person, and when death is only postponed a bit, not prevented, often everyone—the person him/herself, family and friends, the medical personnel involved, and experts on medical ethics—agree that it is better that the life not be prolonged.

Killing the person in this state is illegal and widely thought immoral. On the other hand, many people would think it okay not to have attached the person to the life-support systems in the first place. But suppose that the person has already been attached to those systems before the decision not to prolong life is made. In order to end that person's life now, someone would have to switch off the life-support; but this would be *doing something* that results in death, not merely refraining from doing something. The acting/refraining principle we have been discussing would count this as morally forbidden. It is murder.

This is where ethics-tech comes to the rescue. A simple addition to the life-support system puts a timer on it, designed to shut it off after, say, twenty-four hours. If, before this time runs out, a button is pushed, an additional twenty-four hours is added to the timer, and the machine stays on for one more day. Pushing this button once every day can keep the machine on indefinitely, if that's what's desired.

You can see how this "solves" the ethical problem. If it is decided that prolonging the life would be a bad idea, nobody has to *do* anything. All that we have to do is to *refrain* from pushing the button; the timer would run out, all by itself, with the desired result.

There's a danger in using this adapted machine: what if someone prematurely just forgets to push the button? But this danger is outweighed, in the

---

1   A version of this story is told by James Rachels in "Active and Passive Euthanasia."

eyes of some people who take the acting/refraining distinction seriously, by the moral advantage this adapted machine sometimes gives us.

But there's something very bizarre about this ethical "solution." The object, everyone agrees, is to provide an earlier, more humane end to the unfortunate patient's life. Can it reasonably be supposed that using a machine that stops all by itself, as opposed to one that has to be shut off, makes the moral difference between a humane, morally praiseworthy procedure, and a morally hideous, utterly forbidden murder? An ethics that tells us that the addition of this timer makes that difference is clearly an ethics run amok.

Here we have another reason to doubt that the acting/refraining distinction is a morally important one.

Ten-to-One Dilemmas

HERE ARE A COUPLE of additional cases to try out your moral intuitions on.

Imagine you're standing on a railroad line, at a point where the track splits into two. There's a manually operable switch at that point, which can send a train coming down the track into one or the other of the branches at the fork. A short way past the fork, some little children are playing on the tracks. Ten of them are playing on the north fork, and one on the south. You notice that the switch is now set to send a train down the north fork, and a high-speed train is approaching. You can't stop the train, and there's no time to warn the children to get off the tracks. If the train continues, it will kill ten children. But you can throw the switch, sending the train down the south track, where one child will be killed. Should you throw the switch? Here are two possible answers:

1. A horrible tragedy will result whatever you do, of course. But there would be a worse tragedy—the death of ten children—if you don't throw the switch. If you do, only one death will result. It seems that you should throw the switch.

2. But the acting/refraining distinction gives a different answer. If you throw the switch, you are *acting*. If you just stand there and do nothing, you are *refraining*. Your action will save ten lives, but you will knowingly bring about the death of that child on the south track. This is murder, and forbidden.

FOR FURTHER READING: This problem has become a classic in moral philosophy. It's usually called the "Trolley Problem," and among its well-known treatments in the literature are Philippa Foot's "The Problem of Abortion and the Doctrine of Double Effect" and Judith Jarvis Thomson's "Killing, Letting Die, and the Trolley Problem."

How to Get Organ Donors

PERHAPS BY NOW, HAVING been convinced by all these examples, you doubt that the acting/refraining distinction is a morally relevant one. Maybe you think it's clear that the right thing to do is to throw the switch, sacrificing one child's life to save ten.

If that's what you think, here's one final example designed to confuse you.

Suppose you are the physician in charge of the transplant division at a big hospital. Ten children are under your care. All of them are dying from various organ failures, and all of them could be saved only by organ transplants. One needs a heart transplant, two need kidney transplants, three need liver transplants, and four need lung transplants. None of these organs is available, and none will become available until after all ten have died. All you need is one healthy dead body, out of which you can extract a heart, two kidneys, and the liver and lungs, each of which can be cut up into pieces to provide all the transplant material needed to save the lives of your patients. (This is, of course, science fiction. Transplant recipients have to be carefully matched to donors, and it's unlikely that one donor could provide organs for all ten patients. Other features also make this story currently impossible. But ignore all this.)

While you're pondering your problem, you idly glance out the window. There, playing on the sidewalk outside the hospital, is a healthy-looking little girl the same size as your patients. You run outside, grab the child, and carry her to the operating room, where you cut her up to provide the parts necessary for your patients. Ten children are saved; one dies.

Everyone would agree that, at the very least, you should be locked up in some unpleasant prison for a good long time as a result of this. But what's of interest here is the moral reasoning that condemns this. In particular, if you accepted the conclusion in the example just above that you ought to throw the railroad switch, you should consider what makes that case different from this one. In both cases, there are ten children who will die if you do nothing, and in both cases, the life of one innocent child, who would live if you did nothing, is sacrificed to save the ten. What, if anything, is the difference?

How to Assault a Police Officer by Doing Nothing

HERE'S ANOTHER CASE THAT raises questions about acting and refraining. This one is not imaginary.

Fagan is parking his car on a city street, and a constable is guiding him into the space. Without knowing he's doing it, Fagan brings his car to a halt with one of its tires resting squarely on top of the constable's foot. The constable points out that the car is on his foot. Fagan responds with an offensive remark and tells the constable he could wait. Finally, after repeated requests, he moves his car.

Fagan is arrested and charged with assaulting a police officer in the execution of his duty. He pleads not guilty, on the following grounds. An assault is defined in law as an action (of a certain sort) accompanied by a malicious intent. When Fagan's car rolled onto the constable's foot this may be construed as his action, since he was in control of his car; but there was, as yet, no assault, because he did not know that the foot was there. He had no intention to stop his car on the foot, so assault, which presumes intent, had not yet been committed. A moment later the constable made Fagan aware that his tire was on the constable's foot; at that point, Fagan got the malicious intention to leave it there. But leaving the car there is not doing anything—it's not an *action*, so it can't be an assault.

Fagan's defence did not work. In finding him guilty of assault, a judge gave this (perhaps not entirely convincing) reasoning: Fagan's action was an ongoing one, beginning with his rolling his car onto the foot and continuing through the time when he refused to get it off. The malicious intention developed during this extended action, so the requirements for assault were satisfied.

FOR FURTHER READING: The Canadian case of *Fagan vs. Commissioner of Metropolitan Police* (1969) 1 Q.B. 439 is described and analyzed in *An Introduction to Criminal Law* by Graham Parker.

Poor Joshua!

THE ACTING/REFRAINING DISTINCTION IS relevant to other legal debates about genuinely important and tragic cases—not just amusing ones like *Fagan*.

In 1984, four-year-old Joshua DeShaney was beaten so badly by his father that he suffered brain damage so severe he would have to spend the rest of his life in an institution for the "profoundly retarded." His father was convicted of child abuse.

The county Department of Social Services had been aware for a long time that Joshua's father had been abusing him, and took various steps to protect him, including once temporarily removing him from his father's custody. But on this occasion, despite very good reason to think that the child was in real danger, they did not protect him from his father.

Joshua and his mother, acting on his behalf, sued various social workers and their department for failing to protect him. The case reached the US

Supreme Court in 1988, and that Court's decision affirmed the lower courts' judgement that the social workers did not violate Joshua's rights by failing to protect him.

One principle that Supreme Court Justices made much of in their printed opinions accompanying their ruling is that there is a duty to protect someone only when there has been a "special relationship" established that removes the ordinary means individuals have for self-protection. For example, when somebody is in prison, they are deprived of their normal protections and liberties, so the state has a duty to protect them and could be sued if that person is harmed due to the state's failure to protect. But the state had undertaken no "special relationship" with Joshua which made it their duty to protect him.

Justice Blackmun, dissenting from the decision of the Court, wrote:

Poor Joshua! Victim of repeated attacks by an irresponsible, bullying, cowardly, and intemperate father, and abandoned by respondents who placed him in a dangerous predicament and who knew or learned what was going on, and yet did essentially nothing except, as the Court revealingly observes ... "dutifully recorded these incidents in [their] files." It is a sad commentary upon American life and constitutional principles—so full of late of patriotic fervor and proud proclamations about "liberty and justice for all"—that this child, Joshua DeShaney, is now assigned to live out the remainder of his life profoundly retarded.

Chief Justice Rehnquist, delivering the opinion of the Court, wrote:

While the State may have been aware of the dangers that Joshua faced in the free world, it played no part in their creation, nor did it do anything to render him any more vulnerable to them. That the State once took temporary custody of Joshua does not alter the analysis, for when it returned him to his father's custody, it placed him in no worse position than that in which he would have been had it not acted at all; the State does not become the permanent guarantor of an individual's safety by having once offered him shelter. Under these circumstances, the State had no constitutional duty to protect Joshua.

Judges and lawyers, like other humans, are moved by natural sympathy in a case like this to find a way for Joshua and his mother to receive adequate compensation for the grievous harm inflicted upon them. But before yielding to that impulse, it is well to remember once again that the harm was inflicted not by the State of Wisconsin, but by Joshua's father. The most that can be said of the state functionaries in this case is that they stood by and did nothing when suspicious circumstances dictated a more active role for them.[1]

The Bad Samaritan

SALLY IS ON HER way to the coffee shop when Fred, an elderly man walking down the street in front of her, falls to the ground. "Help me!" croaks Fred. "My heart pills—they're in that bag I've dropped over there! Please!" But Sally is just desperate for her daily double shot half decaf skinny latte, so she just steps over the man on the ground and continues on her way.

If Sally were a nurse who was hired to accompany old Fred on his walk and to help him out if he got in trouble, she'd certainly be failing in her duty. But as things are, Sally has no "special relationship" with Fred which gives her a duty to help him.

SOME QUESTIONS TO THINK ABOUT: We can agree that Sally is not the sort of person we'd like as a friend, but has she actually violated a duty? Should there be a law against what she did? (This would have to be a law against not-doing.) Should Fred, if he survives, or Fred's children if he doesn't, be able to sue Sally for not helping him?

Into the Mainstream of Philosophy

THE ACTING/REFRAINING DISTINCTION IS another one considered in action theory. This issue has special relevance in ethics, since we're often supposed to be more to blame for the bad results of our actions than for similar results of our refraining from acting. You might think about this issue by imagining and morally comparing pairs of circumstances that differ only along acting/refraining lines. One currently lively and important debate along these lines concerns euthanasia—mercy killing. It's widely thought that it's morally permissible to let someone die—to refrain from keeping him or her alive—in the terminal and horribly painful stages of a disease, but that it's morally impermissible to act to kill that person. If the acting/refraining distinction makes no sense or is morally irrelevant, then we shouldn't make this distinction. What do you think about euthanasia?

---

1   DeShaney v. Winnebago Cty. Soc. Servs. Dept.

Chapter XV

Law, Action, and Responsibility

1. Why Is That Illegal?

Blackmailing Letterman

WHAT HAPPENED TO DAVID Letterman, the US late-night TV talk-show host, raised an ethical/legal problem. A while back, he had affairs with some of his female staff members—but that's not the issue. It's that a TV producer found out about these affairs and was accused of attempting to blackmail Letterman by threatening to write a screenplay exposing him, if Letterman didn't fork over a large sum of money. No moral problem yet: everyone thinks that blackmail is nasty. But the publicity about this resulted in some discussion of an interesting question: why, exactly, should acts like this be *illegal*? After all, writing a screenplay (even one that exposes bad things that a celebrity did) is not very nice, but it's perfectly legal (at least in the US; other countries, with legal systems that don't emphasize freedom of speech as strongly as the US, sometimes consider this illegal). And asking for money in exchange for doing something (or not doing it) is legal. Why should combining the two be illegal?

Here are some attempts to answer that question that don't seem to work:

It's really nasty, so it should be illegal. No, that's not enough. If someone says, "Here comes that pig-faced lousy pile of excrement" every time she sees you, that's really nasty, but it's not against the law, and it shouldn't be.

Threatening somebody should be illegal. No, it's not illegal to tell somebody, "If you don't keep your dog off my property, I'll call the dog-catcher who'll come and take him away." And it shouldn't be.

Threatening somebody for money should be illegal. No, it's not illegal to tell somebody, "If you don't pay for those chickens of mine your dog killed, I'll take you to court." Nor should it be.

Threatening somebody with public exposure should be illegal. No, it's not illegal to tell somebody, "If you don't keep your dog off my property, I'll write a letter to the editor of our local newspaper telling everyone what a mess your dog made." Nor should it be.

Threatening somebody with public exposure for a secret moral indiscretion you've discovered should be illegal. No, it's not illegal to tell somebody, "If you don't end that affair with your secretary, I'll tell your wife." Nor should it be.

This transaction is typical of capitalistic free enterprise. All capitalistic transactions are exploitative and immoral. Well, maybe they are—but what needs to be explained is why this attempted transaction is especially bad.

This transaction is typical of capitalistic free enterprise. The freedom of the market is a wonderful thing, and shouldn't be infringed on, so this should be legal. Well, maybe any free economic interchange is okay—but what needs to be explained is why all but the most extremely libertarian of capitalists think this is an exception.[1]

How Not to Sell Ice in Alberta

HERE'S ANOTHER REAL CASE that raises questions about illegality. Arctic Glacier, Inc. is the leading seller of ice in Alberta. (Don't laugh. There is, in fact, a summer in Alberta.) They offered a lower wholesale price than their competitor to Sobeys, a supermarket chain, if Sobeys agreed to stock only their brand of ice-cubes. Does this sound like perfectly ordinary business practice to you? In 2007, their competitor, Polar Ice Express, Inc., took Arctic to court, claiming damages for unlawful interference with its economic interests. Polar won the case (and the appeal) and were awarded $50,000 in damages plus nearly $100,000 in legal costs.

---

1   Some of these (inadequate) reasons, and others, were mentioned in an interesting little article about the Letterman case, "Brainteaser: You've Got Mail," by Lizzie Widdicombe. Smilansky's *Ten Moral Paradoxes* contains a worthwhile discussion of the blackmail problem.

What Arctic did was illegal; it counted, under the Alberta Competition Act, as "price discrimination" because Arctic didn't offer *all* its customers that same lower price—only when they faced competition from Polar. And the court ruled that Arctic intended to injure Polar, and that Polar suffered economic loss. A judge called this "outrageous conduct."[1]

The law is a much more complex thing than you would have guessed.

SOME QUESTIONS TO THINK ABOUT: Why should blackmail be illegal? Should Arctic's "price discrimination" be illegal? What it is about a bad act that means it should be illegal?

2. Twilight-Zone Legislation

Legislating π

IN 1897, A BILL was under consideration by the Indiana state legislature. Bill 246, in its preamble, announced that it was "A Bill for an act introducing a new mathematical truth and offered as a contribution to education." The new truth in question was a formula for *squaring the circle*, a problem considered by geometers since ancient times. To "square the circle" is to construct, using compass and straightedge alone, a square equal in area to a given circle. It was proven impossible in 1882.

Section 2 of the bill pointed out that a consequence of the new truth was that "the ratio of the diameter and circumference is as five-fourths to four"— that is, that the value of π is 3.2.

The bill was given first reading in the House, then referred to the Committee on Canals, for some reason; it was then transferred to the Committee on Education, which reported it back to the House with a favourable recommendation. It received second and third reading in the House, was passed 67–0, and was sent to the Senate for consideration. The Senate referred it to the Committee on Temperance (for some reason), which reported it back with a favourable recommendation. But by chance at that point a Purdue University professor happened to see the bill and managed to convince a number of senators that its author was a crackpot; so after second reading, the Senate decided to postpone a decision on the bill indefinitely.

This little story is worth telling as a landmark in the history of silliness; but what's amazing, from a philosophical point of view, is the idea that a mathematical fact (true or false) might be considered the subject of legislation.

---

1 Some details of this case were revealed in "A conspiracy that drove up the price of ice," by Nathan Vanderklippe. Legal particulars can be found at "Alberta Decision...."

Some Unusual Laws

THE FOLLOWING EXAMPLES COME from a website on silly laws:[1]

- An Arkansas law forbids the Arkansas River to rise higher than to the Main Street Bridge in Little Rock.
- In California, animals are banned from mating publicly within 1,500 feet of a tavern, school, or place of worship.
- In Pocatello, Idaho, a law passed in 1912 provided that "The carrying of concealed weapons is forbidden, unless same are exhibited to public view." And in Seattle, it's illegal to carry a concealed weapon over six feet in length.
- It is against the law for a monster to enter the corporate limits of Urbana, Illinois.
- Kirkland, Illinois, law forbids bees to fly over the village or through any of its streets.
- A Texas law requires that when two trains meet each other at a railroad crossing, each shall come to a full stop, and neither shall proceed until the other has gone.
- Horses are forbidden to eat fire hydrants in Marshalltown, Iowa.

These were reported in a newspaper article:[2]

- A 2007 Chinese law requires dead Buddhist monks to get government permission before being reincarnated.
- It's illegal to die in the British Houses of Parliament. (It's a royal palace, and if one dies there, one is entitled to a state funeral.)
- A widely publicized law was passed in 1954 by the little southern French municipality of Châteauneuf-du-Pape prohibiting the landing of flying saucers.[3]

SOME QUESTIONS TO THINK ABOUT: Is there something that these laws have in common? What general principle could you provide to a legislature

---

1   These and similar ones are found at many websites, including "Stupid Laws."
2   Michael Kesterton, "Justice >> Legislative Lolz."
3   The law was passed in response to pressure from vineyard owners (the area is home to the famous wine named after it) who were afraid that flying saucers (which the French call *cigares volantes*, "flying cigars") might disrupt their crops. Apparently the law has been a successful deterrent: no flying saucers or cigars have landed there since. In response to the law, the Bonnie Doon winery in California named a similar wine "Le Cigare Volante," with wine labels picturing one of these spacecraft shining a red ray on a vineyard.

(other than Don't be stupid) that would tell them how to avoid passing this sort of legislation?

3. When Rules Collide

The Immigration Collision

WHEN THE UNIVERSITY DEPARTMENT of which I was chair had a job opening, I found out that Canadian immigration rules required that we present a list showing the citizenship and immigration status of all applicants, and that we institute special procedures when considering non-Canadians, to make sure they were definitely better qualified than any Canadian applicant.

But then I found out there was a provincial human-rights law prohibiting considering or even asking any job candidate about citizenship or immigration status.

Trapped in the Airport

VISITING IN THE US a while back, I carried both my US and Canadian passports (I am a dual citizen). At Immigration Control, when I was returning, I discovered that my Canadian passport was packed in my luggage, so I presented my US passport.

"How long are you going to stay in Canada?" the immigration official asked.

"I live here," I answered.

"Where do you work?"

"At Dalhousie University, here in Halifax."

"May I see your immigrant card or your work visa?"

"I don't have any of these. I'm a Canadian citizen."

"Okay, then, may I see your Canadian passport?"

"It's in my luggage." I looked ahead, and could see my suitcase revolving forlornly around on the luggage carousel. "It's right over there," I said pointing. "I'll go get it."

"No, you can't go through to your luggage till we clear you through immigration."

"But I can't get cleared through immigration till I get my Canadian passport from my luggage, right?"

"Right."

We both stood there thinking about this for a minute.

Finally he called a guard over, and got him to accompany me to my luggage, and I returned with my Canadian passport and all was well. Had the immigration official not been willing to cut through this stalemate, I might be stranded there for eternity, a lost soul haunting the corridor between the arrival gates and the immigration wicket, surviving on discarded pouches of airline peanuts, muttering a mysterious warning to travellers about passports and luggage.

4. Problems for Judges

The Messier Contract

A FEW YEARS AGO, Mark Messier, a hockey player, signed a contract specifying that if he was declared Most Valuable Player at the end of the season, his salary would be raised to be among the top five in the league.

Here's a scenario that would have made for difficulties. Suppose that five other players (call them LaMer, LaPerrier, LaRose, LaFleur, and Gretzky) each held a contract specifying that if he scored a hundred points during a season, then his salary should immediately be raised, if necessary, to put him among the five top-paid players in the league. Imagine that they each succeed in topping one hundred points during a season, and when each does that his salary is raised. By the time the season ends, here are their salaries:

LaMer	$10 million
LaPerrier	$9 million
LaRose	$8 million
LaFleur	$7 million
Gretzky	$6 million

Then Messier is chosen Most Valuable Player. At that point, he is making a mere $5 million. So he goes to his team's owner, contract in hand, demanding a raise to put him in the top five. The owner agrees to raise his salary to $6.5 million. But then Gretzky finds out that he is no longer in the top five, and goes to the owner of his team. His salary is accordingly raised to $6.8 million. But then Messier goes back to his owner demanding and getting an additional raise. But then Gretzky does the same. Pretty soon, both are making more than LaFleur, who demands additional money. And so on.

The team owners notice that this leapfrogging has no end. All six players, with their six respective team owners, appear before a judge whose job it is to sort out this mess.

Let's listen in to the debate in court.

Judge: Here's a solution. Let's go back to the time the problem came up. When Messier was chosen MVP, the salaries of the other five of you were above his. Suppose that Messier's salary be set at $6 million, tied with Gretzky's salary. Then only four players would be making more than Messier, so his salary would be among the top five. Only four players would be making more than Gretzky, so his salary would also be among the top five. It's solved!

Messier: Wait a minute. If Gretzky and I both made $6 million, and if the four others made higher salaries, both of us would be among the top *six*, not among the top *five*. There would be no top five salaries.

Judge: Hmm. Okay. Well, in that case, it appears that it's impossible for all six of you to get salaries among the top five in the league. Contracts specifying that someone do the impossible are invalid. So I think that all six of your contracts are invalid. Go back and negotiate valid contracts.

Messier: Hang on again. I signed my contract before any of these other guys. When I signed it there was nothing wrong with it. It's not my fault that other contracts made for difficulties. Then LaMer signed his, and there was nothing wrong with his either. Then LaPerrier, LaRose, and LaFleur each signed perfectly acceptable contracts. Gretzky signed his contract last; it was only then that a potential problem arose. Gretzky's contract is invalid.

Judge: I guess that's right.

Gretzky: Hold on. None of us signed contracts that were impossible to fulfil when we signed them. When each of us topped one hundred points, we got raises, and there was nothing impossible about our all being in the top five. The problem came up later, at the end of the season, when that damned Messier was chosen MVP. Only at that point did problems arise. So Messier's contract is the one that's invalid.

Judge: Well, okay.

Messier: Not so fast. No team owner has a contract that specifies an impossible action. When I won MVP my owner had to raise my salary, and he could. Then Gretzky wasn't any longer in the top five, so his owner had to raise his salary, and that wasn't impossible either. As salaries go up, one of the owners has to raise somebody's salary, but in no case does an owner

have to do something that's impossible. The poor guys are
just stuck with having to pay leapfrogging salaries.

Judge: That's true.

Owners: [In unison] But! But! But!

What should the judge do?

What Do Judges Do?

A CONTINUING QUESTION IN the philosophy of law is what the job of
judges is supposed to be. What you learned in civics class is that laws are *made*
by legislators, and it's the judge's duty only to *interpret* these laws. But here's a
plausible story that casts doubt on this.

Imagine that years ago, when house-trailers were first produced, Billy-
Bob towed one of them into town, bought an empty plot of land, parked
his trailer on his land, and moved into it. A few months later, Billy-Bob
got a city property tax bill, based on assessment of the land plus the trailer.
Billy-Bob complained to the city that he was taxable for the land, but not for
the trailer on it. Only land and houses were taxable as property. But the city
assessment office insisted that he was living in his trailer, so it was a house.
The matter went to court, where the only matter on which the judge had to
make a decision was whether Billy-Bob's trailer was a house. We imagine the
following arguments made by the two lawyers:

City's Lawyer: It's a house. The word 'house' means "1.a. A structure
serving as a dwelling for one or several families. b. A
place of abode; residence. c. Something that serves as an
abode."[1] It's a structure, and it serves as a dwelling for
Billy-Bob's family. It's Billy-Bob's abode and residence.
It's something that serves as an abode.

Billy-Bob's Lawyer: Gimme that dictionary! The word 'trailer' means "A
furnished van drawn by a truck or automobile and used
as a house or office when parked."[2]

City's Lawyer: Aha! "Used *as a house*"!

Billy-Bob's Lawyer: If my learned colleague would just hang on for a damned
minute. *Using* something as a house doesn't make it a
house. I refer to the case of *Arkansas v. Smedley.* Smedley
was charged with owning a gun without a permit, and

---

1   He was reading from *The American Heritage Dictionary of the English Language*, p. 638.
2   Ibid., p. 1361.

he argued that since he used it only as a paperweight it was a paperweight, not a gun. Smedley lost.

On what basis can the judge make a decision? Clearly there's some "interpretation" of the law necessary here. But what is "interpretation"?

There's no problem in understanding the wording of the law. It's nice and clear. Hard judicial decisions are sometimes made by consideration of precedents in decisions about similar cases. But house-trailers were brand new. There weren't any similar cases. Sometimes judges base decisions on what they think the lawmakers might have had in mind when they wrote the law. Even if this mind-reading trick is a sensible way of "interpreting" some laws, it wasn't useful in this case. The law had been made years before, when house-trailers weren't even imagined: the legislators couldn't have had any intentions about them at all.

What the judges sometimes do is consider what the morally right decision is. But that didn't help in this case. On which side did justice lie? Neither side was trying to cheat the other. Neither was acting out of malice. Neither would have been *unfairly* victimized by a decision for the other side.

There didn't seem to be any good basis for a decision one way or the other. Maybe what would influence the judge's decision was the fact that Billy-Bob was a nice guy, or the fact that the city was running short on money. Such considerations don't appear to provide a good basis for a decision, but a decision had to be made.

Whichever way the decision went, a precedent would have been set: the law would afterwards be taken to read, in effect, that houses *and* installed trailers (or houses *but not* installed trailers) are taxable. This judge *made* the law.

5. Problems about Actions

Why You Don't Drive When You're Drunk

FOLLOWING IS ANOTHER PHILOSOPHICALLY interesting legal argument—this time, an actual case.

LaFontaine, after hours of heavy drinking, crawls out of the tavern utterly soused. Somehow he manages, mostly by random motion, to get in his car and start the motor. While he is slumped over the wheel almost unconscious, his foot presses the accelerator and his car lurches forward, crashing into a building with such force that the building is knocked off its foundation. The police arrive, extract LaFontaine from the wreckage, and (unsurprisingly) arrest him for dangerous driving.

The surprise is that, at his trial, LaFontaine pleads not guilty. His lawyer does not contest the fact that LaFontaine was drunk. Just the reverse: he bases his defence on the fact that he was drunk as a skunk.

This is the substance of the lawyer's argument. Driving a car is something you do *intentionally*. But it's clear that LaFontaine was so drunk that he had no idea what he was doing. He didn't even know that he was in his car. He had no intentions about moving his car. His actions—unbeknownst to him—resulted in his car's motion, but he wasn't *driving* it. LaFontaine might be charged with public drunkenness, and he might be sued by the owner of the building for unintentionally damaging it. But he's not guilty of danger-ous driving. Dangerous, yes. Driving, no.

LaFontaine didn't win his case, but his lawyer's argument is strangely per-suasive. Remember that it's not in question whether there's something wrong with a guy who gets stinking drunk before getting in his car; the answer to that, everyone will agree, is Yes.

Many of the activities mentioned in laws are intentional actions—things that people *do*. A necessary condition of *doing* something is that you're aware of your bodily movements, and that you intend the consequences.

This sort of distinction applies as well in ordinary moral thinking. If Sally tells Fred something that's false, but Sally doesn't want to deceive Fred and believes that what she said was true, then Sally hasn't *told a lie*, and we don't blame Sally for what she did. If Sally is so drunk that she hasn't a clue what she's saying, she isn't *lying* when she says something that's false.

The Lucky Murderer

YOUR WHOLE GANG IS out to kill Vito. You slip some poison in Vito's granola, and he eats it. An hour later, the police, having been tipped off by the extermination company where you bought the poison, arrest you and charge you with murder. At the same time, Vito is rushed to the hospital, where his stomach is pumped, but it is too late—Vito is already showing the signs of serious poisoning. As Vito lies in his hospital room, near death, a fellow member of your gang, wanting to make sure Vito won't recover, slips into the hospital and shoots him in the head, killing him immediately. But now the police have to reduce their charge against you: you are charged only with attempted murder.

You were lucky. Had your pal not shot Vito, he would have died of the poison you gave him, and you would have been convicted of first-degree murder, which carries a much larger penalty than mere attempted murder. The puzzle here is that what your pal did had nothing to do with you. It seems that what crime you commit, and what your punishment is to be, should be a matter only of *what you do*, not of things that happen or don't happen afterwards. But it seems, in this case, that "what you did"—murder or merely attempted murder—depends on things that happen afterwards, and that are totally out of your control.

This puzzle does not merely apply to artificial, imaginary, or unlikely events. Think of all the things people do in real life for which they are praised or blamed. The praise or blame, and the extent of praise or blame, depend on what sort of action it was. And the sort of action depends on circumstances and consequences very often utterly out of control of the doer. An unlucky speeding driver may kill a pedestrian, for example; whether this happens or not depends a good deal on whether any pedestrians happen to be around when the speeder is careening down the road. And, of course, this is a matter over which the driver has no control. The very same behaviour on the driver's part will be punished very differently if it constitutes mere speeding, or if it involves killing a pedestrian. But this difference is merely a matter of good or bad luck for the driver.

A QUESTION TO THINK ABOUT: Is it fair to make our decision on what act was committed, and to adjust the amount of punishment meted out accordingly, on the basis of circumstances utterly beyond the agent's control?

FOR FURTHER READING: "Moral Luck" by Thomas Nagel, and Bernard Williams's book *Moral Luck*.

A Time and a Place for Murder

NOW SUPPOSE YOUR PAL didn't get to the hospital, and Vito dies of the poison you gave him. You have committed murder, but when? Suppose you put poison in his granola on Tuesday, he ate it on Wednesday, and he died on Thursday. Did the murder take place on Tuesday? Or Wednesday? That would be very odd in either case, because he didn't die till Thursday: his death would then retroactively have created an earlier murder, changing the past. Maybe the murder happened on Thursday when he died? But you spent Thursday harmlessly lying around on the beach—*that* couldn't be murder. Or maybe the murder lasted from Tuesday through Thursday?

When the murder happened might have important consequences. Suppose your state legislature, meeting on Wednesday, votes to institute the death penalty for murders. Retroactive legislation isn't allowed, so murders that took place before Wednesday don't carry the death penalty. Is it clear that the murder you are charged with took place entirely before Wednesday? If "part" of it took place on Thursday, perhaps you face the death penalty.

Actions might be seen to be spread out not only in time, but also in space. Suppose you shot Vito instead, and that you were standing in New York at the time, at the Connecticut border, and Vito was standing a few feet away from you in Connecticut. Did the murder take place in New York or in Connecticut? This again might have important consequences (for example, if New York has the death penalty for murder and Connecticut does not). It's tempting to think that the murder took place where you were, in New York. But now let's move you a few feet east, so that your outstretched arm, with the pistol in hand, is across the border in Connecticut while the rest of you is in New York. The hand that pulled the trigger, the gun, the path of the bullet, and Vito were all in Connecticut. But did the murder take place where you (all except for your arm) are—in New York?

Some actual cases:

- Did an extortion take place when and where a threatening letter demanding money was mailed, or when and where it was received? In a 1971 case, the court picked the former.

- Did a libellous radio broadcast take place where it was transmitted, or where it was heard? In a 1952 case, the court picked the latter.

- Did a libel arise when and where an offending message was written, or when and where it was published? In this case, the court opted for both![1]

    The funny thing about all these examples is that the answers to these questions aren't clear, even though all the facts are known. It seems to follow that the answers a court might come up with are simply rather arbitrary decisions, not findings about what the facts really were.

6. Cans and Can'ts

Can Pierre Keep His Promise?

PIERRE HAS PROMISED YOU that he'll show up at noon in his car to drive you to the airport. Noon comes and goes; no Pierre. It turns out that he remembered his promise, but nevertheless he just sat in his room watching TV. Is Pierre to blame for his failure to keep his promise?

---

1   Cases reported by Alan R. White, "Shooting, Killing and Fatally Wounding," and mentioned by Michael Clark in "The Paradox of Jurisdiction."

Clearly he is. He could have kept his promise, but he didn't. It's his fault that he didn't show up to drive you. He's morally responsible for his failure.

But suppose it turns out that Pierre's crazy landlord has locked Pierre's room from the outside. He tries to get out, but he can't. There's no phone in his room, so there's no way for him to warn you that he can't get there. All he can do is to sit there until someone comes by to let him out. Now is he to blame?

This additional information, it seems, absolves Pierre from blame. We wouldn't say that Pierre *ought* to have shown up, because he *couldn't* have.

The only things one ought to do are those things one can do. Philosophers express this general moral principle by the slogan, "Ought implies can."

Ought But Can't?

IT'S WIDELY ACCEPTED THAT *ought* implies *can*. But consider this example:

Sally has promised her son that she'll go to the school Christmas Concert this afternoon, and she's planning to leave work early. But at noon a co-worker, a very good friend of hers, comes into her office in tears: "Please!" the co-worker begs, "I just *have* to get this report done by tomorrow morning—my job's on the line. Please *please* stay a little late today and help me with it, please!"

Sally really should stay to help out her co-worker. She also really should get to that concert. She ought to do both. But she can't do both.

Does this example show that *ought* doesn't imply *can*?

From a certain perspective, it even looks like *ought* implies *can't*. Maybe morality that asks of us only what we can do is too wishy-washy. Maybe real morality is much more demanding than that: it regularly asks of us what we're doomed not to be able to do.[1]

Saving Ought Implies Can

SALLY'S CASE IS AN example of a moral dilemma.

(Be careful using that word. *Dilemma* doesn't just mean *problem*. It means a case in which there are two alternatives, neither of which is satisfactory.)

---

1 Simon Critchley argues that asking the impossible is a theme of Christian moral theology. See his *Infinitely Demanding*.

The reaction to Sally's problem just above, that Sally ought to do what she can't, and we should just abandon the idea that *ought implies can*, seems quite odd. Here's another suggestion for thinking about Sally's case.

> There has to be a resolution of Sally's problem. Is it more important, ethically speaking, that Sally keep her promise to her kid, or help her friend-in-need? Dunno—that depends on filling in more details of the story. It may even be hard for Sally, who knows the details, to figure out which is more important. But it's most likely that, everything considered, it's more important that she do one of the two things. Suppose it's going to the concert. That means that (everything considered) she *ought* to go to the concert; and, given that staying to help her friend will mean that she misses the concert, she *ought not* to stay to help her friend. But suppose the moral score really is tied: they're morally speaking dead even. Then it doesn't matter which one Sally does. She can just flip a coin. She ought to do one or the other, but it doesn't matter morally which. So *ought but can't* doesn't arise. No problem.

Or maybe this is the right approach to Sally's dilemma:

> Maybe we should say: Sally ought to go to her kid's concert. She can go to her kid's concert. No problem about ought-but-can't here. Sally also ought to stay to help her friend. She can stay to help her friend. No problem about ought-but-can't here either. What she can't do is *both* go to her kid's concert *and* stay to help her friend. Nobody's going to ask her to do that! The problem that seems to arise here is the result of thinking that
>
> $$S \text{ ought to do } a \textbf{ and } S \text{ ought to do } b$$
> $$\text{implies}$$
> $$S \text{ ought to do } a \text{ and } b.$$
>
> Why have that as a principle of moral logic? Without that, there's no problem for *ought implies can*.

Two men have a long-standing bitter dispute, which they decide to ask the rabbi for adjudication.

The first man makes his case to the rabbi. When he's finished, the rabbi strokes his beard, thinking, and at last says, "I think you're right."

Then the second man makes his case. When he's finished, the rabbi strokes his beard, thinking, and at last says, "I think you're right too."

The rabbi's wife, who has been overhearing all this, says to the rabbi, "You say that they're both right, but they're asking for opposite things. They can't possibly both be right!"

The rabbi strokes his beard, thinking, and at last says, "I think *you're* right too."

What You Can't Do

WHAT DOES IT MEAN to say that someone *can* or *can't* do something?

> Perhaps we might say: the things you can't do are the things you try your best to do, but don't succeed. We imagine Pierre trying to get out of his room when his door is locked: he pushes on his door, turning the handle one way and the other. He bangs and yells, trying to attract the attention of someone who might be able to let him out. *This* is a case in which Pierre *can't* get out of his room.

But this won't do as an account of 'can't,' because we would agree that Pierre can't get out of the room even if he doesn't actually perform all these frantic attempts. Suppose Pierre hears the door lock, and he knows that now there's no way to get out, so he doesn't even try. He just turns on the TV and settles down for what might be a long wait. It's clear that in this situation Pierre can't get out, even though he doesn't even try to. Can you think of a better account of what it is not to be able to do something?

> Perhaps a better answer is this: To say that Pierre can't get out of the room means that *if* Pierre tried his best to get out, he *wouldn't* get out. Nothing that Pierre might have done would get him out of the room. This means that it can be true that Pierre can't get out of the room, although he doesn't actually try.

But even this won't do. Suppose that Pierre's crazy landlord (who locked him in the room) has installed a hidden button on the lock, which will unlock the door from the inside. The landlord hasn't told Pierre about this, and Pierre has no way of knowing about it. Now there is something Pierre might have done to get him out of his room: he might have pushed the button. It's within Pierre's physical power to push the button. So should we still say that Pierre can't get out of the room?

A QUESTION TO THINK ABOUT: Maybe after some thought about this you might come up with a better account of what it means to say that one *can* or *can't* do something. But this question turns out to be surprisingly complicated and difficult.

The Incapable Golfer

DESPITE THE DIFFICULTIES OF *can* and *can't* we have just noticed, at least one thing seems clear: whenever someone *does* something, then it follows that that is the sort of thing the person *can* do. If we see Matilda driving her car, that proves that Matilda can drive. Of course, this doesn't prove that she'll still be able to drive at any time in the future, because she might suffer a paralyzing stroke or go blind. But at least it proves that she can drive now.

By now you will hardly be surprised to find out that even this very clear principle might be mistaken. Consider this example:

Myrtle hits a golf ball off the tee. It's an ordinary shot. The ball travels down the fairway and finally rolls to a stop at a place we'll call Spot **S**. What Myrtle did was to hit a golf ball from the tee exactly to Spot **S**. Does it follow that Myrtle *can* hit a golf ball from the tee exactly to Spot **S**? Suppose she tries to do it again. Being a good golfer, she hits balls that wind up in the general vicinity of that spot, but after many tries, unsurprisingly, no ball has rolled exactly to Spot **S**. This seems to show that Myrtle *can't* hit a golf ball exactly to Spot **S**. But nothing relevant has changed since the time she actually did it. It seems that, even at the time she did it, she couldn't do it. No golfer, after all, has *that* much ability.

So maybe somebody's doing something doesn't prove that they can do it.

No Absolution for Pierre

A FURTHER COMPLICATION.

Suppose (and here we change the story a bit) that Pierre doesn't know that his door is locked from the outside. Why doesn't Pierre try to get out? He's feeling lazy, and he doesn't feel like driving you to the airport. He remembers his promise, and he knows that you're counting on him. "To hell with that promise!" Pierre thinks. "I'll just stay here and watch TV instead."

Pierre can't get out of his room, but now he *is* to blame. He's responsible for not having done something he nevertheless couldn't have done.

7. Free Will

I Just Had to Do It

IF YOU DO SOMETHING bad, you're not to blame if you were forced to do it. But you are to blame if you did it, as we say, "by your own free will." But philosophers have worried for centuries about what "free will" might amount to, and about when, if ever, we really have it.

Here's one way of looking at the problem. As we've seen, it's very tempting to believe *determinism*, the position that everything has a cause (see **The Incompetent Repairman** in Chapter IX above). I mean *everything*, including all of everyone's actions. If that's so, then whatever you do is the result of the preceding events that caused it, and those events are the result of earlier events, and so on, back into time. Given the earlier causes of an action, it had to happen—the causes *determined* that action. So you had to do what you did—you were forced to by the earlier causes. Given the earlier causes, you could not have acted otherwise. So you're not responsible for anything you do, and neither is anyone else. Our belief in action done by one's own "free will" (whatever that means) is an outdated unscientific myth. Scientific thinking, in terms of cause and effect, does away with all that. And because you're not responsible for anything, you shouldn't be blamed for the bad things you do, or praised for the good things.

Some philosophers accept this reasoning. Many, however, reject its conclusion. We'll look at some ways they've found to avoid it.

Freedom as Uncaused Action

DESCARTES (SEE **Angels and Superman**, Chapter X), the existentialists (see **Sorry, I'm Not Free Right Now**, Chapter VI), and other philosophers think that what has gone wrong with this reasoning is that it puts people in the same category as the other stuff in the universe. All the rest of it might very well be determined by causes, but people aren't like that other stuff. They're radically different: they're not determined by causes. (We've already discussed this sort of dualism, back in Chapter X.)

What makes dualists so sure that humans are undetermined? Just take a look inside yourself, they say: you'll notice that no matter what sorts of events have transpired in the past, you might now do **X** or **Y**.

Other philosophers object to this partitioning of the universe. We should think of things as a unified whole, rather than put humans alone as radically different from—outside of—nature. But how could they believe in free will?

Contemporary physics holds that some events in the physical universe are uncaused and random: the events that quantum physicists talk about (see **Nothing Made That Happen**, Chapter IX). Some philosophically minded physicists and physically minded philosophers have suggested that this randomness might provide for free will in an otherwise determined universe.

SOME QUESTIONS TO THINK ABOUT: So let's see how this indeterminism is supposed to work. Imagine that Fred always gives up his seat on the bus to aged or infirm people, because that sort of pattern of behaviour was instilled in his brain by a lot of training by his mum when he was little. That would be behaviour that was determined in a regular causal manner, and so it would be unfree; he shouldn't be praised for this good action, because he's not responsible for it. But imagine that one day instead of giving up his seat in the bus to an old, infirm woman, Fred stays seated and kicks her crutches right out from under her. Why did he do this? Well, there was a random quantum event in his brain which overrode the normal causal processes and produced this unpredicted and unpredictable behaviour. That would be random behaviour, so that would be free; he should be blamed for this bad action.

Do you think that this reasoning gets things backwards? That giving up the seat is praiseworthy, but that random violence was too bad, but not blameworthy? Where's the mistake? Dualists also think that free actions are the result of uncaused (mental) events. Do they run into the same problem?

An Unfree Ass

HERE'S A VERY OLD philosophical story. Imagine an ass (I mean a donkey, come on now) which is hungry, and positioned half-way between two equal-sized bales of hay. If the causes for going to one are exactly equal to the causes of going to the other, the ass will remain stationary, and starve to death.[1]

Sometimes this story is used to prove free will. A person, it's argued, would never get into this fix, but would always go to one or the other source of food. That's supposed to show that people (unlike the ass) are not determined by causes.

It doesn't. Let's imagine what happens. Faced with two alternative actions which are in some way equally attractive, a person might:

(1) Think about the situation for a while, and as a result of these deliberations, finally go to one.

(2) Decide that there's no reason to choose one or the other, and flip a coin. But then we could say that the coin-flip determined the action.

In both cases (and in any case in which an action resulted), we might say that there were causes.

---

1   This story is always called "Buridan's Ass," but it's not in the work of the fourteenth-century Parisian philosopher John Buridan. It dates at least back to Aristotle, who used the example of a man "who, though exceedingly hungry and thirsty, and both equally, yet being equidistant from food and drink, is therefore bound to stay where he is" (*De Caelo*, Section 13, Part 2). The ass version is probably due to a parody of Buridan's position written by a philosophical opponent.

But suppose that the person actually was (contrary to the story) permanently paralyzed—unable to choose one or the other action. Then we wouldn't say that the person has free will either. Then we'd say the person had a psychological disability which required therapy.

> In the beginning of the novel by John Barth called *End of the Road*, the protagonist is paralyzed—unable to decide between alternatives which seem equally attractive (or unattractive). His psychotherapist gives him two principles for action to get him out of his paralysis: The Principle of Temporal Priority, which says to choose what would come first, and The Principle of Sinistrality, which says to choose the alternative which is to the left of the other. One or the other of these principles applies to just about every situation he's in, and he's no longer paralyzed.
>
> Of course, these are utterly arbitrary principles for choice. But the point is that these are useful exactly when the person has no reason to choose one or the other alternative. Then something has to be chosen, and it has to be arbitrary.

Freedom as Irrationality

IN HIS SHORT NOVEL *Notes from Underground*, Dostoyevsky argues for a weird and interesting position: that the only true freedom is crazy irrationality.

Never mind Dostoyevsky's examples. Consider Sally, who is a rational person. She loves fish and hates hamburgers, so whenever she's in a fast-food joint, she orders the Fishwich and avoids the Whopper. When she has important things to do the next day, she avoids drinking too much the night before and gets a good night's sleep. She knows that she should give up her seat on the bus to someone who's aged or infirm, so whenever such a person gets on her bus, she gets up and offers her seat.

Now, consider Fred, who is irrational. He loves fish and hates hamburgers, so whenever he's in a fast-food joint, he orders the Whopper. Why? No reason. He really hates that Whopper—he just doesn't act to suit his own preferences. He deliberately gets drunk and stays up too late the night before he has something important to do. He'll be in trouble the next day, and he knows this, but he doesn't act to further his own advantage. When he's on the bus and someone aged and infirm gets on, Fred stays seated and kicks her crutches out from under her. He knows that this is nasty, but he is irrational, and he sometimes quirkily does what he knows is nasty and wrong, just on a whim.

Sally is predictable; what she does is determined by her preferences, her advantage, the useful, and the good. She's just like a machine. Fred, by contrast, is not. He acts ... well, just out of his own freedom.

> "Ah, ladies and gentlemen, don't talk to me of free will when it comes to timetables and arithmetic, when everything will be deducible from twice two makes four! There's no need for free will to find that twice two is four. That's not what I call free will!"—Fyodor Dostoyevsky[1]

Freedom means being able to say 2+2=4.—George Orwell[2]

The Unpredictable Dealer

SUPPOSE YOU HAVE A deck of cards. Someone claims to be able to predict what colour of card you're going to put on the table next. But you intend to prove that person wrong, so if she predicts a red card, you choose a black one to put on the table, and if she predicts a black card, you choose a red one.

The author of the article with this example in it argues that the fact that she can't predict what you'll do shows that you have free will.[3]

SOME QUESTIONS TO THINK ABOUT: Doubts can be raised whether we really know what we mean when we talk about free will. If we say that someone has free will, does that mean that that person is utterly free from outside influence? Does it mean that that person is unpredictable? Or irrational? Would someone acting utterly randomly have free will?

Compatibilism

THE POSITION ON FREEDOM and determinism that most philosophers believe nowadays is called *compatibilism* or *soft determinism*. According to this view, the difference between a free action—one a person is responsible for—and compelled action—for which the person is not responsible—is not that one action is determined by antecedent causes but the other isn't. If you like the idea that everything, including human actions, is determined by antecedent causes, you can keep believing this, but believe that some actions are free and that their doers are responsible for them, anyway.

---

1   *Notes from Underground* (1864).
2   *1984*.
3   Ardon Lyon, "The Prediction Paradox."

Well, then, what do they suppose is the difference between free and un-free action? A free action, they suggest, is one that's caused by a decision the person makes, but an unfree action isn't. So, for example, if you spill your coffee all over my computer keyboard because you decided to do it, I blame you for this. But if there are other causes—if a decision played no part in this—for example, if somebody jostled your arm while you were holding a full coffee cup—then you're not to blame. Note that we don't need any un-determined, random actions anywhere in this story. When you spilled your coffee on purpose, the spill was determined by a decision, and this decision (no doubt) by other earlier events, maybe including your bad upbringing.

The Evil Physiologist

BUT IMAGINE THAT THERE'S an evil physiologist who has your brain wired up to a computer under his control; when he types a command into the computer, it sends electric signals into your brain, causing you to develop the decision to kill somebody. When you do that, it's an action caused by a decision of yours, so (according to the Compatibilist) that's a free action, and you're responsible for it.

But that seems wrong, doesn't it?[1]

FOR FURTHER READING: Just about any general introductory philosophy textbook you pick up will have a section on freedom and determinism, and just about all of these sections will have something about the three sorts of views we have been talking about (hard determinism, which accepts deter-minism and denies freedom; libertarianism, which denies determinism and accepts freedom; and soft determinism, which accepts both). So I won't even bother to mention particular readings.

Into the Mainstream of Philosophy

LAWS EXIST TO PREVENT immoral action, but it's clear that the fact that something is not immoral is not sufficient grounds for saying that there ought to be a law against it.

When they make you Prime Minister of Klopstokia, you'll be able to get the parliament to make any law you want. One thing that's always been a minor annoyance to you is that some people show up late for appointments. It's not controversial whether this sort of thing is immoral—everyone agrees

---

1   In *Metaphysics*, Richard Taylor gives this example and uses it to argue against compatibilism.

that showing up late is wrong. It's obvious, however, that it would be stupid to make lateness illegal, punishable by law. In this case, the reason is that it's such a trivial matter. But there are other, much less trivial wrongs that should also not be a matter of law. For example, some parents bring up their children with very low self-respect, with unfortunate psychological consequences on the kids for the rest of their lives. I don't think you'll want to create a law against this, either. You should start designing the new Klopstokian legal code soon, but first you'll have to decide on some principles for deciding which wrong things should be prevented by law, and which should not.

Another sort of issue dealt with in Philosophy of Law is the nature of the actual (or the proper) function of judges and juries. Do they *make* the law, or merely *interpret* it? If the latter, what exactly is *interpretation*? This issue is raised in the example above concerning the house-trailer. It's a philosophical question, not a factual one; it's not easily answerable even after we've observed the actual procedures followed by judges. You probably know enough about what actually goes on in courts (from watching all that legal-drama TV) to think about this question.

Several interesting philosophical questions arise not only in Philosophy of Law, but also when we consider ordinary matters of action and responsibility in everyday contexts. We have seen how questions arise concerning the time and place of an action. These questions might be important to answer not only in legal contexts. The notion of an *action* is philosophically interesting. Sometimes we describe actions in terms merely of intentional bodily movements. But sometimes action-descriptions include what happens outside the doer's body, as a result of the bodily motions. In the philosophical area called Theory of Action, philosophers consider questions about delimiting and counting such actions.

Another interesting, difficult, and often important family of questions concerns responsibility. It seems we're not always responsible for the unintended consequences of otherwise intentional actions. For example, if you intentionally hit a golf ball, but unintentionally hit a golfer in front of you on the head, you're (in a sense) not responsible for harming the other golfer. But things are not this simple. You might justly be blamed for the harm even if you didn't anticipate it (for example, if you should have made sure you wouldn't hit her, but you didn't). Can you give a general account of what sort of bad results one is responsible for?

A related issue concerns what we can and can't do. Maybe you're not to blame for not doing something you can't do, but it's sometimes not clear what you can't do. It seems plausible to think of a person's actions as being caused, but if the causes of a person's actions actually took place, could that person have acted otherwise? This issue is one of the questions raised in conjunction with the general topic of freedom—it's the issue of free will. Do we actually have free will? What is free will supposed to be, anyway?

You'll often find articles dealing with the issues raised in these chapters in introductory anthologies. A very good, somewhat more advanced book on action theory is Alvin I. Goldman's *A Theory of Human Action*. There are plenty of books available dealing with practical ethical problems in many areas; in these, you'll often find philosophical discussion of law, action, and responsibility.

Chapter XVI
Deep Thoughts

Why, back where I come from there are people who sit around all day
and do nothing but think deep thoughts. They're called phila ... philo
... uh, deep-thought-thinkers—and with no more brains than you.
But they do have something you don't have—a diploma.
—*The Wizard of Oz*

Two Jews are sitting silently over a glass of tea.

"You know," says the first man, "life is like a glass of tea with
sugar."

"A glass of tea with sugar?" asks his friend. "Why do you say
that?"

"How should I know?" replies the first man. "What am I, a
philosopher?"

> Calvin: Bugs fly in such crazy loops and zigzags. I wonder why
> they don't get dizzy and barf.
> Hobbes: Maybe they do.
> Calvin: Eww, gross! Ha ha ha! But then why would they keep
> flying that way?
> Hobbes: Maybe bugs *like* to barf!
> Calvin: EWWWW! They WOULD! Ha ha ha ha! BLAUGH!
> Calvin: I tell you, Hobbes, it's great to have a friend who ap-
> preciates an earnest discussion of ideas.
> —Calvin and Hobbes comic strip, July 15, 1992

"If I became a philosopher, if I have so keenly sought this fame for
which I'm still waiting, it's all been to seduce women basically."—
Jean-Paul Sartre

Wisdom

MAYBE THIS BOOK HASN'T given you what you expected from philosophy. Perhaps you have been wondering why there are so many quite particularized problems in this book, and so little in the way of the generalized "wisdom" people expect to get from philosophy. I have talked about a great number of philosophical positions, but almost none of them are advice about how to live your life. You might find it surprising that so little of philosophy is concerned with "philosophy of life." When philosophers try to give this sort of advice, they don't do much better than anyone else. In fact, some philosophers who have discussed other problems brilliantly say some quite peculiar things when they try to give practical advice on how to live. Two rather strange examples of this are the ancient philosopher Pythagoras of Samos and the seventeenth-century Irish clergyman-philosopher George Berkeley.

Yes, Pythagoras (c. 560–c. 480 BCE) is the man associated with the theorem that gave you such a headache back in high-school geometry. But he was also apparently responsible for a religious order whose tenets included (among much else) the prohibitions on looking into a mirror beside a light, touching a white rooster, and eating beans. It's supposed that the problem Pythagoras found with beans derived from the Egyptian view that beans contained the souls of dead people. It's said that while fleeing for his life, Pythagoras ran up to a field of beans, and declared that he'd rather die than step on any of the plants. His pursuers obliged him.

George Berkeley (1685-1753) also has a name familiar to non-philosophers: the city in California was in fact named after him.[1] He was a hugely important figure in the development of British empiricism, but in later life he devoted a significant part of his writing to the practical virtues of tar-water. This stuff is made by stirring tar with water, and letting the solids settle out. Berkeley wrote at length extolling its properties as a medicine capable of curing every ailment, recommending it especially for "seafaring persons, ladies, and men of studious and sedentary lives."[2]

Alice Toklas, the companion of the great English writer Gertrude Stein, wrote this account of their last conversation in a Paris hospital:

---

1   The city's name was suggested by a trustee of the College of California who was impressed by Berkeley's 1726 poem lamenting the decay of Europe and predicting the rise of a new golden age in the West. You can read the poem at "Verse on the Prospect of Planting Arts and Learning in America." Berkeley lived for a short time in the US but never made it west of Providence, Rhode Island.

2   *Siris: A Chain of Philosophical Reflexions.*

"I sat next to her and she said to me early in the afternoon, What is the answer? I was silent. In that case, she said, what is the question?"[1]

A man who was desperate to find meaning in his life heard about a holy sage living high on a mountain top in the Himalayas, who had the reputation of great wisdom, and he decided that he must find out the secret of life from this holy man. Saving as much money as he could, and selling everything he owned, he at last had enough money to fly to northern India; there he set off on foot on a steep rocky path miles long to the top of the mountain where the sage lived. At last, exhausted, he staggered into the temple where the holy man spent his days, and knelt before him.

"I must know, oh holy sage! What is the secret of life?"

The holy man opened his eyes, and at last spoke. "Life," he said, "is a fountain," and closed his eyes again.

The man, hearing this, stayed motionless for minutes. At last he said, "I'm terribly sorry—that really doesn't make any sense to me. What do you mean, life is a fountain? I can't see how that is at all."

The holy man at last opened his eyes again. "So, maybe, life isn't a fountain?"[2]

It's a fairly common experience to have a dream in which the secret of the universe is revealed, but it's forgotten when the dreamer wakes up. The American psychologist/philosopher William James reports a case in which the person had repeated dreams in which the secret was revealed to him, and he forgot it each time; but at last he managed to remember it long enough to write it down. In the morning, he found that what he had written was "A smell of petroleum prevails throughout."

During a faculty meeting, an angel suddenly appeared before a philosopher.

"I shall grant you one wish," said the angel to the philosopher. "You may receive wisdom, or beauty, or ten million dollars. Choose!"

The philosopher immediately said, "Wisdom!"

There was a flash of light, and the angel said, "It is done!" and disappeared.

---

1   *What Is Remembered.*

2   A somewhat ponderous analysis of the significance of this old joke is given at the beginning of "Philosophy and the Meaning of Life," by Robert Nozick.

The philosopher sat there for a minute, staring at the desk. Another person said, "Is something wrong?"

The philosopher replied, "I should have taken the money."

Cheer

ONE TIME WHEN I was feeling grumpy and annoyed about something, my wife asked me, "Why can't you take a philosophical attitude toward it? You're a philosopher, after all." I told her that, unfortunately, the sort of philosophy we do over there at the university's philosophy factory has almost nothing to do with what's called a "philosophical attitude" of good cheer in the face of adversity, or at least of resignation. If anything, philosophy seems to accentuate the negative. Finding out about something doesn't necessarily make you jollier.

> "Philosophy teaches us to bear with equanimity the misfortunes of others."—Oscar Wilde[1]

> "He who laughs hasn't heard the bad news."—Bertolt Brecht

> "I have a new philosophy. I'm only going to dread one day at a time."—Charles Schulz, "Peanuts" comic strip

My dictionary gives this definition of one sense of 'philosophical': "Characteristic of a philosopher; wise; calm; temperate; frugal." But almost no philosophers I know show those characteristics to a large extent, and many of them are just the reverse.

So if philosophy is unlikely to make you wiser or more cheerful, then what good is it?

Sub Specie Aeternitatis

THAT LATIN PHRASE MEANS *under the aspect of eternity*.[2] It describes what's often supposed to be the basis of real wisdom—seeing things in their eternal, universal, essential nature, that is, not dependent on one's particular interests or viewpoints, or on the perspective in which *the now* looms larger than *the eternal*. So, *sub specie aeternitatis*, our small and temporary yearnings

---

1   Quoted in Winokur, *The Portable Curmudgeon*, p. 217.

2   In case you want to impress somebody at a party with the Latin phrase, you should know it can be pronounced *soob SPEE-keay eye-tairn-ee-TAH-tees*.

and dislikes drop away, replaced by a philosophical calm, or something. The phrase is especially associated with Spinoza, who thought that this larger perspective could show you that whatever is bothering you is just the result of your narrow perspective; true blessedness results when we realize that from the eternal perspective, there's no such thing as a human problem, a catastrophe, an injustice. There's just the overall goodness of the universe. Okay?

Slogans advising you how to live your life often advise you try to see things from the long view. A very corny song tells us that things look difference "from a distance." An inspirational quotation on the web tells us that ten thousand years from now, none of this will matter. An unusual saying in this genre is what's supposed to be a Chinese proverb: "How does it look underwater?"

But what, really, follows from the fact that things look different from a perspective that's not ours?

> Yet humans have the special capacity to step back and survey themselves, and the lives to which they are committed.... They can view it *sub specie aeternitatis*—and the view is at once sobering and comical.—Thomas Nagel[1]

Doubt

PHILOSOPHY HAS MANY MORE questions than answers, and you'll have noticed that this is true of this book as well. Puzzle books often contain, at the end, a section of answers, but you won't find that sort of section in here. That's not because there are no answers. In many cases, philosophers have found what they take to be answers to these questions; and in some cases I have hinted at what these answers are, or at least at the way one might begin thinking to arrive at them. To understand these answers, however, you must go a good deal further and deeper than we have. That's what the serious study of philosophy is for.

"It is easy to build a philosophy. It doesn't have to run." Thus spake Charles Kettering (1876–1958), US engineer, the inventor of the electric starter and the electric ignition system for cars, and of the electric cash register. I guess that what he meant is that in philosophy you can say any old thing you want, without worrying about whether it works or not. Well, that just goes to show you that if you want to find out something about Subject X, you don't ask an expert in Subject Y. After all, you wouldn't want to ask a philosopher about

---

1   "The Absurd."

how electric cash registers work. I think that you may have discovered, while reading this book, that there are some real questions in philosophy (though many of them have little or no practical upshot), and that there's a difference between a right and a wrong answer to a philosophical question.

In many cases, however, there is no general agreement, and a lot of controversy, about what the answers are. Unanswered questions are what make philosophy interesting and fun.

"It is better to know some of the questions than all of the answers."—James Thurber

The first job of philosophy is to question what other people take as given. Philosophy is the doubting profession.

"The believer is happy; the doubter is wise."—Hungarian Proverb

"Men become civilized, not in proportion to their willingness to believe, but in proportion to their readiness to doubt."—H.L. Mencken

"To believe is very dull. To doubt is intensely engrossing. To be on the alert is to live, to be lulled into security is to die."—Oscar Wilde[1]

"Objection, evasion, joyous distrust, and love of irony are signs of health; everything absolute belongs to pathology."—Friedrich Nietzsche[2]

"The whole problem with the world is that fools and fanatics are always so certain of themselves, and wiser people so full of doubts."—Bertrand Russell

"I am plagued by doubts. What if everything is an illusion and nothing exists? In that case, I definitely overpaid for my carpet."—Woody Allen[3]

---

1   This quotation, and the two preceding, are in Winokur, *The Portable Curmudgeon*, p. 8.
2   *Beyond Good and Evil*, Chapter V, No. 154.
3   *Without Feathers*.

Bibliography

Notes:

Because items published before the twentieth century almost always appear in a variety of modern editions, I have not specified more than their original date of publication here.

Unsigned magazine, newspaper, and internet articles are alphabetized by the first letter in their titles.

Adams, Douglas. *The Hitchhiker's Guide to the Galaxy.* New York: Crown, 2004.

Adams, Douglas, and Mark Carwardine. *Last Chance to See.* London: Pan Books, 1991.

"Alberta Decision Contemplates Novel Use of the Price Discrimination Provision of the Competition Act." <http://www.blakes.com/english/view.asp?ID=2230>.

Alexander, Lawrence. "The Doomsday Machine: Proportionality, Punishment, and Prevention." *The Monist* 63 (1980): 199–227.

Allemang, John. "On a fearful day, you can see forever." [Toronto] *Globe and Mail* 7 Nov. 2009.

Allen, Woody. "My Speech to the Graduates." *Side Effects.* New York: Random House, 1980.

_____. "Selections from the Allen Notebooks." *Without Feathers.* New York: Random House, 1975.

The American Heritage Dictionary of the English Language. New York: American Heritage, 1969.

Anderson, David G. "Primal Life Force Under the Ice." *Times Higher Education Supplement* 8 Aug. 2003.

Andrews, Kristin. "Animal Cognition." *The Stanford Encyclopedia of Philosophy* (Fall 2010 Edition), ed. Edward N. Zalta. <http://plato.stanford.edu/archives/fall2010/entries/cognition-animal/>.

"Animal Language." Wikipedia. <http://en.wikipedia.org/wiki/Animal_language>.

Aristotle. The following of his works: *De Caelo, Nicomachean Ethics, Physics* (4th century BCE).

Austin, J.L. "A Plea For Excuses." Originally published as "The Presidential Address to the Aristotelian Society, 1956."*Proceedings of the Aristotelian Society, 1956–1957*, Vol. LVII; reprinted in *Philosophical Papers*. Oxford: Clarendon Press, 1961.

Ayer, A.J. *Language, Truth, and Logic*. Oxford: Oxford University Press, 1946.

_____. *The Problem of Knowledge*. London: MacMillan, 1956.

Baggini, Julian. "Knowledge in Retrospect," "Don't Misunderestimate Me," and "What Right Have You Got?" *The Duck That Won the Lottery: 100 New Experiments for the Armchair Philosopher*. London: Plume, 2009.

Barber, Katherine, ed. *Canadian Oxford Dictionary*. 2nd ed. Don Mills, ON: Oxford University Press, 2004.

Barry, Dave. *Dave Barry Does Japan*. New York: Fawcett Columbine, 1992.

_____. *Dave Barry Is from Mars and Venus*. New York: Ballantine Books, 1997.

Barth, John. *The End of the Road*. Garden City, NY: Doubleday & Company, 1967.

Bennett, Jonathan. "The Difference Between Right and Left." *American Philosophical Quarterly* 7 (July 1970): 175–91.

_____. "Substance, Reality and Primary Qualities." *American Philosophical Quarterly* 2 (1965): 1–17.

Bentham, Jeremy. *Anarchical Fallacies*. 1843.

_____. *Rationale of Reward*. 1825.

Berkeley, George. *Siris: A Chain of Philosophical Reflexions and Inquiries Concerning the Virtues of Tarwater and Divers Other Subjects Connected Together and Arising One From Another*. 1744.

Bertrand, Joseph. *Calcul des probabilités*. Paris: Gauthier-Villars et fils, 1889.

Blackburn, Simon. *Spreading the Word*. Oxford: Clarendon Press, 1984.

Block, N.J. "Why Do Mirrors Reverse Right/Left but Not Up/Down?" *The Journal of Philosophy* 71 (May 1974): 259–76.

Block, Ned J. "Troubles with Functionalism." *Minnesota Studies in the Philosophy of Science* 9 (1978): 261–325.

Bornstein, M.H. "On the development of color naming in young children: Data and theory." *Brain and Language* 26 (1985): 72–93.

Boswell. *Life of Johnson*. 1763.

Bower, Bruce. "The Piraha challenge: an Amazonian tribe takes grammar to a strange place." *Science News* 10 Dec. 2005. <http://findarticles.com/p/articles/mi_m1200/is_24_168/ai_n16029317/pg_2/?tag=content;col1>.

"Brave Thinkers: Alex de Waal." *The Atlantic* Nov. 2009: 75.

Britt, Robert Roy. "Pluto Demoted: No Longer a Planet in Highly Controversial Definition." <http://www.space.com/scienceastronomy/060824_planet_definition.html>.

Brody, Baruch A. *Identity and Essence.* Princeton: Princeton University Press, 1980.

Byrne, Robert. *1,911 Best Things Anybody Ever Said.* New York: Fawcett Columbine, 1988.

Campbell, Brian. "The Largest Single Organism on Earth." <http://briancampbell. blogspot.com/2005/05/largest-single-organism-on-earth.html>.

Camus, Albert. *The Outsider.* Trans. Stuart Gilbert. London: Hamish Hamilton, 1946.

Carroll, Lewis. *Alice's Adventures in Wonderland.* 1865.

_____. *Through the Looking Glass, and What Alice Found There.* 1871.

Castañeda, Hector-N. "'He': A Study in the Logic of Self-Consciousness." *Ratio* 8 (1966): 130–57. Reprinted in A. Brook and R.C. DeVidi, eds. *Self-Reference and Self-Awareness.* Amsterdam: John Benjamins, 2001.

Cathcart, Thomas, and Daniel Klein. *Plato and a Platypus Walk into a Bar: Understanding Philosophy Through Jokes.* New York: Abrams Image, 2006.

"Chess Fans Overload IBM's Web Site." 3 May 1997 <http:// articles.cnn.com/1997-05-03/world/9705_03_chess. rematch_1_chungjen-tan-garry-kasparov-games-kasparov?_s=PM:WORLD>.

Chisholm, Roderick M. *The Problem of the Criterion.* Milwaukee: Marquette University Press, 1973.

_____. *Theory of Knowledge.* 3rd. ed. Englewood Cliffs, NJ: Prentice-Hall, 1989.

Churchland, Paul. *Matter and Consciousness.* Cambridge, MA: MIT Press, 1984.

Clark, Kelly James, ed. *Readings in the Philosophy of Religion.* Peterborough, ON: Broadview Press, 2008.

Clark, Michael. *Paradoxes from A to Z.* 2nd ed. London: Routledge, 2007. Articles cited in this book include "The Paradox of the Ravens," "Self-Fulfilling Belief," and "The Paradox of Jurisdiction."

Cline, Austin. "Evolution Textbook Disclaimers: Should Biology Texts Have Disclaimers?" <http://atheism.about.com/od/aboutevolution/a/ EvolutionTextbookDisclaimers.htm>.

Cole, Chris, ed. "Puzzles/Archive/Logic." <http://www.faqs.org/faqs/puzzles/archive/ logic/>.

Cortesi, David E. "Dostoevsky Didn't Say It: Exploring a widely-propagated misattribution." <http://www.infidels.org/library/modern/features/2000/cortesi1.htm>.

Cosmides, L. "The Logic of Social Exchange: Has Natural Selection Shaped How Humans Reason? Studies with the Wason Selection Task." *Cognition* 31 (1989): 187–276.

Craig, William Lane. "Theistic Critiques of Atheism." *The Cambridge Companion to Atheism,* ed. Michael Martin. Cambridge: Cambridge University Press, 2006.

Crick, Francis. *The Astonishing Hypothesis: The Scientific Search for the Soul.* New York: Charles Scribner's Sons, 1994.

Critchley, Simon. *Infinitely Demanding.* London and New York: Verso, 2007.

Daniels, C.B., and S. Todes. "Beyond the Doubt of a Shadow." *Selected Studies in Phenomenology and Existential Philosophy,* ed. D. Ihde and R.M. Zaner. The Hague: Martinus Nijhoff, 1975.

Davidson, Donald. "Knowing One's Own Mind." *Proceedings and Addresses of the American Philosophical Association* 60 (1987): 441–58. Reprinted in Davidson's *Subjective, Intersubjective, Objective.* Oxford: Oxford University Press, 2001.

Davis, Lawrence H. "Disembodied Brains." *Australasian Journal of Philosophy* 52 (August 1974): 121–32.

Dayton, Leigh. "Livestock of the Future Has Hump." *The Australian* 14 Sept. 2009.

De Kruif, Paul. *Microbe Hunters.* New York: Harcourt, Brace and Company, c. 1926.

Denes-Raj, V., and S. Epstein. "Conflict between intuitive and rational processing: When people behave against their better judgment." *Journal of Personality and Social Psychology* 66 (1994): 819–29.

Dennett, Daniel. "Quining Qualia." This can be found in several anthologies: *Consciousness in Contemporary Science,* ed. A. Marcel and E. Bisiach (Oxford: Oxford University Press, 1988); *Mind and Cognition: A Reader,* ed. William G. Lycan (Oxford: Basil Blackwell, 1990); *A Historical Introduction to the Philosophy of Mind: Readings With Commentary,* ed. Peter A. Morton (Peterborough, ON: Broadview, 2010). Online: <http://ase.tufts.edu/cogstud/papers/quinqual.htm>.

Descartes, René. *Meditations on First Philosophy.* 1681.

DeShaney v. Winnebago Cty. Soc. Servs. Dept., 489 U.S. 189 (1989).

Desharnis, Raymond, et al. "Aerobic Exercise and the Placebo Effect: A Controlled Study." *Psychosomatic Medicine* 55 (1993): 149–54. Online: <http://www.psychoso-maticmedicine.org/cgi/reprint/55/2/149.pdf>.

Devlin, Keith. "The Two Envelopes Paradox." <http://www.maa.org/devlin/dev-lin_0708_04.html>.

Dostoyevsky, Fyodor. *The Brothers Karamazov.* 1880.

———. *Notes from Underground.* 1864.

Douglas, Ann. "Boy or Girl?" *Canadian Living Magazine* 25.10 (Oct. 2000): 79–80.

Eire, Carlos. *A Very Brief History of Eternity.* Princeton: Princeton University Press, 2009.

Elga, Adam. "Self-Locating Belief and the Sleeping Beauty Problem." *Analysis* 60 (2000): 171–76.

Emerson, Ralph Waldo. "Self Reliance." *Essays: First Series.* 1841.

Eternal Earth-Bound Pets USA. <http://eternal-earthbound-pets.com/>.

Fagan vs. Commissioner of Metropolitan Police [1969] 1 Q.B. 439.

"Female medics 'to outnumber male.'" 2 June 2009. <http://news.bbc.co.uk/2/hi/health/8077083.stm>.

Fitzgerald, F. Scott. "The Crack-Up." *Esquire Magazine* Feb. 1936.

Flew, Antony. *Thinking about Thinking: Or, Do I Sincerely Want to Be Right?* Glasgow: Fontana/Collins, 1975.

Flew, Antony, R.M. Hare, and Basil Mitchell. "Theology and Falsification." *New Essays in Philosophical Theology*, ed. Antony Flew and Alasdair MacIntyre. New York: Macmillan, 1955.

Fodor, Jerry. "The Big Idea. Can There Be a Science of Mind?" *Times Literary Supplement* 3 July 1992: 5.

Fojo, Tito, and Christine Grady. "How Much Is Life Worth: Cetuximab, Non-Small Cell Lung Cancer, and the $440 Billion Question." *Journal of the National Cancer Institute* 101 (2009): 1044–48.

Folger, Tim. "Contact: The Day After." *Scientific American* Jan. 2011: 40–45.

Foot, Philippa. "The Problem of Abortion and the Doctrine of Double Effect." *Oxford Review* 5 (1967): 5–15.

Frayn, Michael. *The Human Touch: Our Part in the Creation of a Universe*. London: Faber and Faber, 2006.

Frege, Gottlob. *Grundgesetze der Arithmetik (The Basic Laws of Arithmetic)*. Trans. Montgomery Furth. Berkeley: University of California Press, 1964.

Freud, Sigmund. *Die Zukunft einer Illusion (The Future of an Illusion)*. Trans. W.D. Robson-Scott. London: Hogarth Press, 1928.

Gardner, Martin. "Mathematical Games." *Scientific American* Oct. 1959.

Gauthier, David. "Assure and Threaten." *Ethics* 104 (1994): 690–721.

Giere, Ronald N. *Understanding Scientific Reasoning*. 3rd ed. Fort Worth: Holt, Rinehart and Winston, 1991.

Goldacre, Ben. *Bad Science*. Toronto: McCelland & Stewart, 2010.

Goldberg, Stanley. *Understanding Relativity*. Boston: Birkhäuser, 1984.

Goldman, Alvin I. *A Theory of Human Action*. Princeton: Princeton University Press, 1970.

Goodman, Nelson. *Fact, Fiction and Forecast*. 2nd ed. Indianapolis: Bobbs-Merrill, 1965.

Gottlieb, Anthony. "What Do Philosophers Believe?" *Intelligent Life* Spring 2010. Online: <http://www.moreintelligentlife.com/content/ideas/anthony-gottlieb/what-do-philosophers-believe>.

Gray, William D. *Thinking Critically about New Age Ideas*. Belmont, CA: Wadsworth, 1990.

Haidt, J. "The Emotional Dog and Its Rational Tail: A Social Intuitionist Approach to Moral Judgment." *Psychological Review* 108 (2001): 813–34.

Haidt, J., H. Koller, & M.G. Dias. "Affect, Culture, and Morality, or Is It Wrong to Eat Your Dog?" *Journal of Personality and Social Psychology* 65 (1993): 191–221.

Hallpike, C.R. *The Foundations of Primitive Thought.* Oxford: Oxford University Press, 1979.

Hardin, Garrett. "The Tragedy of the Commons." *Science* 162 (1968): 1243–48.

Harman, Gilbert. *Thought.* Princeton: Princeton University Press, 1973.

Harris, John. *Wonderwoman and Superman: The Ethics of Human Biotechnology.* Oxford: Oxford University Press, 1992.

Harris, Sam. *The End of Faith.* New York: W.W. Norton, 2004.

Hawking, Stephen W. *A Brief History of Time: From the Big Bang to Black Holes.* New York: Bantam Books, 1988.

Heidegger, Martin. *An Introduction to Metaphysics.* New Haven: Yale University Press, 1959.

Heller, Joseph. *Catch-22.* New York: Dell, 1961.

Hempel, Carl. *Aspects of Scientific Explanation and Other Essays in the Philosophy of Science.* New York: The Free Press, 1945.

Hines, Terence M. Review of Geoffrey C. Kabat, *When Science Gets Distorted for Nonscientific Reasons. The Skeptical Inquirer* 33.4 (July/Aug. 2009). Online: <http://www.csicop.org/si/show/when_science_gets_distorted_for_nonscientific_reasons/>.

Hitchens, Christopher. *God Is Not Great: How Religion Poisons Everything.* New York: McClelland & Stewart, 2008.

_____. "Mommie Dearest: The pope beatifies Mother Teresa, a fanatic, a fundamentalist, and a fraud." <http://www.slate.com/id/2090083/>.

Hobbes, Thomas. *De Corpore.* 1650.

_____. *Leviathan.* 1651.

Hofstadter, Douglas R., and Daniel Dennett. *The Mind's I.* New York: Basic Books, 1981.

Horowitz, Alexandra. *Inside of a Dog.* New York: Scribner, 2010.

Hume, David. *Dialogues Concerning Natural Religion.* 1779.

_____. *An Enquiry Concerning Human Understanding.* 1748.

Hunter, James Davison, and Carl Desportes Bowman. *Politics of Character: Survey of American Public Culture.* Charlottesville: Institute for Advanced Studies in Culture, University of Virginia, 2000.

James, William. *The Varieties of Religious Experience.* New York: Longmans, Green, 1902.

_____. "What Pragmatism Means." (Lecture, 1904.) *Essays in Pragmatism.* New York: Hafner, 1948.

_____. "The Will to Believe." *The New World* 5 (1896): 327–47. Reprinted in *The Will to Believe and Other Essays in Popular Philosophy.* New York: Longmans, Green, 1897.

Jamieson, Dale, and Tom Regan. "On the Ethics of the Use of Animals in Science." *And Justice for All: New Introductory Essays in Ethics and Public Policy*, ed. Tom Regan and Donald Van De Veer. Totowa, NH: Rowman & Allenheld, 1982.

Jeffrey, Richard C. *The Logic of Decision*. 2nd ed. Chicago: University of Chicago Press, 1983.

Johnson-Laird, P., and Peter C. Wason, eds. *Thinking*. Cambridge: Cambridge University Press, 1977.

Johnston, Mark. *Saving God*. Princeton: Princeton University Press, 2009.

Kabat, Geoffrey C. *When Science Gets Distorted for Nonscientific Reasons*. New York: Columbia University Press, 2008.

Kahneman, Daniel, and Amos Tversky. "On the Psychology of Prediction." *Psychological Review* 80 (1973): 237–51.

Kahneman, Daniel, and S. Frederick. "Representativeness Revisited: Attribute Substitution in Intuitive Judgment." *Heuristics and Biases: The Psychology of Intuitive Judgment*, ed. T. Gilovich, D. Griffin, and D. Kahneman. Cambridge: Cambridge University Press, 2002.

Kahneman, Daniel, Paul Slovic, and Amos Tversky, eds. *Judgement Under Uncertainty: Heuristics and Bias*. Cambridge: Cambridge University Press, 1982.

Kass, Leon R. "The Wisdom of Repugnance." *New Republic* 216.22 (2 June 1997).

Kavka, Gregory S. "Some Paradoxes of Deterrence." *The Journal of Philosophy* 75 (June 1978): 285–302.

Keillor, Garrison. *Lake Wobegon Days*. New York: Viking, 1985.

Kekulé, August. Speech given in the Berlin City Hall, 1890. Trans. O. Theodor Benfey. *Journal of Chemical Education* 35 (1958): 21–30.

Kesterton, Michael. "Justice >> Legislative Lolz." *The* (Toronto) *Globe and Mail* 24 April 2010: F4.

Kirk, Robert, and J.E.R. Squires. "Zombies v. Materialists." *Aristotelian Society Supplementary Volume* 48 (1974): 135–63.

Kirkpatrick, L.A., and S. Epstein. "Cognitive-experiential self-theory and subjective probability: Evidence for two conceptual systems." *Journal of Personality and Social Psychology* 63 (1992): 534–44.

Krech, Shepard, III. *The Ecological Indian: Myth and History*. New York: W.W. Norton & Co Ltd, 1999.

Laudan, Larry. *The Book of Risks: Fascinating Facts about the Chances We Take Every Day*. New York: John Wiley & Sons, 1994.

Leibniz, Gottfried. *Monadology*. 1714.

———. "The Principles of Nature and of Grace, Based on Reason." 1714.

LePan, Don. *The Cognitive Revolution in Western Culture*. Vol. 1: *The Birth of Expectation*. London: Macmillan, 1989.

Lewis, David. "Attitudes De Dicto, and De Se." *Philosophical Review* 88 (1979): 513–43.

_____. *Counterfactuals.* Oxford: Blackwell, 1973.

_____. "Sleeping Beauty: Reply to Elga." *Analysis* 61 (2001): 171–76.

Lipton, Peter. *Inference to the Best Explanation.* 2nd ed. London: Routledge, 2004.

Locke, John. *Essays on the Law of Nature.* 1677.

_____. *An Essay Concerning Human Understanding.* 1690.

Look Magazine. 28 March 1950.

Lucretius. *De Rerum Natura.* 50 BCE.

Lyon, Ardon. "The Prediction Paradox." *Mind* 68 (1959): 510–17.

Malcolm, Norman. *Ludwig Wittgenstein: A Memoir.* Oxford: Oxford University Press, 1984.

Malinas, Gary, and John Bigelow. "Simpson's Paradox." *The Stanford Encyclopedia of Philosophy,* (Fall 2009 Edition), ed. Edward N. Zalta. <http://plato.stanford.edu/archives/fall2009/entries/paradox-simpson/>.

Mann, Thomas. *The Magic Mountain.* Trans. John E. Woods. New York: Knopf, 1991.

Marshall, Kenneth G. "Population-Based Fecal Occult Blood Screening for Colon Cancer: Will the Benefits Outweigh the Harm?" *Canadian Medical Association Journal* 163 (5 Sept. 2000): 545–46. Online: <http://www.pubmedcentral.nih.gov/articlerender.fcgi?artid=80462>.

Martin, Robert L. "On Grelling's Paradox." *Philosophical Review* 77 (1968): 321–31.

Martin, Robert M. *The Meaning of Language.* Cambridge, MA: MIT Press, 1987.

_____. *Scientific Thinking.* Peterborough, ON: Broadview Press, 1997.

"Martingale Roulette System." <http://www.roulette-systems.com/martingale-roulette.html>.

Maugham, W. Somerset. "Appointment in Samarra." Excerpt from his play *Sheppey.* London: Heinemann, 1933.

Meakin, Budgett. *Life in Morocco and Glimpses Beyond.* London: Chatto and Windus, 1905.

Mencken, H.L. *In Defense of Women.* New York: A.A. Knopf, 1928.

_____. *Prejudices: Third Series.* New York: A.A. Knopf, 1922.

Mercado, Samuel. "The International Date Line and the Mark of the Beast." <http://www.chcpublications.net/idlmark.htm>.

Nagel, Thomas. "The Absurd." *The Journal of Philosophy* 68 (21 Oct. 1971): 716–27. Reprinted in his *Mortal Questions.* Cambridge: Cambridge University Press, 1979.

_____. "Moral Luck." *Proceedings of the Aristotelian Society* Supplementary 50 (1976): 137–55. Reprinted in his *Mortal Questions.* Cambridge: Cambridge University Press, 1979.

Naiman, Arthur. *Every Goy's Guide to Common Jewish Expressions.* New York: Ballantine Books, 1981.

Nerlich, B.C. "Popular Arguments for the Existence of God." *The Encyclopedia of Philosophy*, ed. Paul Edwards. New York: Macmillan, 1967.

Nietzsche, Friedrich. Works referenced by him are *The Antichrist* (1895), *Beyond Good and Evil* (1886), *Thus Spake Zarathustra* (1883), and *Twilight of the Idols* (1889).

Norton, Amy. "Regular drinkers get more exercise: study." <http://www.reuters.com/article/healthNews/idUSTRE57U3V820090831>.

"Not knowing is not the answer." Ad for Colon Cancer Canada. *The* [Toronto] *Globe and Mail* 2 Sept. 2009: L5.

Nozick, Robert. "Philosophy and the Meaning of Life." *Life, Death and Meaning: Key Philosophical Readings on the Big Questions*, ed. David Benatar. Lanham, MD: Rowman & Littlefield, 2004.

Nussbaum, Martha. "Discussing Disgust: On the folly of gross-out public policy." Interviewed by Julian Sanchez, 15 July 2004. <http://reason.com/archives/2004/07/15/discussing-disgust>.

Olds, James. "Pleasure Centers in the Brain." *Scientific American* Oct. 1956: 105–16.

Orwell, George. *1984*. New York: Knopf, 1992.

Orwin, Clifford. "Can we teach ethics? When pigs fly." *The* [Toronto] *Globe and Mail* 6 Nov 2009.

Pacini, R., and S. Epstein. "The relation of rational and experiental information processing styles to personality, basic beliefs, and the ratio-bias phenomenon." *Journal of Personality and Social Psychology* 76 (1999): 972–87.

"Padre Pio the Mystic." <http://www.ewtn.com/padrepio/mystic/bilocation.htm>.

Parfit, Derek. "Personal Identity." *The Philosophical Review* 80 (Jan. 1971): 3–27. Reprinted in *Personal Identity*, ed. John Perry. Berkeley: University of California Press, 1975.

Parker, Graham. *An Introduction to Criminal Law*. Agincourt, ON: Methuen Publications, 1977.

Pascal, Blaise. *Pensées*. 1670.

Paulos, John Allen. "Animal Instincts: Are Creatures Better than Us at Computation?" *Scientific American* Jan. 2011: 18.

————. "Do the Math: Why You're Probably Less Popular than Your Friends." *Scientific American* Feb. 2011: 33.

————. *Innumeracy: Mathematical Illiteracy and Its Consequences*. New York: Vintage Books, 1990.

————. *I Think, Therefore I Laugh: The Flip Side of Philosophy*. New York: Columbia University Press, 2000.

Perry, John. *A Dialogue on Personal Identity and Immortality*. Indianapolis: Hackett, 1978.

————, ed. *Personal Identity*. Berkeley: University of California Press, 1975.

————. "The Problem of the Essential Indexical." *Nous* 13 (1979): 3–21. Reprinted in Perry's *The Problem of the Essential Indexical and Other Essays* (Oxford: Oxford

University Press, 1993); and in A. Brook and R.C. DeVidi, eds., *Self-Reference and Self-Awareness*. Amsterdam: John Benjamins, 2001.

PhilPapers. <http://philpapers.org/surveys/>.

Pigafetta, Antonio. *Relazione del primo viaggio intorno al mondo (Report on the First Voyage Round the World)*. 1525 and later.

Pile, Stephen. "The Most Boring Lecture." *The Book of Heroic Failures: The Official Handbook of the Not Terribly Good Club of Great Britain*. London: Routledge & Kegan Paul, 1979.

Pinker, Steven. *The Blank Slate*. New York: Viking, 2002.

_____. *How the Mind Works*. New York: W.W. Norton, 1997.

Plato. References to the following of his works: *Apology, Cratylus, Meno, Republic, Theaetetus*. 4th century BCE.

Plutarch. *Life of Theseus*. 1st century CE.

"Police force's signs mocked for stating the obvious: 'Don't commit crime.'" *The Daily Mail* 13 Sept. 2007. <http://www.dailymail.co.uk/news/article-481569/Police-forces-signs-mocked-stating-obvious-Dont-commit-crime.html#ixzz0RrFWSolQ>.

Postman, Neil. *Crazy Talk, Stupid Talk*. New York: Dell, 1976.

Poundstone, William. *Labyrinths of Reason*. New York: Doubleday, 1988.

Price, Marjorie S. "Identity through Time." *Journal of Philosophy* 74 (1977): 201–17.

Proudhon, Pierre-Joseph. *What Is Property?* 1840.

Putnam, Hilary. *Reason, Truth and History*. Cambridge: Cambridge University Press, 1981.

Quine, W.V.O. "On a So-Called Paradox." *Mind* 62 (1953): 65–67. A slightly amended version of his article, titled "On a Supposed Antinomy," was printed in *The Ways of Paradox and Other Essays*. New York: Random House, 1966.

_____. "Paradox." *Scientific American* 206 (1962): 84–95. Reprinted as "The Ways of Paradox," in *The Ways of Paradox and Other Essays*. New York: Random House, 1966.

_____. "Two Dogmas of Empiricism." *Philosophical Review* 60 (1951): 20–43. A slightly amended version is in Quine's *From a Logical Point of View*. Cambridge, MA: Harvard University Press, 1953.

_____. *Word and Object*. Cambridge, MA: MIT Press, 1960.

Quinn, Warren S. "The Puzzle of the Self-Torturer." *Philosophical Studies* 59 (1990): 123–32.

"Rabbis fight flu pandemic on a wing and a prayer." <http://www.reuters.com/article/2009/08/11/idUSLB163764?feedType=RSS&feedName=swineFlu&virtualBrandChannel=10521>.

Rachels, James. "Active and Passive Euthanasia." *New England Journal of Medicine* 292 (9 Jan. 1975): 78–80.

"Reversion to the mean, regression to the mean." <http://www.ddnum.com/articles/meanreversionregression.php>.

Right to Play Canada. <http://rtpca.convio.net/>.

Rivers, W.H.R. "Primitive Color Vision." *Popular Science Monthly* 59 (May 1901): 44–58.

Robertson, Peter. *The Early Years: The Niels Bohr Institute, 1921–1930.* Copenhagen: Akademisk Forlag, Universitetsforlaget i København, 1979.

"Rome Statute of the International Criminal Court."International Criminal Court. <http://www.icc-cpi.int/>.

Rosten, Leo, et al. *The New Joys of Yiddish.* New York: Random House, 2003.

Rowe, William L. "The Problem of Evil and Some Varieties of Atheism." *American Philosophical Quarterly* 16 (1979): 335–41.

Russell, Bertrand. *The Analysis of Mind.* New York: Macmillan, 1921.

_____. *The Autobiography of Bertrand Russell.* Boston: Bantam Books, 1967.

_____. *Introduction to Mathematical Philosophy.* London: George Allen and Unwin, 1919.

_____. "On the Notion of Cause." *Proceedings of the Aristotelian Society* 13 (1912–13): 1–26. Reprinted in *Mysticism and Logic.* London: Allen & Unwin, 1918.

_____. "On the Value of Scepticism." *Sceptical Essays.* London: George Allen & Unwin, 1928.

_____. "The Philosophy of Logical Atomism." *Monist* 28–29 (1918–19); reprinted in *Logic and Knowledge.* London: George Allen and Unwin, 1956.

_____. *The Principles of Mathematics.* 2nd ed. London: Allen & Unwin, 1937.

_____. *The Problems of Philosophy* London: Williams and Norgate, 1912.

_____. *Sceptical Essays.* London: George Allen & Unwin, 1928.

_____. "Why I Am Not a Christian." *Why I Am Not a Christian and Other Essays on Religion and Related Subjects.* New York: Simon and Schuster, 1957.

Ryle, Gilbert. *The Concept of Mind.* Chicago: University of Chicago Press, 1949.

Sagan, Carl. "The Abstractions of Beasts." *The Dragons of Eden.* New York: Random House, 1977.

Sainsbury, R.M. *Paradoxes.* 2nd ed. Cambridge: Cambridge University Press, 1995.

Santayana, George. *Reason in Religion (The Life of Reason,* vol. 3). New York: Collier Books, 1962.

Searle, John R. "Minds, Brains, and Programs." *The Behavioral and Brain Sciences* 3 (1980): 417–24.

_____. *Speech Acts.* Cambridge: Cambridge University Press, 1969

Sextus Empiricus. *Outlines of Pyrrhonism.* c. 200 CE.

Shaw, George Bernard. *Collected Letters, 1898–1910.* Vol. 2. Ed. Dan H. Laurence. London: Viking, 1972.

Simpson, Edward H. "The Interpretation of Interaction in Contingency Tables." *Journal of the Royal Statistical Society* (Series B) 13 (1951): 238–24.

Sizzi, Francesco. *Dianoia Astronomica, Optica, Physica.* 1611.

Skidelsky, Edward. "Words that think for us: Beyond inappropriate." *Prospect Magazine* 165 (18 Nov. 2009).

Skyrms, Brian. *Choice and Chance.* 4th ed. Belmont, CA: Wadsworth Publishing, 1999.

Slater, Lauren. "DR. DAEDALUS: A radical plastic surgeon wants to give you wings." *Harper's Magazine* 303.1814 (July 2001): 57–67.

Smilansky, Saul. *Ten Moral Paradoxes.* Oxford: Blackwell, 2007.

Smith, Russell. "Let me be clear: we can't always banish tricky words: Phrases that make no sense are nothing if not annoying, but we're stuck with them." *The* [Toronto] *Globe and Mail* 11 Feb 2010.

Smullyan, Raymond. *What Is the Name of This Book?* Englewood Cliffs, NJ: Prentice-Hall, 1978.

Solomon, Henry A. *The Exercise Myth.* New York: Harcourt Brace Jovanovich, 1984.

Sorensen, Roy A. *Blindspots.* Oxford: Clarendon Press, 1988.

_____. "Seeing Intersecting Eclipses." *Journal of Philosophy* 96 (1999): 25–49.

Stangroom, Jeremy. "Philosophy Experiments: What Does Mary Do?" <http://philosophyexperiments.com/mary/Default.aspx>.

Stanovich, Keith E. "Rational and Irrational Thought: The Thinking That IQ Tests Miss." *Scientific American Mind* 30 Oct. 2009. Online: <http://web.mac.com/kstanovich/iWeb/Site/Research%20on%20Reasoning_files/Stanovich_IQ-Tests-Miss_SAM09.pdf>.

Sterne, Laurence. *The Life and Opinions of Tristram Shandy, Gentleman.* 1759–69.

Stewart, Ian. *Concepts of Modern Mathematics.* Harmondsworth: Penguin Books, 1975.

Stich, Stephen. *The Fragmentation of Reason.* Cambridge, MA: MIT Press, 1990.

Stoppard, Tom. *Rosencrantz and Guildenstern Are Dead.* London: Faber and Faber, 1967.

Strawson, P.F. "On Referring." *Essays in Conceptual Analysis*, ed. Anthony Flew. London: Macmillan and Company, 1956.

"Stupid Laws." <http://www.stupid-laws.net/>.

Sussman, Dalia. "See Spot Go to Heaven? The Public's Not So Sure." <http://www.beliefnet.com/Inspiration/Angels/2001/05/See-Spot-Go-to-Heaven-The-Publics-Not-So-Sure.aspx>.

Taylor, Charles. "Rationality." *Rationality and Relativism*, ed. Martin Hollis and Steven Lukes. Oxford: Basil Blackwell, 1982.

Taylor, Richard. *Metaphysics.* 4th ed. Englewood Cliffs, NJ: Prentice-Hall, 1991.

"Things People Said: Bad Predictions." <http://www.rinkworks.com/said/predictions.shtml>.

Thomson, James F. "Tasks and Super-Tasks." *Analysis* 15 (Oct. 1954): 1–13.

Thomson, Judith Jarvis. "Killing, Letting Die, and the Trolley Problem." *The Monist* 59 (1976): 204–17.

Tierney, John. "Behind Monty Hall's Doors: Puzzle, Debate and Answer?" *The New York Times* 21 July 1991.

Toklas, Alice B. *What Is Remembered*. New York: Holt, Rinehart and Winston, 1963.

Turing, A.M. "Computing Machinery and Intelligence." *Mind* 59 (1950): 433–60.

Twain, Mark. *Following the Equator*. 1897.

U.S. Centers for Disease Control and Prevention. "Age-adjusted death rates for 113 selected causes by race and sex: United States, 2005." <http://www.disastercenter.com/cdc/>.

Updike, John. *Self-Consciousness: Memoirs*. New York: Alfred A. Knopf, 1989.

Urgesi, Cosimo, et al. "The Spiritual Brain: Selective Cortical Lesions Modulate Human Self-Transcendence." *Neuron* 65 (Feb. 2010): 309–19.

Vale, Brenda, and Robert Vale. "How Green Is Your Pet?" *New Scientist* 2731 (23 Oct. 2009. For an online article on this study, see Kate Ravilious, "How Green Is Your Pet." <http://wincoast.com/forum/showthread.php?93106-How-Green-is-Your-Pet-Measuring-the-Carbon-Paw-Print>.

van Fraassen, Bas C. *Laws and Symmetry*. Oxford: Clarendon Press, 1989.

Vanderklippe, Nathan. "A conspiracy that drove up the price of ice." *The* [Toronto] *Globe and Mail*, October 22, 2009. pp. 1, 11.

"Verse on the Prospect of Planting Arts and Learning in America." Department of Mathematics, University of California website. <http://math.berkeley.edu/aboutus_viewpoints_berkeley.html>.

Visser, Margaret. *The Rituals of Dinner: The Origins, Evolution, Eccentricities and Meaning of Table Manners*. Toronto: HarperCollins, 1991.

von Däniken, Erich. *Chariots of the Gods*. New York: Bantam, 1968.

Warhaft, Sidney. *Francis Bacon: A Selection of His Works*. Toronto: MacMillan of Canada, 1967.

Wason, Peter C. "Reasoning about a Rule." *Quarterly Journal of Experimental Psychology* 20 (1968): 273–81.

_____, and P. Johnson-Laird. "A Conflict between Selecting and Evaluating Information in an Inferential Task." *British Journal of Psychology* 61 (1970): 509–15.

White, Alan R., "Shooting, Killing and Fatally Wounding." *Proceedings of the Aristotelian Society* 80 (1979–80): 1–15.

Whitman, Walt. "Song of Myself." *Leaves of Grass*. 1855.

"Why I Believe in God." *Ebony Magazine* Nov. 1962.

Widdicombe, Lizzie. "Brainteaser: You've Got Mail." *The New Yorker* 18 Oct. 2009.

William of Ockham. "Quodlibetal Questions." c. 1300. A multi-volume collection of Ockham's surviving work—in Latin—is now available (*Opera Philosophica et Theologica*, G. Gal et al., eds. [New York: The Franciscan Institute, 1967–88]), but there are several partial English translations, e.g., Alfred J. Freddoso and Francis E. Kelly, trans., *Quodlibetal Questions*. New Haven: Yale University Press 1991.

Williams, Bernard. *Moral Luck*. Cambridge: Cambridge University Press, 1981.

_____. "The Self and the Future." *The Philosophical Review* 79 (April 1970): 161–80. Reprinted in *Personal Identity*, ed. John Perry. Berkeley: University of California Press, 1975, pp. 179–98.

Williams, Patricia J. "No Vengeance, No Justice." *The Nation* 2 July 2001: 9.

Winch, Peter. "Understanding a Primitive Society." *American Philosophical Quarterly* 1 (1964): 307–24.

Winokur, Jon. *The Portable Curmudgeon*. New York: New American Library, 1987.

Wisdom, John. "Gods." *Proceedings of the Aristotelian Society* (1944–45), reprinted in *Logic and Language*, ed. Antony Flew (Garden City, NY: Anchor Books, 1965).

Wittgenstein, Ludwig. *Philosophical Investigations*. Oxford: Basil Blackwell, 1958.

_____. *Tractatus Logico-Philosophicus*. 1921. A standard translation is by David Pears and Brian McGuinness. London: Routledge, 1961.

"Women poised to dominate doctors' offices." <http://www.scwist.ca/index.php/main/entry/women-poised-to-dominate-doctors-offices/>.

Zweig, Janet. "Public Art." <http://www.janetzweig.com>.

Disclaimer

NO ANIMALS WERE INJURED in the creating of this book. Void where prohibited by law. All rights reserved. Your mileage may vary. Available while quantities last. Used with permission. Information was current at time of printing. Abandon hope all ye who enter here. For information purposes only. Any resemblance to real persons, living or dead, is purely coincidental. Author does not carry cash. Limitations on coverage and remedies may apply. Formatted to fit this book. Please remain seated until the book has come to a complete stop. All names listed are proprietary trademarks of their respective corporations. Use only as directed. No purchase necessary. Must be over 18. Avoid contact with skin. May be too intense for some readers. Some restrictions may apply. Not affiliated with the American Red Cross. Not responsible for direct, indirect, incidental, or consequent damages resulting from any defect, error, or failure to perform. This is not an offer to sell securities. Views expressed may not be those of the publisher. No other warranty expressed or implied. Contains a substantial amount of non-tobacco ingredients. Inspired by a true story. Not responsible for typographical errors. Specifications subject to change without notice. Prerecorded for this time zone. All models over 18 years of age.

RECYCLED
Paper made from
recycled material
FSC
www.fsc.org FSC® C103567

LIST
of products used:

2,218 lb(s) of Rolland Enviro100 Print
100% post-consumer

RESULTS
Based on the Cascades products you selected
compared to products in the industry made with
100% virgin fiber, your savings are:

19 trees
1 tennis court

18,350 gal. US of water
198 days of water consumption

2,320 lbs of waste
21 waste containers

6,030 lbs CO2
11,434 miles driven

29 MMBTU
143,002 60W light bulbs for one
hour

18 lbs NOx
**emissions of one truck during 25
days**